D1567693

BRICKLAYING

Brick Institute of America, 11490 Commerce Park Drive, Reston, VA 22091

BRICKLAYING
Brick and Block Masonry

Brick Institute of America

8-97

#20363636

ISBN: 0-15-505548-8

Printed in the United States of America

CONTENTS

Chapter 8   BLUEPRINT READING   276

Chapter 9   MASONRY MATH AND ESTIMATING   308

PREFACE

Both knowledge and technique are required to build a sound and lasting masonry structure. *Bricklaying* is a comprehensive introduction to the craft and art of working with masonry units. It is written for the beginning student, the journeyman, the professional craftsman, the supervisor in the building trades, and the homeowner.

Current building techniques and practices are covered throughout. Special emphasis is given to the requirements of masonry apprenticeship and to safe working procedures and practices on the job.

The coverage begins with basic information and techniques, and progresses to advanced tools, equipment, materials, and safety in all areas of masonry work. There is extended coverage of brickwork and concrete block work. Labor-saving procedures and special hints on how to get the job done with the least pain and effort, and still maintain high professional standards, are mentioned throughout the text.

Bricklaying is designed not only as a "how to" guide to current practices, but also as a continuing reference. No matter how much work you do in the masonry field, unfamiliar problems and questions continue to come up. This text is designed as a source for solving new problems encountered on the job. The many illustrations throughout offer a quick and easy reference to standard professional procedures—in both hot weather and cold.

The manufacture of brick and concrete masonry units is covered to provide a more thorough knowledge of the materials used. Basic mortars and mortar mixes are described and related to the material standards in the field. Correct trade terminology is emphasized throughout. Standard grades, types, and sizes are discussed in detail.

Basic masonry tools, their safe use, and proper techniques for their use are covered. Knowledge of tools, professional and safe tool use, and proper tool care are necessary to do a good job.

Brick and concrete block, bonds, layout, joints, and finishes are covered. Construction of one-wythe walls, solid two-wythe walls, and cavity walls are illustrated, including the use of steel reinforcement and grouting procedures. Special techniques for constructing window and door openings are also covered. Other topics include columns, piers, pilasters, chases, corbelling, lintels, veneer, arches, fireplaces, chimneys, capping, coping, control joints, flashing installations, and paving. Both basic and advanced work is discussed. Use of masonry for solar storage is also described.

Layout and design of basic walls, techniques for building leads, and procedures for leveling and plumbing the finished wall are illustrated and discussed. The final construction steps—striking of joints, finishing, and cleaning of the finished masonry work—complete the discussion.

For professionals—for journeymen, supervisors, and contractors—an extensive introduction to interpretation of blueprints and estimating is provided. Estimation is required for takeoff, bidding of jobs, and economical construction practices. The extensive Glossary contains over 300 key terms and definitions most commonly encountered on the job.

Bill W. Weaver
Director
Manpower Development

MODERN MASONRY

Chapter 1

MASONRY TODAY

After studying this chapter you should be able to:
- State six advantages of masonry construction.
- Define twelve different types of masonry walls.
- Describe the two types of basic masonry construction.

- Describe the types of masonry structural units.
- Describe the energy-efficient uses of masonry.
- List the requirements of a masonry apprenticeship.
- Define what a mason does and the training needed.

Masonry building units, along with shaped stone, are possibly our oldest manufactured building materials. They are also, when used well, two of the most beautiful and enduring. Brick, for example, when used with imagination and care, with good design, and with attention to color and texture, can create a structure that is both aesthetically appealing and functional (Figure 1–1). Brick and stone suggest quality and sound, enduring construction.

Masonry units are long lasting, maintenance free, and energy efficient. When in place, they create a water resistive and sound-proof barrier that is extremely fire resistant. Masonry building units are available in a great number of types, sizes, textures, and colors, and are our most versatile building material today.

Anyone with some help and training can do a fairly good job laying masonry units in a simple wall. Only a trained and experienced professional, however, can build the more complex building elements to the high standards required in today's construction. It takes thousands of hours of on-the-job work to get the experience and technical facility to become a masonry journeyman. A masonry journeyman can do a job to the highest and

FIGURE 1–1
Brick construction can create an architecturally interesting and attractive structure. (Masonry Institute of Wisconsin, Inc.)

most exacting standards and do it quickly. The experienced journeyman will know the different masonry units, such as stone, brick, concrete block, structural tile, and glass block, and the type of mortar to use for a specific application. He will also know the different patterns, textures, colors, and hues that can be used to create an attractive and satisfying whole—a building or structural element that is appealing to the eye and that will be a commercial success, and, at the same time, possess structural integrity. The mason is both a craftsman and an artist. He or she will be expected to build (and estimate and design, if necessary) a wide variety of structural parts to the highest professional standards: exterior walls, retaining walls, interior walls, columns, piers, pilasters, buttresses, window and door openings, arches, fireplaces, floors, walks, and patios.

TYPES OF MASONRY CONSTRUCTION

There are basically two types of masonry construction recognized in the field: conventional and engineered. *Conventional masonry construction* is the type commonly seen in regular garden wall or residential construction. Figures 1–2 to 1–6 show examples of conventional masonry construction. Little, if any, steel reinforcement is used in the structural elements; the primary strength comes from the bonding of the masonry units themselves. *Engineered masonry construction* is a designed construction based on recognized engineering principles. It frequently employs steel reinforcement as an integral part of the structural element or building. The vertical steel reinforcement (if used) is embedded into the masonry

FIGURE 1–2
Brick used in simple residential construction. (Cherokee Brick and Tile Co.)

FIGURE 1-3
Two-story traditional brick home with outside chimney and turret. (Cherokee Brick & Tile Co.)

FIGURE 1-4
Auto dealership structure made using solid concrete block. A one-wythe wall is shown on the garage side. (Masonry Institute of America)

FIGURE 1-5
Brick used for traditional two-story houses with chimneys. (Cherokee Brick & Tile Co.)

FIGURE 1-6
Brick used in housing development. The houses have party walls.

FIGURE 1-7
Vertical steel reinforcement used in wall. Bottom detail shows how vertical reinforcement is wired into horizontal steel reinforcement. (*Bottom:* Masonry Institute of America)

is reinforced brick masonry, often simply referred to as RBM. Reinforced brick masonry is designed to resist forces that produce bending, breaking, or compression. All joints and openings are filled with cementitious material; steel reinforcement is used throughout.

Within the two basic types of conventional and engineered masonry construction, various standard structural units or elements are built. Walls, both exterior and interior, are the most common type of masonry construction.

Wall Construction

Most people, when they think of masonry walls, think of a solid wall. Some masonry walls used in construction for exterior walls, however, are the *cavity wall* type (Figure 1-14). The cavity wall is sometimes used because the space of two inches or more between the two wythes allows insulation

units, as shown in Figure 1-7. Engineered masonry construction with reinforcement is commonly associated with commercial and industrial construction and with larger residential or multi-unit residential construction. Figures 1-8 to 1-13 show structures built with reinforced masonry. Reinforced masonry is required in earthquake areas. The most widely used reinforced masonry

FIGURE 1-8
Reinforced brick used in church construction. (Masonry Institute of America)

FIGURE 1-9
Apartments used for student housing. This traditional design uses exterior insulated brick and concrete block load bearing walls with interior concrete masonry walls. Exterior face brick uses English bond pattern accentuated by bands of soldier coursing, recessed and corbelled brick, arches, circles, and rowlocks. (Masonry Institute of Michigan, Inc. Photo © Jadel.)

to be added. The air space itself is an important insulator. It is a common practice today to use rigid foam insulation board in the cavity while still retaining an air space. If grout and vertical reinforcing bars are added in the space, a *reinforced masonry wall* is created in addition to a soundproof and fireproof wall.

Frequently, a brick wythe is used as the exterior wall, and concrete block forms the interior or backing wythe. This is called *composite construction*. Not only is a strong, attractive wall created but also one that, because of its resistance to heat transfer, gives high insulation. Good insulation, of course, makes for energy-efficient construction.

Internal, non-bearing masonry walls or *partitions* carry no building weight; they are designed as room dividers and support only their own

FIGURE 1-10
Split concrete block and brick used in decorative pattern in reinforced high-rise construction. (W.R. Grace & Co.)

FIGURE 1–11
Eight-story office building. Brick is used as an outer skin on a steel frame. Medium dark red-brown brick is used, accented by black brick in single courses. (Masonry Institute of Michigan, Inc., Photo by Balthazar Korab)

weight. These partitions are frequently only one building unit wide. Figure 1–4 shows a simple one-wythe concrete masonry unit wall; this wall does support the garage roof, however.

There are several other wall types you will encounter in masonry construction. *Bearing walls* are walls that hold part of the weight of the building. *Non-bearing walls* carry only their own weight; they do not carry any of the building load. A *curtain wall* is an outside wall attached to the building framework; it is a non-bearing wall. A *veneer wall* is also a non-load bearing wall laid on the foundation and attached to the building framework. A

party wall is a common wall between two separate living units. A *fire wall* is a wall designed to contain a fire; the efficiency of a fire wall is noted in the number of hours it will prevent the spread of a fire. A *garden wall* is a free-standing wall used outside; it is used to surround property, a yard, or a garden area. A *decorative screen* is a free-standing masonry wall that has a decorative pattern. A *retaining wall* is a wall built to hold earth in place, as on a slope or hillside. A *tree wall* is a special retaining wall built around the trunk of a tree; it is designed to hold back the earth.

FIGURE 1-12
Government building made using reinforced brick construction. Exterior walls are brick-bearing walls and brick-on-concrete frame. This is the Skagit County Administration building, Mount Vernon, Washington. (Masonry Institute of America)

Veneers

A veneer is a non-bearing wall attached to structural backing (Figure 1–15). Brick veneer is also used with a concrete block wall. The veneer is attached to the bearing wall with metal ties. There is always an air space and, if desired, insulation may also be used.

FIGURE 1-13
Commercial lease office building in post-modern design. Utility size brick is used with carnelian granite decoration. (Masonry Institute of Michigan, Inc.)

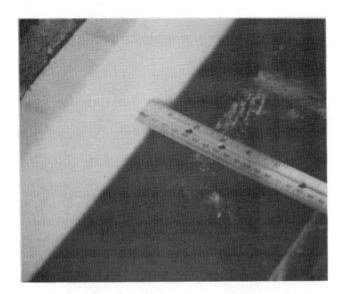

FIGURE 1–14
Cavity wall: brick on concrete block with solid foam insulation in the cavity.

Column

Brick and concrete block columns are used to support overhead beams or part of a floor. Figure 1–16 shows typical masonry columns. The masonry units are interlaid to form a strong locking pattern. Columns may be solid masonry or laid to cover reinforced concrete or steel columns. Figure 1–17 shows two columns being laid with concrete block. The block is laid around the vertical reinforcing steel; then, after the masonry units are in place, a cementitious material (called grout) is poured into the open spaces.

FIGURE 1–16
Masonry columns. *Top:* Brick and concrete column laid around steel column. *Bottom:* Ashlar on reinforced concrete column.

FIGURE 1–15
Brick veneer on frame building. (Non-Stop Scaffolding)

FIGURE 1–17
Two reinforced concrete block columns under construction. Block is laid around the vertical reinforcing steel and the opening is then filled with concrete or grout. (Masonry Institute of America)

FIGURE 1–18
Free-standing brick piers.

Piers

Masonry piers are sometimes used under the crawl space of a house to support a girder or beam. A pier is a short column. Free-standing piers (Figure 1–18) are used in garden walls at corners or openings; free-standing piers only tie into the wall and do not carry any overhead load. Figure 1–19 shows a brick wall with piers.

Arches

Various masonry arches are used to create an attractive opening. Figure 1–20 shows common types of curving masonry arches. A support, called centering, is used under the arch while it is being built to hold the masonry units in place until they set. Decorative circle openings (Figure 1–21) are also increasingly used today. They are nonfunctional but do create a more open space and let in sunlight. Many designers today like to use this kind of an opening because it creates a great deal of interest in the architecture.

Fireplaces

Masonry fireplaces traditionally lend an air of distinction and interest to a home. They are, however, expensive and difficult to construct and must be carefully designed to create the proper draft and to prevent heat loss when they are not in use. Masons require extensive experience before they can build a sound fireplace and chimney.

Manufacturers' and architects' drawings show, of course, the dimensions required. The art of constructing a fireplace requires more knowledge than the information or dimensions supplied on the drawings. Figure 1–22 shows several brick fireplaces. Note the wide variety of effects that may be created.

FIGURE 1–19
Brick wall with brick piers on each side of walkway. (Stark Ceramics, Inc.)

FIGURE 1-20
Typical brick arches.

FIGURE 1-21
Decorative circular opening used in brick wall.

Decorative Work

A great variety of decorative work can be created using different patterns of layout, different sizes, and different colored and textured masonry units. Figure 1-23, for example, shows different patterns, different sizes, and different colors used to achieve an architecturally distinctive feature. Light and dark courses of brick are used to create architectural bands in the wall. The set back of the dark brick lends a distinctive effect and emphasis. The light, six-brick squares in the dark brick band create a kind of geometrical sculpture.

Paving

Attractive walks and patios can be created using brick, shaped concrete paving, and flat stones. Figure 1-24 shows an attractive walkway made by using paving brick. Well-planned and carefully laid-out walkways are an important feature of successful house design and sales, as well as recreational and public developments.

Masonry paving units may be laid in a concrete base and bonded with mortar. Also, the paving can be laid in sand or other flexible bases with no mortar between units. Paving units without bonding are laid separately, and sand is swept between the units. Stones are also used as paving, both outside in walkways and inside buildings.

FIGURE 1–22
Typical brick fireplaces. (Mid East Region, Brick Institute of America)

FIGURE 1-23
Decorative brickwork. (Judith Uphoff, Warden, Wyoming Women's Center)

FIGURE 1-24
Brick paving used as outside walkway. (Higgins Brick Co.)

ENERGY EFFICIENCY

Masonry units, when used in exterior walls, have traditionally been noted for their resistance to heat transfer. Thomas Jefferson wrote that "brick houses have the advantage of being warmer in winter and cooler in summer than those of wood. . . ." When cavity walls are used, especially with insulation, an even greater insulative value is achieved. The sheer mass of the masonry creates a thermal barrier which slows heat transfer in or out of the building. On a hot summer day, because of the masonry mass, the heat does not have time during the sunlight hours to flow through a well-constructed masonry wall. The reverse is true on a cold winter day. Heat doesn't have time during the day to flow out through the masonry wall. On the other hand, heat that has collected in the wall during the day can then, during the low-heat night hours, flow back into the living area. In this case, the masonry wall acts as a thermal storage wall during the night. Of course, with lower heat loss, the designer can install a smaller, less costly heating unit in the house.

With the increased cost of fuel, energy-efficient designs and the use of energy-efficient materials have become very important. Masonry units can contribute to this energy efficiency.

With the advent of energy-efficient designs and passive solar heating, there has been an expanded use of brick and other masonry units in both the home and in light industrial and commercial construction.

JOB TRAINING

Masonry training programs are widely available in vocational programs associated with local high schools and post-secondary schools. Special skill or career centers are frequently available where students can learn basic theory and hands-on masonry skills and techniques. Beyond this basic introduction, many students go on to enter apprenticeship programs. Apprenticeship programs last three or sometimes four years, and thousands of hours of experience are required.

APPRENTICESHIP TRAINING

The normal apprenticeship for bricklayer apprentices lasts approximately 4,500 hours over a period of three years. Most of this time is on-the-job training. The apprentice is paid, of course, for all work in the field. Hourly wages are based on the amount of experience but are a percentage of what a qualified journeyman receives. Once the apprenticeship period is completed, the apprentice becomes a journeyman at full pay.

Requirements for entering a masonry apprenticeship program are that the applicant should be at least 17 years old, have completed two years of high school, and be physically fit. Applicants will also be required to take a qualifying aptitude test. Specific information on requirements and on the conditions of indenture in the apprenticeship program can be obtained from the U.S. Department of Labor, a local masonry union, or the International Union of Bricklayers and Allied Craftsmen. Applicants accepted for apprenticeship will sign an agreement, usually with the local joint apprenticeship and training committee, stating that they will complete the training program. Responsibilities and obligations of the apprentice are as follows, as recommended by the U.S. Department of Labor:

1. To perform diligently and faithfully the work of the trade and other pertinent duties as assigned by the contractor in accordance with the provisions of the standards.

2. To take care of materials and equipment and abide by the working rules of the Contractor and the local Joint Apprenticeship Committee.

3. To attend regularly and complete satisfactorily the required hours of instruction in subjects related to the trade, as provided under the local standards.

4. To maintain such records of work experience and training received on the job and in related instruction, as may be required by the local joint committee.

5. To develop safe working habits and conduct themselves in such manner as to assure their own safety and that of their co-workers.

6. To work for the contractor to whom assigned to the completion of the apprenticeship, unless the apprentice is reassigned to another contractor or the agreement is terminated by the local joint committee.

7. To conduct themselves at all times in a creditable, ethical, and moral manner, realizing that much time, money, and effort are spent to afford them an opportunity to become skilled craft workers.

8. To abide by the work rules of the Collective Bargaining Agreement negotiated and administered by the local Joint Apprenticeship Committee.

Training in the 4,500-hour apprenticeship program covers all areas of job skills plus related training. Training and completion is organized in six-month periods. Once one six-month training period is satisfactorily completed, the apprentice advances to the next level. The following course outline, recommended by the U.S. Department of Labor, is generally followed for the bricklayer apprenticeship.

First and Second Years

Masonry Material

1. Masonry Units
   History, description, manufacture, classification, types, special units, structural characteristics, physical properties, color, texture, and uses for:
   a. Clay and shale brick
   b. Fire brick
   c. Sandlime brick
   d. Concrete masonry units
   e. Tile (structural and facing)
   f. Stone (granite, limestone, sandstone, marble)
   g. Acid brick
   h. Glass block
   i. Terra cotta

2. Mortar
Properties, description, uses, workability, water retentiveness, bond, durability, and admixtures for:
   a. Hydrated lime
   b. Cement lime
   c. Cement mortar
   d. Prepared masonry cement mortar
   e. Special mortars for:
      (1) Firebrick
      (2) Glass block
      (3) Acid brick
      (4) Stone (granite, limestone, sandstone, marble)

3. Sand
Classification, description, selection, tests, types, and uses

Tools and Equipment

Use, care, operation, and safe practices for:

1. Brick trowel

2. Brick hammer, blocking chisels, six-foot rules, levels, and jointing tools

3. Story pole and spacing rule

4. Stone setting:
   a. Woodwedges
   b. Setting tools
   c. Caulking gun
   d. Chain hoists
   e. Cranes
   f. Hangers

5. Accessories:
   a. Wall ties
   b. Expansion strips
   c. Clip and angles
   d. Nailing blocks
   e. Reinforced steel for grouted walls and lintels
   f. Steel and precast lintels
   g. Flashing materials
   h. Anchor bolts
   i. Steel-bearing plates

6. Welding equipment

Trade Arithmetic

1. Review of the fundamental operations of arithmetic including:
   a. Fractions
   b. Decimals
   c. Conversions
   d. Weights
   e. Measures

2. Reading the rule:
   a. Six-foot rule
   b. Spacing rule

Plan Reading, Blueprint Reading, and Trade Sketching

1. Fundamentals of plan and blueprint reading:
   a. Types of plans
   b. Kinds of plans
   c. Conventions
   d. Symbols
   e. Scale representation
   f. Dimensions

2. Trade Sketching:
   a. Tools (types)
   b. Straight-line sketching
   c. Circles and arcs
   d. Making a working sketch

Construction Details

1. Trade terms, motion study, bonds (structural and pattern), laying of units, joints, and so forth, for:
   a. Walls
   b. Footings
   c. Pilasters, columns, and piers
   d. Chases
   e. Recesses (corbelling)
   f. Chimneys and fireplaces

2. Cleaning, caulking, and pointing

3. Reinforced masonry lintels

Shop Practices

1. Spreading mortar

2. Laying brick to line (building inside and outside corners for a four-, eight-, and twelve-inch wall)

3. Layout and erect:
   a. Walls and corners with:
      (1) Flemish and Dutch bond
      (2) Tile backing
      (3) Pilasters and chase
      (4) A cavity
      (5) Reinforced grouted brick

   b. Brick piers
   c. Chimneys (single and double flues)

4. Setting sills, copings, and quoins

5. Laying paving brick

Safety

Third Year

Tools and Equipment

Use, care, operation, and safe practice for:

1. Builder's level and transit
2. Frames, beams, lintels, and rods
3. Welding equipment

Blueprint Reading

1. Specifications
2. Job layout
3. Shop drawings
4. Modular measure

Construction Details

1. Arch construction
2. Modular masonry
3. Firebox construction
4. Layout of story poles and batter boards

Estimating

1. Mortar
2. Masonry units (modular and nonmodular types)
3. Concrete footings

Shop Practice

Lay out and erect:

1. Reinforced masonry lintels
2. Story pole and batter boards
3. Fireplaces (with and without steel fireplace forms)
4. Project with glazed tile leads and panels
5. Project with marble or granite setting, adhesive, terra cotta, glass block
6. Modular wall
7. Circular corner

Prefabricated Masonry Panels

1. Layout
2. Assembly
3. Welding and erection
4. Installation
5. Caulking, pointing, and cleaning

Application of Insulating Materials for Masonry Walls

1. Theory
2. Care and preparation of area
3. Types of application

Safety

1. Valid safety certificate
2. Valid first aid certificate

After successful completion, the apprentice is awarded a certification of completion of apprenticeship (Figure 1–25). At that time the apprentice becomes a fully qualified journeyman, a mason.

FIGURE 1–25
Certificate of completion for bricklayers apprenticeship.

MASON

A mason is someone who lays masonry units in a mortar to build a structural unit or element. The mason works with brick, block (concrete, clay, and pumice), structural tile, terra cotta, and stone (natural or manufactured, both shaped and rough). The key to defining a mason's work is that the unit be laid in a mortar (or sometimes an adhesive) to bond the sides of the masonry unit.

A masonry apprentice is required to complete a total of 4,500 hours working in the field, usually over a three-year period. A wide and varied work experience is required. All work by the apprentice is performed under the supervision of a journeyman. Table 1–1 shows the number of hours recommended in the various areas.

In addition to the time on the job, 144 hours of related instruction are required each year. This instruction will cover theory, terminology, and general trade information and practices, including blueprint reading and safety. The 144 hours of related training, usually in a classroom situation, is included in the overall 4,500 hours. After successful completion of the apprenticeship, the apprentice becomes a journeyman.

TABLE 1–1

Work Experience	Approximate Hours
Laying of masonry units	3,000
Laying of stone	450
1. Cutting and setting of rubblework or stonework	
2. Setting of cut-stone trimmings	
3. Butting ashlar	
Pointing, cleaning, and caulking	150
1. Pointing brick and stone, cutting and raking joints	
2. Cleaning stone, brick, and tile (water, acid, sandblast)	
3. Caulking stone, brick, and glass block	
Installation of building units	525
1. Tile cutting and setting	
2. Cutting, setting, and pointing of special masonry units	
3. Blockarching	
4. Mixing mortar, cement, and patent mortar; spreading mortar; bonding and tying	
5. Building footings and foundations	
6. Plain exterior brickwork (straight wall work, backing up brickwork)	
7. Building arches, quoins, columns, piers, and corners	
8. Planning and building chimneys, fireplaces and flues, and floors and stairs	
9. Building masonry panels	
10. Laying paving brick	
Fireproofing	225
1. Building party walls (partition tile, gypsum blocks, glazed tile)	
2. Standardized firebrick	
3. Specialities	
Care and use of tools and equipment	150
1. Trowels	
2. Brick hammer	
3. Plumb rule	
4. Scaffolds	
5. Cutting saws	
6. Welding equipment	
Total	4,500

MASON'S HELPER

A shorter apprenticeship is required for a mason's helper or tender. The training program for the cleaner, pointer, and caulker apprenticeship lasts between 2,500 and 3,000 hours over a period of not less than one year. The helper mixes mortar, carries mortar and brick or other masonry units to the mason, strikes off the completed joints, and does caulking. The helper sets up and moves any scaffolding needed on the job. The helper also wets and cuts brick as needed and cleans up after the masonry work is completed. Table 1-2 shows the training required for the cleaner, pointer, and caulker apprentice.

TABLE 1-2

Work Experience	Approximate Hours
Cleaning	1,000

1. Use, care, and maintenance of tools and equipment
2. Sandblasting
3. Grinding
4. Chemical washing
5. Etching
6. Pressure cleaning

Pointing	250

1. Mixing mortar
2. Tuckpointing and striking joints
3. Dry packing

Caulking	1,125

1. Use, care and maintenance of tools and equipment
2. Mixing and applying primers
3. Mixing and applying sealants
   a. Oil base
   b. Butyls
   c. Neoprenes
   d. Acrylics
   e. Polysulfides
   f. Urethanes
   g. Silicones
4. Masking
5. Waterproofing

Scaffolding and rigging	125

1. Swinging stages
2. Single basket

Total	2,500

CHAPTER REVIEW

QUESTIONS

1. Why are brick and other masonry units so versatile and capable of being used in many ways in a structure?

2. List six advantages of masonry construction.

3. Describe the two basic types of masonry construction.

4. Describe the types of masonry walls.

5. What is a veneer wall? How does it differ from a bearing wall?

6. What is paving? How is paving laid?

7. Describe how masonry can create energy-efficient construction.

8. What are the requirements for entering a masonry apprenticeship?

9. How long does the masonry apprenticeship normally last?

10. What trade arithmetic and blueprint reading skills must the masonry apprentice have?

11. What is the job of a mason?

12. How many hours are required to complete a masonry apprenticeship?

13. List the major areas of study and experience required in the masonry apprenticeship.

14. How many hours of related instruction is required each year? What does it cover?

15. What does a mason's helper do?

ACTIVITIES

1. Survey brick structures in your area and identify basic types of masonry construction: free-standing walls, bearing walls, veneers, columns, arches, and fireplaces.

2. By observation of finished structures, identify and make rough sketches of two or three types of support over windows or doors in a masonry wall.

3. Locate a masonry arch or curved opening and sketch the pattern of masonry units in the arch. (If there are no examples, use figures in this chapter.)

4. Note any examples of masonry paving in your area and sketch two examples. (If there are no examples, use figures in this chapter.)

5. Find examples of interesting or unusual masonry patterns or decorative work. Sketch the most interesting pattern. Try to write up a description of how the pattern is created. Why do you think it is interesting?

6. Talk with masons on the job and find out:
   a. What training they had.
   b. What kind of work schedule they follow—especially what the work conditions are in cold weather.
   c. What employment opportunities there are in your area.

Chapter 2

TOOLS, EQUIPMENT, AND SAFETY

After studying this chapter you should be able to:

- Identify mason's tools used on the job and describe their use.
- Describe the measuring instruments and guides used to lay out masonry work.

- Describe how masonry units and materials are handled on the job.
- Describe scaffolding used on the job; list scaffolding safety rules.
- Describe safe work practices on the job.

Proper, top-condition tools for the job, proper equipment, and safe, standard work practices are the mark of the professional. Not only must you use the correct tools for a specific job but they must be clean and in top condition. Of course, all work must be done following safe, established practices and masonry techniques. There are no short cuts to a good, professional job that meets specifications and will not fail or weaken in a few years. Always buy the best quality tools available and learn to use them correctly. Start out slow and practice, practice, practice. Speed counts only if the job is done right.

TROWELS

Mason's Trowel

The most often used masonry tool is, of course, the mason's trowel. Figure 2-1 shows a typical trowel and the terms for its parts. The trowel is held by the handle, as shown in Figure 2-2, and the mortar is loaded on the blade. Note how the handle is grasped. The thumb should be to the front of the handle (on the ferrule), not over the front or to the side. It should be held naturally but firmly. The front of the trowel blade is used for furrowing the mortar bed (Figure 2-3). The toe or point may be used on occasion for finishing mortar joints. The side of the blade is used for cutting off excess mortar from the laid joint (Figure 2-4,

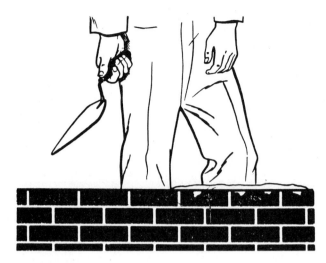

FIGURE 2-2
Grasp the trowel handle firmly with thumb on the ferrule.

bottom). The blade side or edge is also used for breaking brick and for tapping brick into place or alignment (Figure 2-4). The ferrule, or metal band, secures the metal shank to the wooden handle. Plastic handles are also available, but most masons prefer the feel and performance of the wooden handle. The end of the handle is used for tapping the masonry units to level or settle them into place (Figure 2-5).

Masonry trowels are available in various sizes. Common lengths vary from 10 inches to 12 inches and common widths from $4\frac{3}{4}$ inches to $5\frac{7}{8}$

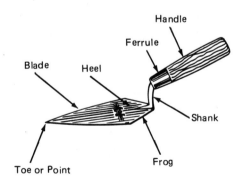

FIGURE 2-1
Mason's trowel and terminology. (Marshalltown Trowel Co.)

FIGURE 2-3
The front of the trowel blade is used for furrowing the mortar bed. (Richard Hardesty)

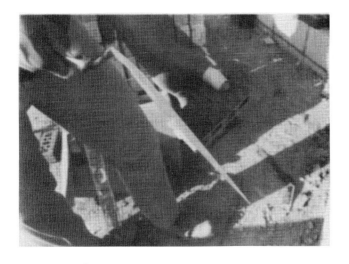

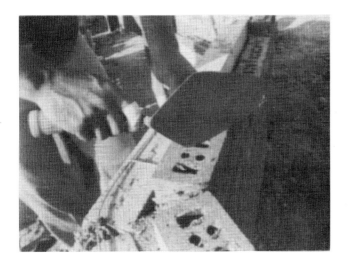

FIGURE 2-5
The end of the handle is used for tapping the masonry unit down into place. (Richard Hardesty)

FIGURE 2-4
The side of the trowel blade is used for breaking bricks, for tapping bricks into place, and for cutting off excess mortar. (Richard Hardesty)

inches. The heel shape also varies. Figure 2-6 shows two of the most common mason's trowels: Philadelphia and London. The Philadelphia pattern has a wide heel and can load more mortar and is preferred by many masons, especially when laying block. The London pattern has a sharper angle on the heel.

Pointing Trowel

Figure 2-7 shows a pointing trowel. Note how much narrower the pointing trowel is than the mason's trowel. The pointing trowel is, as the name implies, used for pointing or making a V-joint in the mortar between the masonry units. It is sometimes used to apply mortar in small areas. The pointing trowel is commonly $4\frac{1}{2}$ inches to 7 inches long and $2\frac{1}{4}$ inches to 3 inches wide.

Caulking Trowels

Caulking trowels (Figure 2-8) are used for caulking or for filling and finishing joints that have been cleaned or raked out and refilled with mortar

PHILADELPHIA PATTERN

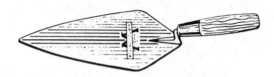

LONDON PATTERN

FIGURE 2-6
Common mason's trowels. (Marshalltown Trowel Co.)

or special adhesive. Figure 2-9 shows a caulking trowel being used. The length is commonly 6 inches; widths vary from $\frac{1}{4}$ inch up to 1 inch. The flat blade is also used for striking the mortar joint flat.

FIGURE 2-7
Pointing trowel. (Marshalltown Trowel Co.)

FIGURE 2-8
Caulking trowel. (Marshalltown Trowel Co.)

FIGURE 2-9
Using the caulking trowel. (Hyde Tools)

JOINTERS

Jointers are used to shape the finished masonry joints. Figure 2-10 shows a typical jointer. This jointer makes a concave or curved joint. The jointer is used to strike or shape the masonry joint after it has set slightly (Figure 2-11). The mortar should be hard enough that a fingerprint can be seen when pressed. This usually takes around five minutes. If the mortar is too hard, however, metal will wear off the jointer and cause streaks.

Jointers come in different sizes depending on the thickness of the joints: $\frac{3}{8}$ inch, $\frac{1}{2}$ inch, $\frac{5}{8}$ inch, $\frac{3}{4}$ inch, and $\frac{7}{8}$ inch.

Figure 2-12 shows *sled runners*. These tools are used for quickly finishing long horizontal joints. A V-joint or half-round sled runner is used. Sizes vary depending on the thickness of the joints. Figure 2-13 shows a sled runner being used on a concrete block wall.

Joint rakers (Figure 2-14) are used for raking or cutting back the mortar in a joint. The square

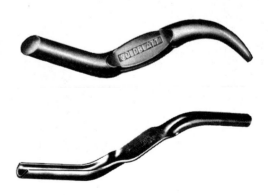

FIGURE 2-10
Jointers. (Goldblatt Tool Co.)

FIGURE 2–11
Using the jointer. (Masonry Specialty Co. Division of Bon Tool Co.)

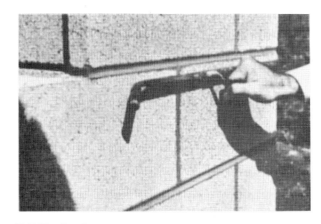

FIGURE 2–13
Using the sled runner. (National Concrete Masonry Association)

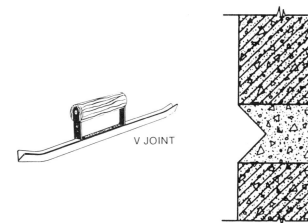

V JOINT

V-Joint

HALF ROUND

Concave Joint

FIGURE 2–12
Sled runners. *Top:* V-joint. *Bottom:* half round. (Marshalltown Trowel Co.)

point pushes out the mortar. Either a plain jointer raker or a wheeled joint raker is used. Figure 2–15 shows the joint rakers being used to rake out joints.

HAMMERS

Hammers are used for either striking (with the flat head) or cutting, chiseling, or trimming (with the blade). Wear eye protection when using hammers.

FIGURE 2–14
Joint rakers. *Top:* Plain joint raker. *Bottom:* Wheeled joint raker. (Goldblatt Tool Co.)

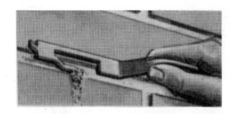

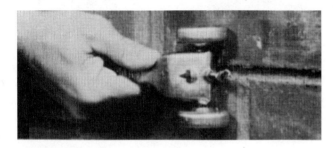

FIGURE 2–15
Using the joint rakers. (Goldblatt Tool Co.)

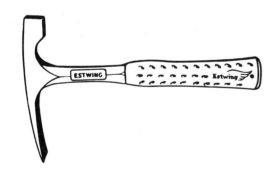

FIGURE 2–16
Brick hammers. *Top*: Wooden handle. *Bottom*: Vinyl grip.
(*Top*: Stanley Works. *Bottom*: Estwing Manufacturing Co.)

Brick Hammers

Figure 2–16 shows common brick hammers. Both wooden and fiberglass handles are used. Some hammers have a vinyl grip to help absorb shocks. Figure 2–17 shows the proper way to hold the hammer when striking.

Brick hammers are identified by weight. A light 10-ounce or 12-ounce hammer is used for working with hollow tile; heavier hammers run 16, 18, 20, and 24 ounces.

FIGURE 2–17
Using the brick hammer. Wear eye protection. (*Top*: Masonry Specialty Co. Division of Bon Tool Co.)

FIGURE 2–18
Mashing hammer. (Goldblatt Tool Co.)

Before use, always check to be sure the handle is tight and secure in the head. If the blade becomes dull or nicked, file it smooth and sharp. Always wear eye protection when using the brick hammer.

Mashing Hammer

A mashing hammer (Figure 2–18) is a type of sledge hammer. It is used for heavier work. Figure 2–19 shows the mashing hammer being used to strike a brick set. Weights vary from two pounds to four pounds.

FIGURE 2–20
Stone mason hammer. (Goldblatt Tool Co.)

Stone Mason Hammer

The stone mason hammer (Figure 2–20) is used for trimming and splitting stone. One end has a wedge for breaking and trimming the sides of the stone. A four-pound weight is commonly used. Figure 2–21 shows a stone mason hammer being used to trim and shape a stone. Note that eye protection is worn. The stone mason hammer is sometimes called a spalling hammer.

CHISELS

Various chisels are used to cut or break building units. All of the chisels are struck with a hammer. Various lengths and blade widths are used. Figure 2–22 shows the chisels used in masonry. The *brick*

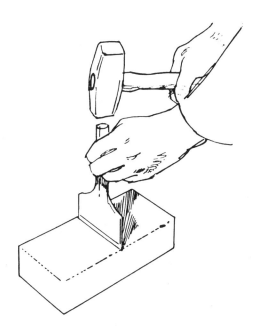

FIGURE 2–19
Using the mashing hammer to strike a brick set. Wear eye protection. (Hyde Tools)

FIGURE 2–21
Using the stone mason hammer. Wear eye protection. (Hand Tool Institute)

FIGURE 2-22
Chisels used in masonry work. (Goldblatt Tool Co.)

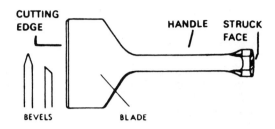

FIGURE 2-23
Terminology used with chisels; the brick set is shown. (Hand Tool Institute)

When using a single bevel chisel, such as the brick set, turn the bevel *away* from the piece that is to be used after it is cut. The bevel should face away from you. The brick section to be saved and used should be pointed towards you. Keep the cutting edge sharp. Always wear eye protection when using. It's a good idea to place the brick on a fairly soft base, such as sand, when breaking.

MASONRY SAWS

Power masonry saws are commonly used on the job for cutting brick or concrete block to the exact shapes and sizes needed. The masonry saws do a much faster and more accurate cutting job than breaking with a brick set or mason chisel. Figure 2-24 shows a typical portable masonry saw used on the job. The masonry unit is held on the base and the saw blade is pulled into the unit. A special diamond-tipped or abrasive circular saw blade is used. Masonry saws cut either wet or dry. Diamond-tipped blades may cut wet or dry. Check manufacturer's instructions to determine if the blade is to be used wet or dry. If it is to be used wet, water is run over the blade and the masonry unit while being cut. Abrasive blades, such as silicon carbide, can cut dry. Abrasive blades must be especially reinforced to prevent their breaking.

When using the masonry saw, it is very important that proper safety measures be taken. You should *always* wear eye protection when using the saw, as shown in Figure 2-25.

set (top left) is used for cutting brick and is used with a brick hammer or mashing hammer. The *pitching tool* (middle left) is used to size and trim hard stone. The *tooth chisel* (top right) is used for cutting soft stone only. The *plugging chisels* (bottom right) are used to clean mortar from brick joints; a tapered blade is used. The plugging chisel is sometimes called a joint chisel. The *point chisel* (bottom left) is used for trimming stone.

Figure 2-23 shows the terminology associated with a chisel; a brick set is shown. Note that chisel cutting edges have either a single or double bevel.

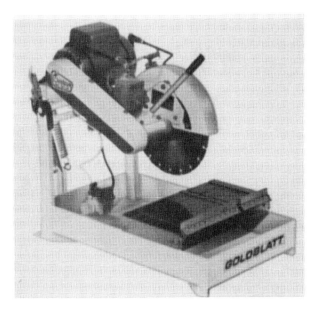

FIGURE 2-24
Masonry saw. (Goldblatt Tool Co.)

MASON'S LINE

Mason's line (Figure 2–26) is used to guide the mason when laying the units in place. A long, horizontal line is run between corners to serve as a guide to the masonry units in a course. This allows a straight and true course of masonry units to be laid. Nylon line is used with a 150-pound to 170-pound test. A colored line is used for contrast

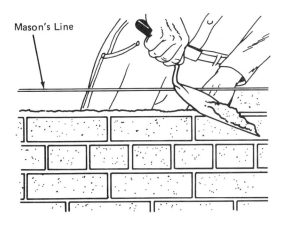

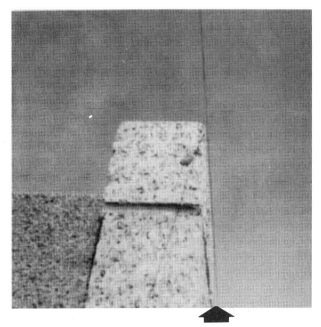

Brick Laid Approximately 1/16" to the Line

FIGURE 2-26
Mason's line. The masonry unit is set about 1/16 inch from the line.

against the masonry units—yellow and green are commonly used. Line is held at the corners by special *line blocks* (Figure 2–27). Both wooden and plastic line blocks are used. The line blocks stretch the mason's line under tension to each corner; the tension holds the line and the blocks in place.

Line Support

Several devices are used to hold the mason's line in place. The most commonly used are line blocks

FIGURE 2-25
Using the masonry saw. Always wear eye protection. (National Concrete Masonry Association)

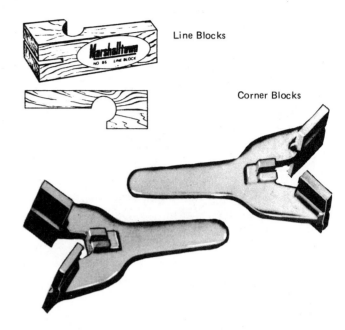

Line Blocks

Corner Blocks

FIGURE 2-27
Line and corner blocks. (*Left:* Marshalltown Trowel Co. *Right:* Goldblatt Tool Co.)

Mason's Line Held by Line Blocks

Line Pin

FIGURE 2-28
Methods of supporting the mason's line. *Top right:* Line blocks. *Left:* Line pin. *Bottom:* Adjustable line stretchers. (Portland Cement Association)

Adjustable Line Stretchers

or corner blocks. Figure 2–28 (top) shows a mason's line in place, held at the corners by line blocks. Knots are made at each end of the line and slid into the slot on the line block. The line blocks are then fit onto the corners to stretch the line taut. The line is set about $\frac{1}{16}$ inch from the face of the brick. When laying the masonry units, the line is used as a guide to keep the unit level. When the course is completed, the line and blocks are moved up for the next course.

Steel *line pins* are also used at each end of the wall to support the line. The line is tied to the pins and the pins are inserted into the mortar between two masonry units. Figure 2–28 (center) shows how the steel line pin is used. After the pins are removed, the holes should be patched with mortar.

Line stretchers (Figure 2–28, bottom) are used on wide brick or concrete block. The stretcher is adjustable and is fitted over the top of the wall at a convenient location.

For long lines, a support is sometimes required in the center. A metal fastener called a *trig* is placed somewhere near the center of the wall

being built. This serves to support the line so it doesn't sag. The trig is laid between two masonry units for support and is removed when the course is completed. Figure 2–29 shows how a trig is used.

Line Level

A line level (Figure 2–30) is used on the mason's line to check its level. It is hung on the line and is easily attached and removed.

Chalk Line

A chalk line (Figure 2–31) is used to snap a straight line down as a guideline. The line is attached at each end of the edge or straight line to be established. The line is stretched taut, then picked up, as shown in Figure 2–31, and snapped. Since the line is coated with chalk, it leaves a straight chalk line where it hits the surface.

Trig Detail

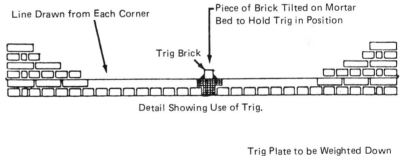
Detail Showing Use of Trig.

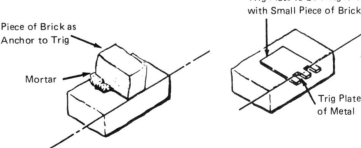

FIGURE 2–29
Mason's line can be supported at the center by a trig. (*Left:* Portland Cement Association. *Right:* Brick Institute of America)

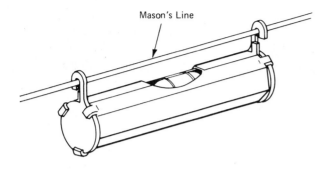

FIGURE 2–30
Line level.

FIGURE 2–31
Snapping a chalk line.

Straightedge

The straightedge is a long wooden layout guide used for leveling surfaces some distance apart, as shown in Figure 2–32. The bottom and top edges are true and flat, and a level can be placed on the top to get an overall reading. The straightedge is usually several feet long. It is also used for checking the alignment of masonry units. A handle is cut near the top so it can be easily picked up.

LEVELS

Levels are used to check the trueness of the masonry units already laid. Both horizontal and vertical trueness is checked. Figure 2–33 shows a level used in masonry work. Generally a long level is used: 36-inch, 42-inch, and 48-inch levels are popular. Hand holes are provided so the level can be easily positioned and moved. Spirit vials with a bubble are used to determine horizontal and vertical trueness.

Figure 2–35 (top) shows a level being used to *level* (horizontally true) masonry units. The bubble in the spirit vial is centered when the surface is true. Different spirit vials are used when checking horizontal or vertical surfaces, as shown in Figure 2–34. Horizontal readings always use the vial and bubble located in the middle of the level. Check-

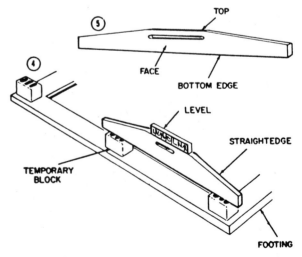

FIGURE 2–32
Straightedge.

FIGURE 2-33
Levels. (Goldblatt Tool Co.)

FIGURE 2-35
Using the level. (*Top*: U.S. Department of Labor)

ing the trueness of a vertical surface is called *plumbing*, as shown in Figure 2-35 (bottom).

Before using the level, it's a good idea to check the trueness of the bubble in each vial. This can be quickly done by finding a surface where the bubble sits exactly in the center of the vial.

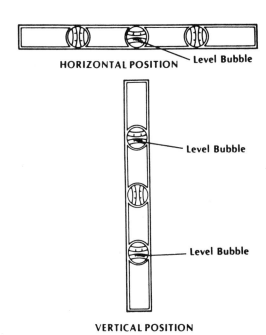

HORIZONTAL POSITION — Level Bubble

— Level Bubble

— Level Bubble

VERTICAL POSITION

FIGURE 2-34
Reading the level.

Reverse the end of the level and measure the same surface. The bubble should still be exactly centered. If not, the level is not true.

MASONRY RULERS

Both folding rulers and push-pull steel tapes are used for masonry work. A regular inch measure is used on one side of the rule or tape, and a special masonry measure is used on the other side. Two special masonry measures are used: brick spacing measure and a modular measure.

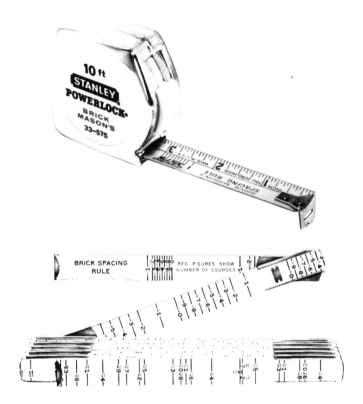

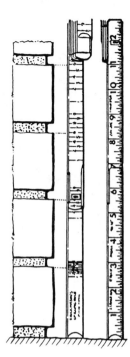

FIGURE 2–37
Using the brick spacing rule. (Brick Institute of America)

FIGURE 2–36
Brick mason's spacing rules. (*Top and bottom:* Stanley Works. *Middle:* Lufkin Rule Co.)

Brick Spacing Measure

Figure 2–36 shows a push-pull rule and a six-foot brick mason's folding rule with a brick spacing measure on one side. A detail of the measure is shown at the bottom of Figure 2–36. The brick spacing rule has ten different brick spacing scales, numbered 1 to 0. The "0" represents "10." The different spacing scales or numbers correspond to different sized mortar joints that depend on the brick unit being used. That is, the thicker the mortar joint, the higher the spacing number. The numbers in red on the rule represent the course number. You can easily determine the height of any number of courses once you know the measure or spacing of one brick with mortar in place. For example, eight courses of a brick that measures 7 on the brick spacing rule would be $22\frac{1}{2}$ inches high. You find the red number 8 (for eight courses) and then the black number 7 (for #7 spacing). Once this is found you turn the rule over to read the other side. The eighth course of a #4 spacing, on the other hand, would only be 21 inches high.

Use of the brick spacing rule is a quick and easy method to determine course height once one course with mortar is laid. It is assumed, of course, that the same mortar thickness is used for all courses.

The brick spacing measure is also available on a ten-foot retractable or push-pull rule. Most masons prefer the folding rule because it is more rigid and doesn't bend or sag when opened out. Figure 2–37 shows a brick spacing rule being used. For comparison a regular inch rule is also shown. When using the folding rule you should oil the joints from time to time.

Modular Spacing Measure

The modular spacing rule (Figure 2–38) has a regular inch scale on one side and a modular scale on the other. The modular scale has six different scales all based on the four-inch module, as measured to a larger module or increment of 16 inches. It is easy to read and understand the modular scale. The number of the scale represents the number of courses, in place with mortar, it takes to reach a height of 16 inches. The #2 modular scale, for example, represents two courses with mortar that reaches a 16-inch height. The #2 modular scale is used with concrete block. The following are the modular scales:

Scale No. 2	2 courses = 16 inches Concrete block
Scale No. 3	3 courses = 16 inches Modular $5\frac{1}{3}$ tile
Scale No. 4	4 courses = 16 inches Modular economy brick
Scale No. 5	5 courses = 16 inches Modular engineer brick
Scale No. 6	6 courses = 16 inches Modular standard brick
Scale No. 8	8 courses = 16 inches Modular Roman brick

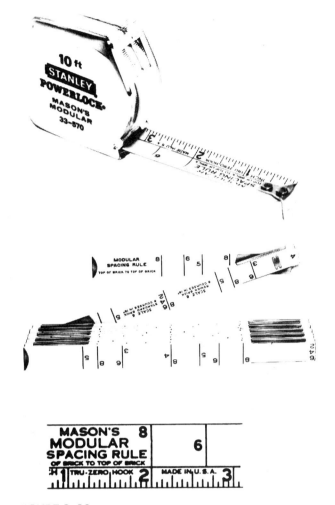

FIGURE 2–38
Modular spacing rules. (*Top and bottom:* Stanley Works. *Middle:* Lufkin Rule Co.)

STEEL SQUARE

A large steel square (Figure 2–39) is used for checking right angles. A large 24-inch square is used for checking corners; a smaller square, usually 12 inches, is used for squaring window and door opening corners.

MASONRY GUIDES

Masonry guides are used at the corners of the building to establish course levels. Figure 2–40

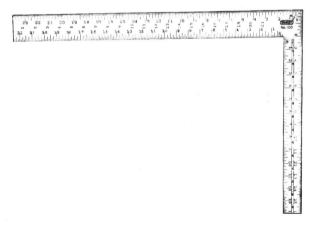

FIGURE 2–39
Steel square: 24 inch. (Stanley Works)

FIGURE 2-40
Masonry guides are used at the corners to attach the mason's line. (Masonry Specialty Co. Division of Bon Tool Co.)

shows two masonry guides being used to set guidelines on two sides of a building. Guides are attached at each corner. A line runs from each guide to establish the course height and to keep the course level. The guide is held away from the building to allow room for the masonry units. Using a masonry guide saves time because corners

(leads) do not have to be carefully built up to serve as a guide.

Figure 2-41 shows a masonry guide and its parts. The line holder slides up and down to the desired level. Some masonry guides are marked for different heights. Standard brick and modular scales may be marked on the guide. Masonry

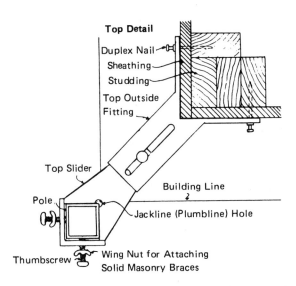

Top Detail
Duplex Nail
Sheathing
Studding
Top Outside Fitting
Top Slider
Pole
Building Line
Jackline (Plumbline) Hole
Thumbscrew
Wing Nut for Attaching Solid Masonry Braces

Line Holder Detail

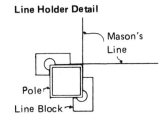

Mason's Line
Pole
Line Block

Base Detail

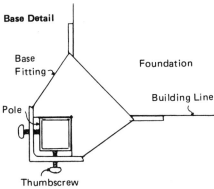

Base Fitting
Foundation
Pole
Building Line
Thumbscrew

Top Extension
Top Adapter
Adjustable Steel Tape (Modular Spacing)
Aluminum Clamp
Line Holder
Bronze Clip
Base Adapter
Base Extension

FIGURE 2-41
Masonry guide. (Masonry Specialty Co. Division of Bon Tool Co.)

guides are designed for one story heights and are nine-feet long.

Heavier masonry construction may require separate support poles for the masonry guide, as shown in Figure 2-42. The two telescoping pole braces are used with solid-bearing masonry and with multi-story construction. Wall clips are used to attach the base of the support poles at higher levels.

STORY POLES

Story poles are marked wooden poles that are used as guidelines for course heights or window sill and head heights. Figure 2-43 shows a simple story pole being used to check concrete block courses. Story poles can be easily made from a 1" × 2" lumber piece; heights needed can be marked and noted. Masonry guides have replaced story poles for most uses.

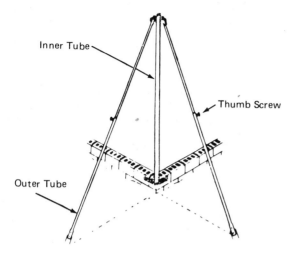

Ground Level Installation

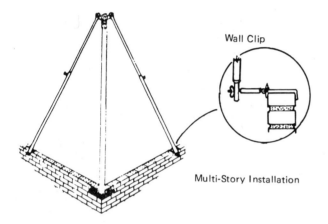

Multi-Story Installation

FIGURE 2–42
Telescoping pole braces are used in heavier construction.
(Masonry Specialty Co. Division of Bon Tool Co.)

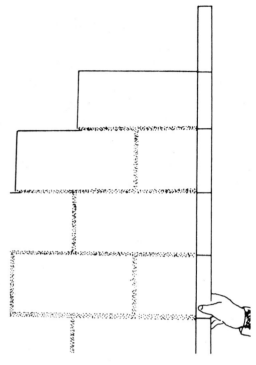

FIGURE 2–43
Story pole. Course heights are marked on the pole as a guide.

Brushes are also used to wash the wall with an acid solution. A long handle is normally used with an acid brush.

TOOL BAG

The mason commonly carries his work tools in a canvas tool bag. Figure 2–46 shows a tool bag with typical tools needed by an apprentice. It's a good idea to identify your tool bag by lettering your name on it.

BRICK TONGS

Brick tongs (Figure 2–47) are used to easily carry brick. Pulling or lifting up the carrying handle presses the two ends of the tongs together to clamp the brick for carrying.

MASON'S BRUSHES

Various stiff bristle brushes are used for cleaning the face of the masonry wall. Figure 2–44 shows several common brushes. Some brushes are simply used to brush down the masonry surface to remove masonry stains or powder left from mortar droppings. Large mortar droppings or tailings should be chipped off with a trowel before brushing. Figure 2–45 shows a bricklayer's brush being used to remove small mortar stains left on the wall. Brushes with soft bristles are used for walls with fresh mortar; stiff brushes are used on walls with set mortar.

Bricklayer's Brush

All Purpose Brush

Wire Brush and Scraper

Acid Brush (Handle Required)

Acid Brush (Short Handle)

Acid Brush

FIGURE 2-44
Mason's brushes. (Masonry Specialty Co. Division of Bon Tool Co.

MORTAR BOX

For small jobs, a mortar box or tub is used. This is merely a shallow container about five-feet wide and ten-feet long with ten-inch sides. The ingredients are placed in the box and mixed, usually with a special mortar hoe. Mortar boxes are not often used on the construction site because they take too much time. For patch work or for home use, they are still used.

MORTAR MIXER

Mortar is mixed on the site for use when needed. A mechanical mortar mixer (Figure 2–48) is nor-

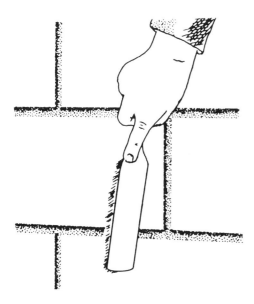

FIGURE 2-45
Using a bricklayer's brush to clean masonry surface.

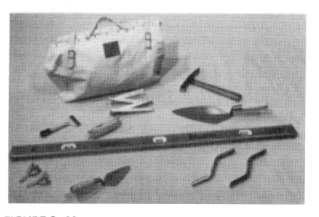

FIGURE 2-46
Typical bricklayer's apprentice tool kit. (Masonry Specialty Co. Division of Bon Tool Co.)

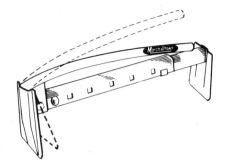

FIGURE 2–47
Brick tongs. (*Top:* Marshalltown Trowel Co. *Bottom:* Goldblatt Tool Co.)

mally used for mixing each batch. Either electric or gasoline-operated mixers are used. Various capacities are available but a mixer that will handle four cubic feet is popular.

FIGURE 2–48
Mortar mixer. (Goldblatt Tool Co.)

HOD

A hod (Figure 2–49) is used to carry the mixed mortar up to where the mason is working. A long handle is attached to the hod so the mortar can be lifted up to the work area.

MORTAR BOARD

Wood, fiberglass, or polyethylene mortar boards are used to hold the mortar at the work area. Figure 2–50 shows a 30-inch × 30-inch polyethylene mortar board. Fiberglass or polyethylene boards are easy to clean, don't absorb water, don't splinter, and are long lasting. The mortar carried in the hod is emptied onto the mortar board. If a wheelbarrow or power buggy is used, an appropriate amount is delivered to the mortar board at each work station.

POWER BUGGY

Hand-pushed wheelbarrows were normally used in the past to carry larger quantities of mortar.

FIGURE 2–49
Hod. (Masonry Specialty Co. Division of Bon Tools Co.)

FIGURE 2-50
Mortar boards. (*Top*: Masonry Specialty Co. Division of Bon Tools Co. *Bottom*: Goldblatt Tool Co.)

They are still used, of course, on small jobs and for work around the home. On the large construction site today, however, gasoline-powered buggies (Figure 2-51) are normally used to deliver large quantities of mortar to the work area. Ramps are used to allow the wheelbarrow or power buggy to reach the work area. In higher construction, elevators are used.

HAND CARTS

Hand carts (Figure 2-52) are used to move sections of the masonry cube over to the work area.

FIGURE 2-51
Power buggy. (Mueller Machinery Co., Inc.)

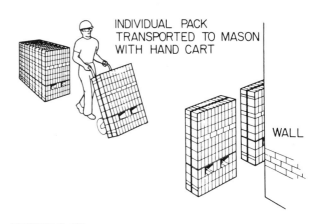

FIGURE 2-52
Hand cart being used to move bricks. (Mason Contractor's Association of America)

Each masonry cube or package is designed so it can be broken down and moved in hand carts or can be lifted as a unit by a fork lift. Voids are left in the cube so the fork lift arms can fit in for lifting.

FORK LIFTS

On the construction site, especially for large jobs, mechanical lifts are used to deliver the masonry units to the work area. Various types of fork lifts, often with telescoping arms, are used to deliver materials as high as the fifth story. Figure 2-53 shows a fork lift being used to deliver a concrete block package to the mason's scaffold. Fork lifts are also used to lift large batches of mortar up to the work area. In some cases, the fork lift may simply lift a mortar box or wheelbarrow load of mortar up to the work platform and hold it suspended there until the mortar is emptied out by the mason's helper.

MASONRY PUMPS

In larger construction projects, such as high-rise construction, pumps may be used to lift the mortar to the work station. The mortar is mixed on the ground and then pumped up to each work station

FIGURE 2-53
Fork lift being used to deliver concrete block to work platform. (JCB Inc.)

through a long hose or pipe (Figure 2-54). Of course, this is only practical when a large number of masons are on the job. Crane-hoisted concrete buckets are also used to lift mortar to where it is needed.

Pumps are commonly used in reinforced masonry construction where the wythes are separated and grout is poured between them. Figure 2-55 shows a two-wythe reinforced brick masonry wall with a $2\frac{1}{2}$-inch space between the two wythes. Grouting is pumped between the two wythes to completely fill the space. This is sometimes referred to as the *high-lift grouting system*. The wythes are commonly built to a considerable height before a lift or pour of grout is pumped in; a lift (layer) as deep as four feet may be poured at one time between the two wythes. Deeper lifts may be pumped, but special wall reinforcement may be required.

Pumps can lift the grout as high as 20 floors. The grout is pumped through a standpipe anchored to the side of the building. A flexible hose is attached to the standpipe. This allows the grout

Flexible Hose

FIGURE 2-54
Masonry or grout pump. (Morgan Manufacturing Co.)

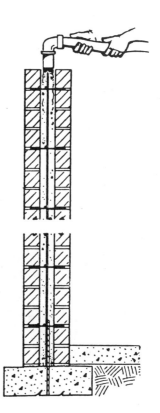

FIGURE 2-55
Grouting being pumped into a reinforced brick wall.

to be delivered to exactly where it is needed. If the grout has to be delivered higher than 20 stories, a second pump is used at the floor where pumping becomes difficult. For high quantity use like this, the grout is usually not mixed on site; it is delivered to the site in ready-mix trucks.

READY-MIX TRUCKS

Many of the mortars used today are designed for long life. Since they may be stored without setting for some time, over a day for some mortars, they are sometimes mixed away from the job site on large jobs. The mortar is mixed in a plant away from the site and delivered to the site in ready-mix trucks.

SCAFFOLDING

Mason's scaffolding must not only provide a safe place to work but also provide a very strong area on which to store mortar and masonry units. Only the beginning of a masonry wall can be laid working from the ground. As the wall gets higher, some safe support is needed. Scaffolds are used to build a temporary, movable work platform. It is very important that mason's scaffolds be carefully built and erected. A great deal of weight may be put on the scaffold. Always follow the recommended erection procedure and follow all safety rules. Your life and the lives of your fellow workers depend on the safe erection of the scaffolding.

Both wood and steel scaffolding is used. Most scaffolding on the job today is erected by assembling steel pieces together. This is much faster than framing wooden scaffolds. Figure 2–56 shows a steel scaffold being assembled.

Figure 2–57 shows a low-level steel scaffold assembled for working on a concrete block wall. The worker stands on the lower planking; the mortar and concrete block units are supported for convenience on a higher shelf. Figure 2–58 shows scaffolding in place for a brick wall. Again, a higher shelf is used to hold the building material.

FIGURE 2–56
Steel scaffold being assembled. (Patent Scaffolding Co. Division of Harsco Corp.)

FIGURE 2–57
Low-level steel scaffold. (Non-Stop Scaffolding)

FIGURE 2-58
Scaffolding in place for a brick veneer wall. (Non-Stop Scaffolding)

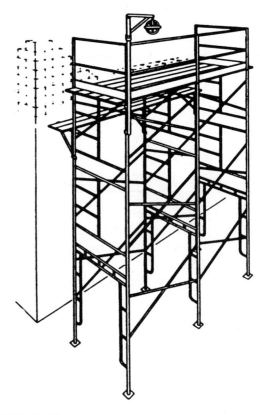

FIGURE 2-59
Heavy duty, tubular, steel mason's scaffold. (Bil Jax Scaffolding and Equipment Co.)

Figure 2-59 shows a heavy duty, tubular steel mason's scaffold. A platform is always provided to hold mortar and masonry units. This scaffold is erected to the height needed, floor by floor. Note that hand rails are used. Steel base plates are always used under the scaffold support frame to give a wider and safer support area. Note that a pulley is provided for winching materials to the top of the scaffolding.

Figure 2-60 shows a mason's steel scaffold for a high wall. Fork lifts are used to deliver material to the top of the scaffolding. Beyond five floors, elevators or cranes are used to lift the materials. This is an adjustable scaffold. As the wall is built, the scaffold platform is cranked higher by a winch (Figure 2-61). This allows the masons to always work at a comfortable height. Motor-driven adjustable scaffolding is also used. Figure 2-62 shows adjustable scaffolding; two motors are used to lift and lower the platform. Platform lengths vary from 20 feet to 50 feet; the tower can reach heights up to 350 feet. Adjustable scaffolding

FIGURE 2-60
Mason's scaffold. Work heights can be adjusted as needed. (Morgan Manufacturing Co.)

allows the masons to work at comfortable heights and increases overall job speed.

SAFETY ON THE JOB

Safety on the job is a must. Unsafe and unprofessional practices can cause injuries and can result in lost work time. Don't take short cuts. Don't break safety rules. Don't use faulty or broken equipment or tools. Use all recommended safeguards. Always report any unsafe conditions.

Personal safety is also a must. Wear a hard hat, as shown in Figure 2–58. A hard hat is a must when any part of the building or work is over your head. Wear steel-toed work shoes. *Always wear eye protection when breaking or sawing masonry units.* Report and take care of any injury, no matter how minor.

Personal Protection

1. Wear a hard hat.
2. Wear steel-toed safety shoes.

3. Wear eye protection when breaking or sawing masonry units.

4. Wear gloves when lifting or carrying rough or broken material or when working with caustic material.

5. Remove all rings and jewelry so they don't interfere with your work. Never wear rings or jewelry around electrical equipment.

6. Wear proper protective clothing, as recommended by the manufacturers, when working with chemicals.

7. Wash off mortar from your hands and skin, and use a hand lotion to prevent chapping. Mortar dries the skin.

FIGURE 2–62
Adjustable, motorized scaffold used on the job. (Access Engineering U.S.A., Inc.)

FIGURE 2–61
A winch is used to raise and lower the adjustable platform. (Non-Stop Scaffolding)

Work Habits

1. Do the work following safe, professional standards.

2. Don't horse around on the job or in the work area.

3. Don't throw objects, tools, or materials.

4. When working high, take care to avoid dropping objects, such as tools. Never place tools or other objects at the edge of the scaffold or at the edge of an open floor or ledge.

5. Use only the proper tools and only tools that are in top condition. Store tools that you are not using.

6. Check any electrical equipment before using it.

7. Keep work area as clean as possible.

8. Spread sand on slippery walkways. Calcium chloride is used to melt ice on walkways.

Material Handling

1. When lifting heavy loads, lift with your legs, not your back. Squat down and pick up the load by straightening your legs. *Never* bend over to pick up a heavy load. Get help to carry heavy loads.

2. Do not overload a wheelbarrow or power buggy. Place the load forward toward the front wheel. Never use a wheelbarrow or buggy with a loose, cracked, broken, or faulty handle or a twisted or out-of-round wheel.

3. Store masonry units on a paved surface, on planks, or on shipping paper. Don't set directly on the ground; Figure 2–63 shows brick cubes stored on the job site.

4. The maximum height for open, unsupported piles of brick is seven feet. A pile should be set back one inch at the four-foot level, and one inch at every foot thereafter.

5. Block and brick should always be stacked in tiers on a solid foundation. Stacked piles should be limited to a height of six feet whenever possible. When block and brick are stacked higher than

FIGURE 2–63
Store masonry units on the job so they are not in direct contact with the ground.

six feet, the pile must be stepped back, braced, and propped.

6. Cut stone for sills, door, and window trim must be stored level and on planks. Stone is packed with sisal to prevent chipping (Figure 2–64). Support is important since the stone could crack or break if improperly stored. Flagstone or any thin stone should be stored on edge to prevent breaking.

7. When stacking cement or lime sacks, stack in a pile with mouths facing inward. Cross-pile the sacks; that is, lay every other layer at right angles to each other. Set sacks back one-sack

FIGURE 2-64
Cut stone sills are stored level and off the ground. Note sisal used between stone members to prevent chipping.

length at every sixth layer in height. Do not build stacks over ten-feet high unless they are stored in a bin or enclosure. The stack or pile must be stable so it won't slip or tilt.

8. Do not store materials near a walkway or near a doorway or hoist. Keep materials at least six feet away from a doorway or hoist. If stored above the first floor in a building, keep material at least ten feet away from the outer floor edge, including stairwells and hoistways.

9. If masonry units are in an exposed area where they may be rained on, the package should be covered. Vinyl is commonly used.

Electrical Equipment

1. Check electrical equipment before using. Equipment must be grounded. Don't use if there are frayed cords, damaged insulation, or exposed wires.

2. Never operate electrical equipment when standing in wet or damp areas.

3. Keep electrical wires off the ground. Never run over wires with any moving equipment.

4. Shut off power in case of a problem or accident.

5. Do not touch anyone in contact with live electrical current. Instead, first shut off the power.

Then move the person by pushing him or her with a dry piece of lumber. Give mouth to mouth resuscitation if the victim is not breathing. Call an ambulance.

TOOL CLEANING AND MAINTENANCE

Good, sound tools are important to doing a professional job. Over time, of course, tools will wear out and can no longer do the job they were designed for. When worn, they should be replaced. Don't try to do the job with a faulty tool. Simple cleaning will extend tool life and keep your tools in good shape.

Trowel Care. When finished, wash or wipe off mortar. Dry mortar can be scoured off with sand. A board or broken brick can also be used to remove dry mortar. If the trowel is washed, be sure to dry off all moisture. Rust causes pitting, which makes the trowel unsuitable for professional use. If the trowel is not going to be used for a few days, wipe the blade with a light coat of oil to prevent rusting.

Mason's Rule. The joints of the folding rule should be lightly oiled to prevent binding or rusting. The metal blade of the push-pull rule can be wiped with oil.

Level. Both metal and wooden levels should be cleaned of all masonry splatter. Remove any mortar stains by rubbing with a damp cloth. Always take care to dry off any moisture. Difficult stains can be cleaned by rubbing with steel wool. The wood in wood levels should be wiped periodically with boiled linseed oil. Rub the wood with a linseed-soaked rag. This keeps the wood in good condition. Allow the linseed oil to dry into the wood. Wipe off any linseed oil that gets on the metal parts. Keep the linseed oil off the glass; oil will cause staining or clouding and make it difficult to see the bubble. If any linseed oil gets on the glass, wipe it off immediately with a clean, dry cloth.

SCAFFOLDING SAFETY RULES

as Recommended by

SCAFFOLDING AND SHORING INSTITUTE

(SEE SEPARATE SHORING SAFETY RULES)

Following are some common sense rules designed to promote safety in the use of steel scaffolding. These rules are illustrative and suggestive only, and are intended to deal only with some of the many practices and conditions encountered in the use of scaffolding. The rules do not purport to be all-inclusive or to supplant or replace other additional safety and precautionary measures to cover usual or unusual conditions. They are not intended to conflict with, or supersede, any state, local, or federal statute or regulation; reference to such specific provisions should be made by the user. (See Rule II.)

I. **POST THESE SCAFFOLDING SAFETY RULES** in a conspicuous place and be sure that all persons who erect, dismantle or use scaffolding are aware of them.

II. **FOLLOW ALL STATE, LOCAL AND FEDERAL CODES, ORDINANCES AND REGULATIONS** pertaining to scaffolding.

III. **INSPECT ALL EQUIPMENT BEFORE USING**—Never use any equipment that is damaged or deteriorated in any way.

IV. **KEEP ALL EQUIPMENT IN GOOD REPAIR.** Avoid using rusted equipment—the strength of rusted equipment is not known.

V. **INSPECT ERECTED SCAFFOLDS REGULARLY** to be sure that they are maintained in safe condition.

VI. **CONSULT YOUR SCAFFOLDING SUPPLIER WHEN IN DOUBT**—scaffolding is his business, **NEVER TAKE CHANCES.**

A. **PROVIDE ADEQUATE SILLS** for scaffold posts and use base plates.

B. **USE ADJUSTING SCREWS** instead of blocking to adjust to uneven grade conditions.

C. **PLUMB AND LEVEL ALL SCAFFOLDS** as the erection proceeds. Do not force braces to fit—level the scaffold until proper fit can be made easily.

D. **FASTEN ALL BRACES SECURELY.**

E. **DO NOT CLIMB CROSS BRACES.** An access (climbing) ladder, access steps, frame designed to be climbed or equivalent safe access to the scaffold shall be used.

F. **ON WALL SCAFFOLDS PLACE AND MAINTAIN ANCHORS** securely between structure and scaffold at least every 30' of length and 25' of height.

G. **WHEN SCAFFOLDS ARE TO BE PARTIALLY OR FULLY ENCLOSED,** specific precautions must be taken to assure frequency and adequacy of ties attaching the scaffolding to the building due to increased load conditions resulting from effects of wind and weather. The scaffolding components to which the ties are attached must also be checked for additional loads.

H. **FREE STANDING SCAFFOLD TOWERS MUST BE RESTRAINED FROM TIPPING** by guying or other means.

I. **EQUIP ALL PLANKED OR STAGED AREAS** with proper guardrails, midrails and toeboards along all open sides and ends of scaffold platforms.

J. **POWER LINES NEAR SCAFFOLDS** are dangerous—use caution and consult the power service company for advice.

K. **DO NOT USE** ladders or makeshift devices on top of scaffolds to increase the height.

L. **DO NOT OVERLOAD SCAFFOLDS.**

M. **PLANKING:**
1. Use only lumber that is properly inspected and graded as scaffold plank.
2. Planking shall have at least 12" of overlap and extend 6" beyond center of support, or be cleated at both ends to prevent sliding off supports.
3. Fabricated scaffold planks and platforms unless cleated or restrained by hooks shall extend over their end supports not less than 6 inches nor more than 12 inches.
4. Secure plank to scaffold when necessary.

N. **FOR ROLLING SCAFFOLD THE FOLLOWING ADDITIONAL RULES APPLY:**
1. **DO NOT RIDE ROLLING SCAFFOLDS.**
2. **SECURE OR REMOVE ALL MATERIAL AND EQUIPMENT** from platform before moving scaffold.
3. **CASTER BRAKES MUST BE APPLIED** at all times when scaffolds are not being moved.
4. **CASTERS WITH PLAIN STEMS** shall be attached to the panel or adjustment screw by pins or other suitable means.
5. **DO NOT ATTEMPT TO MOVE A ROLLING SCAFFOLD WITHOUT SUFFICIENT HELP**—watch out for holes in floor and overhead obstructions.
6. **DO NOT EXTEND ADJUSTING SCREWS ON ROLLING SCAFFOLDS MORE THAN 12".**
7. **USE HORIZONTAL DIAGONAL BRACING** near the bottom and at 20' intervals measured from the rolling surface.
8. **DO NOT USE BRACKETS ON ROLLING SCAFFOLDS** without consideration of overturning effect.
9. **THE WORKING PLATFORM HEIGHT OF A ROLLING SCAFFOLD** must not exceed four times the smallest base dimension unless guyed or otherwise stabilized.

O. For **"PUTLOGS"** and **"TRUSSES"** the following additional rules apply.
1. **DO NOT CANTILEVER OR EXTEND PUTLOGS/TRUSSES** as side brackets without thorough consideration for loads to be applied.
2. **PUTLOGS/TRUSSES SHOULD EXTEND AT LEAST 6"** beyond point of support.
3. **PLACE PROPER BRACING BETWEEN PUTLOGS/TRUSSES** when the span of putlog/truss is more than 12'.

P. **ALL BRACKETS** shall be seated correctly with side brackets parallel to the frames and end brackets at 90 degrees to the frames. Brackets shall not be bent or twisted from normal position. Brackets (except mobile brackets designed to carry materials) are to be used as work platforms only and shall not be used for storage of material or equipment.

Q. **ALL SCAFFOLDING ACCESSORIES** shall be used and installed in accordance with the manufacturers recommended procedure. Accessories shall not be altered in the field. Scaffolds, frames and their components, manufactured by different companies shall not be intermixed.

FIGURE 2-65

Scaffolding safety rules. (Scaffolding, Shoring, & and Forming Institute)

Hammers. Replace any splintered or broken handles. If the hammer head is loose, drive an additional wedge in the end or replace the handle. Grind out any nicks in the blade of the brick hammer.

Chisels. Do not use chisels or brick sets with a mushroomed head. Grind the head to restore it to its original shape.

SCAFFOLDING

Assemble scaffolding following manufacturer's recommendations. Install and use all safeguards. Support on firm ground and use steel support plates. The Scaffolding, Shoring & Forming Institute has a set of recommended safety rules for scaffolding. See Figure 2–65. *Follow these rules.*

FIRST AID

Immediately treat and report all injuries. If chemicals, cement, or lime gets into your eyes, flush profusely with clean water and see a doctor. Chemical burns should be treated with burn first aid and then checked by a doctor. *Remember the following:*

1. Seek first aid immediately.

2. See a doctor for serious injuries or chemicals in eyes.

3. Report all accidents.

CHAPTER REVIEW

QUESTIONS

1. What is the difference between a mason's trowel and a pointing trowel?

2. How is a tuckpointing trowel used?

3. What are jointers used for? A sled runner?

4. What does a joint raker do?

5. Describe the use of a brick hammer.

6. What is the difference between a stone mason hammer and a mashing hammer?

7. What is the mason's chisel used for?

8. How does a pitching tool differ from the tooth chisel? What are they each used for?

9. How is a plugging chisel used?

10. How does a masonry saw work? Describe wet sawing. Dry sawing.

11. Describe how a mason's line is placed and held in place.

12. What is the mason's line used for?

13. What is a trig? How is it used?

14. How are levels used?

15. Describe the difference between a brick spacing measure and a modular spacing measure.

16. How many courses are laid out in 16 inches using a #6 modular scale?

17. How are steel squares used for alignment or truing?

18. Describe how masonry guides are used.

19. What is a story pole?

20. What are mason's brushes used for?

21. What is a power buggy?

22. What are fork lifts used for on the job?

23. Why is scaffolding used? Describe a mason's scaffold.

24. When should eye protection be worn?

25. List seven guides for safe work habits on the job.

26. Describe how to lift heavy objects.

27. What should you do if you get lime or other chemicals in your eyes?

28. What should you do if someone comes in contact with a live electrical current?

29. Refer to figure 2–65 for scaffolding safety and list at least 20 guidelines or safety rules.

30. What are the three basic rules of first aid?

TOOL IDENTIFICATION

1. Identify the parts of the trowel:

2. Identify the following tools:

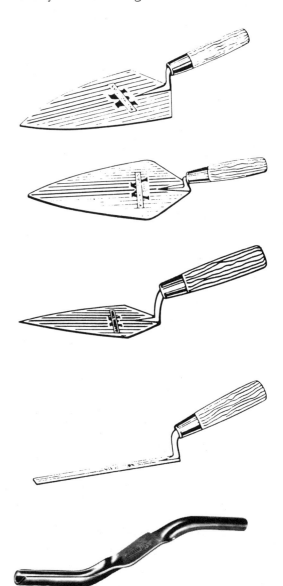

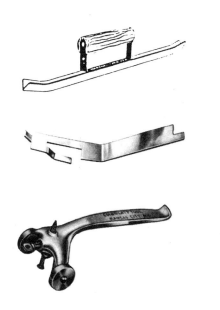

3. Identify the following chisels:

4. Identify the parts of the chisel

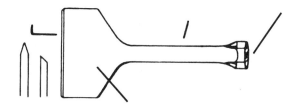

5. Locate and circle (a) course 2 for #5 spacing; (b) course 2 for #10 spacing, and (c) course 1 for #3 spacing.

Brick spacing rule

						Small numbers show number of courses						
1	2	4	6	8	0		1	2	4	6	8	0
1	3	5	7	9	1		2	3	5	7	9	2

ACTIVITIES

1. Make a list of basic tools you feel you need to start work on the job. Check manufacturer's catalogs and tool supply stores for prices. Add up your total beginning investment. *Remember:* Only use quality tools. Cheap tools cost too much!

2. Talk to experienced journeymen and masonry masters. What brands of tools do they use and recommend? Check the trowels they use. What kind of material is used for the trowel handles?

3. With permission, observe work conditions on a job site.
   a. How are masonry materials and units stored?
   b. How is the mortar mixed?
   c. How are materials and mortar delivered to the masons at the work station?
   d. What scaffolding or material supports are used?
   e. Describe what tools, measures, and guides are used.
   f. Describe how masonry units are cut.
   g. Describe any safety guidelines or practices followed. What safety violations, if any, are visible?
   h. What jobs do the mason's helpers do?

4. Obtain a mason's rule with either a modular scale or a brick spacing scale. Use the rule to measure at least three different standing brick walls and identify the measure used in laying the wall.

Chapter 3

MASONRY BUILDING UNITS

After studying this chapter you should be able to:

- Describe the types of structural clay masonry.
- Describe how brick is manufactured.
- Describe the three brick grades based on weather.
- List at least seven common brick types and describe how they are used.
- Explain the difference between nominal and actual sizes.
- Define different masonry units by how they are laid in a wall.

- Describe hollow masonry units and their grades.
- Explain what terra cotta is and how it is used.
- Describe how concrete masonry units are manufactured.
- Define concrete block grades.
- Describe at least fourteen different types of concrete block.
- List the basic block sizes used.
- Describe the parts of a concrete block.
- List common glass block sizes.
- Describe the three types of natural stone.
- Describe seven types of natural stone.
- Describe what manufactured stone is.

The mason uses a wide variety of building units, mortars to bond the units, and, if needed, different ties, anchors, and reinforcements. There are thousands of different shapes, textures, and colors available in the basic building units. Building units are basically made from fired clay (such as brick or tile), concrete (concrete block), and glass (glass block). In addition, of course, natural stone is used.

The general term used for all masonry units made from fired clay or shale is *structural clay masonry*. Structural clay masonry includes brick, structural clay tile, and architectural terra cotta.

BRICK MASONRY UNITS

Brick is made of fired clay and shale mixtures. In addition to brick, hollow tile and terra cotta are produced from structural clay although only a small quantity of either is produced today. Brick are either solid or cored.

Brick Manufacturing

Clay and shale, the raw materials for brick manufacturing, are mined or quarried out of the ground with heavy equipment. The quarrying process is called *winning*. A wide variety of clays that are suitable for brickmaking are available. Generally, local clays are used. The clay itself is created by the weathering and breakdown of rocks over millions of years. Clay is mainly composed of silica and alumina. Metallic oxides in the clay create different colors in the fired brick.

Each clay deposit has its own characteristics. Shale, which is also used in brick manufacture, is a hard, compressed clay. It must be broken up and ground before it can be used.

After winning, the raw materials are crushed and ground. Water is added, and the mixture is shaped into brick. Figure 3–1 shows the brickmaking process. Two processes are currently being used for shaping the brick units: the soft mud molding process and the stiff mud extrusion process.

Soft Mud Molding Process. In the soft mud molding process, a liberal amount of water is mixed with the ground clay blend, and the soft mud or mixture is then pressed into forms or molds. Figure 3–2 shows the molding process. Multiple brick molds are used so a large number of brick can be formed at one time. The molds are coated with sand or water so the soft clay doesn't stick to the sides. Brick made by this process are sometimes referred to as sand mold or water struck brick. After inspection, the green brick are removed from the molds, stacked, and placed in a drying chamber to remove excess moisture. Figure

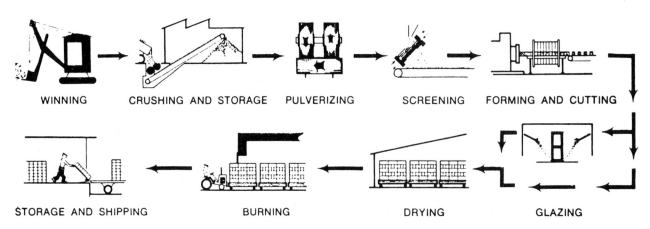

WINNING   CRUSHING AND STORAGE   PULVERIZING   SCREENING   FORMING AND CUTTING

STORAGE AND SHIPPING   BURNING   DRYING   GLAZING

FIGURE 3–1
Brick manufacturing process. (Brick Institute of America)

FIGURE 3-2
Soft mud process of forming brick. Multiple molds are used to form individual brick. (Old Carolina Brick Co.)

3-3, left, shows brick exiting a drying chamber. Figure 3-3, right, shows a carload of dry brick ready to enter the kiln for firing.

The soft mud molding process is the way brick were originally made by hand. Today, of course, the process is usually automated. Custom brick in special shapes and made-to-match old or antique brick are still made by hand.

Stiff Mud Extrusion Process. In the stiff mud extrusion process, only about half as much water is used as in the soft mud process. The brick materials are mixed with water in a pug mill and then the mud is forced out of the mill through a die. Figure 3-4 shows the formed mud being forced out of the pug mill. Note that the shaped clay comes out in a continuous column or ribbon. Tubes or rods may be used within the die to create holes. This continuous ribbon or column then runs through a wire-cutting machine (Figure 3-5) where it is cut to the size desired. A revolving reel holding the cutting wires turns 90° at each cut. After cutting, the unfired or "green" brick are in-

FIGURE 3-3
Drying chamber is shown to the left. Dry brick is shown entering the kiln at right. (Lingl Corp.)

FIGURE 3-4
Stiff mud process. Formed mud column being extruded from pug mill. (J.C. Steel & Sons, Inc.)

spected, stacked, and placed in a drying chamber, as shown in Figure 3-3.

Note in Figure 3-3 that the green brick are stacked on a flat kiln car, something like a small railroad car. This car, along with other cars, is placed in the drying chamber. The brick are left in the drying chamber for 24 to 48 hours until they lose a good part of their moisture, from 7 to 30 percent, depending on whether the stiff mud or soft mud process is used. Heat and humidity are regulated in the drying chamber to allow an even drying process.

Brick Kilns. There are three basic types of kilns: the tunnel, periodic, and scove or field kiln. The most widely used and more modern type is the tunnel kiln. It is a continuous chamber several hundred feet long. Periodic kilns may be round or rectangular and are usually 30 to 50 feet across. These kilns operate in a batch fashion much like a kitchen oven. The waste heat from these two types of kilns is often used in the drying of the green brick.

The scove or field kiln is the oldest and least-used variety. It consists of a house-like structure built of green brick with a fire inside. When the brick is fully fired, the kiln is disassembled and the brick is removed.

Kilns are usually lined inside with firebrick. Oil or gas and sometimes sawdust and coal are used to fuel the kiln. At the hottest part of the kiln, the heat reaches an average temperature of 1950°F (1065°C). Temperatures may be varied depending upon the particular clay used. It takes around 30 hours for the brick to pass through the kiln. Figure 3-6 shows a carload of fired brick emerging from the end of a tunnel kiln.

FIGURE 3-5
Stiff mud process. Wire cutting machine cuts the column into individual bricks. (J.C. Steel & Sons, Inc.)

FIGURE 3–6
Brick kiln: carload of fired Norman brick leaving the kiln.
(Lingl Corp.)

Coloring and Texturing

Most clays fire to either a red or buff color. The red color is created by the ferrous (iron) oxides in the clay. Variations of white or cream are also produced. Black or gray are produced by adding manganese oxides.

Color variations are also produced by temperature variations in the kiln. Higher temperatures create darker brick. A purple-colored brick is produced from red brick clays by *flashing* the brick in the kiln. Flashing creates a very high temperature for a short time and burns up all the oxygen in the kiln. This creates an atmosphere short of oxygen, which changes or reduces the iron oxides on the brick surface to give a purple color. Brick color varies, however, even with the same kiln and the same firing.

Brick Coatings. Additional colors are often produced on ordinary red clay brick by coating the outside of the green brick before firing. This gives a large variety of colors on the brick surface. White, creams, grays, browns, and black pigments are commonly used. Pigment can be applied to the surface by a clay slurry or by dusting with colored sand. The sand is only used to carry the pigment. The colored mineral coating is then fired on the outside of the brick. These different colored brick are often laid out together to create an interesting, multi-colored wall. By using computer-controlled color blending, an almost endless color variety can be achieved. The color can be duplicated if additional brick of exactly the same color are required.

Textures. Brick are textured while still wet, usually just after they are extruded from the mill. The brick face may be scored, scraped, or cut to give different shapes. Special rollers may be used to press different designs on the surface. A very wide variety of textures are available from the different brick manufacturers.

Packaging

After cooling, the brick are restacked and banded with steel bands. Approximately 100 brick, depending on the brick size, are banded together in a pack and five packages are rebanded into a cube. The number of brick in a cube may vary slightly depending on the size and manufacturer. Figure 3–7 shows a cube containing 500 standard brick. Note that two openings are left in the side of the packages. These openings are where the two arms of the fork lift fit when the cube is being carried.

Modular and standard brick usually have 500 brick per cube while larger sizes may have as few as 200.

Brick Grades

Brick are generally graded according to their ability to resist exposure or weathering and as to surface perfection. The American Society of Testing and Materials (ASTM) has established the grade standards. Three basic weathering grade classifications have been developed for clay or shale brick: Grades SW, MW, and NW.

Grade SW. Grade SW describes clay or shale brick that can withstand exposure to below freezing temperatures where there is frost, freezing,

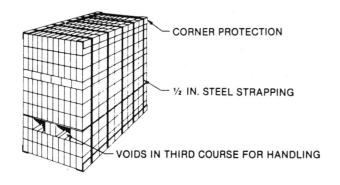

FIGURE 3-7
Brick cube. For convenience, cube may be broken down into smaller packs. (Mason Contractors Association of America)

and thawing. Grade SW is used in the northern, moist areas of the United States. SW stands for *severe weathering*.

Grade MW. Grade MW describes clay or shale brick that can withstand exposure to freezing temperatures in a drier climate. MW stands for *moderate weathering*.

Grade NW. Grade NW is used to describe clay or shale brick that *cannot* withstand freezing or thawing. Grade NW is used in areas where there is no freezing or frost or in areas where there is some frost but the area is generally dry (annual rainfall less than 15 inches). This brick is primarily intended for interior or backup brick. Brick *not* exposed to weather may be grade NW if used in walls but should be SW when used in floors. NW stands for *no weathering*.

Brick Types

There are various types of brick in common use. Some are defined by their composition, and some are defined by their use or finish. Clay and shale brick are the common red brick seen universally in construction. Most brick are defined by how they are used in the structure.

Facing Brick. Facing brick, as the name implies, is used on the exposed face of the wall. They are a high quality select unit of great durability. Special firing and texturing techniques may be followed to produce a uniform brick. Various shades of red, brown, gray, yellow, and white are produced. Different surface textures or special scorings or markings are available. Figure 3-8 shows face brick with different face finishes.

Grades SW and MW are recommended for facing brick, as shown in Figure 3-9. In addition to weathering grades, facing brick are further specified by type. Three types of facing brick are used: Types FBS, FBX, and FBA. *Type FBS* facing brick are for general use in exposed exterior and interior masonry walls and partitions where some variety and color differences are permitted. *Type FBX* is for walls where a high degree of perfection and consistency is required. Very little variation or color range is permitted. *Type FBA* is special facing brick selected for its variety in color and texture; its nonconformity is designed to give an architectural effect.

Building Brick. Building brick, sometimes called common brick, is made from ordinary pit-run clay or shale and follows a routine firing procedure in the kiln. No special firing or texturing is done. Building brick is used as backing or backup brick behind the face brick. Grades SW, MW, and NW are used. Building brick are often red.

Clinker Brick. If the kiln heat is too high, the brick may overburn. Overburnt brick are called clinker brick. These brick are rough and very hard and usually dark in color and may have black spots. They may also be misshaped or distorted. Clinker brick may, however, be used to create spe-

SANDMOLD FACE, SMOOTH WITH COLOR VARIATION

WIRE CUT, ROUGH FINISH

DIE SCORED FINISH

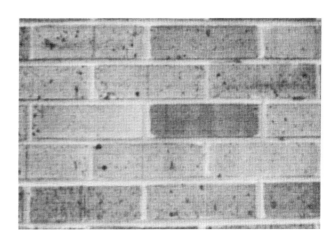

DIE SCORED FINISH

STIPPLED FINISH

STIPPLED FINISH

FIGURE 3-8
Typical face brick.

COLOR VARIATIONS CAUSED BY FLASH
(HIGH TEMPERATURE)

PAINTED SURFACE FINISH

PRESSED SURFACE TEXTURE

PRESSED SURFACE TEXTURE

FIGURE 3–8 (*continued*)

cial or unusual effects in the construction. Figure 3–10 shows an example of clinker brick used in a decorative wall.

Glazed Brick. Glazed brick is a type of face brick that has the outside face covered with a ceramic glaze. This creates a very hard, glass-like

	Weathering Region		
Use	Negligible	Moderate	Severe
In vertical surfaces:			
In contact with earth—	MW	SW	SW
Not in contact w/earth—	MW	MW	MW
In horizontal surfaces:			
In contact with earth—	SW	SW	SW
Not in contact w/earth—	MW	SW	SW

FIGURE 3–9
Grade requirements for clay or shale facing brick. (ASTM #C-62 Standard)

FIGURE 3-10
Clinker brick used in decorative wall.

coating. Various colored glazes are available, such as white, black, red, and blue. Different surface color patterns are also available. Figure 3-11 shows samples of glazed brick. Glazed brick or tile is often used in areas or buildings where a very hard nonporous surface is needed; that is, a surface that cannot collect and conceal dirt and a surface that is easy to clean. Glazed brick or tile is commonly used in hospitals and laboratories where cleanliness is very important. Glazed brick is also used strictly for its beauty and decorative effect.

Firebrick. Firebrick is made out of a special fire clay and is used to line the inside of fireplaces and boilers. The brick is larger than a regular building brick and is designed to withstand very high temperatures. Firebrick are not made by the manufacturers who make regular structural brick.

Solid Brick. Most extruded brick have small cores running through them that are designed to reduce the weight of the unit and to improve drying and firing characteristics. Although these brick have small holes or cores they are still called solid brick. *Solid brick* is defined as having at least 75 percent of its cross-sectional area solid. Small holes or cores, up to 25 percent, therefore, are allowed in "solid" brick. Some brick have no cores at all and are truly solid. Don't be confused when cored brick is called solid; this is the technical convention in the field. Three-core or ten-core brick, therefore, is still considered solid brick if the cores

take up no more than 25 percent of the area. Brick-type units with large hollows or cores in excess of 25 percent are called *hollow brick* or *hollow masonry units or tile.* (These are covered in the next section.)

Paving Brick. Paving brick is a type of brick used on floors, walkways, driveways, and patios (Figure 3-12). Paving brick is usually harder and more durable than ordinary brick. They are completely solid with no holes or cores. Paving brick are classified in two ways, either by weathering or by type of traffic.

Paving brick is defined in terms of three classes of weathering: Classes SX, MX, and NX.

RED GLAZED BRICK

WHITE GLAZED BRICK

FIGURE 3-11
Typical glazed brick. *Top:* Red glazed brick with different shades of red. *Bottom:* White glazed brick with black specks caused by manganese.

FIGURE 3-12
Paving brick. (Higgins Brick)

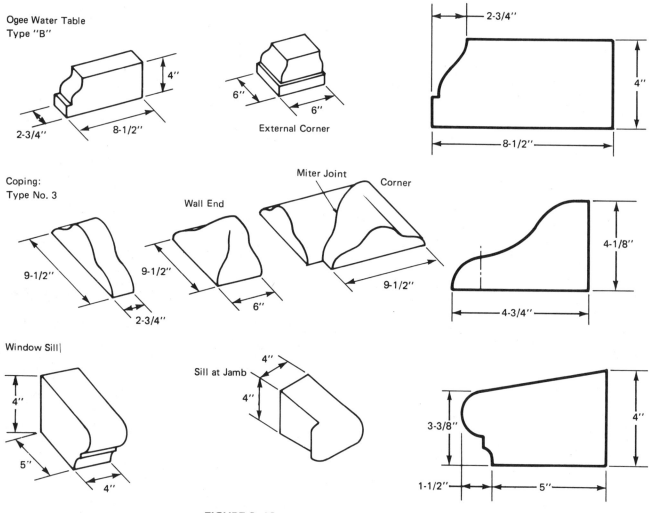

Ogee Water Table
Type "B"

4"

2-3/4"

8-1/2"

6"

6"

External Corner

2-3/4"

4"

8-1/2"

Coping:
Type No. 3

Miter Joint

Corner

Wall End

9-1/2"

9-1/2"

9-1/2"

6"

2-3/4"

4-1/8"

4-3/4"

Window Sill

4"

Sill at Jamb

4"

4"

4"

5"

4"

3-3/8"

4"

1-1/2"

5"

FIGURE 3-13
Special brick shapes. (Old Carolina Brick Co.)

Class SX is for paving brick that is used in areas of high moisture and freezing. *Class* MX is for brick designed for exterior use where freezing is not a factor. *Class* NX is for interior use where a sealer or coating will be applied to the brick, such as on factory floors.

Paving brick is also defined by *traffic use*. *Type I* is for paving brick exposed to extensive abrasion. Type I brick would be used in driveways or as a paving in front of public entrances. *Type II* brick is exposed to intermediate traffic. Type II would be used on exterior walkways or the floor in a store or restaurant. *Type III* brick is exposed to low traffic use, such as a family patio.

Special Shapes.   Ordinary brick is made in a simple rectangular shape. Various special brick shapes are sometimes offered by brick manufacturers. For example, special brick are available for making odd-angle building corners. Rather than a right angle (90°) corner, a sharp 60° corner can be laid using special-shaped brick. Wedge-shaped brick are also sometimes used for building arches. In addition, it is possible to have shaped brick custom made. Of course, shaped brick, especially custom-made brick, are more expensive. Figure 3–13 shows a few special types of brick offered by one brick company. Special handmade brick is used to lay the fireplace shown in Figure 3–14.

Used Brick.   Used or salvaged brick is sometimes specified for use in areas that are not exposed to the weather. Since old brick is salvaged from demolished buildings, face brick and backing brick are often mixed together. Salvaged brick should not be used for exterior work since the backing brick would not hold up to the weather. Used brick makes an attractive, interesting wall and is frequently used inside buildings.

Some brick manufacturers make new brick that are designed to look old. If these new "used" brick are manufactured to face-brick standards, they can be used in exterior walls.

Brick Sizes

A number of different brick sizes are used to produce different characteristics when in place. The larger sizes are limited by the weight of the unit—the brick must be easy to handle in one hand. Another consideration for brick size is that when in place with mortar it fits to a modular layout. Modules are based on four-inch units. Modular masonry construction allows the use of standard-size modular windows and doors. Use of standard sizes cuts down on cost.

Brick are characterized by actual size and nominal size. *Actual size* relates to the measured size of the brick. *Nominal size* relates to the overall size of the brick, including the thickness of the joint. An actual $11\frac{1}{2}''$ brick laid with $\frac{1}{2}$-inch joints would have a nominal length of $12''$ ($11\frac{1}{2}'' + \frac{1}{2}''$). A standard modular brick may have a nominal size of $4'' \times 2\frac{2}{3}'' \times 8''$, yet have an actual manufactured size of $3\frac{5}{8}'' \times 2\frac{1}{4}'' \times 7\frac{5}{8}''$. With mortar, the nominal size is reached. This unit would require $\frac{3}{8}$-inch thick joints.

FIGURE 3–14
Fireplace made using special handmade brick. (Old Carolina Brick Co.)

Unit Designation	Nominal Dimensions, in.			Joint Thickness in.	Manufactured Dimensions in.		
	T	H	L		T	H	L
Standard Modular	4	$2\frac{2}{3}$	8	$\frac{3}{8}$	$3\frac{5}{8}$	$2\frac{1}{4}$	$7\frac{5}{8}$
				$\frac{1}{2}$	$3\frac{1}{2}$	$2\frac{1}{4}$	$7\frac{1}{2}$
Engineer	4	$3\frac{1}{5}$	8	$\frac{3}{8}$	$3\frac{5}{8}$	$2\frac{13}{16}$	$7\frac{5}{8}$
				$\frac{1}{2}$	$3\frac{1}{2}$	$2\frac{11}{16}$	$7\frac{1}{2}$
Economy 8 or Jumbo Closure	4	4	8	$\frac{3}{8}$	$3\frac{5}{8}$	$3\frac{5}{8}$	$7\frac{5}{8}$
				$\frac{1}{2}$	$3\frac{1}{2}$	$3\frac{1}{2}$	$7\frac{1}{2}$
Double	4	$5\frac{1}{3}$	8	$\frac{6}{8}$	$3\frac{5}{8}$	$4\frac{15}{16}$	$7\frac{5}{8}$
				$\frac{1}{2}$	$3\frac{1}{2}$	$4\frac{13}{16}$	$7\frac{1}{2}$
Roman	4	2	12	$\frac{3}{8}$	$3\frac{5}{8}$	$1\frac{5}{8}$	$11\frac{5}{8}$
				$\frac{1}{2}$	$3\frac{1}{2}$	$1\frac{1}{2}$	$11\frac{1}{2}$
Norman	4	$2\frac{2}{3}$	12	$\frac{3}{8}$	$3\frac{5}{8}$	$2\frac{1}{4}$	$11\frac{5}{8}$
				$\frac{1}{2}$	$3\frac{1}{2}$	$2\frac{1}{4}$	$11\frac{1}{2}$
Norwegian	4	$3\frac{1}{5}$	12	$\frac{3}{8}$	$3\frac{5}{8}$	$2\frac{13}{16}$	$11\frac{5}{8}$
				$\frac{1}{2}$	$3\frac{1}{2}$	$2\frac{11}{16}$	$11\frac{1}{2}$
Economy 12 or Jumbo Utility	4	4	12	$\frac{3}{8}$	$3\frac{5}{8}$	$3\frac{5}{8}$	$11\frac{5}{8}$
				$\frac{1}{2}$	$3\frac{1}{2}$	$3\frac{1}{2}$	$11\frac{1}{2}$
Triple	4	$5\frac{1}{3}$	12	$\frac{3}{8}$	$3\frac{5}{8}$	$4\frac{15}{16}$	$11\frac{5}{8}$
				$\frac{1}{2}$	$3\frac{1}{2}$	$4\frac{13}{16}$	$11\frac{1}{2}$
SCR brick *	6	$2\frac{2}{3}$	12	$\frac{3}{8}$	$5\frac{5}{8}$	$2\frac{1}{4}$	$11\frac{5}{8}$
				$\frac{1}{2}$	$5\frac{1}{2}$	$2\frac{1}{4}$	$11\frac{1}{2}$
6-in. Norwegian	6	$3\frac{1}{5}$	12	$\frac{3}{8}$	$5\frac{5}{8}$	$2\frac{13}{16}$	$11\frac{5}{8}$
				$\frac{1}{2}$	$5\frac{1}{2}$	$2\frac{11}{16}$	$11\frac{1}{2}$
6-in. Jumbo	6	4	12	$\frac{3}{8}$	$5\frac{5}{8}$	$3\frac{5}{8}$	$11\frac{5}{8}$
				$\frac{1}{2}$	$5\frac{1}{2}$	$3\frac{1}{2}$	$11\frac{1}{2}$
8-in. Jumbo	8	4	12	$\frac{3}{8}$	$7\frac{5}{8}$	$3\frac{5}{8}$	$11\frac{5}{8}$
				$\frac{1}{2}$	$7\frac{1}{2}$	$3\frac{1}{2}$	$11\frac{1}{2}$

* Reg. U.S. Pat. Off., SCPI.

FIGURE 3–15
Nominal and manufactured dimensions: modular solid brick. (Brick Institute of America)

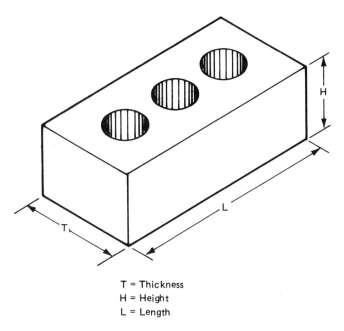

T = Thickness
H = Height
L = Length

FIGURE 3-16
Brick dimensions.

Modular Solid Brick. Figure 3–15 shows modular sizes of different brick. Thickness (T) is the front-to-back dimension or bed depth, height (H) give top-to-bottom size, and length (L) gives the left-to-right distance (Figure 3–16). Note that different manufactured sizes are available for any one nominal size. This allows either a $\frac{1}{2}$-inch or $\frac{3}{8}$-inch mortar joint thickness to be used.

Figure 3–17 shows different types of common modular solid brick. These are called *solid* brick because the holes (cores) do not exceed 25 percent of the cross-sectional area. The names for the units shown are generally accepted although some brick manufacturers may use their own designation. The wider 6-inch and 8-inch bricks are commonly used for laying one-wythe walls, such as house walls. Other sizes, different from the ones shown, are also produced. You should always check with your local brick manufacturers to see what sizes they produce.

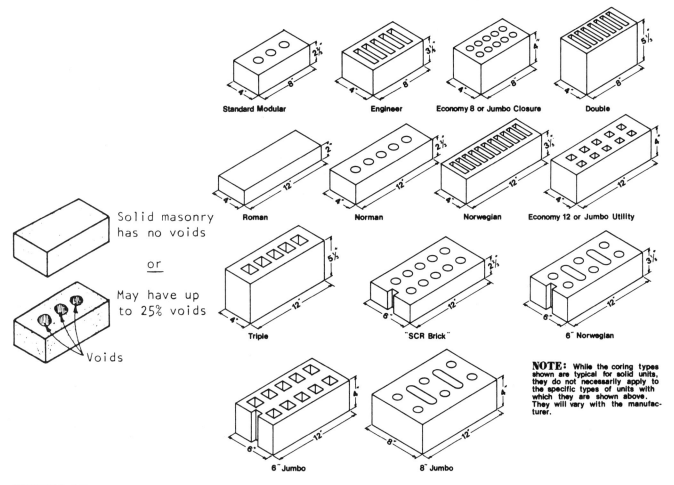

FIGURE 3-17
Modular solid brick. (Brick Institute of America)

Nonmodular Solid Brick. Nonmodular solid brick is also used. Figure 3–18 shows the three common nonmodular brick used. The "three-inch" brick is used in veneer work and for cavity walls. The larger, oversized brick is used because the larger size allows a greater square-foot area to be laid by the mason in a set time.

Paving Brick. Special brick are made for paving. These brick have no opening or cores. Figure 3–19 shows common modular paving brick and their sizes. Note that some paving brick are much thinner than regular brick. Their height varies from $\frac{1}{2}$-inch up to $2\frac{1}{4}$-inches. Paving units less than 1 inch in thickness are usually referred to as tiles.

Brick Weight

Brick weight, of course, varies depending on the size and number of the cores. In general, a solid cubic foot of brick varies in weight from 100 pounds to 150 pounds. The average weight of a building brick is around $4\frac{1}{2}$ pounds to 5 pounds each.

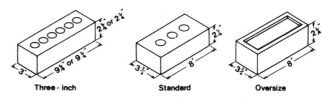

Unit Designation	Manufactured Size, in.		
	T	H	L
Three-inch[1]	3	2⅝	9⅝
	3	2¾	9¾
Standard	3¾[2]	2¼	8
Oversize	3¾[2]	2¾	8

[1]In recent years, the so-called "three-inch" brick has gained popularity in certain areas. The term "three-inch" designates its thickness or bed depth. The sizes shown in the table are the ones most commonly produced under the designation "Kingsize". Other sizes of 3-in. brick are also produced under such designations as "Big John", "Jumbo", "Scotsman" and "Spartan". Originally developed primarily for use as a veneer unit, it is also used to construct 8-in. cavity walls and 8-in. grouted walls.

[2]The manufactured thickness of standard or oversize nonmodular brick will vary from 3½ to 3¾ in. Therefore, if other than a running bond is desired, the designer should check with the manufacturer of the brick selected.

FIGURE 3–18
Nonmodular solid brick. (*Bottom*: Brick Institute of America)

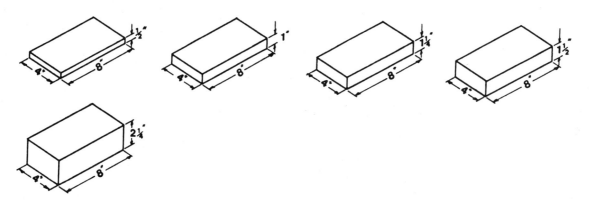

FIGURE 3–19
Modular paving brick (nominal dimensions).

Brick Terminology

Various standard terms are used to refer to parts of the brick and to broken or cut brick pieces. Figure 3–20 shows the names of the brick surfaces. Some molded bricks have a recessed panel called a *frog*, or *frogging*, on one of the beds. The oversized brick, Figure 3–18, top right, shows a frog.

When the brick is in place, the bottom where the brick rests in the mortar is referred to as the *bed joint* (Figure 3–21). The end, with mortar, is referred to as the *head joint*. The head joint is also sometimes called a *cross joint*. The mortar joint between two wythes (vertical walls) is called a *collar joint*.

Different names are used to describe cut or broken brick, as shown in Figure 3–22, top. A half brick, for example, is called a *bat*. Three-fourths of a brick is called a *three-quarter closure*; one-fourth, a *quarter closure*. Figure 3–22, bottom, shows how three-quarter and quarter closures are used. One corner may be cut off to make a *king closure*. A brick cut lengthwise across the end is called a *queen closure*. A brick cut lengthwise parallel to the bed is called a *split*.

Brick are also described by how they are laid in the wall. Figure 3–23 shows the different common positions. This terminology applies to all masonry units including concrete block and structural tile. Most masonry units are laid out as *stretchers*. A *header* is laid in the wall so the end is exposed. *Headers* are used in a solid wall to tie the parts (wythes) together. If the masonry unit is laid on the side (Figure 3–23, center) either a *rowlock stretcher* (parallel to the wall) or a *rowlock header* (perpendicular to the wall) is created. Any masonry unit laid on its side is referred to as a *rowlock*. Sometimes masonry units are laid on end. If the side or face faces out it is called a *soldier* (Figure 3–23, bottom). If the bed faces out it is called a *sailor*. Soldier and sailor brick are sometimes used at the top of a wall for decorative effect.

A continuous row or level of horizontal masonry units is called a *course* (Figure 3–24, left). A single vertical tier or wall of masonry units is called a *wythe* (Figure 3–24, right).

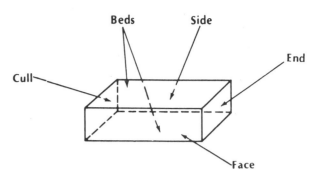

FIGURE 3–20
Brick surface terminology.

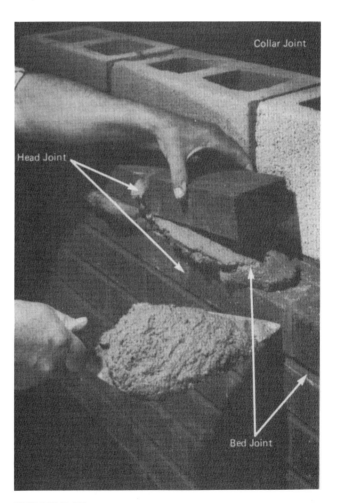

FIGURE 3–21
Joint terminology. (Master Builders)

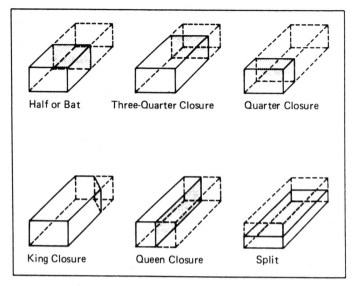

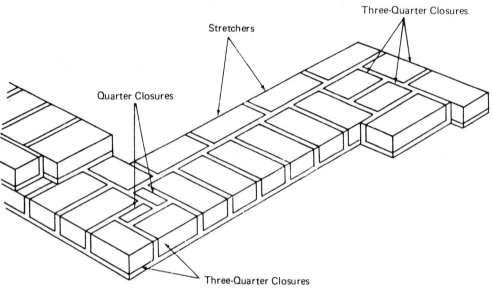

FIGURE 3-22
Brick parts or sections.

High-Suction Bricks

Brick may sometimes absorb a high amount of water. If brick absorbs too much water out of the mortar, then the mortar will not set properly—there will be insufficient water in the mortar mix to cause the chemical reaction with the cement, called hydration. If brick have a high absorption rate, they must be thoroughly wetted before being laid. They must be completely covered with water, as by careful hosing, before they are laid in the mortar. *Note:* There should be no standing or observable water on the hosed brick when they are being laid. Allow them to surface dry before using.

Brick can be tested for absorption by a simple test: (1) Draw a circle of one-inch diameter on the brick surface (bed) using a pencil; then trace the circle with a wax crayon. Use a quarter as a guide

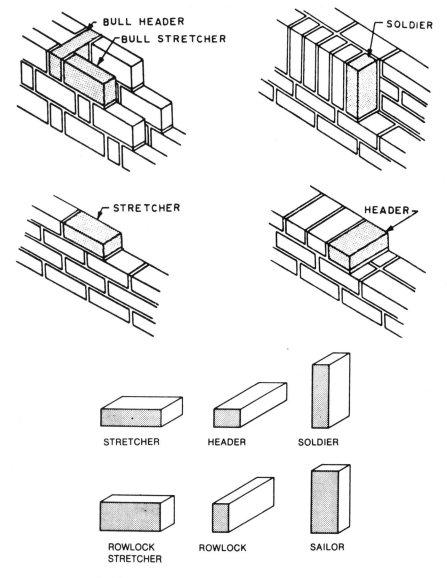

FIGURE 3–23
Brick units in place in the wall. (*Bottom*: Brick Institute of America)

when drawing the circle. (2) Using an eye dropper, very quickly drop 20 drops of water within the circle. The circle should be full of water but should not overflow. (3) Wait $1\frac{1}{2}$ minutes. If all the water is absorbed, you have a high-suction brick. All high-suction brick must be thoroughly wetted before being laid. If the time of absorption exceeds $1\frac{1}{2}$ minutes, the brick does not have to be wetted.

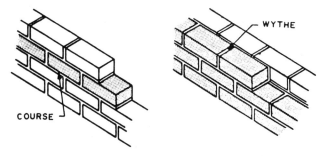

FIGURE 3–24
Brick wall: A horizontal row of brick is called a course. A vertical wall one-brick thick is called a wythe.

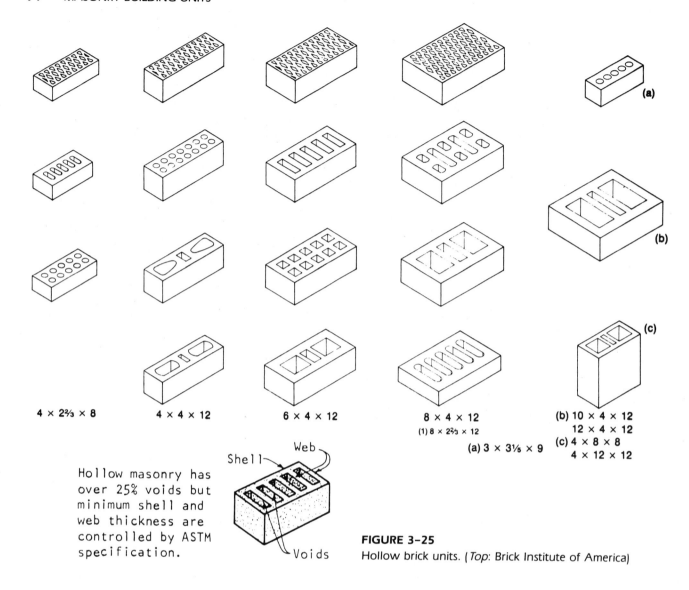

4 × 2⅔ × 8   4 × 4 × 12   6 × 4 × 12   8 × 4 × 12   (b) 10 × 4 × 12
                                                      (1) 8 × 2⅔ × 12   12 × 4 × 12
                                                      (a) 3 × 3⅛ × 9   (c) 4 × 8 × 8
                                                                            4 × 12 × 12

Hollow masonry has over 25% voids but minimum shell and web thickness are controlled by ASTM specification.

Shell   Web

Voids

FIGURE 3-25
Hollow brick units. (*Top:* Brick Institute of America)

HOLLOW BRICK UNITS

Hollow brick are widely used as a backing material. Hollow brick units have voids or openings of between 25 percent and 40 percent of their cross-sectional area. They are, therefore, at least 60 percent solid. Hollow brick units are made by forcing the clay mix through shaped dies. They are cut to the length needed. Hollow brick units are fired in the same manner as solid brick.

Figure 3–25 shows examples of different hollow brick units. Note the large size of the cells. Special shapes are available for use around windows and doors. Hollow masonry units are very popular today in reinforced brick construction.

Grading

Two grades are used based upon weather: Grade SW and Grade MW. These grades are the same as for solid brick. *Grade SW* hollow brick units are designed for use in areas of high moisture and freezing. *Grade MW* units are designed for use in moderate areas where there is some frost but a low amount of moisture.

Types

Hollow brick units are also classified (ASTM C652) by where they are used. *Type HBX* is for general use in exposed exterior and interior masonry walls and partitions where a high degree of mechanical perfection is required. Little color or size variation is allowed. *Type HBS* is also for general use in walls but a wider size and color variation is permitted. *Type HBA* is selected to allow a wide variation in color, size, and texture for planned architectural effect. *Type HBB* is for general use where color and texture is not a consideration. Figure 3–26 shows grading and types for hollow brick units.

Sizes

As shown in Figure 3–25, nominal widths of 4-inch, 8-inch, and 12-inch modular sizes are common.

The larger $6'' \times 4'' \times 12''$, $8'' \times 4'' \times 12''$, and $8'' \times 4'' \times 16''$ hollow brick do, of course, allow a much higher cubic footage to be laid by the mason in any time period. An $8'' \times 4'' \times 12''$ hollow brick, for example, produces a full 8-inch thick wall. It only takes three $8'' \times 4'' \times 12''$ hollow bricks to produce the same square foot, 8-inch thick wall produced by 13 standard-sized, solid brick. The labor savings and cost efficiency are considerable. These large or jumbo brick are called through-the-wall (TTW) masonry units.

Grade	Type	Use
SW MW	HBS	For general use in exposed exterior and interior masonry walls and partitions where wider color ranges and greater variation in size is permitted than specified for Type HBX
SW MW	HBX	For general use in exposed exterior and interior masonry walls and partitions where a high degree of mechanical perfection, narrow color range, and minimum permissible variation in size are required
SW MW	HBA	For brick manufactured and selected to produce characteristic architectural effects resulting from non-uniformity in size, color and texture of the individual units
SW MW	HBB	For general use in masonry walls and partitions where color and texture are not a consideration, and a greater variation in size is permitted than is specified for Type HBX

FIGURE 3–26
Grade requirements for hollow masonry units made from clay or shale. (ASTM #C652)

STRUCTURAL GLAZED FACING TILE

Structural clay units, or structural clay tile, has even larger voids or cells than the hollow brick units. Openings take up as much as 75 percent of their surface area. Tile is a much older masonry system, but it is still used as a glazed facing unit. A variety of sizes are available. Joints of $\frac{1}{8}$-inch to $\frac{1}{4}$-inch are used.

Figure 3–27 shows examples of facing tile. Note that the outside face is especially glazed and finished. Some of the tile faces have holes designed to trap sounds. This acoustic tile (see Figure 3–27 bottom) is widely used to cut down noise. Figure 3–28 shows structural glazed facing tile (SGFT) used in a commercial kitchen. A glazed finish is used on the face. Glazed finishes are widely used in hospitals and institutions where cleanliness is of great importance.

FIGURE 3–27
Structural glazed facing tile. (Stark Ceramics, Inc.)

FIGURE 3-28
Structural glazed facing tile used in a commercial kitchen. (Stark Ceramics, Inc.)

Both single-faced and double-faced units are available. Double-faced units are used in single-wythe walls; both sides of the wall will have glazed facing.

TERRA COTTA

Architectural terra cotta is another type of fired clay. Terra cotta is a Latin word that means "cooked earth." It is an ancient process that has been used for thousands of years. A special aged clay is used. It can be molded into simple building units or into very ornate three-dimensional figures. It is fired at high temperatures to give a hardness and compactness that cannot be obtained with ordinary brick.

Terra cotta differs from other fired clay units in that it can be molded into any design or architectural shape needed. It is frequently used for special ornamental work and architectural detail (Figure 3–29). Once a mold is made, any number of identical units can be cast and fired. Frequently, the face of the terra cotta is glazed. Since glazing is used, any number of colors are available.

Today terra cotta is used mostly in remodeling and restoration work. Architectural terra cotta is important in the restoration of historical build-

FIGURE 3-29
Decorative terra cotta used around a door opening to a clothing store. (Gladding, McBean & Co.)

ings. Existing terra cotta architectural features are molded and replaced as needed.

CONCRETE MASONRY UNITS

Concrete masonry units (CMU) are made from portland cement, sand, and coarse aggregate. A mixture by volume of one part cement, 5.3 parts sand, and 2.7 coarse aggregate is typical. The mix is kept dry and stiff so the molded green block can be easily stripped from the mold without deforming.

Both normal and lightweight concrete masonry units are manufactured. The dense or normal weight concrete block uses sand, gravel,

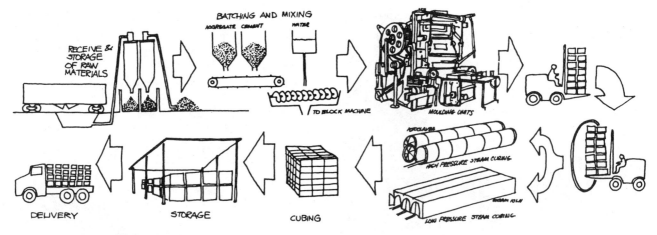

FIGURE 3–30
Manufacturing steps in making concrete block. (National Concrete Masonry Association)

crushed stone, or crushed blast furnace slag as the aggregate. The lightweight masonry units use expanded shale, clay, slate, crushed blast furnace slag, fly ash, crushed coal cinders, or pumice as aggregate. Figure 3–30 shows the manufacturing process for making concrete block masonry units.

Concrete masonry units are molded, several units at a time, in a concrete block machine. Figure 3–31 shows molded units leaving the molding machine. After the green block are removed, they are stacked for curing.

Curing is done in steam kilns (under low pressure) and in autoclaves (under high steam pressure). Figure 3–32 (left) shows concrete block being transported to the curing kiln and in the curing chamber (right). Curing is done by injecting live steam into the curing chamber until the temperature reaches 180°F. The steam provides the moisture to hydrate the cement and accelerate the curing process.

Low pressure steam curing uses steam at temperatures around 150°F to 180°F. The block are stored in long, tunnel-like kilns. They are treated with low temperature steam for about 24 hours. *High-pressure steam curing* takes place in a special airtight autoclave. The block are treated in the autoclave at temperatures around 360° F with an air pressure of 150 pounds per square inch (psi). Block

are treated in the autoclave for 5 hours to 10 hours.

After curing, the concrete block are stacked into cubes and banded with steel or plastic straps. Cubes of 108, 90, and 72 block are made. Figure 3–33 left, shows a cube of 72 standard-size concrete block. Note that the bands or straps run around the cube to hold the block together. The block are cubed so that smaller packages of 24 block each can be broken away. This allows for easier han-

FIGURE 3–31
Molded concrete block exiting the molding machine. (Southern Cast Stone Co., Inc.)

FIGURE 3-32

Left: Concrete block being transported to curing kiln: 240 eight-inch-block are held on the transporter. *Right:* Block in the curing chamber. (Southern Cast Stone Co., Inc.)

8" BLOCK
3 PACKS—24 BLOCKS/PACK—TOTAL 72 BLOCKS

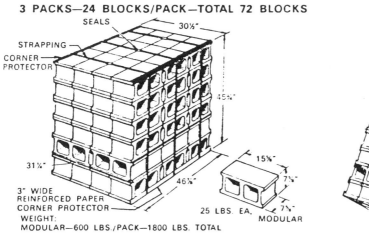 

FIGURE 3-33

Concrete block is packaged into a cube. Smaller sections can be broken away for easy handling. (Masonry Contractors Association of America)

dling on the job. Figure 3–33, right, shows a break-away package of 24 block being moved on a dolly. Note that a band runs around the block.

Block Terminology

Block may be flat or plain on the end or concave. Plain end block are used at corners. Block with concave ends have two *ears* or *ends*. Figure 3–34 shows the basic difference between block with ends or ears on the face shell (with a concave depression) and the plain end block. Block may have ears on one or both ends; plain or smooth finish may also be on one or both ends. Block that are plain at one end and have ears at the other end are used at corners. Block that are plain on both ends, Figure 3–34, are used as headers in two-wythe walls or in piers. Block with ears on both ends are called stretcher block, Figure 3–34. Stretcher block are used in the center part of the course.

Note that the openings or voids in the block are called *cells* or *cores* (Figure 3–34). The wall be-tween the cells or cores is called a *cross web*. The outside face of the concrete block is called the *face shell*.

Block Grades

Load-bearing block are graded according to resistance to weathering. Two ASTM grades are used. Grade N and Grade S. *Grade N* block are designed for use in areas of freezing and thawing where they will be in contact with moisture. *Grade S* block are designed for use in areas not subject to weathering, such as interior walls or exterior walls with special protective coatings.

Block are also classified by the amount of moisture retained in the cured block. *Type I* block have a low retained moisture content. They are used in dry, desert areas of the country. *Type II* block have no specific moisture content. They are used throughout the United States where the mosiure content is fairly high.

Block are specified both by grade and by type: Grades N-I, N-II, S-I, and S-II.

Non-load bearing block are also available.

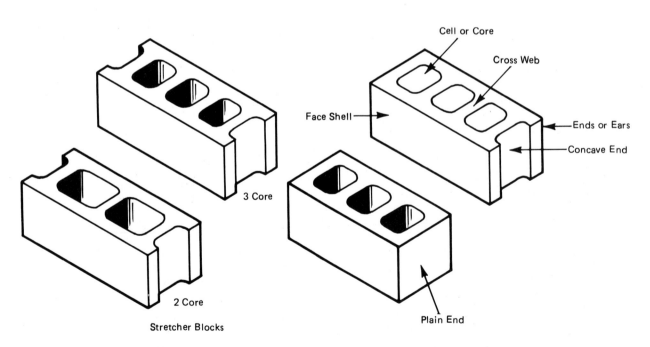

FIGURE 3–34

Concrete block terminology. (*Left:* National Concrete Masonry Association)

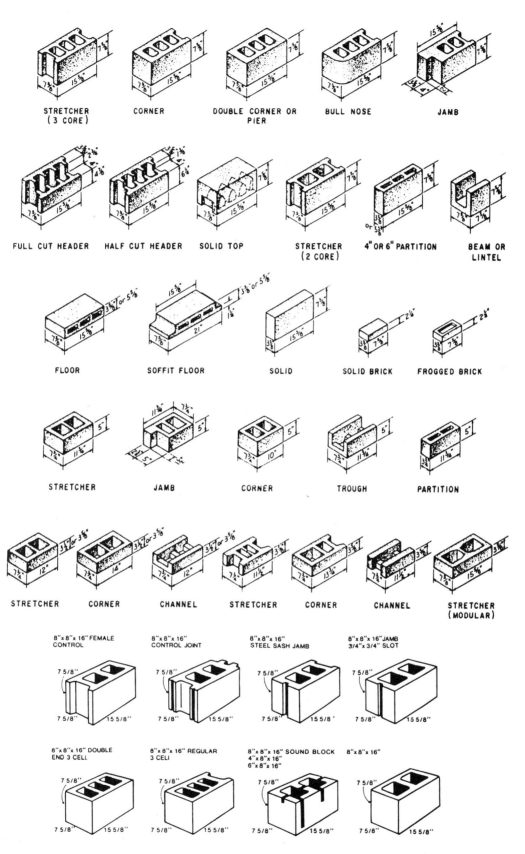

FIGURE 3-35

Concrete block types. Actual or manufactured sizes are shown.

Non-load bearing block are used for interior partitions where no loading is planned. They only carry their own weight.

Block Types

Concrete block units are available in a wide number of shapes, over 1,000 different sizes and shapes are available, many designed for very specialized use. Figure 3–35 shows a selection of typical concrete block.

Stretchers. The most common types of concrete block is the stretcher (Figure 3–35, top left). The stretcher is used in laying out walls. Stretchers have either three cells (cores), as shown in Figure 3–35, or two cells (cores). Most manufacturers today produce the two-cell block. The two-cell block has thicker walls or web. Note that some stretchers have two "ears" or end projections. Mortar is applied to the ears when the stretchers are used in the wall. Stretchers are usually flat on the exposed face; they may, however, be scored, nibbed, or fluted to give a special effect. Some stretchers are *split-faced*—the exposed face is rough where the block has been split off a larger piece.

Corner Block. Some stretchers are flat on the end. These are called corner block and are used at the corner of a wall.

Bull-Nose Block. Bull-nose block are also used to form corners. The bull-nose shape gives a rounded corner.

Jamb Block. Jamb block (Figure 3–35, top right) are used to form door or window openings. The set back in the block leaves room for the door or window jamb to fit in. Many jamb block are grooved (as shown in Figure 3–35, bottom center) to receive the edge of the metal door or window buck.

Header Block. Header block have a side cut down to form a shelf. Header block are used when laying a composite wall with brick. Brick units are laid on the shelf formed on the headers.

Partition Block. Partition block are thin blocks—less than half the thickness of standard block. Partition block are used for laying single-wythe partitions inside the building. Partitions are non-load bearing.

Beam or Lintel Block. Beam or lintel block are used at the top of an opening. The opening between the two arms of the block are filed with concrete with reinforcing bars. This forms a strong support beam over any opening. Figure 3–36 shows beam or lintel block used over a door opening. Different shaped lintel block are used (Figure 3–37).

Sound Block. Concete block form a very effective sound absorbing wall. Some block have specially designed cuts in them to enhance their acoustic qualities. These are called sound block or acoustic block. Figure 3–35, bottom center, shows a sound block.

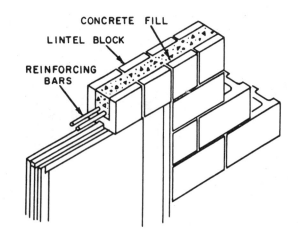

FIGURE 3–36
Lintel block used over opening.

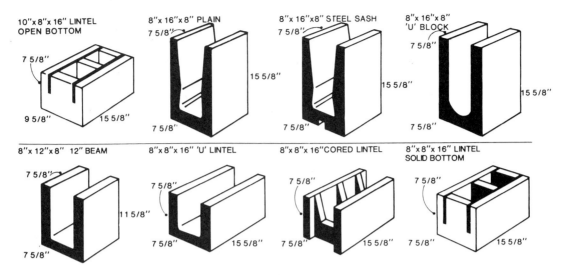

FIGURE 3–37
Lintel block. (U.S. Department of Energy)

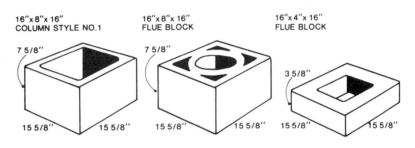

FIGURE 3–38
Column and flue block. (U.S. Department of Energy)

Column and Flue Block. Special hollow block are cast for laying columns and flues. Figure 3–38 shows typical column and flue block.

Pilaster Block. Pilaster block are special block used to build pilasters in the wall for additional support. A pilaster is an integral part of the wall and acts like a support column. Pilaster block look like flue block, but they are often filled with concrete grouting for extra strength. Figure 3–39 shows pilaster block in use.

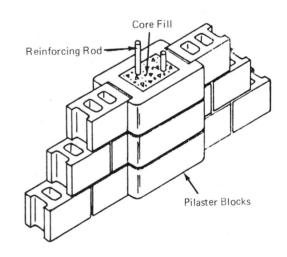

FIGURE 3–39
Pilaster block in use.

FIGURE 3-40
Insulated block. (Southern Cast Stone Co., Inc.)

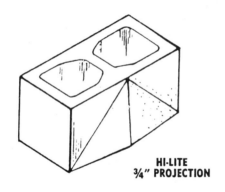

**HI-LITE
¾" PROJECTION**

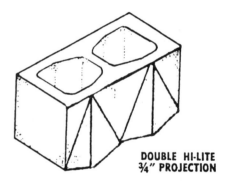

**DOUBLE HI-LITE
¾" PROJECTION**

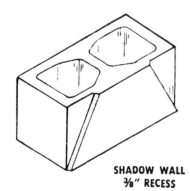

**SHADOW WALL
⅜" RECESS**

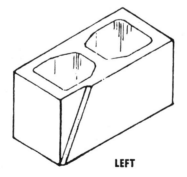

LEFT

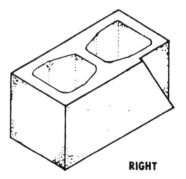

RIGHT

FIGURE 3-41
Typical shadow block. (Concrete Masonry Association of California and Nevada)

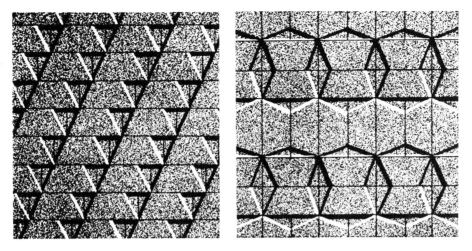

FIGURE 3–42
Shadow block walls. (National Concrete Masonry Association)

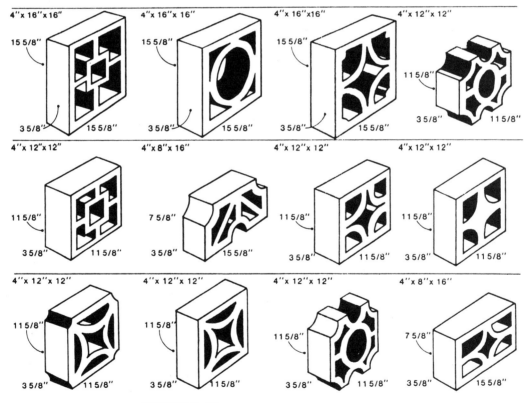

FIGURE 3–43
Typical grill block. (U.S. Department of Energy)

Insulated Block. Because of the great importance today in energy conservation, some block are manufactured with thermal insulation in place in the cells (cores). Figure 3–40 shows typical concrete block with polystyrene inserts. This greatly increases the insulative value of the block.

Glazed Block. Face glazing is also available on almost all block shapes. Almost any color is available. Glazed block has a wide use in hospitals, institutions, and public buildings where easily cleaned walls are critical.

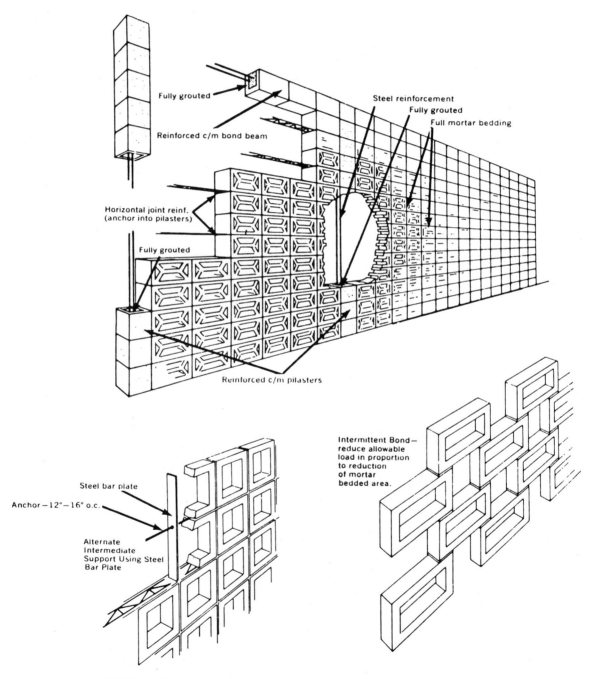

FIGURE 3–44
Techniques for laying grill block. (National Concrete Masonry Association)

Shadow Block. Shadow block are a type of face block with a specially shaped face. The face may be ribbed or molded in special geometrical shapes. Figure 3–41 shows samples of shadow block. These block, when laid in an exterior wall, create an interesting effect by their shadow pattern. Figure 3–42 shows walls laid with shadow block. Note the interesting pattern formed by the shadows. Of course, the shadow pattern changes as the angle of the sun changes. Shadow block are also called pattern block.

Grill Block. Grill block is used for laying decorative walls. Decorative walls are normally used outside to creat privacy screens and sun screens to cut down direct sunlight. They may be used directly in front of the building windows. Figure 3–43 shows a few samples of grill block. The different shapes and designs are endless. When laid together in a wall they form an attractive and very useful architectural feature. Figure 3–44 shows techniques for laying grill block in a wall. A reinforced masonry framework or steel beams are used for support in larger walls. Thicknesses of 4", 6", and 8" are used.

Slump Block. Slump block is made by using an extra-wet concrete mixture. The wet mixture slumps or sags to create irregular surfaces when removed from the mold.

Split Block. Split block is made by casting large block, usually made double, then splitting the unit into two parts. A heavy splitting knife is used in a machine to break the block unit. Split block gives a rough stone-like texture on the face. Various split-face block types are used. Figure 3–45 shows a few sample split block.

Customized Block. An almost limitless variety of special shapes and face textures are available from the various manufacturers. Check with local suppliers to see what is available. Figure 3–46 shows a few samples of customized face block. Note that some customized block have their faces shaped to resemble natural stone. As noted, split block are made by breaking apart a larger unit; the

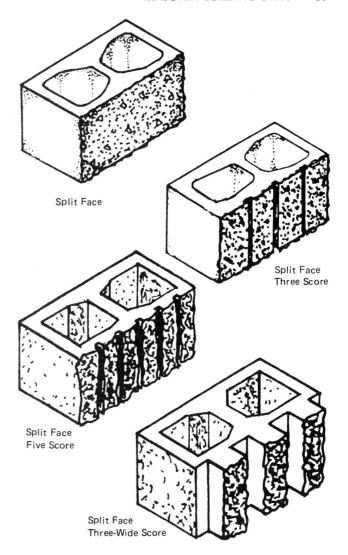

Split Face

Split Face Three Score

Split Face Five Score

Split Face Three-Wide Score

FIGURE 3–45
Typical split block. (*Top*: Concrete Masonry Association of California and Nevada)

8"x 8"x 16"
VERTICAL PATTERN

7 5/8"

7 5/8"   15 5/8"

8"x 8"x 16"
VERTICAL PATTERN

7 5/8"

7 5/8"   15 5/8"

8"x 8"x 8"
VERTICAL PATTERN

7 5/8"

7 5/8"   7 5/8"

8"x 8"x 16"
FLUTED

7 5/8"

7 5/8"   15 5/8"

8"x 8"x 16"
FLUTED & SPLIT

7 5/8"

7 5/8"   15 5/8"

8"x 8"x 16"
FLUTED & SPLIT

7 5/8"

7 5/8"   15 5/8"

4"x 8"x 16"
FLUTED & SPLIT

7 5/8"

3 5/8"   15 5/8"

8"x 8"x 16" 3 SCORE

7 5/8"

7 5/8"   15 5/8"

4"x 4"x 16"
SLUMP BLOCK

3 5/8"

3 5/8"   15 5/8"

4"x 3"x 16"
SLUMP BLOCK

2 5/8"

3 5/8"   15 5/8"

4"x 2"x 16"
SLUMP BLOCK

2"

3 5/8"   15 5/8"

4"x 2 1/4"x 16"
SPLIT FACE

2 1/4"

3 5/8"   15 5/8"

8"x 8"x 16" SPLIT

7 5/8"

7 5/8"   15 5/8"

8"x 4"x 16" SPLIT

3 5/8"

7 5/8"   15 5/8"

8"x 4"x 16" SPLIT

3 5/8"

7 5/8"   15 5/8"

8"x 4"x 16"
SLUMP BLOCK

3 5/8"

7 5/8"   15 5/8"

FIGURE 3–46
Customized block. (U.S. Department of Energy)

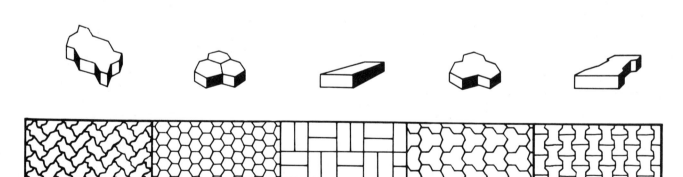

FIGURE 3–47
Typical paving block. (U.S. Department of Energy)

broken face resembles stone. The possibilities are endless since you can, if need be, have your own customized block produced by the manufacturer.

Concrete Brick.   Concrete brick is a solid masonry unit used in much the same manner as regular clay brick. The concrete brick is commonly sized 4″ × 2⅔ × 8″ (nominal dimensions) and is used widely for veneer walls.

Sand-Lime Brick.   Sand-lime brick are a type of formed solid brick similar to a concrete brick except little if any portland cement is used. They are formed of a mixture of fine sand, lime, and crushed stone or crushed blast furnace slag. They are molded under mechanical pressure and are hardened by high pressure steam. Grade SW is for sand-lime brick exposed to freezing temperatures in the presence of moisture. Grade MW is for sand-lime brick exposed to temperatures below freezing but unlikely to be saturated with water.

Paving Block.   Paving block are solid, flat units used to lay floors, walkways, patios, and driveways. Figure 3–47 shows a few patterns. As shown, interlocking patterns are normally used. This creates a more stable floor.

Block Sizes

Block sizes are designed on a nominal 4-inch measure. The basic, standard concrete block, for example, is designed to a nominal size of $8″ × 8″ × 16″$. Figure 3–48 shows the standard stretcher block with an actual manufactured size of $7\frac{5}{8}″ × 7\frac{5}{8}″ × 15\frac{5}{8}″$ compared to the nominal size of $8″ × 8″ × 16″$. A $\frac{3}{8}$-inch mortar joint is assumed to give the nominal size. Half block or solid block are calculated with a nominal size of $8″ × 4″ × 16″$. Figure 3–49 compares a 4-inch thick half block or solid block to a regular 8-inch thick block.

Some block, however, are designed to form a wide, single-wythe bearing wall and have greater thicknesses. Thicknesses of 10 inches and 12 inches are available. Block for non-bearing partition walls in thicknesses of 4 inches and 6 inches are also used.

Block Terminology

The terms used in describing concrete masonry units are the same as those noted for brick. See Figures 3–20, 3–23, and 3–24. The void in the block is properly called a *cell* because of its size, although they are sometimes referred to as *cores*. (Small voids in brick are properly called *cores*.) The wall between the cells in the masonry unit is called

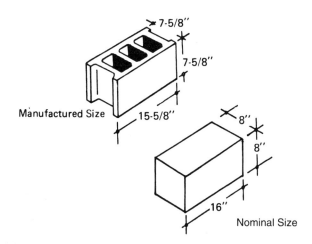

FIGURE 3–48
Manufactured actual and nominal sizes.

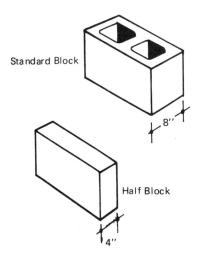

FIGURE 3–49
The half block has a four inch thickness.

a *web*. The outside walls are referred to as the *shell* or *face shell*. The two projections on the end of the stretcher block are commonly called *ears*.

GLASS BLOCK

Glass block are hollow glass units that are used in window openings and to create walls that allow diffused light through. Glass block are made by molding the two separate sections and sealing them together in a permanent bond. The outside edge of the glass block is left rough with a special coating so it will readily take mortar.

Figure 3–50 shows typical glass block. Note that the glass is distorted and only semi-transparent. It will admit light, yet you cannot see through it. This is an important advantage if light is needed, but privacy and security are a consideration.

Glass block are usually square and are commonly made in nominal 8″ × 8″ and 12″ × 12″ sizes. Nominal 6″ × 8″, 6″ × 6″, and 4″ × 8″ sizes are also used. A wide number of glass patterns are available. Figure 3–51 shows a window wall made with patterned glass blocks. An attractive wall is created that allows light in but is still private and secure. Glass block is non-load bearing, however. Also, glass has a high expansion rate and an expansion strip will be required between glass block and brickwork. Take care when handling glass block to prevent chipping. Figure 3–52 shows glass block being installed.

STONE

Natural stone is used either rough or cut. Rough, unshaped natural stone is called fieldstone. Rough

FIGURE 3–50
Typical glass block. (Pittsburg Corning Corp.)

FIGURE 3–51
Window wall made with glass block. (Pittsburgh Corning Corp.)

stone may also be dressed or shaped to fit better in the wall; shaped stone is called ashlar. Cut stone is taken from quarries and is cut to various sizes, some weighing thousands of pounds. Because of the cost of obtaining stone, especially quarried stone, and the difficulty in laying it, it is very expensive. Stone is mostly used in veneer work and in flooring.

All types of stone are used in construction as long as they are stable and do not flake or break in use when exposed to weathering. There are three kinds of natural stone: igneous, sedimentary, and metamorphic.

Igneous Stone. Igneous stone comes from molten magma deep in the earth. Granite is the most common igneous stone used in construction. It is very hard and tough and takes a very high polish. Granite slabs are frequently used as a veneer on very large buildings as an attractive architectural finish.

Sedimentary Stone. Sedimentary stone is formed by deposits under water. The deposits are compressed until they become a hard mass. Limestone, sandstone, and shale are common examples.

widely used metamorphic stone; marble is lime-stone that has been changed by heat and pressure to a denser, more crystalline form. Quartzite (changed from sandstone) and slate (changed from shale) are other metamorphic stone used in construction.

Stone Types

Natural stone is available in several forms, and each has its own uses in construction and stone-work. Stone is a basic building material and is used as veneers and as paving material.

Fieldstone.   Fieldstone is natural stone just as it is found in the field. It is usually rounded from wear. In use the stone must be carefully selected so they fit together.

Flagstone.   Flagstone or flags are flat stone. They are used for paving walkways or floors. Flagstone are often split off of larger pieces. Figure 3–53 shows slate flagstone used to make a lobby floor.

Cobblestone.   Cobbles are rough stone around four inches in diameter. They are used for paving. Figure 3–54 shows cobblestone used in paving an entryway.

Paving Block.   Paving block are rough-shaped, square stone from three inches to five inches square. They are used in paving driveways and streets.

Rubble.   Rubble is coarse, broken stone. It is generally collected near sites where stone beds are exposed. Figure 3–55 shows rubble used in a wall. This shows random rubble, no courses are used. Great care may be taken to fit the stone together.

Ashlar.   Ashlar stone are stone that have been individually cut and shaped. Figure 3–56 shows typical ashlar stone used in a wall and church bell tower. Different sized ashlar stone are used. Ashlar is commonly used as a veneer on masonry or

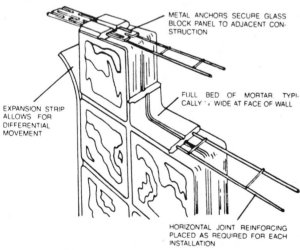

FIGURE 3–52
Installing glass block. (Pittsburgh Corning Corp.)

Metamorphic Stone. Metamorphic stone is formed by changing other types of stone under extreme heat and pressure. Marble is the most

FIGURE 3-53
Slate flooring. (Robinson Flagstones)

FIGURE 3-54
Cobblestone used in paving a front entryway. (North Carolina Granite Corp.)

FIGURE 3-55
Typical anchor system used to hold stone slabs on a masonry wall.

FIGURE 3-56
Ashlar stone used in church construction.
(Vetter Stone Co.)

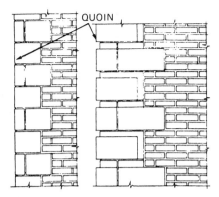

FIGURE 3-57
Cut stone, called quoins, used at corner of brick building.

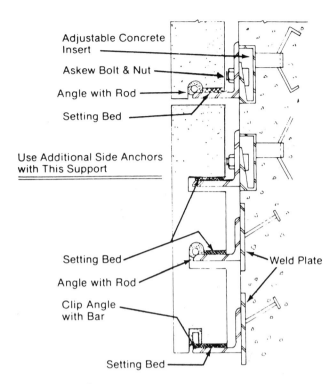

FIGURE 3-58
Typical anchor systems used to hold stone slabs to the base. (Indiana Limestone Institute of America, Inc.)

frame walls. Metal ties are used to hold the veneer to the backing wall.

Quarried Stone. Large stone that are cut out of a quarry are called quarry stone. Limestone, marble, and granite are common stone types that are quarried. Figure 3-57 shows large, cut quarry stone used in the corner of a brick building. Large squared stone used in a corner like this are called quoins. Quarry stone is also commonly cut into slabs for use as veneer on large buildings. Slabs are attached to the building frame with metal anchors. A wide variety of different types of anchors are used. Figure 3-58 shows a typical anchor system used to hold stone slabs on a masonry wall. Room is always left between the veneer slabs for expansion during temperature change.

Cut stone is also used for lintels, sills, and coping. The cut, shaped units are normally laid in a mortar bed and also held with anchors.

Manufactured Stone. Artificial or manufactured stone is also used. Manufactured stone is made by pouring color-tinted, lightweight concrete into shaped forms. The finished product is shaped and textured to look like natural stone. On the job, manufactured stone is mainly used as a veneer and is set into a mortar on the base wall. Since it weighs much less than natural stone, it is very suitable as a veneer. When installed it is difficult to distinguish from natural stone.

CHAPTER REVIEW

QUESTIONS

1. List four types of structural clay masonry.

2. Describe the two processes used for manufacturing brick.

3. What is a brick kiln and how is it laid out?

4. How are brick packaged after firing?

5. Describe the three brick grades based on weather-exposed walls.

6. How is facing brick used? Building brick?

7. What is the advantage of glazed brick?

8. How is "solid brick" defined?

9. Explain the two ways paving brick is graded.

10. What is the difference between actual brick size and nominal brick size?

11. What three nonmodular solid brick are used?

12. Explain the difference between a bed joint and a head joint.

13. Explain the difference between a bat and a quarter closure.

14. What is the difference between a queen closure and a split?

15. What is a rowlock?

16. Explain the difference between a course and a wythe.

17. What is the difference between cored brick and a hollow masonry unit?

18. Explain the grading systems used to describe hollow masonry units.

19. How are terra cotta units used?

20. Describe how concrete masonry units are manufactured.

21. What grades are used to describe concrete block?

22. How are bull-nose block used? Jamb block? Header block? Lintel block?

23. What is insulated block? How is it used?

24. What is split block? How is it made?

25. What are grill block used for?

26. What is the difference between "cores" and "cells"?

27. How is glass block used? What are some advantages of glass block? What common sizes are used?

28. What is the difference between fieldstone and rubble? How do both differ from ashlar?

29. Describe what quarried stone is and how it is used.

30. What is manufactured stone? What is it used for?

ACTIVITIES

1. Visit masonry structures in your area and identify, by their position, stretchers and headers, and by size, any cut units.

2. Of the structures visited make a list with simple sketches of at least five different masonry units. Label each unit with the type of masonry unit it is. Measure each unit and note the actual sizes on each sketch. Measure the masonry joints around each unit. Add the joint width to the dimensions noted. (One-half the masonry joint is used on each side to determine nominal size.) Sketch A shows a sample sketch. Check measured actual and nominal sizes against masonry dimensions given in this chapter.

3. If possible, arrange a visit to a local brick or concrete block manufacturer and observe how their units are manufactured.

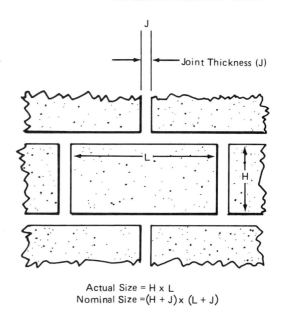

Actual Size = H x L
Nominal Size = (H + J) x (L + J)

SKETCH A
Sample sketch of brick shown in elevation.

Chapter 4

MASONRY CONSTRUCTION: BONDS, JOINTS, AND MORTARS

After studying this chapter you should be able to:

- Define and explain the three different meanings for the term *bond*.
- Identify and describe at least six different bonds.
- Explain why mortar joints should be finished.
- Describe the two most common and recommended joints.
- Recognize six different mortar joints.
- Describe the three portland cements used in mortar.
- Explain what admixtures are.
- Describe how six different mortars are made.
- Describe how grout mortar is made.
- Explain how surface bonding cement is used.
- Explain where damp proofing is used and how it is applied.

- Describe both hand mixing and power mixing of mortars.
- List the different types of heating required in cold weather masonry.
- List the different types of protection required in cold weather masonry.
- List the problems of hot weather work.
- Describe the metal ties used in masonry work.
- Describe the types of joint reinforcement used.
- Describe how metal anchors are used.
- Describe how steel reinforcing bars are used.
- Describe how and where flashing is used in masonry work.
- Explain what an expansion joint is, where it is used, and how it is made.
- Explain what a control joint is, where it is used, and how it is made.

Masonry units are laid together in some set, established pattern. The pattern is called a bond. Each masonry bond has its own particular strength and beauty. The architect, when designing the building, may decide on and specify a particular masonry pattern or bond. Only a few bonds are commonly used and you should become thoroughly familiar with these. More difficult and unusual bonds are sometimes required to create architectural effects.

Probably the most important part of a finished masonry element is the mortar used in the joint. Often, for a specific use, an exact mortar mix may be required. It is very important that the proper mortar type and mix be used. Most masonry problems are caused by errors in mix proportions, poor mortar adhesion, or by weathering or breaking of the mortar.

In some cases, metal ties, anchors, or reinforcements may be required in the mortar joint or in the actual masonry units. After the units are laid in place, the mortar joints are finished or tooled.

The term *bond* is sometimes confusing when used in masonry work. The following three different meanings are commonly used for the term.

Masonry Bond. Masonry bond is the term used to define the *pattern* made by the masonry units set in mortar in the wall. This usage applies only to walls or other vertical elements. Floor or paving patterns are simply referred to as a *pattern.*

Mortar Bond. The adhesion of the actual mortar joint is also referred to as a bond. Bond in the sense of mortar bond refers not only to the adhesion of the mortar to the masonry units but also to the adhesion of the mortar to any metal reinforcement used.

Structural Bond. Structural bond refers to the interlocking of structural units in a wall or masonry element. This is done by overlapping masonry units to tie the parts together, by using metal ties between connecting joints, and by grouting separate parts (wythes) of the wall to form a structural whole.

MASONRY BONDS

Masonry patterns or bonds used in walls are laid out to create a strong masonry element. The basic premise of masonry bonds is that the masonry end joints (head joints) should not line up with end joints on the course above or below. This is true of all bonds except the stack bond, which is mainly a decorative bond and usually carries little structural load. Running joints so they do not line up with joints above or below is called "breaking bond."

Running Bond

The most common masonry bond is the running bond (Figure 4–1, top). In some codes, unless specified otherwise, a standard running bond is required when laying a wall. As you can see in the illustration, the running bond is a very simple pattern. Stretchers are laid in each course; head joints are broken so they do not line up. Note that in the running bond, the head joints in the courses above and below are horizontally offset at least one-quarter the unit length. In alternate courses, however, head joints do line up. With 8-inch brick, as shown in Figure 4–1, head joints are centered on the stretchers above and below. In running bond, for 12-inch or longer units, the head joints will *not* break at the center of the brick above and below. The running bond is widely used in cavity wall construction, brick veneer walls, in single-wythe concrete block walls, and in facing tile walls. Figure 4–2 shows a cavity wall made with running bond. The two wythes are tied together with metal ties. Grouting and steel reinforcing bars may be placed in the wall to create a strong, reinforced wall. Figure 4–3 shows running bond used in a single-wythe concrete block wall. Joint reinforcement is used to control shrinkage of the wall and to add strength.

Common Bond

The common bond, or American bond, as it is sometimes called, uses several courses of running

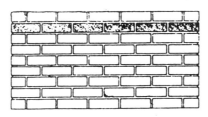

RUNNING

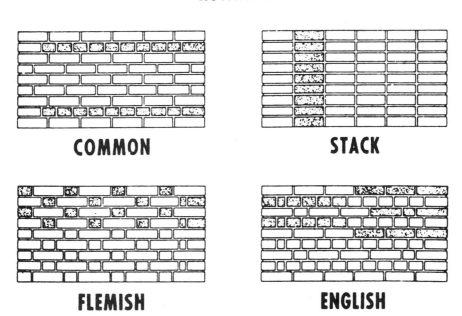

COMMON   **STACK**

FLEMISH   **ENGLISH**

FIGURE 4-1
Common masonry bonds.

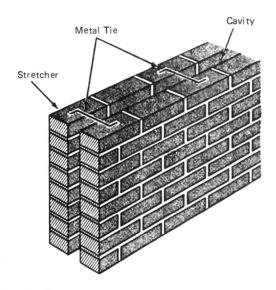

FIGURE 4-2
Two-wythe cavity wall laid in running bond. Wythes are held together with metal ties.

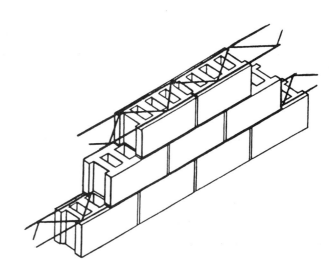

FIGURE 4-3
Single-wythe, concrete block laid in running bond.

bond followed by a course of headers. The headers are used to structurally tie the wall together. Figure 4–1, center left, shows a face view. Header courses are used at every fifth, sixth, or seventh course. Figure 4–4 shows a solid wall using the common bond. The headers run through the wall to tie the parts together. Either a two-wythe or three-wythe wall can be built using this bond.

Note: When laying out the common bond it is very important that the header course be started correctly at the corner. As shown in Figures 4–1 and 4–4, the header course starts with a three-quarter brick. This allows the headers to break properly so they are centered over the stretcher joints.

Flemish Bond

Flemish bond (Figure 4–1, bottom left) is made up of alternating stretcher and header brick in each course. Headers in alternating courses are centered over stretchers. The headers, of course, tie two wythes together to make a structurally sound

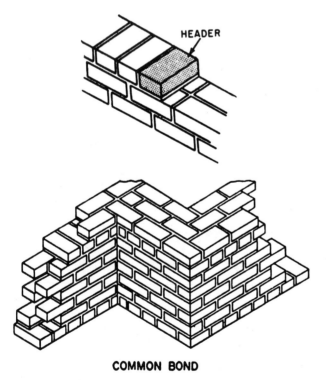

COMMON BOND

FIGURE 4–4
Solid wall laid in common bond.

wall. As shown in Figure 4–1, half brick and three-quarter brick are used at the corners. Figure 4–5 shows different types of Flemish bond solid walls. With the Dutch corner, a three-quarter closure starts the course; with the English corner, a two-inch queen closure is used next to the whole corner brick. Figure 4–6 compares the two corners.

English Bond

English bond (Figure 4–1, bottom right) essentially uses alternate courses of stretchers and headers; headers are centered over stretchers. This is a more complex bond. Figure 4–7 shows two variations of English bond used in a solid wall. The English cross bond is also called the Dutch bond.

Stack Bond

The stack bond (Figure 4–1, center right) is a common, widely used bond. This is not a strong bond since end joints line up one over the other—it is mainly decorative. The stack bond, however, can be load bearing. It is an attractive bond and is widely used for outside walls and for interior partitions, especially with concrete block. With concrete block stack walls, reinforcing bars with grouting are sometimes used in the block cells to provide strength. Joint reinforcement must also be used.

Garden Wall Bonds

Garden wall bonds are variations of the basic Flemish bonds. They are used in outside decorative walls. Figures 4–8 and 4–9 show two garden wall bonds made using different colored brick. Figure 4–8 shows a double stretcher garden wall bond; use of light-colored brick allows emphasis on the diagonal or diamond shape. Figure 4–9 shows a garden wall bond laid in a dovetail fashion. Use of light and dark colored brick to create a pattern is called *pattern bonding*. Pattern refers to the change or varied arrangement of brick, textures or colors used in the face of the wall.

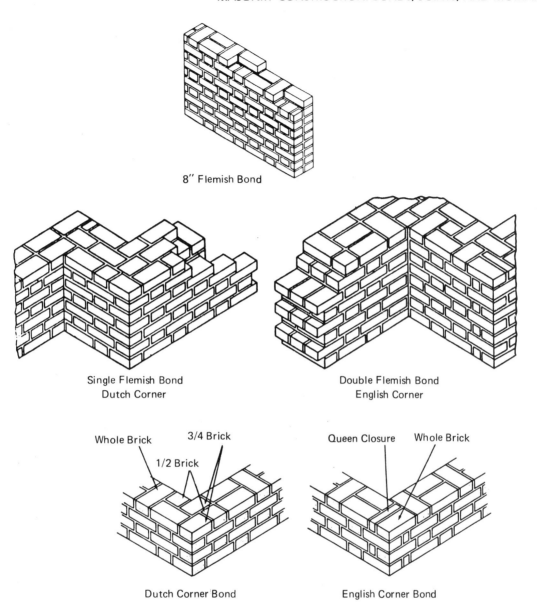

8" Flemish Bond

Single Flemish Bond
Dutch Corner

Double Flemish Bond
English Corner

Whole Brick   3/4 Brick

1/2 Brick

Queen Closure   Whole Brick

Dutch Corner Bond

English Corner Bond

FIGURE 4–5
Flemish bond solid walls. *Bottom left:* Dutch corner; *bottom right:* English corner.
(Brick Institute of America.)

DUTCH CORNER   ENGLISH CORNER

FIGURE 4–6
Flemish bond showing how Dutch (*left*) and English (*right*)
corners are laid. (Brick Institute of America)

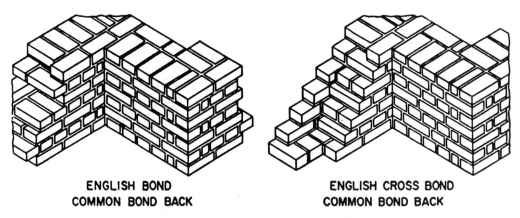

ENGLISH BOND
COMMON BOND BACK

ENGLISH CROSS BOND
COMMON BOND BACK

FIGURE 4-7
English bonds.

Wall Texture

Emphasis and architectural interest can be created in a bond by recessing or allowing masonry units to protrude out. Figure 4-10 shows an example of wall texture created by extending the masonry units. The shadow created by the brick creates interest in the wall. This technique is also referred to as *pattern bonding*. Both extended and recessed brick are sometimes used together with colored brick to create bold effects (Figure 4-11).

Figure 4-12 shows texture and pattern used in a reinforced masonry wall to create an interesting design on the face of a building. Plain red brick is contrasted with textured, light-colored brick to emphasize vertical lines. An offset running bond is used with 12-inch long Norman brick.

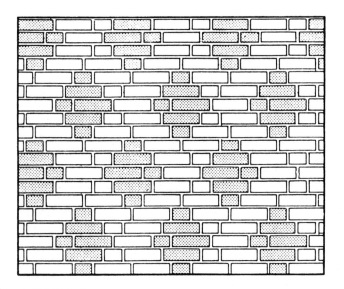

FIGURE 4-8
Double stretcher, garden wall bond with diagonal emphasis to create diamonds. (Brick Institute of America)

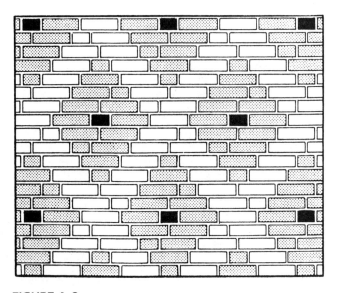

FIGURE 4-9
Garden wall bond with dovetail emphasis. (Brick Institute of America)

FIGURE 4–10
Wall texture created by extending out brick headers.

FIGURE 4–11
Pattern bonding created by using colored bricks and by recessing and extending out bricks. (Judith Uphoff, Warden, Wyoming Women's Center)

FIGURE 4–12
Pattern created by contrasting brick colors. Smooth red brick is used under the windows. Textured off white brick is used for the main part of the wall.

MORTAR JOINTS

The mortar joints between the masonry units should be finished. This creates a stronger, tighter bond between the mortar and the masonry units. Tightness is very important to any joint exposed to weather and especially to moisture. Exterior mortar joints should be watertight.

The joints are first cut flush when the units are laid. If the joints were left unfinished, tiny cracks would develop between the mortar surface and the masonry surface. Finishing or tooling the joints compacts the mortar back in the joints and prevents cracks. The mortar in the joint should be finished after it has been allowed to set for a short period. You can test when it should be finished by pressing it with your thumb. If slight pressure leaves a thumbprint, it is ready for finishing. Always take care *not* to allow the mortar to harden. If the mortar is hard, the metal of the finishing tool (jointer) will rub off the mortar and create streaks.

Figure 4–13 shows masonry joints being finished. The finishing tool, or jointer, is shaped to create an indentation in the mortar. This compacts and forces the mortar back from the face, as shown in Figure 4–14.

Both vertical and horizontal joints, of course, must be finished. Most masons believe in finishing the head (vertical) joints first, as shown in Figure 4–13. A metal jointer is used to finish the head

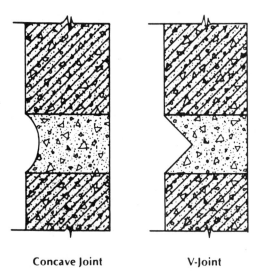

Concave Joint   **V-Joint**

FIGURE 4–14
Mortar is compressed and forced back into the joint to finish the joint. Different-shaped jointers give different-shaped joints; the concave joint (*left*) is most commonly used.

joints. After striking the head joints, the horizontal joints are finished with a sled runner, as shown in Figure 4–15. This is a longer tool and allows the continuous course joint to be quickly struck. The jointing tools used should be selected so that they are slightly larger than the width of the mortar joint being finished.

The most common and the most durable mortar joints are the *concave joint* and the *V-joint* (Figure 4–14). These are the recommended joints, especially in masonry work exposed to weather. The concave and V-joints give a watertight finish.

FIGURE 4–13
Striking or tooling mortar joints. (Brick Institute of America)

FIGURE 4–15
Striking a horizontal joint using a sled runner. (National Concrete Masonry Association)

The mortar is pushed tight against the masonry. In many codes the concave joint is recommended unless specified otherwise. Other joint finishes are also used sometimes. Figure 4–16 shows the other finishes used on joints.

The extruded joint is an unfinished joint made by leaving extruded mortar in place (Figure 4–16, bottom right). This is sometimes used as a decorative joint but is a *very poor* joint when exposed to weather. Water can easily work back into the joint and cause deterioration. This is an especially bad joint if exposed to freezing and thawing cycles. Any water that gets into the joint can freeze, expand, and rupture the joint. Extruded joints are sometimes used on interior, exposed brickwork. This may give an interesting, rough effect.

The *flush joint* (Figure 4–16, bottom left) is also a poor joint. Since it is not compacted, small cracks will develop in the mortar. Any cracks, of course, can hold water. It should only be used for covered work that is not exposed to weather. The flush joint is made by holding the edge of the trowel against the face and cutting away the exposed mortar.

Struck joints and *weathered joints* (Figure 4–16, center) are sometimes used on exposed masonry. They are better than no finish; they are not, however, as weathertight as the concave or V-joints. The struck joint especially causes problems since a small shelf is created that will hold water. The struck joint should only be used on interior work. The weathered joint is better since it is designed to allow water runoff. Both joints are made by pushing in with the point of a trowel. These joints are sometimes specified because of their interesting shadow effect. The deep joints create dark shadow lines.

The *raked joint* is favored by many since it accents the masonry units and creates strong, attractive lines in the finished wall. For that reason, it's sometimes requested by an architect. Raked joints are normally used for interior, decorative work. A special raking tool is used to cut back the mortar for the raked joint.

Other decorative joints, such as the *beaded joint* or *grapevine joint* (Figure 4–16, center and top right) are also used. These give an interesting architectural effect.

MORTAR

Mortar is used to bind masonry units together. Mortar is made from portland cement, lime, aggregate (sand), and water (Figure 4–17). The ingredients are usually specified by parts. Mortar should be used soon after mixing; it should not be left to stand for a long period. Mortar normally should be used within 2 hours after mixing. Some building codes state that mortar *must* be used within $2\frac{1}{2}$ hours following initial mixing. If not too old, mortar may be retempered by adding water and remixing. Mortar that has fallen on the scaffolding or on the wall must *never* be reused.

One design and specification authority gives the following guidelines for retempering mortar:[1]

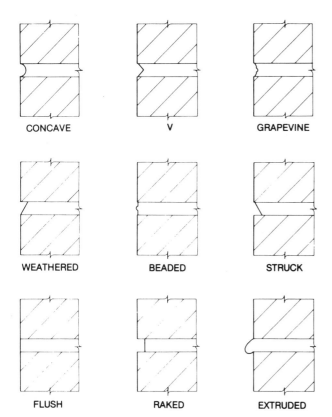

FIGURE 4–16
Joint finishes.

[1]Masonry Industry Advancement Committee, "Guide Specifications for Reinforced Masonry Construction," *Masonry Design Manual*, 1979.

FIGURE 4-17
Setup for mixing mortar.

Mortar may be retempered with water before it has stiffened. Old mortar should not be retempered but should be thrown out and new mortar used.

Mortar should be retempered with water as required to maintain high plasticity. Retempering on mortar boards shall be done only by adding water within a basin formed with the mortar and the mortar worked into the water. Any mortar which is unused after one and one-half hours from the initial mixing time shall not be used.

If mortar stiffens through evaporation, it may be retempered by remixing water in with the trowel. Add only enough water to replace that lost by evaporation—enough to make it workable. Mortar that is stiff because of hydration, however, may not be retempered. If mortar is retempered three hours after initial mixing, bonding and compressive strength will be significantly reduced. Throw away set or hard mortar and get fresh.

Portland Cement

Portland cement is made by burning limestone and clay together; the basic material always contains lime, silica, alumina, and iron. The clinkers that result are ground into a fine powder. Portland cement contains four basic chemical compounds: tricalcium silicate, dicalcium silicate, tricalcium aluminate, and tetra calcium aluminoferride. The tricalcium silicate is largely responsible for initial set and early strength. The ground powder is mixed with two to three percent gypsum to control setting. The powder or cement, when mixed with water, starts a chemical reaction that results in a hard mass. Cement gives durability and strength to the mortar.

Cement standards are established by the American Society for Testing and Materials (ASTM Standard C-150). There are three grades of portland cement recommended for use in masonry mortars: Types I, II, and III. *Type I* is a general purpose cement; it is used when no special requirements are specified. Type I is typically used for normal work. *Type II* is for general use where moderate sulfate resistance or moderate heat of hydration is needed. *Type III* is used where high early strength is needed. Type III is sometimes recommended in colder weather. Other cement types are available but not commonly used for mortar. In no event should air-entraining cements be used. They reduce the strength of the bond. Air-entraining cements are identified as IA, IIA, and IIIA.

FIGURE 4-18
Portland cement (Type I) stored on the job.

Portland cement comes in 94-pound paper sacks (Figure 4–18) and is marked with the type on the side. A sack of cement contains a loose volume of one cubic foot.

Masonry Cement

Masonry cement is a general purpose cement, an inert limestone mixture especially designed for making mortar. It is used in mixtures the same way as portland cement and lime. Of course, if it is used, then no lime is required. Only sand and water need be added. Masonry cement comes in 70-pound paper bags. Masonry cement mortar is in line with building codes for most applications as long as it does not contain additives that would lower the strength or durability of the mortar.

Hydrated Lime

Hydrated lime is made by heating crushed limestone to high temperatures to drive off carbon dioxide. What is left is called calcium oxide (CaO) or quicklime. Quicklime (also called lime putty) is very caustic and reacts violently when it comes into contact with water. Before being used, quicklime must be slaked with water to create calcium hydroxide $(Ca(OH)_2)$ or *hydrated lime*. Hy-

drated lime or simple *lime*, is a dry powder that is used by the mason in mixing portland cement lime mortar.

Lime is supplied in paper sacks in 50-pound quantities. Lime used in mortar is graded by the ASTM as *Type S*. The lime in the mortar is what gives plasticity to the mixture. The more lime in the mortar, the easier it is to work.

Lime Putty

As noted, lime putty is the name used to refer to *quicklime*. Lime putty may contain up to eight percent magnesium oxide (MgO). Some specifications will call for either hydrated lime or lime putty. Lime putty, because of its caustic nature, is not commonly used in the field. It is only used in plant mixing and must be thoroughly slaked before use.

Sand

Sand, of course, is an essential ingredient in any mortar. Sand is a fine aggregate that must be clean and of fairly uniform size. Both natural and manufactured sand may be used. Natural sand is rounded while manufactured sand is sharp and angular. Each produces a mortar with different properties. A well-graded sand will have some variation in size from fine to coarse. Figure 4–19 shows the sand gradations recommended. The smaller the sieve number, the larger the opening. Different percentage requirements are given for natural sand and manufactured sand. Manufactured sand is made from crushed stone, gravel, or blast furnace slag. A mixture of some fine sand with coarse sand allows spaces to be filled and makes a stronger mortar. If all large sand particles are used in the mix, it will be harsh and difficult to spread. If all fine sand is used, it will be weak and too thin.

Water

Water must be clean and free from organic materials, alkalies, acids, and oil. Salts of all kinds and

Mortar Sand Grade By the Amount Passing Through Different Sieves

	Percent Passing	
Sieve Size	Natural Sand	Manufactured Sand
No. 4 (4.75-mm)	100	100
No. 8 (2.36-mm)	95 to 100	95 to 100
No. 16 (1.18-mm)	70 to 100	70 to 100
No. 30 (600-μm)	40 to 75	40 to 75
No. 50 (300-μm)	10 to 35	20 to 40
No. 100 (150-μm)	2 to 15	10 to 25
No. 200 (75-μm)	0 to 2	0 to 10

Source: ASTM Designation: C 144–84.

FIGURE 4–19
Recommended mortar sand. Good mortar sand is a mixture of different sand sizes. The percentage of each size is based on the amount passing through different sieve openings. The smaller the sieve size number, the larger the opening. (American Society for Testing and Materials)

alkaline water can reduce mortar strength and make it unsuitable. Silt or other organic material must be avoided. Generally, if you can drink the water, it can be used for mixing mortar. If in doubt, test batches can be made and setting time and mortar quality can be checked. Water is added to the mortar mix until the batch is workable. In general, the guideline is to add as much water as needed since water is essential to the chemical reaction in the mortar. With insufficient water, the mortar will form a poor bond. Some mixes specify water in pounds—there are 8.33 pounds per gallon of water. The general guideline in adding water is to add the maximum amount consistent with workability to provide maximum tensile bond strength.

Admixtures

Various admixtures (additives) are available to change the property of the mortar. Some admixtures accelerate and others retard the setting of the mortar. In hot weather, a retarding admixture is sometimes used to offset the effect of the heat of the sun. Some admixtures are designed for use in cold weather. Cold weather admixtures that contain calcium chloride should not be used. Calcium chloride can cause corrosion of any metal reinforcement. In addition, air-entraining admixtures should not be used, and antifreeze compounds should not be used to lower the freezing point.

Admixtures are also now available for extending the workability of mortars. This allows mortars to be mixed away from the site and delivered in ready-mix trucks. Some ready-mixed mortars have a work life as long as 40 hours when properly stored.

Check local codes and design information before using any admixture. (This is normally the responsibility of the architect or the contractor.) Some codes do not allow the use of certain admixtures in the mortar. Admixtures should be avoided unless they have been tested and their effects are known. Any admixture used should conform to the American Society for Testing and Materials (ASTM) specifications and should be properly proportioned.

Plasticizers

Some mortar additives are designed to improve the workability of the mortar. Mortar plasticizers add smoothness and plasticity to the mortar—the mortar is easier to spread and finish. Plasticized mortars also adhere to the trowel and to the masonry unit faces better. Some plasticizers, made of a special hydrated clay, are designed to replace hydrated lime in the mortar mix: a mix of portland cement, plasticizer, and sand is used to make the mortar. Follow manufacturer's directions when mixing.

Coloring

Some mortars are colored to give special interest to the bond. Naturally colored sands, ground stone, or finely ground metallic oxides may be used. Carbon black is used to produce a black mortar. Under no circumstances should organic colors be used in the mix; they will create a weakened mortar. As a general guideline, use the minimum amount of coloring possible. If an approved coloring agent is used, it is very important to keep an exact record of the amount used in relation to the other ingredients. It is recommended that in no case should more than ten percent by weight of a metallic oxide be used; carbon black should be limited to two to three percent. Unless there is exact control on the color used, the different mixes will have different color shades. Color variation will create an undesirable visual effect in the bond.

Color is also used to match masonry units in order to avoid contrast. Figure 4–20 shows a mason working on a cavity wall with two different colored mortars. His mortar tub has a divider down the center to separate the mortars. The dark regular mortar is used for the backup wythe. The white mortar is used to match the color of the facing masonry units. White mortar is made using a white sand or ground white marble aggregate. A different trowel is used for each different colored mortar.

Mortar Mix

In building construction, mortar is made by mixing cement, lime, sand, and water. For small jobs, however, and especially for the homeowner, premixed mortars are available. Masonry cement is available in different size sacks, some as small as seven pounds. Types N, S, or M are available. Normally, only water needs to be added to make up this type of mortar. Mortar mix is in line with building codes in most cases.

MORTAR TYPES

Mortar is classified into four basic types depending on the proportion, by volume, of the different ingredients or by the properties developed. Figure 4–21 shows the basic mortars and their mortar proportions by volume or parts. Figure 4–22 gives recommendations for basic mortar uses.

Type M

Type M mortar is a high strength mortar and is recommended for use below grade where it will be in contact with the earth, such as in foundations

FIGURE 4–20
Two different colored mortars used on the job. (Grace Construction Products)

Mortar Proportions by Volume

	Portland Cement-Lime Mortars		
Type	Portland Cement	Hydrated Lime or Lime Putty	Sand
M	1	1/4	3
S	1	1/2	4 1/2
N	1	1	6
O	1	2	9

FIGURE 4–21
Mortar types and proportions of ingredients.

Guide for the Selection of Masonry Mortars[A]

Location	Building Segment	Mortar Type	
		Recommended	Alternative
Exterior, above grade	load-bearing wall	N	S or M
	non-load bearing wall	O[B]	N or S
	parapet wall	N	S
Exterior, at or below grade	foundation wall, retaining wall, manholes, sewers, pavements, walks, and patios	S[C]	M or N[C]
Interior	load-bearing wall	N	S or M
	non-bearing partitions	O	N

Source: ASTM Designation: C 270-86b.

[A]This table does not provide for many specialized mortar uses, such as chimney, reinforced masonry, and acid-resistant mortars.

[B]Type O mortar is recommended for use where the masonry is unlikely to be frozen when saturated or unlikely to be subject to high winds or other significant lateral loads. Type N or S mortar should be used in other cases.

[C]Masonry exposed to weather in a nominally horizontal surface is extremely vulnerable to weathering. Mortar for such masonry should be selected with due caution.

FIGURE 4–22

Guide for the selection of masonry mortars. (Does not cover specialized uses such as chimney, reinforced masonry and acid resistant mortars. (American Society for Testing and Materials)

and retaining walls. It is a mixture of 1 part portland cement, $\frac{1}{4}$ part lime, and 3 parts sand.

Type S

Type S is recommended for exterior use above grade and especially where there are lateral (side) forces on the wall. Type S is used in both rein-

forced and unreinforced masonry; it develops a high tensile bond and is recommended for use where mortar is used between facing and backing. It is a mixture of 1 part portland cement, $\frac{1}{2}$ part lime, and $4\frac{1}{2}$ parts sand.

Type N

Type N is for general use above ground where high compressive or lateral strengths are not required. It is considered to be a medium strength mortar. It is especially recommended for parapet walls, chimneys, and exterior walls with severe exposure. It is a mixture of 1 part portland cement, 1 part lime, and 6 parts sand.

Type O

Type O mortar is a low strength mortar. It is recommended for load bearing walls where the compression does not exceed 100 pounds per square inch, and where the masonry is not subject to freezing and thawing in the presence of a lot of moisture. Type O is recommend for non-load bearing walls and for general interior use. It is a mixture of 1 part portland cement, 2 parts lime, and 9 parts sand.

Refractory Mortar

A special refractory mortar is required for laying firebrick. It is made from fireclay. Refractory mortar is required in the firebox of a fireplace and in flue linings.

Gypsum Mortar

Gypsum mortar is used for laying gypsum block. Gypsum mortar is composed of hydrous calcium sulfate. These recommendations were developed by the American Society for Testing and Materials (ASTM).

SPECIAL MORTARS

Mortars with special properties are used for different specialized types of masonry work. These mortars have additives or properties that are not a part of regular mortars. A wide variety of special mortars are available from different manufacturers. In each case, the mortar must be tested and approved before it is accepted by building codes. Some of the more widely used specialized mortars are discussed below.

Tuckpointing Mortar

Type N or O mortar is used for tuckpointing. If possible, the same proportions should be used as for the original mortar. In any event, the mortar should be prehydrated to reduce excessive shrinkage. This gives a harder, doughlike mortar. Prehydrated mortar is made in the following three steps: *Step 1.* Thoroughly dry mix all the ingredients except water. *Step 2.* Mix again adding only a small amount of water; the mix should be damp and doughlike and able to be formed into a ball. *Step 3.* After one or two hours, add additional water to make it workable although drier than normal mortar.

Dirt-Resistant Mortar

Dirt-resistant mortar is made to resist staining. Calcium stearate or ammonium stearate, up to two or three percent of the weight of the portland cement, is added. Follow the manufacturer's recommendations when mixing.

Grout

Grout is used in reinforced walls, in bond beams, or inside the masonry cells themselves. Steel reinforcement bars are placed in the space to be filled with grout. Bars are always placed first, followed by the grouting material. Since grout is poured or pumped into the area filled, it needs to have a soupy consistency. Larger aggregate sizes are used when large spaces are being filled. After the grout is placed, it is consolidated by puddling or by mechanical vibration.

A recommended general grout specification would be, by volume, 1 part portland cement, 2 parts sand, and 2 parts coarse aggregate, with a maximum size of $\frac{3}{8}$-inch. Fine grout should use 1 part cement and $2\frac{1}{4}$ parts to 3 parts sand. Sufficient water should be added to produce a fluid mix.

Both fine and coarse grout are prepared. Fine grout is used in grout spaces not exceeding 2 inches in thickness. Coarse grout is used in spaces exceeding 2 inches in thickness. Fine grout uses sand as the aggregate; coarse grout uses sand and pea gravel; gravel up to $\frac{3}{8}$ inch is used. In both cases, the grout must be fluid so it can be pumped. ASTM standard C-476 is followed in mixing and proportioning the grout. If even larger spaces, over 5 inches or 6 inches, must be filled, conventional concrete with maximum 1-inch gravel may be used, if special placement procedures are used.

Latex Mortars

Latex or polymer mortars are used for setting facing on a backing wall. The latex gives higher bonding. Latex mortars are made by using a special latex or polymer mortar additive. This gives a high strength mortar to hold facing units such as granite, marble, or slate to the backing. Manufacturer's recommendations must be carefully followed. Non-mortar latex or rubber emulsions must never be used as additives. Figure 4–23, top, shows a latex mortar used to set thin brick on a concrete block backing. The concrete block is covered with felt and wire mesh and then a scratch coat. The latex mortar is applied to the scratch coat; ceramic tile, thin brick, or natural stone is then set into the latex, usually by a tilesetter. Figure 4–23, bottom, shows the finished building with the thin brick set in place.

Epoxy Mortars

Epoxy mortars are made by mixing an epoxy resin together with a catalyst to form a very strong

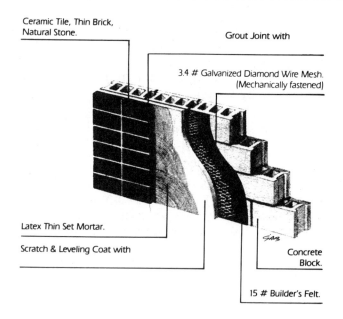

Ceramic Tile, Thin Brick, Natural Stone.

Grout Joint with

3.4 # Galvanized Diamond Wire Mesh. (Mechanically fastened)

Latex Thin Set Mortar.

Scratch & Leveling Coat with

Concrete Block.

15 # Builder's Felt.

bonding material. Manufacturer's instructions for mixing and using must be strictly followed. Epoxy mortars are used for bonding facing to a backing material.

Surface Bonding Cement

Special mortar or cement is used for plastering the face of masonry walls. Plastering coats are used to build a base on which masonry units may then be attached. Cement coats are also used in dry bonding. In *dry bonding*, no mortar is used between the masonry units; the wall is held by the exterior cement coat on the face of the masonry units. Many tests show that dry bonding walls are as strong as conventional walls with units set in mortar.

Surface bonding cement is made of a mixture of portland cement, glass fibers, and other ingredients. It is trowelled onto the outside surfaces of the wall. Both sides of the wall are covered with the cement. Figure 4–24 shows surface bonding cement being trowelled onto a concrete block

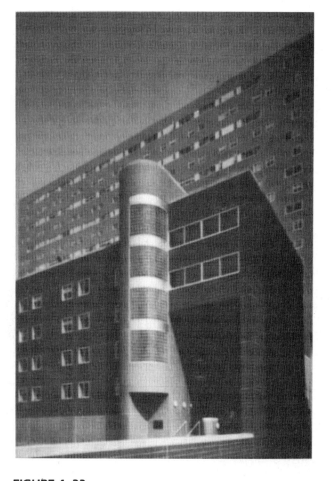

FIGURE 4–23
Latex mortar used to set thin brick on a backing. (Laticrete International, Inc.)

FIGURE 4–24
Surface bonding cement used on the face of dry-stacked concrete blocks. Both sides of the wall are surfaced. (W.R. Bonsal Co.)

wall. Note that the blocks are drystacked; that is, no mortar is used between the joints. A single ⅛-inch coat is used on the wall surface. In addition to creating a strong wall, the wall is made damp proof.

Damp Proofing

Special mortars are used to completely cover the outside surface of basement walls. The technique of plastering the wall is called *parging*. The parge coat is trowelled on after the wall is in place. A surface bonding cement, with or without fiberglass, may be used to make the hard, crack-resistant surface to seal the wall. In addition, special damp-proofing mortar mixes are available. Damp-proofing mortars, or bituminous coatings, are

placed on the exterior face of the wall below grade.

Some outside walls are treated in a two-step, damp-proofing process. First, the wall is parged with mortar. A special damp-proofing membrane is then applied (Figure 4–25). Parging is also done on the *back* of the face brick, as shown in Figure 4–26, when concrete block is used. When the inside face is parged, the mortar joints must be cut flush so the parging mortar can be applied. A rich mortar ⅜-inch thick is used.

Ready-Mix Mortars

Today, mortars are frequently mixed away from the building site and delivered in a ready-mix truck. This guarantees that the consistency of the

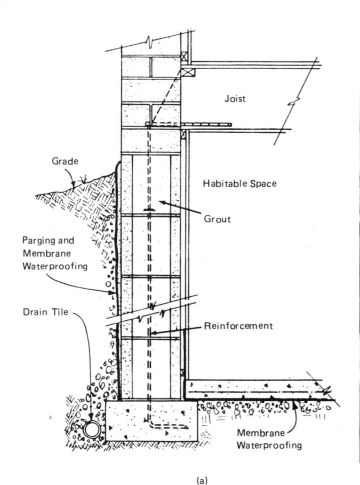

(a)

(b)

FIGURE 4–25

Damp proofing is used on the outside of masonry foundation walls.

FIGURE 4–26
Parging the back of concrete block.

mortar mix is maintained and saves time on the job. Ready-mix mortars have an additive to extend their work life. Some ready-mix mortars, if covered and protected from evaporation, may be used for up to 40 hours after delivery.

MIXING MORTAR

Mixing of mortar is done by hand for small batches, or by power mixing on the site. Both hand and power mixing is done by the mason's helper. In addition, on large construction sites, the mortar may be mixed off site in a plant, then delivered in ready-mix trucks. Mortar for very small jobs, as for patchwork or repair, can be mixed in a five-gallon bucket.

Hand Mixing

As mentioned, hand mixing is normally only done for small jobs, as for repair work, or for work around the home. The mortar ingredients are mixed dry in an appropriate container before adding water. Cement, lime, and sand are measured out by volume, to the parts specified. If mortar mix is used, follow the manufacturer's mixing guidelines. (The complete bag of mortar mix is usually emptied and dry mixed and the amount not needed is returned to the bag. This assures that all the ingredients are mixed in the right proportion.) Figure 4–27 shows the hand mixing of mortar. A mortar hoe is normally used. It is important that the ingredients be thoroughly mixed. Follow these guidelines when hand mixing:

1. Assemble all dry ingredients at the mixing area. Have ready a clean five-gallon container of

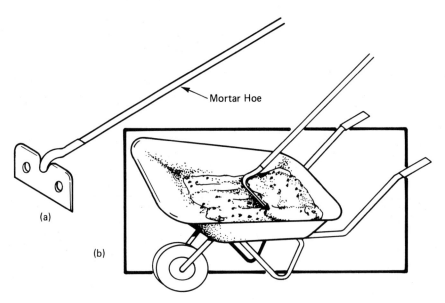

FIGURE 4–27
Hand mixing of mortar. (*Bottom:* Sakrete, Inc.)

water and a clean mixing container, such as a steel mortar box. If only a small amount of mortar is needed, it's best to mix it in the wheelbarrow or in a separate five-gallon bucket.

2. Be sure the mortar box or mixing container is level. An uneven floor will cause the liquid to run to one side or one corner.

3. Determine the mortar mixture proportions you are going to use. This is by part or volume, as noted in Figure 4–21.

4. Determine the amount of mortar you are going to mix. Only mix enough mortar for two hours of work.

5. Proportion out half the sand into the mortar box. Dry ingredients may be measured by the shovelful unless this is specifically prohibited. Some jobs require that the number of shovels it takes to fill up a cubic foot be measured. A measuring box or batcher is sometimes used to measure the number of shovelsful it takes to make a cubic foot. You can then use this number when mixing the dry ingredients. Spread the sand across the bottom of the mortar box.

6. Add all of the cement and lime. Measure by shovel count or, for a large batch, by the bag. Spread over the sand.

7. Add the second half of the sand over the dry ingredients. Adding the sand in two parts makes for a better blend.

8. Dry mix the ingredients together using a mortar hoe or the shovel. Mix thoroughly. After mixing, push all the ingredients to one end of the mortar box.

9. Add water from the five-gallon container. The amount of water depends on the size of the mix. Use a measured container so the amount of water added can be controlled. Do not run water in from a hose since the exact amount added cannot be determined.

10. Mix water into the dry mixture with the mortar hoe or shovel. After mixing, push together at one end of the mortar box. This cuts down on evaporation.

After the mix is completed, check the mortar to see if it has the right plasticity and adhesiveness. Check by cutting ridges with the trowel (Figure 4–28) or spade. Well-mixed mortar will form sharp ridges. If mortar is to be moved in a wheelbarrow, be sure the inside is clean before shoveling in mortar. To prevent sticking, wet the sides of the wheelbarrow before shoveling in the mortar. The mixed mortar is then delivered to each work station. Figure 4–29 shows a mortar board being filled with mortar. Keep the mortar piled high toward the center to cut down on evaporation. Wet down any dry areas on a wooden mortar board before placing any mortar on it. This will

FIGURE 4–28
Testing the mortar. Well-mixed mortar should have the consistency of soft mud. Sharp ridges should form in the mortar when cut with a trowel. (Grace Construction Products)

FIGURE 4–29
Placing mortar on the mortar board.

prevent the dry wood from taking moisture from the mortar.

All tools used in the mix should be washed after use. Never let mortar cake and dry on the shovel or mixing hoe. Hose off tools after use. It's a good idea to have a second five-gallon container just for cleaning tools. Tools can be set in the water when not in use.

Power Mixing

Power mixing is used on almost all construction sites, for both mortar and for grout. Either a gasoline-powered or an electrical mechanical mixer is used. As in hand mixing, all materials must be assembled near the mixer and the mortar proportion must be determined. *Caution:* Wear eye protection when power mixing mortar.

Proportioning the Material.   Material is proportioned according to the same ratios for hand mixing. Of course, large amounts of mix are usually made at one time. The dry materials are frequently added by the bag. If measurements are critical for sand, one-cubic-foot batching boxes may be used. Figure 4–30 shows batching boxes being used to determine the number of shovels in a cubic foot. Checking may be required at least once, and sometimes twice, a day. As sand loses or gains moisture, the number of shovels it takes to fill a cubic foot will differ.

For ease of mixing and for control of ingredients, mortar is mixed in batches proportioned to one bag of cement. A one-batch mix contains one bag of cement plus other ingredients; a two-batch mix contains two bags of cement plus other ingredients.

Figure 4–31 shows a nine-cubic-foot batcher. This simplifies the work and controls the ingredients. The helper fills the batcher, drops the sand into the mixer, then adds two bags of cement and one bag of lime to make a Type S mortar. This is a two-bag mix.

Adding the Ingredients.   A small amount of water is first placed in the drum. Often the drum is

FIGURE 4–30
Batching boxes are used to determine the number of shovelsful in a cubic foot. (Brick Institute of America)

already damp from mixing the last batch, so adding a small amount of water first prevents the dry ingredients from caking or balling up. The drum should be turning when dry ingredients are added. About one-third of the sand and all of the cement and lime should then be added and mixed for a least one minute. Figure 4–32 shows the sequence for adding material. Normally, after adding a small amount of water, some sand is added next, followed by all of the cement and lime. After the initial one minute of mixing, the rest of the water and sand should be added and the ingredients mixed until thoroughly blended, usually around three minutes but no more than five minutes. Do not overmix. Overmixing causes air to become en-

FIGURE 4–31
A nine-cubic-foot batcher. (Brick Institute of America)

Adding Water

Adding Sand

Adding Cement and Lime

FIGURE 4–32
Power mixing. Ingredients are placed into the mixing drum. *Top,* adding water, etc; *Center,* adding sand; *Bottom,* adding water. (*Top:* American Colloid Co., Contractor Products Division. *Center and bottom:* Masonry Institute of America)

trapped in the mortar. While the mixer is still running, tilt the mixer over and discharge the mix into a wheelbarrow or mortar box (Figure 4–33). The turning blades will cause most of the mortar to run out. Turn off the mixer and take the blades out of gear before scraping any remaining mortar out of the mixer.

Mixing the mortar and grout varies. Always check the mixing specifications before going ahead.

Cleaning Mixer.   The mixer is cleaned by turning the motor on and engaging the blades. Hose out the inside while the blades are turning. Turn the mixer down to let water and residue run out. Then turn the mixer off and disengage the paddle. If any material remains stuck, scrub with a stiff brush, and then rinse again with water. Hosing out the drum prevents mortar from drying and caking inside the drum.

Safety.   Safety is very important when running any power equipment. Follow these guidelines when working with a power mixer:

1. Always wear eye protection.

2. When adding ingredients, never allow the shovel to go beyond the safety grate on top of the mixer.

FIGURE 4–33
After mixing, the mortar is discharged into a mortar box or wheelbarrow.

3. *Never,* for any reason, reach into the mixer when the blades are turning. Turn off the mixer and disengage the blades before reaching in for any reason.

COLD WEATHER WORK

Special precautions are necessary during cold weather to keep the mortar from freezing. This involves warming the mortar and the actual work area. Use of antifreezes or admixtures to lower the freezing point of the mortar is *not* recommended. Using calcium chloride in the mortar can cause corrosion of the steel reinforcing or metal ties in the mortar. Frozen mortar must never be used. Mortar must never be laid on ice or frost.

At freezing temperatures, two dangers exist: the mason getting frostbitten and water freezing in the mortar. Protection must be provided for both the mason and the work. The temperature of the mortar must be raised to around 70°F(21°C). The masonry units should be around 40°F. Store mortar ingredients in a heated area; cover and protect the masonry units from the weather. If possible, the mortar should be mixed in a sheltered area. Heating is recommended.

Special, high early strength portland cement (Type III) may be used for cold weather work. Type S hydrated lime is recommended.

The International Masonry Industry All-Weather Council recommends the following general guidelines:[2]

1. The cold weather construction and protection recommendations of this recommended practice should be closely followed.

2. Construction materials should be received, stored, and protected in ways that prevent water from entering the materials.

3. If climatic conditions warrant, temperatures of construction materials should be measured—frozen sand and wet masonry units must be thawed. Masonry units below 20°F must be heated above 20°F without overheating.

4. Sufficient mortar ingredients should be heated to produce mortar temperatures between 40°F and 120°F. Every effort should be made to produce consecutive batches of mortar with the same temperatures falling within this range. The mortar temperature after mixing and before use should be above 40°F. Maintain temperature either by auxiliary heaters under the mortar board or by more frequent mixing of mortar batches. Heated mortar on mortar boards should not become excessively hot (greater than 120°F).

5. During below-normal temperatures, masonry should be placed only on sound unfrozen foundations. Masonry should never be placed on a snow or ice-covered surface because of the danger of movement when the base thaws and the possibility of very little bond being developed between the mortar and the supporting surface.

6. At the end of the day, the top surface of all masonry should be protected to prevent moisture, such as rain, snow or sleet, from entering the masonry. This protection must cover the top surface and should extend a minimum of 2 feet down all sides of the masonry.

Heating

The sand used in the mortar may be heated when temperatures are below 32°F(0°C). If this is not done, any moisture in the sand will turn to ice. Sand is heated by piling it over steam pipes or piling it around a heated horizontal metal culvert or stove, as shown in Figure 4–34. Special steamer units (Figure 4–34, bottom) are also used. The unit is heated by a propane torch. Sand piled over the chamber is steam heated; at the same time, water is heated for use on the job. Sand must not be

---

[2]International Masonry Industry All-Weather Council, "Guide Specifications for Cold Weather Masonry Construction," 1984. This organization represents the masonry industry. Its members are: the International Union of Bricklayers and Allied Craftsmen, Laborer's International Union of North America, Mason Contractors Association of America, National Concrete Masonry Association, Portland Cement Association, Brick Institute of America.

Steam Heating with Propane

FIGURE 4-34
Heating sand on the job. (*Top:* Brick Institute of America. *Bottom:* Ste Genevieve Building Stone Co.)

scorched, however, as this will decrease its strength in the bond.

Warming of the mortar mixture can also be achieved by heating the mixing water to at least 70°F(21°C). Water can be heated in 55-gallon drums, as shown in Figure 4-35. Water should not, however, be heated over 160°F(71°C). If the hot water causes too hot a mortar mixture, flash set could occur when the cement is added. The temperature of the combined ingredients, after heating the sand and the water, should be between 70°F and 120°F(21°C and 49°C).

Mortar should be delivered to the masons at the work station in small amounts so it can be quickly used before it gets too cold. The masonry units themselves may have to be heated if it gets below 20°F(−7°C). Heat the units to about 40°F(4°C).

Once the masonry units are laid in the mortar, the complete building element must be protected. Coverings may be placed over the freshly laid area to protect it against direct cold and any wind chill. If possible, if the area is enclosed, it may be warmed by the heat of salamanders (portable stoves), space heaters, or electric blowers.

The Brick Institute of America recommends the following construction requirements for masonry being worked in:[3]

Air Temperature 40°F to 32°F:
Heat sand *or* mixing water to minimum of 70°F and maximum of 160°F.
Air Temperature 32°F to 25°F:
Heat sand *and* mixing water to minimum of 70°F and maximum of 160°F.

[3]Brick Institute of America, "Technical Notes on Brick Construction," No. 1A, 1982.

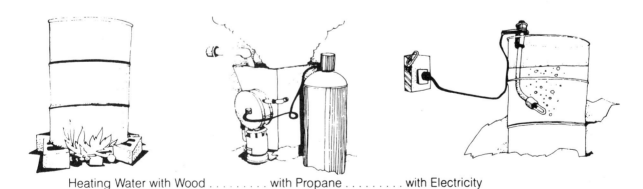

Heating Water with Wood . . . . with Propane . . . . with Electricity

FIGURE 4-35
Heating water on the job; 55-gallon drums are commonly used. (Brick Institute of America)

Air Temperature 25°F to 20°F:

Heat sand *and* mixing water to minimum of 70°F and maximum of 160°F. Use salamanders or other sources of heat on both sides of walls under construction. Employ windbreaks when wind is in excess of 15 mph.

Air Temperature 20°F and Below:

Heat sand *and* mixing water to minimum of 70°F and maximum of 160°F. Provide enclosure and auxiliary heat to maintain air temperature above 32°F. Temperature of units when laid shall be not less than 20°F.

Protection

Protection may be required for the mason on the job and for the newly laid building elements. At low temperatures, below 25°F (−4°C), and with wind above 15 mph, windbreaks should be provided to protect the masons on the job. Windbreaks will also reduce the heat loss of the masonry area. At temperatures of 20°F to 25°F (−7°C to −4°C), the completed masonry can be covered with an insulating blanket. Electric blankets (on both sides of the wall) can also be used at freezing temperatures. Above 25°F (−°C), a plastic or canvas covering can be used.

The Brick Institute of America recommends the following protection requirements for completed masonry sections not being worked on:[4]

Mean Daily Air Temperature 40°F to 32°F:

Protect masonry from rain or snow for 24 hours.

Mean Daily Air Temperature 32°F to 25°F:

Completely cover masonry for 24 hours.

Mean Daily Air Temperature 25°F to 20°F:

Completely cover masonry with insulating blankets for 24 hours.

Mean Daily Air Temperature 20°F and Below:

Maintain masonry temperature above 32°F for 24 hours by enclosure and supplementary heat, by electric heating blankets, infrared heat lamps, or other approved method.

If Type I portland cement is used in the mortar mixture, protection should be increased to 48 hours.

If the building can be enclosed, heat can be provided from within. Some buildings can be completely enclosed with plastic and heated from inside. Figure 4–36 shows a plastic-covered lean-to that can be constructed to protect the wall and

[4]Ibid.

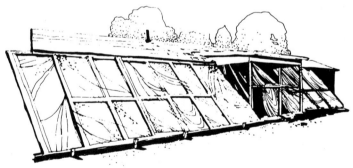

LEAN-TO ENCLOSURE FOR BRICK VENEER

INSIDE OF LEAN-TO

FIGURE 4–36
Plastic lean-to covering may be used to protect fresh mortar in cold weather. Heat is provided from inside. (Brick Institute of America)

the mason on the job. Portable space heaters or electric blowers can then be used inside the building for heat.

HOT WEATHER WORK

When the air temperature exceeds 100°F(38°C), the masonry units will have to be cooled. A fine spray of water over the masonry units should lower the temperature. This can be done several times just prior to their use. Allow units to surface dry before putting into place.

All dry ingredients should be stored in the shade, out of direct sunlight. Ice can be used to lower the temperature of the mixing water.

If possible, shading can be erected over the work area. Try to work only on the shaded areas of the building. Work can be scheduled for the cool, early morning and late evening to avoid mid-day heat.

Only small batches of mortar should be mixed at any one time. No more than 30 minutes worth of mortar should be prepared for each mason. Mortars have a very short work life on hot days. If the weather gets too hot, *flash set* may occur.

METAL TIES

Metal ties or anchors are used in masonry to tie two or more masonry wythes together. Figure 4–2 shows metal ties used to tie together a two-wythe cavity wall. Ties are also used to fasten veneer to structural backup systems. Figure 4–3 shows joint reinforcement used in the joint for concrete block work. Ties are either plain steel or zinc-coated (galvanized) steel. They are specified by gauge size or by diameter. A 9-gauge wire or $\frac{3}{16}$-inch diameter wire is commonly used.

Veneer Wall Ties

Veneer wall ties are used to tie the veneer (nonbearing wall) to the backing (load bearing wall). Either corrugated, flat metal ties or rigid, bent wire ties are used. Figure 4–37 shows the types of common ties used. Various shapes and sizes are used. The corrugated metal tie should be used only to attach veneer to a wood frame construction. The bent tie is nailed onto the wooden stud. Typically, a one-inch air space is left between the backing and the veneer. Rigid insulation is sometimes placed in the space between backing and the veneer.

Requirements for the use and spacing of ties vary depending on code. Typically, codes require metal ties for every $2\frac{2}{3}$ square feet of wall area. Ties should be completely surrounded by mortar in the brick veneer. A minimum embedment of two inches into the bed joints of the veneer is normally required.

Cavity Wall Ties

As already noted, metal ties are used to tie the two wythes of a cavity wall together. Cavity wall ties are designed to tie the two wythes together so lateral loads are transferred between wythes. They may be used to replace header units in the wall.

Rectangular or Z-shaped ties are commonly used (Figure 4–38). The Z-shaped ties are normally used only with solid backing units. Some ties may have a small bend or dip in the center. This is a drip and must be turned *down* when placed in the wall. This allows any water that might condense to drip into the cavity, rather than run into the masonry unit. Some authorities recommend use of the dripless metal tie since it develops greater strength. Adjustable ties are used when the courses of the two wythes are not at the same height. Figure 4–39 shows the use of rectangular adjustable ties. Adjustable ties are used every other block course, 16 inches on center (O.C.).

Joint reinforcement may also be used as ties. Figure 4–40 shows different types of joint reinforcement. Note (Figure 4–40, left) that ties are

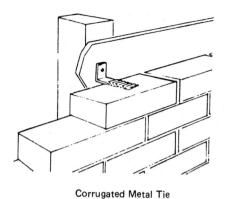

Corrugated Metal Tie

Masonry Veneer
Units

Bric-Brac
Veneer
Clip

Longitudinal
Wires

Cross Wires
Welded 16"
O.D.

Corrugated Metal Tie With Two Wires

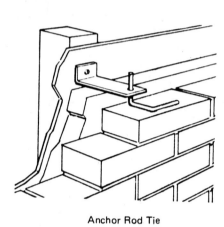

Anchor Rod Tie

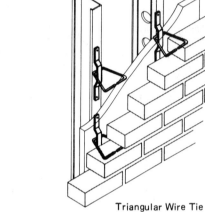

Triangular Wire Tie

FIGURE 4-37

Common veneer wall ties. (Left: Dur-O-Wal, Inc. *Top right:* Concrete Masonry Association of California and Nevada. *Bottom right:* Baltimore/Birmingham Ty-Wal Masonry Products, Division of Jim Taylor, Inc.)

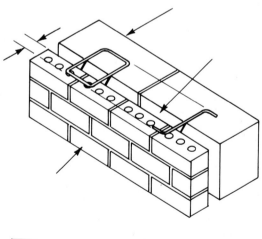

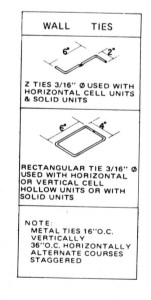

WALL TIES

6" 2"

Z TIES 3/16" Ø USED WITH HORIZONTAL CELL UNITS & SOLID UNITS

6" 4"

RECTANGULAR TIE 3/16" Ø USED WITH HORIZONTAL OR VERTICAL CELL HOLLOW UNITS OR WITH SOLID UNITS

NOTE:
METAL TIES 16" O.C. VERTICALLY
36" O.C. HORIZONTALLY
ALTERNATE COURSES
STAGGERED

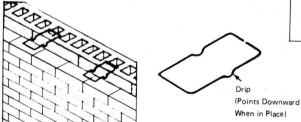

Drip
(Points Downward
When in Place)

FIGURE 4-38

Common cavity wall ties. (Brick Institute of America)

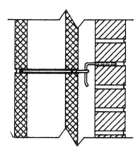
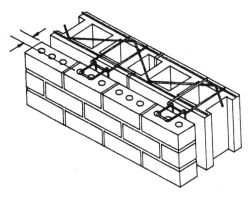

FIGURE 4–39
Adjustable joint reinforcement. (Brick Institute of America)

Cavity Wall

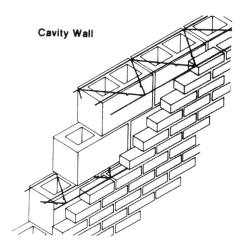

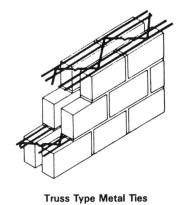

Truss Type Metal Ties

Ladder Type Metal Ties

FIGURE 4–40
Metal ties used to tie cavity walls. (*Top left:* Baltimore/Birmingham Ty-Wal Masonry Products, Division of Jim Taylor, Inc. *Bottom left:* Dur-O-Wal, Inc.)

used across every second course, or 16 inches vertically.

Cavity wall ties are required for every so many square feet of wall area. Z-shaped ties and square ties, for example, may be required for every 3 square feet to 4½ square feet. Ties are normally used for every 16 inches vertically and 36 inches apart on center (O.C.). Closer O.C. spacing is required as the cavity width is increased.

JOINT REINFORCEMENT

Joint reinforcement is used to strengthen the wall and to control cracking. Three types of joint reinforcement are used: truss, ladder, and tab. Figure 4–41 shows examples of the three basic types. The reinforcement is laid on top of the masonry units and centered on the wall. The two edges of the reinforcement should be laid back about 1 inch from the front and the back of the wall. The metal should never run to the edge or up to the face of

the wall. After the reinforcement is located, the mortar bed is placed over it and the next course of masonry units is laid.

Joint reinforcement is normally used every 16 inches vertically in the wall. Reinforcement is used 8 inches above lintels and 8 inches below sills in wall openings. Figure 4–42 shows recommended vertical joint reinforcement spacings for a concrete block wall laid in running bond. Note that extra reinforcement is used under and above the window opening.

Joint reinforcement can be cut if need be by using the edge of the trowel. Place the reinforcement on a hard surface such as a concrete slab or masonry course. Strike the metal wire sharply with the trowel edge to make a nick in the metal. Bend the metal back and forth to break at the nick.

Wire mesh or metal lath may also be used as joint reinforcement. Wire mesh is used as reinforcement where two walls join together, as shown in Figure 4–43.

Metal ties, such as those used to tie cavity walls together, are also used as reinforcement in

TRUSS TYPE

The Regular Truss design gives the greatest possible lateral, tensile and compressive values in single and multi-wythe, as well as cavity walls. Normally specified and used 16" o.c.

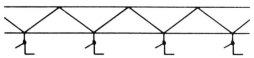

Adjustable Truss Type is ideal when using insulation or when brick & block do not align properly. Manufactured with 3/16" galvanized eye sections welded to truss. Male pintles tie brick to back-up wythe.

LADDER TYPE

Regular Ladder Type is used where reinforcing is desired and at the lowest cost. Manufactured with longitudinal side rods connected by butt welded cross rods.

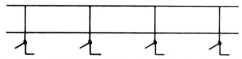

Adjustable Ladder Type provides two longitudinal rods on the face shell of the block with a galvanized eye and pintle for multi-wythe walls. Ideal when insulation is used or courses are misaligned.

TAB TYPE

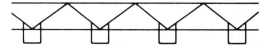

Truss Tab-Ty gives the block back up wythe the added shrinkage crack control of the truss material and ties the exterior wall with rectangular box ties.

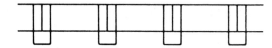

Regular Tab-Ty is basically a ladder type design with the side rods reinforcing both face shells of the block with 4" box tabs that anchor the exterior wythe.

FIGURE 4–41
Basic types of joint reinforcement. (Baltimore/Birmingham Ty-Wal Masonry Products, Division of Jim Taylor, Inc.)

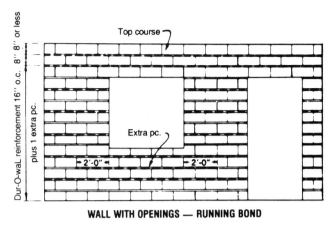

FIGURE 4–42
Spacing of joint reinforcement in a typical wall. (Dur-O-Wal, Inc.)

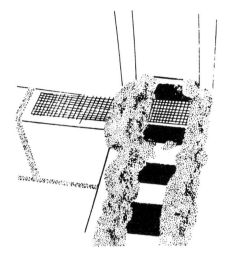

FIGURE 4–43
Wire mesh used as reinforcement where two walls join together.

double-wythe walls. Wire ties are used as a replacement for headers. Figure 4–44, right, shows how metal ties are used in a two-wythe wall. A metal tie is required for every $4\frac{1}{2}$ square feet of wall area. When the metal ties are used, headers (Figure 4–44, left) may be omitted.

ANCHORS

Metal anchors are used to hold stone and masonry units to backing and to tie separate wall parts together. Figure 4–45 shows several typical metal dovetail anchors that are used for holding stone or

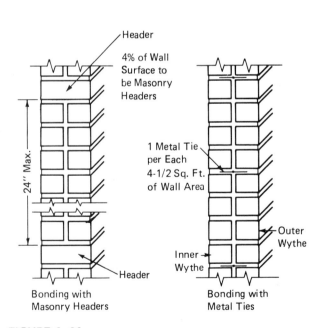

FIGURE 4–44
Metal ties may be used in a solid two-wythe wall (*right*) to replace headers (*left*) (U.S. Department of Housing and Urban Development)

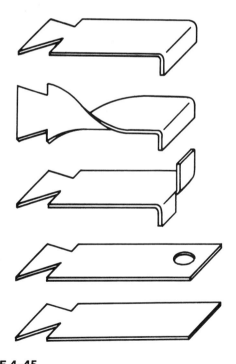

FIGURE 4–45
Typical metal anchors used to hold stone facing to the building. (Southern Slab Products Co., Construction Materials Division)

masonry facing to a backing. The dovetail fits into special slots. Figure 4–46 shows typical uses of metal anchors used to attach limestone slabs to the face of a building. Slots are made in the concrete to receive the shaped end of the anchors. Figure 4–47 shows how a dovetail anchor fits into a concrete column; the other end bends down into the concrete block cell, which is grouted to secure the anchor. A wide variety of different anchors are available.

Metal anchors are also used for tying intersecting bearing walls together. Figure 4–48 shows a rigid steel anchor used for this purpose. Note that wire mesh or metal lath is placed over the open concrete block cell to the right. This prevents the grout from falling through into the course below. The concrete block cell at the left end of the strip will also be filled with grout. After the steel anchor is placed, concrete blocks are laid

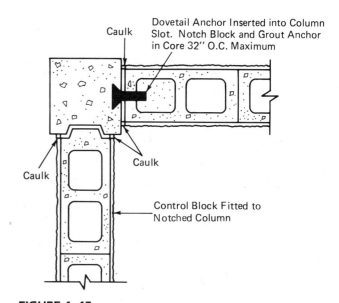

FIGURE 4–47

Dovetail anchor used to attach concrete block to a reinforced concrete column. (W. R. Bonsal Co.)

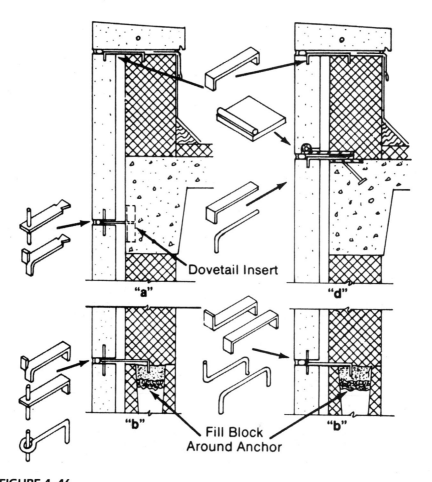

FIGURE 4–46

Typical metal anchors used to hold stone, masonry units, or panels to the building. (Indiana Limestone Institute of America)

1-1/4″ x 1/4″ x 28″ metal strap anchor with ends bent 2″ at right angles as shown. Provide at least 3 in each story height. Metal lath can be substituted for strap anchor in nonbearing walls.

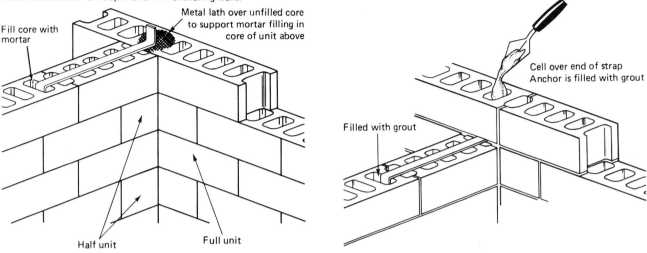

FIGURE 4–48
Rigid steel anchor used to tie intersecting bearing walls together.

to cover the anchor. The concrete block cell over the anchor is grouted to further secure the anchor in place.

Figure 4-49 shows typical metal anchors used in stone and masonry construction. Of course, many additional varieties will be found on the job.

A special anchor bolt is frequently grouted into the top of a foundation wall. Anchor bolts are used to bolt down the sill for a frame building. Figure 4-50 shows how anchor bolts are used. Usually $\frac{1}{2}$-inch diameter, 15-inch long anchor bolts are used, spaced 6 feet apart. The end of the bolt is set down inside the block cells and grouted. Metal

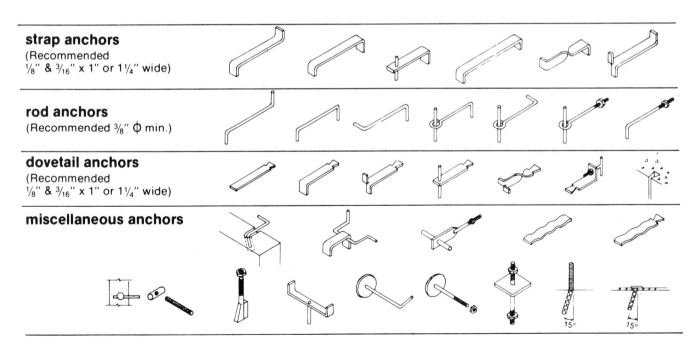

FIGURE 4–49
Typical metal anchors. (Indiana Limestone Institute of America)

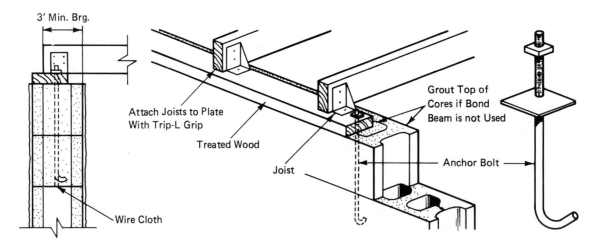

FIGURE 4-50
Typical use of anchor bolt used to hold wood sill. (W. R. Bonsal Co.)

lath or wire mesh is used at the bottom of the cell to hold the grout. Later, the wood sill is bolted to the threaded end of the anchor bolt that projects above the top of the wall.

Special anchors are also used to anchor joist ends on to masonry. Figure 4-51 shows two different wall anchors or ties that are used. Note on Figure 4-51, right, that the end of the wooden joist is cut at an angle. This is called a *fire cut*. In case of fire, this prevents the top corner of the joist, in case it collapses, from acting as a lever and prying the wall apart.

STEEL REINFORCING BARS

Steel reinforcing bars are used in the cells of hollow brick or concrete block to create a strong structure. Any steel used must be completely surrounded by grout or mortar and bonded into the masonry units to add strength to the system.

Reinforcing steel is deformed bars, such as the one shown in Figure 4-52, left. The number stamped on the bar gives the diameter of the bar. The number is read in one-eighths of an inch. The

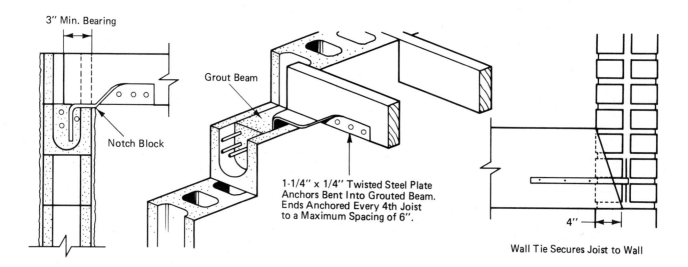

FIGURE 4-51
Wall anchors used to anchor joist ends to masonry wall. (*Top:* W. R. Bonsal Co.)

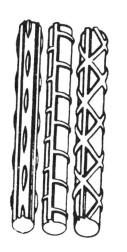
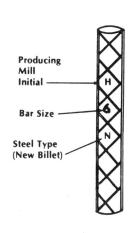

Bar Designation Number †	Unit Weight, lb/ft	Diameter, in	Area, sq in	Perimeter, in
3	.376	0.375	0.11	1.178
4	.668	0.500	0.20	1.571
5	1.043	0.625	0.30	1.963
6	1.502	0.750	0.44	2.356
7	2.044	0.875	0.60	2.749
8	2.670	1.000	0.79	3.142
9	3.400	1.128	1.00	3.544
10	4.303	1.270	1.27	3.990
11	5.313	1.410	1.56	4.430
14	7.65	1.693	2.25	5.32
18	13.60	2.257	4.00	7.09

* The nominal dimensions of a deformed bar are equivalent to those of a plain round bar having the same weight per foot as the deformed bar.

† Bar numbers are based on the number of eighths of an inch included in the nominal diameter of the bars (example: a #3 bar is 3/8 of an inch in diameter).

FIGURE 4–52
Reinforcing steel.

"6" shown means the bar is $\frac{6}{8}$ inch or $\frac{3}{4}$ inch in diameter. The table in Figure 4–52, right, gives information on the different sized reinforcing bars.

Reinforcing steel is commonly used in grouted walls to add strength to the wall. Both ver-tical and horizontal steel bars are used, as shown in Figure 4–53. It is important that the bars be positioned so they do not touch the masonry unit. They must be completely surrounded by grout. If necessary, bar positioners, as shown in Figure 4–54, may be used.

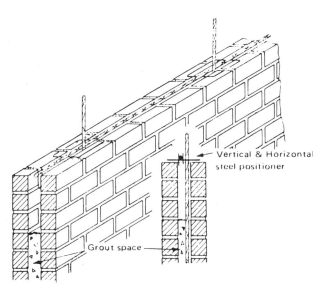

FIGURE 4–53
Reinforcing bars used in two-wythe wall. After bars are located, wall cavity is filled with grouting. (Masonry Institute of America)

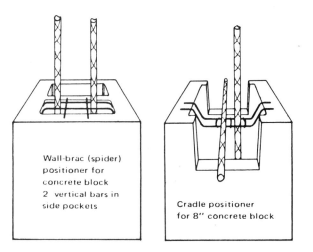

FIGURE 4–54
Bar positioners may be used to properly locate steel in the masonry wall. (Masonry Institute of America)

Figure 4–55 shows a cross-sectional view of steel reinforcing bars placed in a cavity foundation wall. Brick wythes are used; the diagonal lines shown in the two wythes are the standard symbols for brick in a section view. The dashed lines show bars running vertically; the black dot shows the end of bars running horizontally. The drawing shows and specifies how the steel reinforcement is to be placed. Note that the #5 ($\frac{5}{8}$-inch) vertical steel bars are tied at the base to the #5 reinforcing bars set into the concrete footing. In this case #5 vertical bars are 3'–10" long and placed every 20 inches on center (O.C.). The three horizontal reinforcing bars are $\frac{3}{8}$ inch in diameter, running 16 inches apart on center vertically. They rest on the $\frac{3}{16}$-inch Z-shaped ties that are used to tie the two brick wythes together. Use of reinforcement is always very carefully detailed by the architect in the blueprints.

Figure 4–56 shows use of steel reinforcement in an insulated concrete block wall. Both vertical and horizontal steel reinforcement is used. The horizontal steel reinforcement at the top of the wall is used to create a reinforced bond beam. Ladder-type, horizontal joint reinforcement is also used. All block cells not filled with grout to bond the steel bars are filled with lightweight granular insulation. Use of insulation will create an energy-efficient wall.

STEEL ANGLES

Steel angles are sometimes used over openings to support the masonry units. Figure 4–57 shows a typical use; two angles are used. Different sized

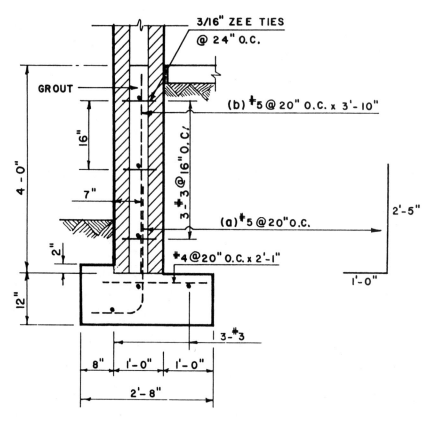

FIGURE 4–55
Placement of reinforcing steel in brick foundation wall. (Brick Association of North Carolina)

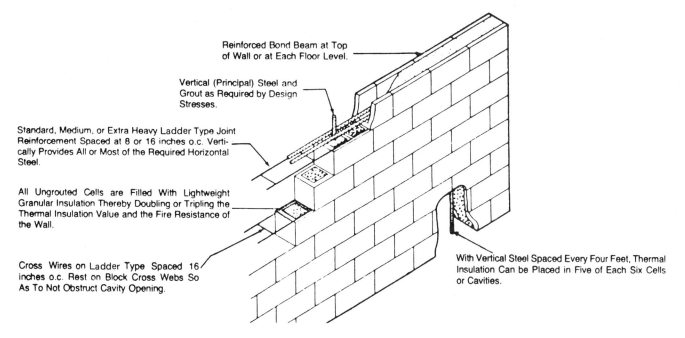

Reinforced Bond Beam at Top of Wall or at Each Floor Level.

Vertical (Principal) Steel and Grout as Required by Design Stresses.

Standard, Medium, or Extra Heavy Ladder Type Joint Reinforcement Spaced at 8 or 16 inches o.c. Vertically Provides All or Most of the Required Horizontal Steel.

All Ungrouted Cells are Filled With Lightweight Granular Insulation Thereby Doubling or Tripling the Thermal Insulation Value and the Fire Resistance of the Wall.

Cross Wires on Ladder Type Spaced 16 inches o.c. Rest on Block Cross Webs So As To Not Obstruct Cavity Opening.

With Vertical Steel Spaced Every Four Feet, Thermal Insulation Can be Placed in Five of Each Six Cells or Cavities.

FIGURE 4–56
Typical steel reinforcement in a concrete block wall. (Dur-O-Wal, Inc.)

angles are used for different opening lengths and for different wall thicknesses. T-shaped steel beams are also used as lintels.

FLASHING

Metal or plastic is commonly used for flashing around masonry elements. Flashing is installed in all types of construction to prevent moisture from entering into the structure. Flashing is installed between the masonry units and the top and bottom of openings and at the intersection of masonry walls with horizontal building elements, such as around chimneys or where the wall meets the roof. Flashing is also used where exterior masonry work meets another material, as at the bottom of a veneer wall.

Figure 4–58 shows a typical use of flashing over heads and under window sills in a brick wall. The flashing completely covers the brick to prevent moisture from entering the wall. Mortar is spread over the top of the flashing. Note that the flashing turns upward at both ends. This stops any moisture that might get in. Metal anchors are re-

quired to bond the brick sill to the course below since the mortar will not bond to the flashing. Weep holes should be provided just above the flashing at 24 inches on center. Flashing is required at both the top (or head) and at the bottom (or sill) of window openings. The flashing should extend out past the jamb lines and be turned up into a head joint to form dams at each end.

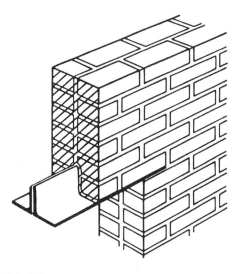

FIGURE 4–57
Steel angles used over masonry opening.

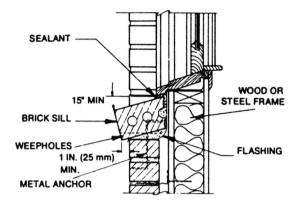

Sill in Frame/Brick Veneer Construction

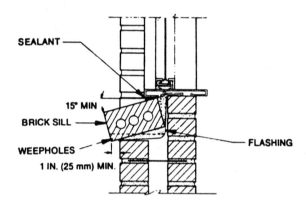

Sill in Cavity Wall Construction

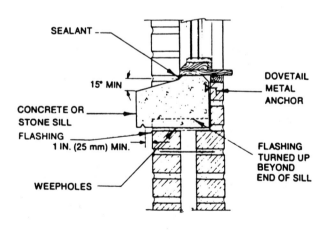

Concrete or Stone Sill

FIGURE 4-58
Flashing used around openings in brick walls. (Brick Institute of America)

Figure 4–59 shows flashing used underneath a brick veneer. The flashing is turned up behind the veneer brick 8 inches. It is very important that weep holes be made in the veneer to allow a way out for any moisture that does get behind the brick veneer. Weep holes are made by omitting the mortar from head joints every 2 feet on center.

Figure 4–60 shows flashing used at the intersection of an outside parapet wall and a flat roof. One end of the flashing runs up the side of the parapet, and the other end of the flashing runs out on the flat roof and is covered with felt strips mopped with hot asphalt. The flashing runs the entire length of the wall. Note that flashing is also used at the top of the wall under the coping. This is designed to prevent water from entering in under the coping and getting into the interior of a building.

Figure 4–61 shows use of masonry wall flashing in different situations at the base of a wall. Remember that the intent is to always prevent water and moisture from entering into the wall.

Figure 4–62 shows flashing used around a brick chimney where it passes through the roof. Two layers of flashing are used to assure that water does not run into the opening.

EXPANSION JOINTS

Expansion joints are built into brick masonry walls to control random cracking caused by expansion. They are located over major breaks in the wall; for example, by openings, by major changes in wall height, by columns and unbonded pilasters, and by wall intersections. Figure 4–63 shows areas for typical locations of expansion joints. Figure 4–64 shows an expansion joint constructed by window openings in a wall. Expansion joints are also used to break a very large wall, usually at a corner, and at return angles in L-, T-, and U-shaped buildings. Expansion joints run in a straight, vertical line from the wall base to the top. This allows the wall to move slightly without cracking or breaking. Figure 4–65 shows how different expansion joints are made in brick walls. Bent copper, neoprene, premolded foam rubber or plastic, and extruded plastic fillers are used in the expansion joint.

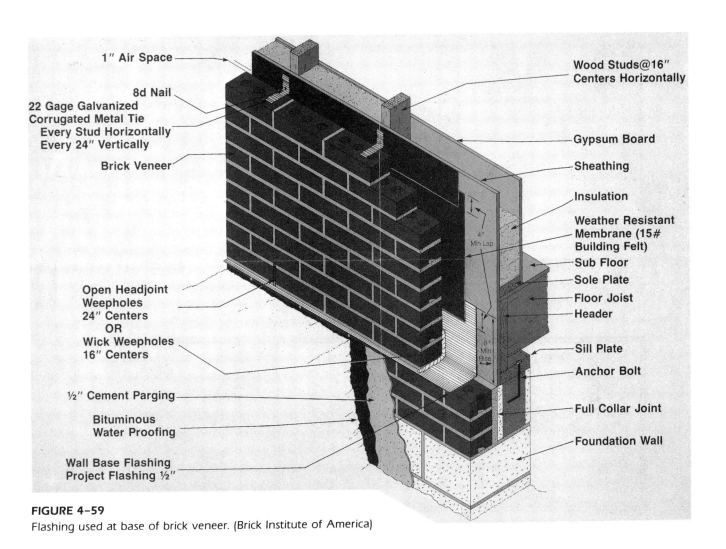

1″ Air Space

8d Nail

22 Gage Galvanized Corrugated Metal Tie Every Stud Horizontally Every 24″ Vertically

Brick Veneer

Open Headjoint Weepholes 24″ Centers OR Wick Weepholes 16″ Centers

½″ Cement Parging

Bituminous Water Proofing

Wall Base Flashing Project Flashing ½″

Wood Studs@16″ Centers Horizontally

Gypsum Board

Sheathing

Insulation

Weather Resistant Membrane (15# Building Felt)

Sub Floor

Sole Plate

Floor Joist

Header

Sill Plate

Anchor Bolt

Full Collar Joint

Foundation Wall

4″ Min Lap

8″ Min Rise

FIGURE 4–59
Flashing used at base of brick veneer. (Brick Institute of America)

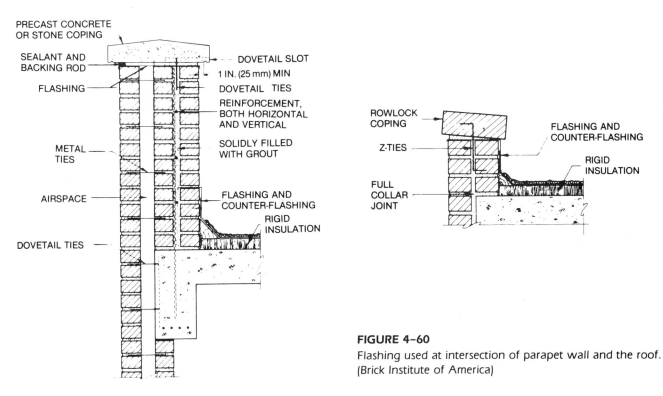

PRECAST CONCRETE OR STONE COPING

SEALANT AND BACKING ROD

FLASHING

METAL TIES

AIRSPACE

DOVETAIL TIES

DOVETAIL SLOT 1 IN. (25 mm) MIN

DOVETAIL TIES

REINFORCEMENT, BOTH HORIZONTAL AND VERTICAL

SOLIDLY FILLED WITH GROUT

FLASHING AND COUNTER-FLASHING

RIGID INSULATION

ROWLOCK COPING

Z-TIES

FULL COLLAR JOINT

FLASHING AND COUNTER-FLASHING

RIGID INSULATION

FIGURE 4–60
Flashing used at intersection of parapet wall and the roof.
(Brick Institute of America)

135

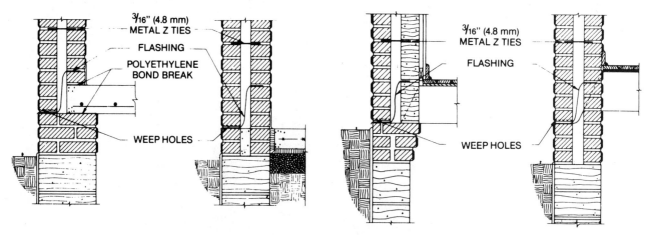

FIGURE 4-61

Flashing used at the base of different masonry wall structures. (Brick Institute of America)

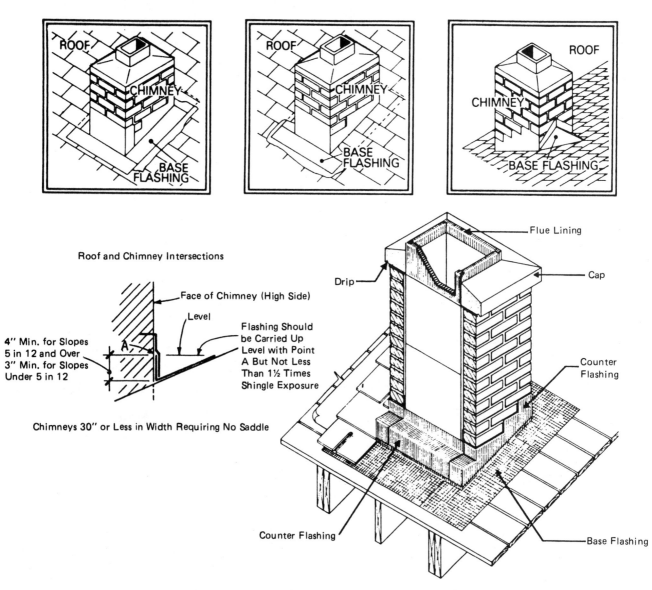

FIGURE 4-62

Flashing used around chimney at the roof. (Brick Institute of America)

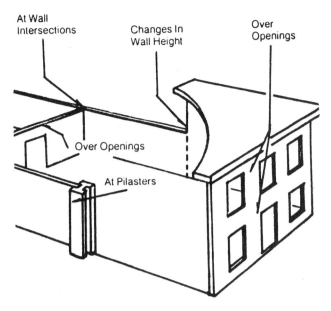

FIGURE 4-63
Typical location of expansion joints and control joints. (W.R. Bonsal Co.)

CONTROL JOINTS

Control joints are very similar to expansion joints, but they are used in concrete block walls (and in concrete work). Control joints are used in the same manner and the same places as expansion joints.

Figure 4-66 shows a control joint made in a concrete block wall using special tongue and groove control blocks and half blocks. This vertical joint would extend all the way from the base to the top of the wall. Control joints may be laid up as any other joint with full mortar. However, after

FIGURE 4-64
Expansion joint constructed in a multi-story brick building. The expansion joint runs from the foundation to the roof top at the side of the window.

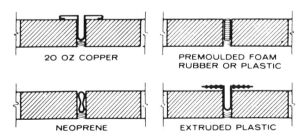

FIGURE 4-65
Expansion joints in brick wall. (Brick Institute of America)

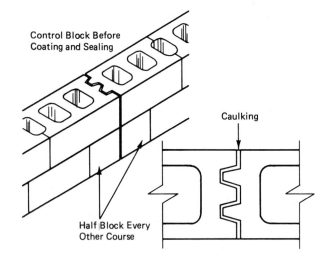

FIGURE 4-66
Control joint constructed in a concrete block wall using special blocks. (*Top:* W. R. Bonsal, Inc.)

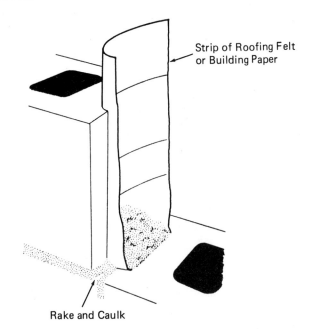

FIGURE 4-67
Control joint constructed using roofing felt or building paper.

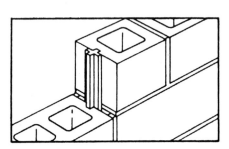

Gasket Used With Standard Sash Block

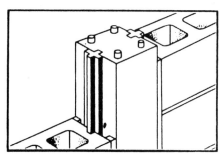

Gasket Used With Concrete Column or Unbonded Pilaster

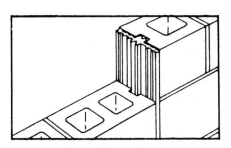

Wide Flange Gasket for 6" and 8" Walls (Standard Sash Block)

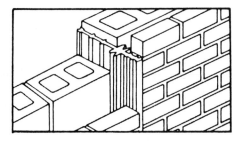

Wide Flange Gasket Used in Composite Wall (With Concrete Brick)

FIGURE 4-68
Control joints constructed using special neoprene gaskets. (Dur-O-Wal, Inc.)

the joint is made, it is raked back about $\frac{3}{4}$ inch and the recess is then filled with a caulking compound or elastic sealant.

Control joints can also be made by using a strip of roofing felt or building paper in the head joint as shown in Figure 4–67. The joint is filled, but the felt or paper prevents the mortar from bonding on one side of the joint. Use control joint blocks if possible. Rake back any mortar on the outside, and caulk each side of the joint.

Control joints are also made in a concrete block wall by using a sash block and a specially molded neoprene gasket, as shown in Figure 4–68.

Three conditions must be achieved to make a good, sound expansion or control joint.[5]

[5]Dur-O-Wal, "Unit Masonry: Ties and Reinforcement," 1982.

1. *Stress Relief:* The joint must cut the masonry wall completely from top to bottom, so as to truly form a stress relieving point.

2. *Shear Strength:* The joint must be structurally sound in that sufficient strength is developed to provide for lateral stability.

3. *Weather Tight:* The joint must be either self-sealing or one that can be easily caulked to prevent moisture penetration.

All expansion or control joints required on the job will be located and marked on the blueprints by the architect.

CHAPTER REVIEW

QUESTIONS

1. Define masonry bond. Mortar bond. Structural bond.

2. Describe how a running bond is made. A common bond.

3. What is a stack bond? How is it used?

4. What is pattern bonding when used on a wall?

5. Why are mortar joints finished?

6. How are mortar joints finished? What are the two common, recommended mortar joint finishes?

7. How are struck joints and weathered joints made? Which is more durable?

8. How and where are raked joints used?

9. When is retempering allowed?

10. What types of portland cement are used in mortar? Describe the types.

11. What is masonry cement? How is it used? What is mortar mix?

12. What kind of lime is used in mortar? What is lime putty?

13. What are the two types of sand used in mortar?

14. What conditions should be met by the water used in mortar?

15. What are admixtures? Describe several admixtures that are available.

16. What is used to give color to mortar?

17. Describe the four basic types of mortar used.

18. How is refractory mortar made? Gypsum mortar?

19. What is tuckpointing mortar? How is it used?

20. What is grout? How is it used and how is it made?

21. Describe how latex mortars are used. Epoxy mortars.

22. What is dry bond?

23. What is surface bonding cement? How is it used?

24. Describe how damp proofing is done.

25. What are ready-mix mortars?

26. Describe how mortar is mixed by hand.

27. Describe power mixing. List the safety precautions that should be followed.

28. Describe the problems associated with cold weather work. List six basic guidelines recommended for cold weather work.

29. For cold weather work, describe heating requirements for the following temperatures:
    a. 40°F to 32°F
    b. 32°F to 25°F
    c. 25°F to 20°F
    d. 20°F and below

30. For cold weather work, describe the protection required for the following temperatures:
    a. 40°F to 32°F
    b. 32°F to 25°F
    c. 25°F to 20°F
    d. 20°F and below

31. Describe problems and solutions associated with hot weather work.

32. Describe at least four metal ties used in masonry work.

33. What is joint reinforcement? How is it used?

34. How are anchors used in masonry work?

35. How are steel reinforcing bars used? What provisions can be made for aligning them when in place?

36. What is an angle iron? How is it used?

37. What is flashing? Why is it used? List four places where flashing is used in masonry work.

38. Describe how flashing is used in brick veneer work.

39. What are expansion joints? Where are they used?

40. Describe three different ways of making an expansion joint.

41. What is a control joint?

42. What is the difference between an expansion joint and a control joint?

ACTIVITIES

1. Check masonry work in your area and identify at least four different brick bonds.

2. Examine the finish on different mortar joints. Identify four different types of finish. Examine the joints for evidence of failure, such as cracking or breaking away. Make a list of failures observed. What could have caused the failure?

3. Visit a local building supply house and make a list of the portland cements, masonry cements, and mortar mixes available. List the weight of the different types. Make a list of the steps recommended for use for three different types.

4. If possible, visit a local building site and observe how mortar is mixed on the job. Write down the sequence in which the ingredients are added; time how long the mixing takes. After mixing, how is the mortar delivered to the mason? What cleanup is followed after each mixing? Note any safety precautions followed. Did you observe any unsafe practices?

5. Observe large masonry structures in your area and identify expansion joints. Make a list of where expansion joints are located.

Chapter 5

BASIC BRICKWORK

After studying this chapter you should be able to:

- Outline the steps to follow when starting work on a job.
- Describe and practice two methods for loading mortar on the trowel.
- Describe and practice throwing the mortar.
- Describe and practice furrowing the mortar bed.
- Lay brick in a mortar bed and cut off mortar.
- Butter brick.
- Lay out a lead in single-wythe running bond.
- Lay out a lead in double-wythe common bond.
- Lay out a 12-inch solid wall in common bond.

- Set mason's line from corner leads.
- Set mason's line from masonry guides.
- Build a trig.
- Set closures in a brick course.
- Strike a concave joint.
- Tuckpoint.
- Describe brick veneer construction.
- Describe the caulking needed in masonry construction.
- Describe on-the-job work practices designed to keep the brickwork clean.
- Describe and practice brickwork cleaning with a brush and water.
- Describe cleaning with muriatic acid and the safety practices to follow.
- Describe what efflorescence is and how it is caused.

Like any craft, bricklaying involves knowledge and experience of the basic technique. Once the basics are thoroughly understood, you can advance to more complicated techniques and jobs. Good workmanship, good tools, the proper materials, a knowledge of what is specified for the job, and careful planning and layout are what make for a professional job.

The first step in bricklaying is to have good tools available. To start, you should have a 6-foot brick spacing rule, 4-foot brassbound level, 2-foot brassbound level, brick trowel, pointing trowel, brick set, brick hammer, bricklayer's brush, mason's line and line blocks, and jointing tools for finishing the mortar joint. The second step is to know exactly what job needs to be done. On the job, you may have to consult blueprints to determine exactly what is required. Lastly, of course, you must have the building materials needed: brick, any reinforcement or ties required, and well-mixed mortar. The brick size, pattern, and joint size must be known.

You may want to check your brick for suction. High-suction brick will absorb water out of the mortar and prevent proper bonding of the mortar. The water test for suction was described in Chapter 3. High-suction brick must be thoroughly wetted by hosing. They must be surface dry before being laid.

A planned layout of the work is essential. This may involve locating corners of the building, establishing wall lines, and measuring and laying out dry brick. Take time to plan. Don't begin until you know exactly where you are going.

For efficient work on the job, all materials should be laid out at your work station. Figure 5–1 shows a well laid out work area. Brick and mortar are at hand; scaffolding is adjusted to a comfortable work height.

Before starting work, follow these steps:

1. Have all your tools ready. Make sure they are in top condition.

2. Know what is required to do the job.

3. Plan the layout of the required masonry element. Locate corners, wall lines, openings, and so forth.

FIGURE 5–1
Mortar and brick must be laid out so they can be easily reached when working.
(Non-Stop Scaffolding)

4. Have brick and mortar at hand.

5. Have a well-organized work station.

BASIC TECHNIQUES

A good job depends on good workmanship. You should practice using and manipulating the brick trowel until it feels comfortable when loaded. Figure 5–2 shows the correct way to hold the trowel. Hold it firmly with your thumb resting on the top of the handle on the ferrule.

Hint: To get used to working with a trowel, you should practice basic techniques. Practice loading mortar, throwing the mortar, furrowing the mortar bed, and cutting off excess mortar after a brick is laid. Work with someone who is experi-

enced so any bad habits or wrong techniques can be quickly spotted and corrected.

Mortar can be loaded in several ways. You can load from the side toward the center, build and cut from the middle, or pull from the side of the pile and scoop. You will have to develop a technique that is sure and easy for you.

When starting work on fresh mortar, you can build the mortar toward the center. The mortar should have good plasticity. If it is too hard, water may have to be added. On hot days, evaporation may dry out the mortar. In that case, water can be added. If hydration has started in the mortar, throw it away and get new.

The size of the trowel you use is also very important. When you're first starting out, it's a good idea to use a smaller trowel until your coordination and muscle tone are built up. Try working with a 10-inch trowel.

Testing the Mortar

The quality of mortar is extremely important. The proper mix, of course, must be followed. Mortar type and any mixing information will be given by the architect in the written specifications.

On the job, the freshness and spreadability of the mortar can be quickly tested with the trowel. Using the point of the trowel, pull the mortar into small, sharp ridges. If the ridges hold, the mix, in terms of the amount of water, is well proportioned. If there is too much water, the ridges will run down and slump. If there is not enough water, the ridges will break and crumble. Good mortar has the consistency of soft mud.

Cupping the Mortar

The technique of cupping the mortar is commonly used when mortar is placed on a mortar board. Figure 5–3 shows this technique. The mortar is cut or sliced off the side of the pile and pushed or rolled away from the main pile. The mortar is then shaped by the trowel to form a roll that is then picked up. As you are lifting the mortar away from the board, give the trowel a slight snap or jerk to seat the mortar. Use your thumb to steady and control the trowel.

FIGURE 5–2
Correct way to hold the trowel. (U.S. Department of Labor)

FIGURE 5-3
Cutting the mortar. When loading, cut into the mortar with the side of the trowel.

Note in Figure 5-3 that the left edge of the trowel is used to cut into the mortar pile. This is the method for those who are right handed. Left-handed masons cut in with the right edge of the trowel.

Clock Method

When a mortar pan is used, a technique called the clock method is used for loading mortar on the trowel. This is so named because the movement of the trowel is described in relation to the hands of the clock. Figure 5-4 shows the steps in loading mortar using this technique. The steps are described in relation to a clock face, assuming that

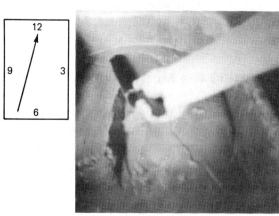
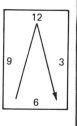

Step 1: Cut from Bottom to Top

Step 2: Cut Back at Angle to Right to Make Pie Wedge

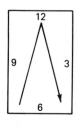
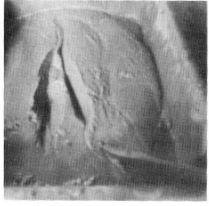

Inverted "V" Pie Wedge

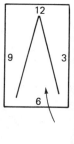

Step 3: Load Pie Wedge on Trowel

FIGURE 5-4
Clock method of loading mortar from a mortar pan. (1) Cut a furrow from the bottom to top. (2) Cut return furrow from top to bottom, leaving a wedge of mortar. (3) Cut into the right side of the prepared wedge from bottom to top to remove mortar.

the bottom of the pan as you face it is at 6 o'clock (6:00). Three basic steps are followed:

1. With the trowel edge, cut across the mortar from the bottom (at the 6:30 position) to the top (12:00 position). This cut makes a furrow to the top of the mortar.

2. Cut back down from the top to the bottom (at the 5:30 position). This cuts another shallow trough. Steps 1 and 2 together have created a narrow, upside-down "V" in the mortar. Steps 1 and 2 prepare the mortar for cutting out a pie wedge or inverted "V."

3. Finally, cut back towards the top, running from the 5:30 position to the 12:00 position in the mortar pan. Cut the trowel into the pie wedge or inverted "V" to remove a trowel-load of mortar. If done correctly, the trowel should be fully loaded.

The clock method, when learned, is a quick, efficient method of loading the trowel. The upside down "V" or pie wedge and the cut for loading the trowel are done in three quick back and forth motions. Practice the method until it feels natural. If you're in doubt about the efficiency of the method, try loading the trowel without first preparing the pie wedge or inverted "V."

Trowel Load

Figure 5–5 shows a fully loaded trowel. The mortar should be enough to form a bed sufficient to lay three or four brick. When first practicing loading mortar, it's a good idea, for control, to pick up smaller amounts on the trowel. As you gain experience, work up to a full trowel load.

Throwing the Mortar

The loaded trowel is swung over to where the brick course is being laid, and the *mortar* is laid out in a straight line of even width to make the mortar bed. Figure 5–6 shows the mason starting the mortar bed. As the trowel is moved along, it is turned over. The mortar is not simply allowed to slide off—it is strung in a sweeping line to form

FIGURE 5–5
A full trowel-load of mortar.

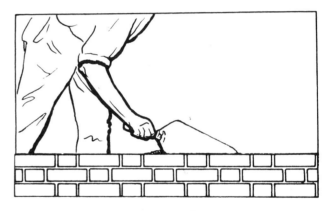

Starting to spread mortar

Spread the mortar with a smooth swing of the arm
with fingers relaxed.

FIGURE 5–6
The trowel is turned and moved along the bed to deposit the mortar. Lay the mortar in the center of the bed area. (Brick Institute of America)

FIGURE 5–7
The trowel is moved until all the mortar is deposited.

the mortar bed. Throwing the mortar allows it to seat into any irregularities in the brick. Deposit the mortar in the center of the bed area. The mortar is thrown off the left edge of the trowel; the trowel is moved to the right in a quick, steady sweep until all the mortar is deposited (Figure 5–7). (A left-handed mason works best throwing to the left.) With a full load of mortar on the trowel, a bed long enough for three or four brick will be laid. When starting, only try to lay a bed for two or three brick. Take care that the mortar bed is of equal thickness throughout, about one-inch thick.

When beginning, only partially load the trowel. Practice throwing mortar for one or two brick and work up to a full load for three or four brick.

Furrowing the Mortar Bed

After the mortar bed is placed, it is furrowed to spread it out. Figure 5–8, top, shows a mortar bed being furrowed. The trowel is held at an angle and the tip of the trowel is moved through the mortar bed with a tapping motion to make the furrow. Do not simply drag the trowel—this may break the mortar. Use a tapping motion. Furrow only enough to spread out the mortar across the brick thickness. Figure 5–8, bottom, shows a completed furrow. Note where the trowel tip has tapped into the mortar. Do not furrow too deeply or a gap will be left in the center when the brick are laid. Try not to lap the mortar over the edge of the brick. If mortar laps too far over the edge, cut it off with the edge of the trowel and return it to the mortar pile.

Beveling the Bed Mortar

When mortar is laid for a *cavity wall*, the mortar on the cavity edges is beveled with the flat of the trowel. (The process is illustrated in Chapter 6.)

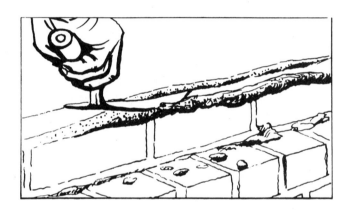

FIGURE 5–8
Furrowed mortar bed. Use the tip of the blade and move along in a tapping motion to spread the mortar across the bed area. (Top: Brick Institute of America)

Beveling prevents mortar from squeezing out and falling into the cavity opening. When brick units are laid, mortar should be kept to the outside. Any mortar fins that project out into the cavity opening should be *flattened* to prevent mortar from falling off. Never cut off the mortar. A smooth surface is often required so insulation can be placed in the cavity.

Holding the Brick

The brick should be held with the thumb and fingers well up from the bed. As shown in Figure 5-9, the brick should be securely held, but there should be a space between the tip of the thumb and fingers and the brick. Note that a sort of open

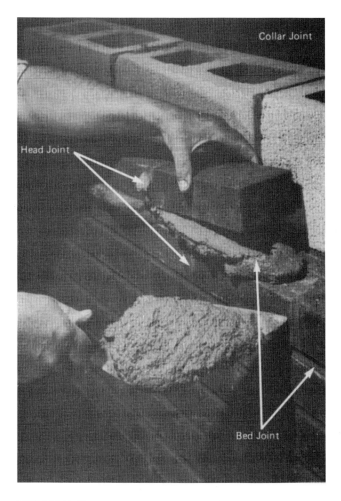

FIGURE 5-9
Holding the brick. Thumb should be well up from the bottom (bed) of the brick. (Master Builders)

V is made between the face of the brick and the end of the thumb and the fingers. When a mason's line is used, this allows the brick to be laid to the line without the thumb or fingers striking the line.

Laying to the Line

It is very important that the thumb, fingers, or brick *not* hit the mason's line when laying the brick. Hitting the line causes it to jiggle or bounce so other masons working with you cannot lay their brick until the line stops moving. Hitting the line with your thumb is called *thumbing the line*. Thumbing the line is a very unprofessional practice and can disqualify you for work on the job. Brick laid to the line are set back about $\frac{1}{16}$ of an inch from the line. Brick should never touch the line. The line is located on the face side of the wall. However, either the thumb or fingers may hit the line depending on which side of the wall the mason is working from. Figure 5-10 shows how the thumb (top) or fingers (bottom) are lifted to avoid hitting the line.

Buttering

Before each brick is laid, mortar is wiped on the end, as shown in Figure 5-11. This common technique is called *buttering* or *buttering the brick*. The buttered brick is then laid into the mortar bed, as shown in Figure 5-9. When buttering, slap the mortar on the end of the brick. This assures a good bond; mortar will go into voids on the brick end. The mortar must fully cover the end of the brick so that when it is shoved into place there will be no voids. Voids will allow water into the joint.

Laying the Brick

Brick should be set or pushed downward into the mortar and shoved against the end of the previously laid brick (Figure 5-12). Shoving the brick pushes mortar out of the top of the head joint. This guarantees that the head joint is full of mor-

Hold thumb out to avoid hitting the line

Hold fingers out to avoid hitting the line

FIGURE 5–10
When holding the brick, hold it high and point thumb or fingers away from the face of the brick to avoid hitting the mason's line when laying.

tar. As a guideline, shove the brick about $\frac{1}{2}$ inch into the head joint. This makes a good joint. A "fin" of mortar must appear above the top of the head joint. Shoving allows the mortar to work itself into the bed of the brick and at the same time it tightens the head joint. The size or thickness of the bed joint will be determined by how far into the mortar bed the brick is pushed. The thickness of the mortar in the head joint is also adjusted or determined by how the brick is shoved against the brick already in place. Square and align the brick by eye when setting it in place. The brick is pressed down to the proper level. You can check the depth and level by resting your hand flat across the end of the brick just laid and the one already in place (Figure 5–12, bottom). With practice you can feel if they are level to each other. Set it square and level so it won't have to be aligned too much later. Naturally, some aligning is required for most masonry units. Brick are tapped by the trowel to level, align, and plumb.

Take care if a brick must be lifted once it has been seated. Lifting breaks the bond. If the brick must be lifted for realignment, do this before tapping the brick down in place. Never lift a brick for reseating if the mortar has begun to set. If mortar has begun to set and the brick is lifted, remove all the mortar, lay a new bed, and reset the brick.

FIGURE 5–11
Buttering the brick.

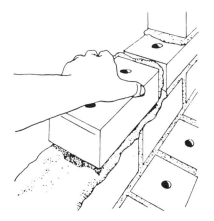

FIGURE 5-12
Shove the brick in to make sure mortar completely fills the head joint. (*Top left:* Brick Institute of America. *Bottom:* Richard Hardesty)

Cutting off Mortar

When a brick is laid in the mortar bed, some mortar will project out over the edge beyond the face of the brick. This extruded or excess mortar on the face side of the wall is cut off with the trowel, as shown in Figure 5-13. The edge of the trowel is held at an angle and lightly scraped across the joint to pick up the mortar. Take care not to smear any mortar on the face of the brick—it will have to be cleaned off later. This mortar is used to butter the end of the next brick to be laid, or it can be laid against the end of the brick just laid, or it can be returned to the mortar pile.

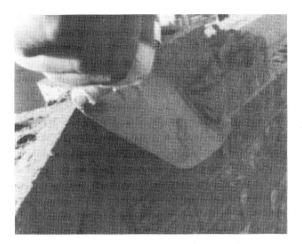

FIGURE 5-13
Cutting off excess mortar from the joint. (Brick Institute of America)

Another method sometimes used, but not recommended, for filling the head joint is to wipe mortar on the exposed end of the brick just laid. The next brick is then laid in with little or no buttering.

Selecting Brick

Frequently there is color variation in the brick. Most brick manufacturers include a tag on each cube of brick indicating how the cube should be broken down, or used, to obtain the desired blend of brick. If instructions are not given, it is a good idea to unload brick from different packs or cubes to distribute any color changes or variations. If color differences are pronounced or deliberate—for example, a mixture of light or whitish brick and dark brick—take care to distribute the color differences throughout the wall or surface. If brick of one color are all grouped together, the completed wall will look unbalanced. Dark or light clumps of brick create a blotched and unpleasant effect. Remember that there is an infinite variety of brick colors and textures. Use this to advantage to create a pleasing and interesting surface.

Labor Saving Hints

It is not efficient to do only one thing at a time when laying brick. When you have progressed to the point where you can lay a fairly long and even furrow, you should practice picking up a brick the same time as you cut off a trowel load of mortar (Figure 5–14). This is often done on the job when laying brick veneer. Use both hands to save time and increase efficiency. Of course, the mortar and brick must be located so it's easy to cut with one hand while at the same time pick up a brick with the other.

Another labor-saving technique is called *walling*. Walling is used when laying out a solid wall. It involves placing several brick on the wall within easy reach, as shown in Figure 5–15, top. When walling, you can pick up two brick at a time (Figure 5–15, bottom). Study how you work. Always try to use two hands to do the job and cut down on time.

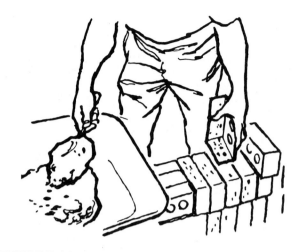

FIGURE 5–14
For efficiency, pick up the brick at the same time you load the trowel with mortar. (Brick Institute of America)

Cutting Brick

You should avoid using short brick in the brick bond if at all possible. Sometimes, however, short brick are needed. Three-quarter brick, for example, are required in the common bond. Cut brick are also needed for brick window sills. As noted in Chapter 2, brick may be cut by (1) striking with the edge of the trowel, (2) hitting with a brick set and hammer, and (3) cutting with a masonry saw.

Brick used in small jobs, as for home use, are frequently cut by using the trowel or brick set and hammer. It's a good idea to score the brick at the point where the break is needed. Scoring can be done by scribing with a hard metal point, such as a nail, or by hitting with the blade of the brick hammer. Use a straightedge to make sure the score is straight. Score on two sides. Then, when the brick is hit on the scored mark, it will break clean at the point where it is scored. Chapter 2 illustrated how a brick set is used to break the brick. The brick can also be cleanly broken by striking sharply with the edge of the trowel. Striking with the trowel is a quick method for cutting the brick but leaves a rough edge unsuitable for quality, exposed work.

On the construction site today, most short brick are cut with the power masonry saw. This is fast and very accurate. Saw cutting is recommended if at all possible. *Remember:* When breaking or cutting a brick always wear eye protection.

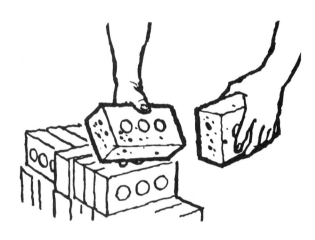

WALL LAYOUT

To do a good, efficient job, the masonry element being worked on must be carefully laid out. Corners must be established, and the line the brick face must follow should be marked.

The location and size of brick walls, or other masonry elements are detailed on the blueprints. The floor plan gives lengths and locations. Elevations show heights and locations; sections show construction details on how the brick are laid in relation to other construction elements. Notes on the blueprints or specifications will spell out types and size of brick, the mortar used, and other information on the quality of the masonry work required.

If a reinforced concrete footing is used to support a brick wall, the wall is centered on the footing. Figure 5–16 shows a concrete footing used to support a double-wythe brick wall. This is a reinforced brick retaining wall. Note that the wall is centered on the footing.

If a concrete slab is used, the wall or veneer will be located at or near the edge of the slab.

FIGURE 5–15
Walling the brick. Pick up and lay out several brick on the wall within easy reach. (*Top:* U.S. Department of Labor. *Bottom:* Brick Institute of America)

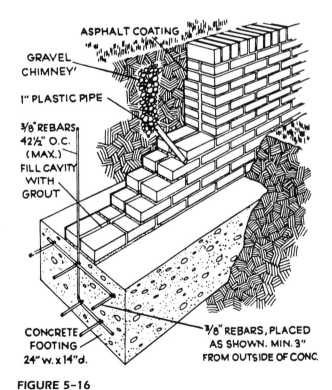

FIGURE 5–16
Reinforced concrete footing support for two-wythe solid brick wall. (Brick Institute of America)

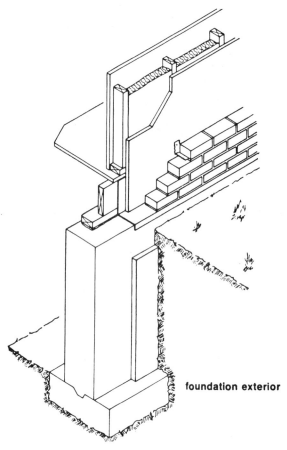

When building on a foundation top, the location depends on the type of masonry wall. If a double-wythe brick wall or a concrete block and brick wall is to be built, the width of the wall will approximately equal the width of the concrete foundation top. When brick veneer is used, both veneer and the building framework are centered on the foundation wall top. Figure 5-17 shows a brick veneer tied to a wood frame wall. With the sheathing between the brick veneer and the wood framework, the total wall thickness equals the width of the foundation top. The veneer is laid even to the outside of the foundation wall.

Some concrete foundation tops are built with a shelf, or built extra wide to hold the brick veneer, as shown in Figure 5-18. The brick are laid flush to the outside edge of the foundation wall (Figure 5-19). If concrete block foundation walls are used, a special header block is laid. The header block is cut back to create a step or shelf on the side. The veneer is laid on the shelf of the header blocks.

Interior brick partitions are laid to a snapped chalk line on the floor. The brick are always laid in a thick bed of mortar placed on top of the support base.

FIGURE 5-17
Brick veneer, wood frame, and sheathing supported by foundation wall. (United States Gypsum Co.)

FIGURE 5-18
Brick veneer is supported by the wide foundation top.

FIGURE 5-19
Veneer is laid flush to front edge of foundation. (Note overlap of flashing beneath veneer base.)

Locating Corners

Corners are located and established by dropping a plumb bob down from building lines supported by batter boards, as shown in Figure 5-20. The exact location of a plumb bob and line may be deter-

mined by measuring over from the building line. The plumb bob locates the outside corner of the brick wall. The exact corner points are located and marked on the foundation or support base. A line is then snapped between corners as a guide for laying the brick. Before laying any one corner, all corners should be located and brick lines snapped on the foundation.

Checking Corner Angle

Measure the angle of the lines at each corner to be sure 90° right angles are laid out. If the walls are long—over 10 feet—check trueness by using the 6-8-10 method. Measure 6 feet along one side (leg) of the corner and mark on the layout line; then measure 8 feet along the other side (leg) and mark. The distance diagonally between the two marks (6 foot and 8 foot) should be exactly 10 feet. Figure 5-21 shows this method of squaring a corner. If more or less than 10 feet is measured, you do not have a true 90° corner.

Note: For walls shorter than 10 feet, the same measure and checking can be done with a 3-4-5 measure. The 6-8-10 measure is more accurate, however.

Right angle corner trueness can also be checked with a square (Figure 5-22). When all

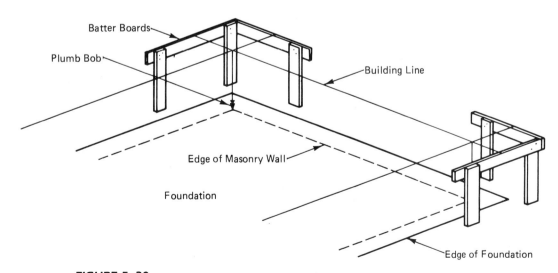

FIGURE 5-20
Corners of brick walls are located by dropping plumb bob down from building lines.

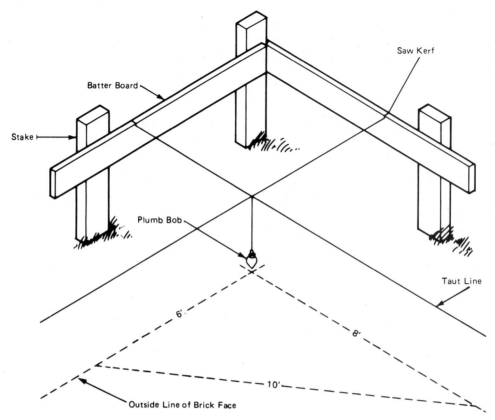

FIGURE 5-21

Checking corner angle: 6-8-10 method. Measure 6 feet and 8 feet on the two wall lines. The distance between the two measured points should measure 10 feet.

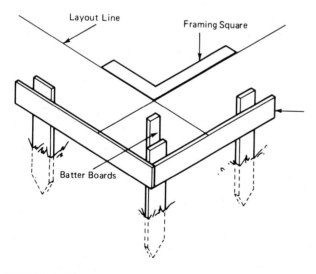

FIGURE 5-22

Checking corner angle with steel square.

four corners are laid out and squared, check trueness by running diagonal lines across from opposite corners (Figure 5-23). If corners are square, the diagonal lines will be of equal length.

Dry Layout

When starting the wall on the support base, the best and safest way to lay out the complete first course of brick, from corner to corner, using no mortar. Laying out a dry run allows you to discover any problems, such as the distance being too long or too short for a set number of full brick.

The first step is to locate exactly the points where the outside corners will rest. You can scratch or pencil an "X" for each corner. A line is established from corner to corner by snapping a chalk line. One end of the line can be attached to

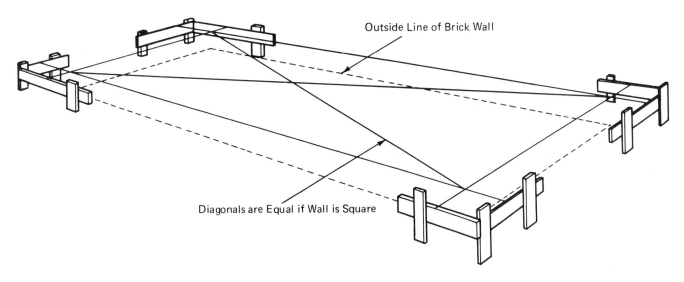

FIGURE 5-23
Measuring across opposite corners. Diagonals should be equal.

a stake driven in the ground. The other is held in the hand just crossing the corner mark. The line is picked up and snapped to leave a chalk mark. The line shows the outside edge or where the face of the wall rests on the support foundation. The brick are laid to this line.

Figure 5-24 shows a row of brick being laid out in a dry run. About $\frac{3}{8}$ inch is left between each brick for the head joint. Place your index finger, sideways, between the ends of the brick; this gives about the right distance for the head joint. Complete the row of brick from corner to corner (Figure 5-25). In doing a dry layout, it is a good idea to work from each corner towards the center. This allows you to make adjustments for the last or closure brick in the center. The ideal situation is to come out even at the center with no part of a brick extending over or running short. If the layout shows that you are going to be a little short or long, you can go back through the course and adjust the head joint openings until the ends are even.

Leave the brick in place when laying the course. Only set back two or three brick at a time for the mortar bed. Lay these brick, then set back two or three more to make room for more mortar bed. If all the brick must be moved, mark each head joint on the foundation (Figure 5-26). A pencil is used to mark the joints; mark both sides of the joint.

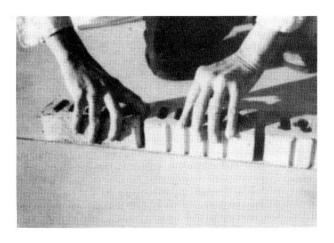

FIGURE 5-24
Laying out a course of dry brick. Use the index finger to make the head joint space, about $\frac{3}{8}$ inch.

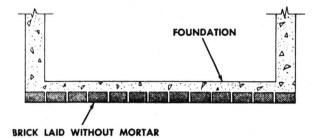

FIGURE 5-25
Row of brick laid dry to check layout.

Laying the Course

Before laying brick, make sure the base is clean. Brush off any dirt before throwing the mortar bed. The first course is laid from *each* corner toward the center. Each corner is built up to make a lead. Then the first course is completed meeting at the center of the wall. By laying toward the center, any problem can be corrected by adjusting head joint openings. If through miscalculation, you find you are considerably off at the center, you should *not* lay in one short brick. Cut two or three short brick of equal length to correct the error. This is not as objectionable as one short brick in the center of the course.

Once the corners (leads) are completed and the first course is laid, the mason's line is stretched from corner to corner to serve as a guide for each course. When laying brick, or any masonry units, it is essential that they be level and plumb. After several brick, five or six, are laid in the course, you should check their horizontal trueness with a level. Position the level on the center of the row of brick. Tap any out-of-level brick down with the end of the trowel handle or the trowel blade to true them. Lay the level or a straightedge on the face of the row of brick to see that they are straight.

Some side adjustments may be made if the brick are not in line. However, if the mortar has begun to set, brick may *not* be slid on their bed joint. Sliding or moving brick on the joints after hydration has started will greatly weaken the bond. If brick must be adjusted after hydration or set has begun, you must remove both the brick and the mortar and lay new mortar. Also, you should not *lift* a brick up from a bed or *pull* the brick from the head joint. This destroys the bond.

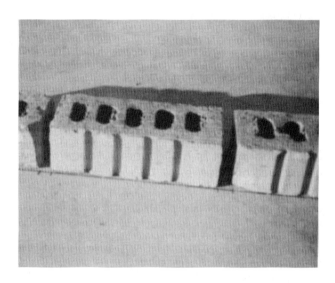

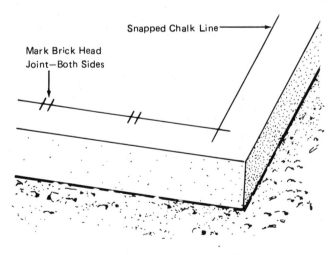

Snapped Chalk Line

Mark Brick Head
Joint—Both Sides

FIGURE 5-26
Mark head joint locations as a guide.

BUILDING CORNERS (LEADS)

It is very important that corners, or *leads*, be very carefully laid out. Corners (leads) are used as a guide for the whole wall. Setting up or laying the corners is called *laying the leads*. Two leads are used, and a line is stretched between them at each course level as a guide for laying the rest of the brick (between the two leads or corners). For very long walls, an intermediate lead, called a *rack-back lead,* is laid between the two corner leads.

The first step is to plan the actual corner size: number of brick in each course and number of courses high. Of course, the length of each side of the corner should be roughly the same. Leads seven or nine courses high are commonly used, depending on the number of stretchers used in each leg of the corner. For example, if four stretchers were used on one side and three on the other side, the lead should be seven courses high. If five and four were used on the corner sides, the lead would be nine courses high. If a short wall was being laid and only three and two stretchers were used on the corner legs, the lead would only be five courses high. A lead eleven courses high would have six and five stretchers laid out on the two legs.

Practice: Corner Lead, Single Wythe (Running Bond)

After the corner points have been marked, chalk lines snapped, and a dry layout of the wall sides made, the corner can be started. First, throw a mortar bed for two or three brick. An unusually thick bed of around 1 inch is recommended for the first course. This bed will be squeezed out to about a $\frac{3}{4}$ inch bed joint when the first brick course is laid. Mortar bed joints for the higher courses is

normally $\frac{3}{8}$ inch. Figure 5–27 shows the start of the first course at the corner. Note that the brick are laid to the chalk line on the foundation. Each head joint is also marked with a pencil as a guide.

Figure 5–28 shows a simple three-course corner lead. This is a single-wythe, running bond corner. Since there is only one wythe, this is a simple lead to lay. If five or seven courses were planned, then the legs would be extended with additional stretchers.

Figure 5–29 shows how this corner lead would relate to an opposing corner lead. A mason's line is used to connect the two leads. This serves as a guide for brick laid between the two leads. The line is raised up for each brick course. Figure 5–30 shows the completed course between two leads.

Once several brick are laid in a course, they should be checked to see that they are level. Figure 5–31 shows the level being checked with a mason's level. Any brick not level can be tapped down with the blade or the handle end of the trowel (Figure 5–32). Outside alignment of the brick is checked with a straightedge or with the level used as a straightedge (Figure 5–33). Straighten any out-of-alignment brick. Any alignment or straightening of brick should be done while the mortar is still very fresh. Once the mortar has started to set, any movement will greatly weaken the bond. If alignment is necessary after set has started, tear out the brick and mortar and re-lay the brick in a new mortar bed. As men-

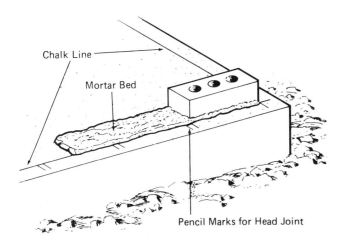

FIGURE 5–27
Start the first course by laying from the corner.

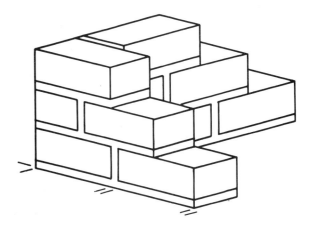

FIGURE 5–28
Three-course corner lead.

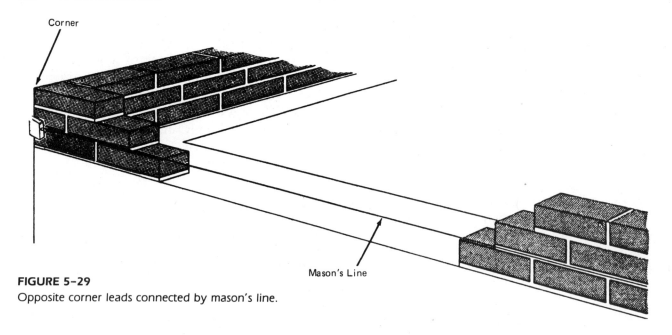

FIGURE 5-29
Opposite corner leads connected by mason's line.

tioned, do not lift or pull brick out of the mortar bed. This will destroy the bond.

Practice: Corner Lead, Double Wythe (Common Bond)

Double-wythe walls are, naturally, much more complicated than single-wythe walls because the two wythes must be tied together. The same steps are followed, including (1) establishing the outside corners, (2) snapping chalk lines for the outside face of the brick wall, and (3) laying out the first brick course dry so any problems can be identified and corrected.

Figure 5-34 shows a sketch for the corner lead for a seven-course, 8-inch wall laid in common bond. Note that the second course is stretchers, four on one side and three on the other.

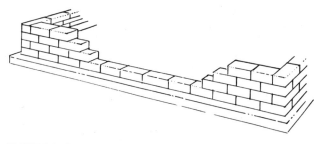

FIGURE 5-30
Completed course between two leads. (Hyde Manufacturing Co.)

FIGURE 5-31
Using level to check trueness or horizontal level of brick course. (Hyde Manufacturing Co.)

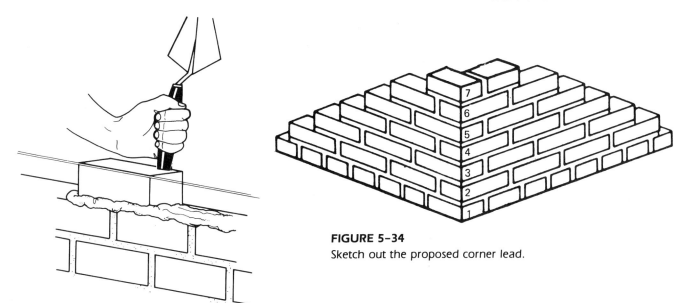

FIGURE 5-34
Sketch out the proposed corner lead.

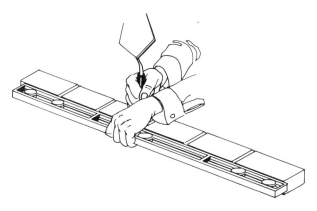

FIGURE 5-32
Tap the brick down until it is level. (Marshalltown Trowel Co.)

FIGURE 5-33
Use a straightedge or level to align the outside face of the brick course.

Note how each side or leg of the corner has stepped back courses. This is called *racking*. Each higher course is laid back half a brick length. The racked courses are used as guides when laying the rest of the brick between the two leads. When all courses for the leads are completed, you will have an even wall running between the top courses of the two leads. At this point, new leads can be constructed on top of the wall. This allows you to continue building until the full height of the wall is reached. When planning the leads it's a good idea to sketch out the corner showing the different brick in place.

Figure 5-35 shows the dry layout for the first course. Only the left leg is shown; the right leg

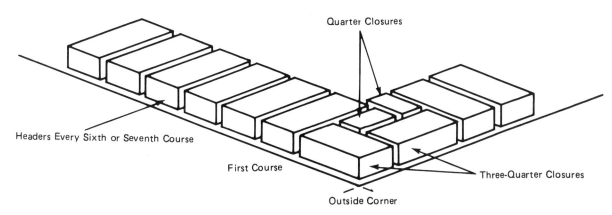

FIGURE 5-35
Dry layout of the first course at the corner.

is identical. Remember that common bond uses headers on the first course and every sixth or seventh course. Quarter closures and three-quarter closures must be cut for the corner.

First Course. The first step in laying out the corner lead is to lay down a mortar bed. A 1-inch mortar bed is used. Figure 5–36, top left, shows the mortar bed laid out for the corner. Step-by-step guidelines for laying the corner are shown. The brick are labeled alphabetically to show the recommended laying sequence.

The corner is started with the two three-quarter brick (Step 2). They are pushed down in

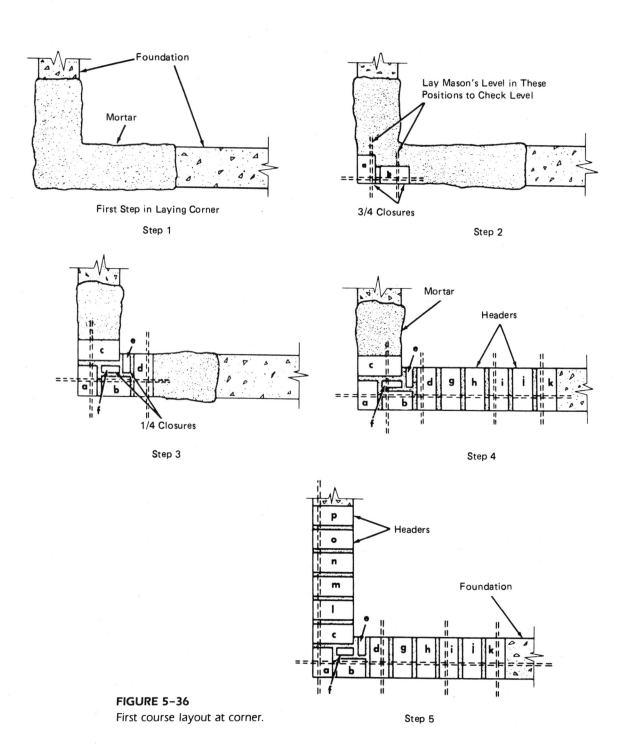

FIGURE 5–36
First course layout at corner.

the mortar to form a $\frac{1}{2}$-inch bed joint. After they are laid and seated, they should be checked with a level to make sure they are not tilted in any way. The dashed lines shown in Step 2 represent the positions of the level. Three level measurements are taken. It is a good idea, however, to take level measurements on both the outside and inside edge of the brick.

Steps 3, 4, and 5 in Figure 5–36 show the sequence for completing the first course. Dashed lines show where the brick are checked with the level. The outside alignment of the brick should also be checked by holding a straightedge against the brick. A 48-inch level is commonly used for aligning the brick. The level can also be placed against the outside face and used as a simple straightedge for checking alignment—the bubbles are not used. Any brick that is out of alignment may be adjusted until it is level and plumb.

Adjustments can be made for any out-of-plumb brick while the mortar is still fresh. Any out-of-adjustment or out-of-plumb brick can be straightened by tapping with either the blade of the trowel or the handle end (Figure 5–32). *Note:* If the mortar has begun to set, brick cannot be adjusted. Any brick that is moved in stiffened, hydrated mortar will lose its bond. If hydration has started, misaligned brick must be removed along with the mortar. New mortar must be placed and the brick re-laid.

Second Course. The second through sixth courses in the common bond shown here use stretchers. Figure 5–37 shows the step-by-step sequence for laying the face stretchers of the second course. The recommended brick sequence is shown alphabetically.

The back wythe or back tier uses the same stretcher layout, but the brick must be offset so the head joints don't align with the head joints of the front wythe. This is called *breaking the bond.* Figure 5–38 shows the backing wythe for this corner. Note how the joints are broken. Three-quarter brick are used in the corner to prevent head joints from lining up. Remember that mortar, called a collar joint, is parged between the two wythes.

Course 3 to 6. Stretcher courses three to six follow the same layout sequence as for course two. Of course, as shown in Figure 5–38, the joints must be broken so they don't line up. Figure 5–39 shows what the corner lead looks like when completed. The top or seventh course is a header course and the whole sequence starts over. After the corner lead is completed, it should be checked for plumb with a level, as show in Figure 5–40. Check the corner and both sides.

The layout of the corner can also be checked by a straightedge or a 48-inch level along the rack

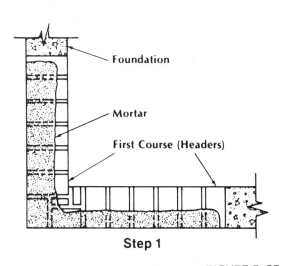

Step 1

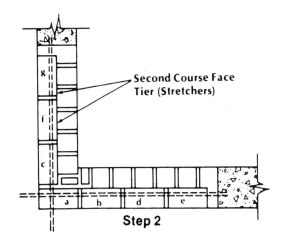

Step 2

FIGURE 5–37
Second course layout at the corner.

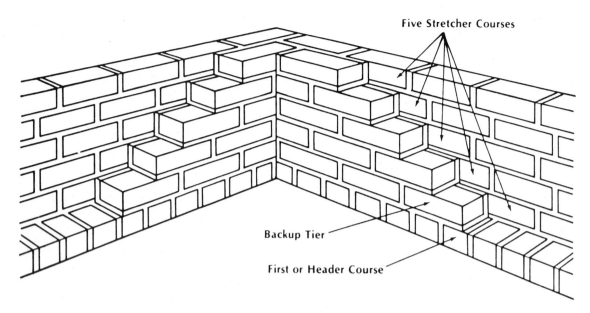

FIGURE 5–38
Completed corner (inside).

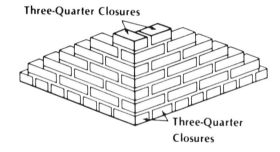

FIGURE 5–39
Completed corner (outside).

or end of each leg, as shown in Figure 5–41. This checks the position of the steps of the rack. The end of each step should exactly touch the bottom of the straightedge or level. Slight adjustments can be made to assure exact alignment.

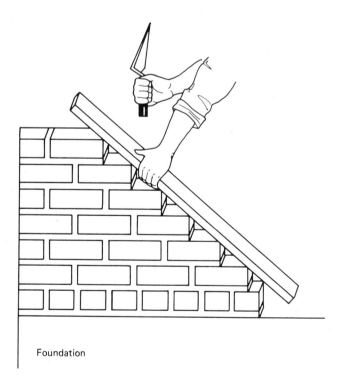

Foundation

FIGURE 5–41
Checking along the rack of the lead.

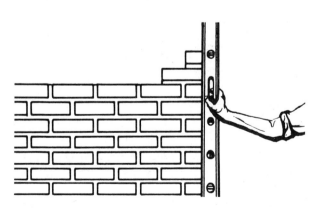

FIGURE 5–40
Plumb the corner with the level. (Brick Institute of America)

Practice: Corner Lead, 12-inch Solid Wall (Common Bond)

A 12-inch solid wall can be built by adding on to the basic two-wythe wall. Figure 5–42 shows the basic steps for constructing a 12-inch wall. In this case, the first course shows how to make both an outside (Figure 5–42, top left) and an inside (Figure 5–42, top right) corner.

Twelve-inch solid walls are used in solar heating for thermal storage. Solid brick are recommended for thermal storage. Dark-colored brick are better since they absorb heat quicker than light-colored ones.

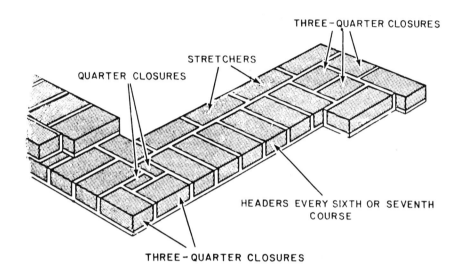

STEP I. FIRST COURSE OF 12-INCH COMMON BOND WALL

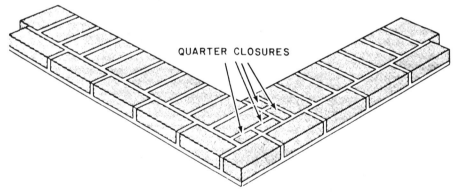

STEP 2. SECOND COURSE

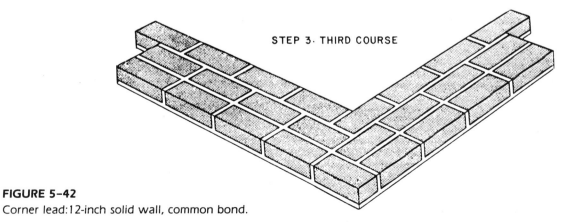

STEP 3. THIRD COURSE

FIGURE 5–42
Corner lead: 12-inch solid wall, common bond.

OPPOSITE CORNER LEADS

Leads are laid at opposite corners so they can be used as guides for the brick laid between them. A mason's line is run between the two corners as a guide for each course. It is very important, therefore, that the courses in each lead be the same height. Bed joint thickness must be the same. A very serious problem occurs if one lead is higher than the other. This can happen if different masons build each corner lead.

To assure that corner leads are built to the same height, you should measure the vertical height of each course with the mason's folding rule. This assures that they are equal.

SETTING LINES

The purpose of corner leads is to provide a guide for the rest of the wall. Two corner leads are built at opposite corners and then a mason's line is run between them as a guide for setting a course of brick between the leads. Using the line to align the brick in the course is called *ranging*. Horizontal brick alignment is adjusted to the line.

A corner block or line block is used at each corner to hold the mason's line. Figure 5–43, top, shows a line supported by a corner block. (Only the left corner block is shown.) As the course is completed, the line block is raised one course on each corner lead. Since the line is under consider-

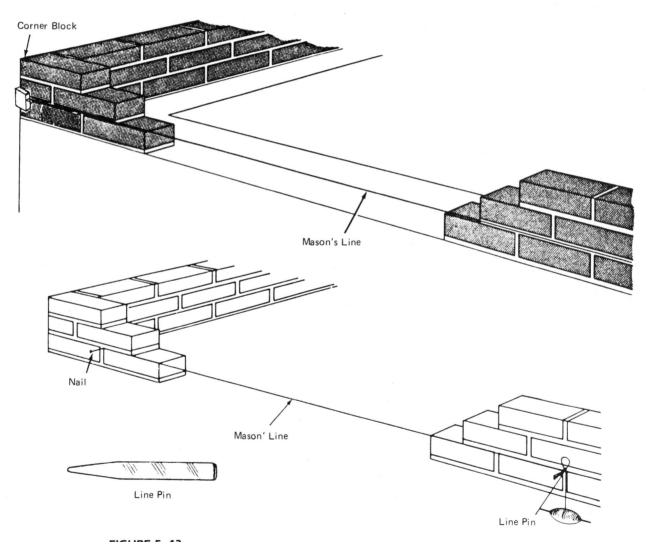

Corner Block

Mason's Line

Nail

Mason' Line

Line Pin

Line Pin

FIGURE 5–43
Mason's line. *Top:* Line set with line blocks. *Bottom;* Line set with nail and line pin.

able tension, it may be difficult to pull the corner block away from the corner. Some corner blocks have handles to make them easier to pull away and lift the line from course to course. The line must be exactly positioned so the course is true and level. (Line levels are available for checking the level of the line.) The line is held away from the face of the brick $\frac{1}{16}$ inch.

Bricklayers' line pins are also used to hold the line. Figure 5-43, bottom, shows a mason's line held between two corner leads by pins. A regular nail and a line pin are used. They are stuck directly into the fresh mortar.

Brick are laid so the face is $\frac{1}{16}$ inch back from the line, and the top bed of the brick is level to the top of the line. Your hand should hold the brick so your fingers or thumb, depending on which side the brick is laid, angle out from the brick when it is laid. Figure 5-10 shows how the thumb (*top*) or fingers (*bottom*) jut out to allow space for the line.

TRIGS

In the case of long walls, a center support may be built up to hold the mason's line. Figure 5-44

shows a trig built in the middle between two corner leads. A piece of broken brick is used on top of the stretcher brick in the center of the course to hold the trig. The trig is a flat piece of metal with a loop on the end. The weight of the broken brick holds the trig in place. No mortar needs to be used. The line is adjusted away from the face $\frac{1}{16}$ inch. When the course is completed, the trig is laid up into the next course and the line is raised.

MASONRY GUIDES

Instead of building up corner leads, masonry guides are often used at the corners to establish course levels. Figure 5-45 shows a masonry guide set up at one corner of a brick veneer house. The mason's line runs from one masonry guide to another guide. The line can easily be slid up or down using the sliding attachments on the pole. Figure 5-45 (details) show how the guide is set for outside and inside corners. Scales are marked on the side of the guide (Figure 5-46) so the line can be exactly adjusted to any specified height. Top and bottom fittings are used to attach the guide

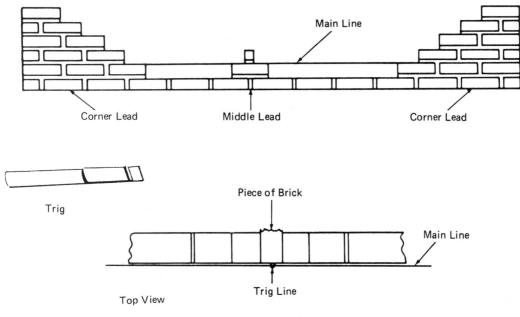

FIGURE 5-44
Using trig to establish center support between corner leads.

Detail of Outside Corner   Detail of Inside Corner

FIGURE 5-45

Mason's line established by masonry guides. (Bottom: Masonry Specialty Co., Division of Bon Tool Co.; Top (details): Goldblatt Tool Co.)

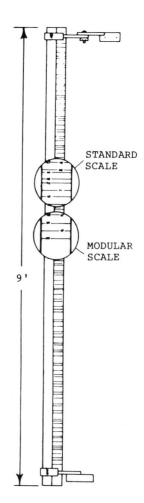

FIGURE 5-46

Scales are located on the side of the masonry guide to establish course height. (Masonry Specialty Co., Division of Bon Tool Co.)

to the corner. Fittings are available so that the pole can be attached to either the outside or the inside corner.

For larger load-bearing and multi-story work, telescoping poles are used to hold and support the guide at the corner.

CLOSURES

As noted earlier, when laying a course in a wall it is advisable to work toward the center from both ends. This allows you to correct and adjust for any miscalculations. Dry layout of the brick allows you to adjust the thickness of the head joint to accommodate a slightly long or slightly short space at the center. If adjustments of the head joints cannot correct any spacing problem at the center, use two or three short brick of equal length. It is much better to use two three-quarter brick together than a one-half brick. Never use a half brick to close a course. It is too obvious and will detract from the overall pattern. The eye will not readily identify two three-quarter brick together in a stretcher course.

If the course is well planned and well laid out, the space at the center should be the exact size needed for the final, standard-sized brick needed in the bond. Figure 5–47 shows the steps for laying a closure brick in a stretcher course. Mortar is placed in both the bed and the head joints (Step 1). The closure brick is then buttered at both ends (Step 2). Finally, the buttered brick is pushed into the closure space. Take care not to disturb the brick already in place. If adjacent brick are moved, they will have to be replaced if the mortar has started to set. Excess mortar is used, so quite a bit will be squeezed out. Cut off all the excess mortar and return it to the mortar pile. The same technique is used for laying a header closure (Figure 5–48). For a header closure, however, the sides of the brick are buttered.

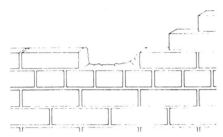

1. Spreading Mortar on Ends of Brick Already Laid

2. Spreading Mortar on Both Ends of Closure Brick

3. Laying the Brick into Position

FIGURE 5–47
Steps for laying a closure brick.

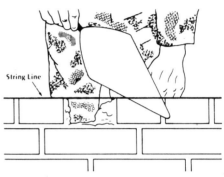

1. Spreading Mortar on Sides of Brick Already Laid

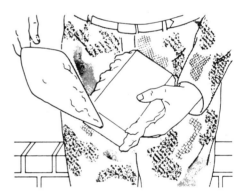

2. Spreading Mortar on Both Sides of Closure Brick

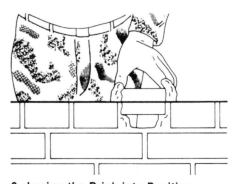

3. Laying the Brick into Position

FIGURE 5–48
Steps for laying a header closure.

Inserting a Brick in the Wall

In repair work, the same technique is used to re-place a brick inside the bond pattern. The old brick is completely removed with all mortar, as shown in Figure 5–49. The opening left in the bond is cleaned, wetted, and spread on all sides with a thick bed of mortar (Figure 5–50). The new, replacement brick is buttered and shoved into the mortared opening (Step 2). Mortar should squeeze out around all four sides of the brick (Step 3). When mortar squeezes out all four sides you know that the joints are full of mortar.

STRIKING JOINTS

Once a section of wall is laid and the mortar has set to some extent, (i.e., is thumbprint hard), the joints should be finished. Finishing mortar joints is called striking, jointing, or tooling. The terms are synonymous and are used interchangeably.

When joints should be finished depends on several factors. The mortar mix and the temperature will significantly affect the setting time. Some mortars should set up so they can be finished in around 30 minutes. You can test the mortar joint with your thumb. If your thumb leaves a thumbprint when pressed on the mortar, it is ready for striking. Figure 5–51 shows a thumbprint test—the mortar is now ready for tooling.

If the mortar is not sufficiently set, both the cement fines and water will come to the joint face, streaking the surface. If it is too far set, it cannot be pressed into the joint to make a tight bond.

The various types of finish on mortar joints were covered in Chapter 4. A jointer slightly larger than the thickness of the joint should be used. The joint profile will be specified by the architect.

Figure 5–52, top, shows a horizontal mortar joint being finished with a convex jointer. A concave finish is commonly used. Striking the joint leaves tailings (Figure 5–52, bottom), which should be scraped off with the trowel edge.

Remember: Finish the joints when they are thumbprint hard. Strike the head joints first, and then strike the bed joints.

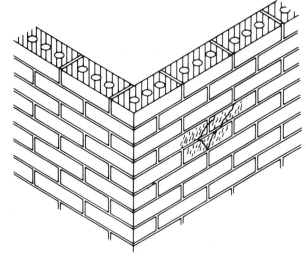

A) DAMAGED BRICK UNITS

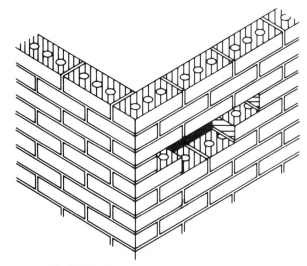

B) CHISEL OUT BRICK UNITS AND MORTAR

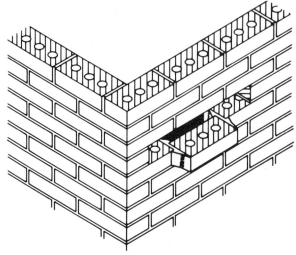

C) BUTTER REPLACEMENT UNITS AND CAREFULLY SHOVE INTO PLACE

FIGURE 5–49
Remove old damaged brick. (Brick Institute of America)

1. Spreading a Thick Bed of Mortar

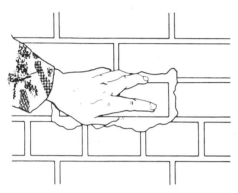

2. Shoving the Brick into Place

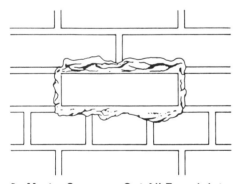

3. Mortar Squeezes Out All Four Joints

FIGURE 5-50
Steps for replacing a brick in a wall.

FIGURE 5-51
Thumbprint test for checking the mortar. Clear thumbprint shows that mortar is ready for tooling. (Brick Institute of America)

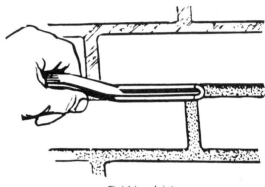

Finishing Joint

Mortar Tailings Left After Finishing Joint

FIGURE 5-52
Top: Finishing a horizontal brick joint with a concave jointer. *Bottom:* Mortar tailings left after finishing; scrape tailings off with the trowel. (*Top:* Marshalltown Trowel Co.)

You will notice that after finishing, short pieces of mortar, called *tailings*, are forced up out of the joint. These raised mortar edges or tailings should be scraped off with the edge of the trowel. After the mortar is dry, the wall should be brushed to remove mortar and dust.

TUCKPOINTING

Tuckpointing is the process of removing old, decayed mortar from a joint and placing in new mortar. Joint decay is caused by moisture entering the joint. When removing the old, decayed or broken mortar, always wear eye protection.

The old mortar is cut out either by a special power grinder or by a chisel. Power grinding is very expensive. Most often the old mortar is chipped out using a special chisel. Figure 5–53 shows a special toothing or plugging chisel being used to break out old decayed mortar. Mortar should be cut back to a uniform depth, approximately $\frac{3}{4}$ inch. If sound mortar is not reached at this depth, a deeper cut must be made. Broken mortar is raked out with a special hooked mortar rake (Figure 5–54). Clean out all old mortar. Make sure the joint is clean and cut out to an even depth.

As noted, a tuckpointing grinder may be used for large jobs to grind out the joints. The grinder uses a thick circular blade to remove the old material.

Figure 5–55, left, shows a deteriorated mortar joint. Figure 5–55, right, shows the mortar cut back to an even depth.

After the mortar is removed and the joint is cleaned, it must be wetted before it can be refilled.

FIGURE 5–54
A hooked mortar rake is used to rake out broken mortar. (Marshalltown Trowel Co.)

The dry joint would take too much moisture out of the mortar. Type N or O mortar is used, and the mortar should be stiff. Use less water than for regular mortar. A small square board called a hawk is often used to hold the tuckpointing mortar. It has a handle on the bottom so it can be held in one hand while filling the joints.

FIGURE 5–53
Cleaning out a decayed head joint. Toothing or plugging chisel and hammer are used to break out broken and decayed mortar. (Marshalltown Trowel Co.)

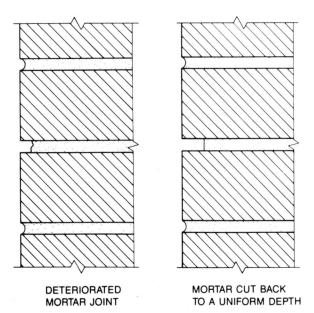

DETERIORATED
MORTAR JOINT

MORTAR CUT BACK
TO A UNIFORM DEPTH

FIGURE 5–55
Left: Deteriorated mortar joint. *Right:* Cut decayed and broken mortar back to a uniform depth. (Brick Institute of America)

A tuckpointing trowel is used to fill (or "tuck") the mortar back into the joint. Mortar is packed in tightly in thin layers until the joint is full. Be sure the joint is completely full. Figure 5–56, left, shows how the raked out joint is filled. Note that two or three mortar layers are used. After it is partially set, it should be finished to match the rest of the mortar finish around the repair (Figure 5–56, right). A special caulking or tuckpointing trowel is used to lay in the mortar. (See Figures 2–8 and 2–9.)

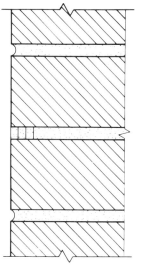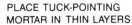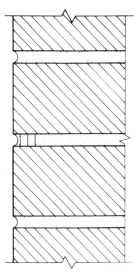

PLACE TUCK-POINTING MORTAR IN THIN LAYERS

TOOL JOINT TO MATCH ORIGINAL PROFILE

FIGURE 5–56
Tuckpointing the cleaned joint. *Left:* Layers of mortar built up flush to the brick face. *Right:* Tuckpointed joint tooled off to match other joints. (Brick Institute of America)

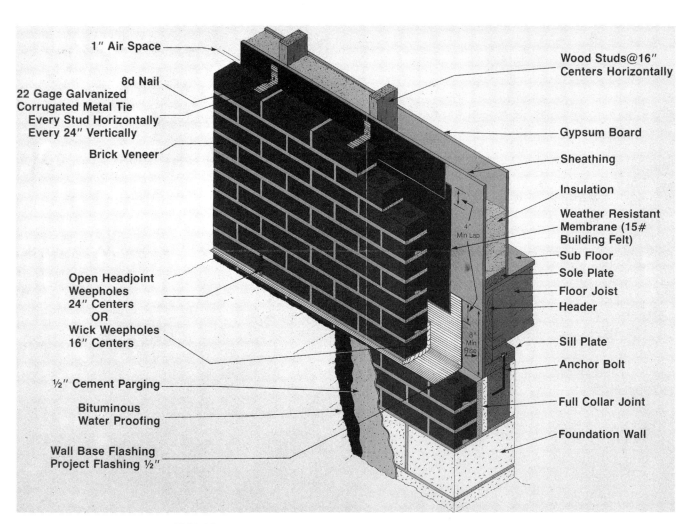

FIGURE 5–57
Flashing is run behind the sheathing. (Brick Institute of America)

VENEER WORK

Brick veneer, as already noted, is non-load bearing. A single-brick wythe is commonly used over a structural "backup" system. Brick veneer is used with both wood and metal studs and is also used with load bearing concrete block walls or reinforced concrete. The brick is laid up after the load bearing framework or masonry backing is in place. The veneer is tied to the framework or backing with metal ties.

Brick veneer commonly uses a running bond. A stack bond is also used with joint reinforcement. Face brick is used. The basic techniques for laying running bond are illustrated in Figures 5–27 to 5–38. The veneer attaches to a frame or masonry backing; an air space is left between the brick and the backing.

Flashing

Flashing is required at the base of the veneer. This is to prevent moisture from seeping to the interior of the wall. Flashing is run back under the building paper or the sheathing at least eight inches, as shown in Figure 5–57. Figure 5–58 shows the sequence for installing veneer flashing. The foundation shelf is shown at the top; the plastic flashing has been nailed on at the center; and the completed veneer with the flashing trimmed is shown at the bottom. *Note:* Flashing must extend through the brick face. Excess flashing is trimmed off after the veneer wall is completed (Figure 5–59).

Weep Holes

Weep holes are required at the base of the veneer in the brick course at the flashing level. Figure 5–60 shows the location of weep holes at the veneer base. This allows any water that condenses in the air space to run out. Weep holes are normally run every 16 inches to 24 inches on center. They can be made by omitting mortar from the head joint or by inserting metal rods, plastic tubing, or cotton

Veneer Shelf on Top of Foundation

Plastic Flashing Nailed in Place

Brick Veneer Laid

FIGURE 5–58
Installing brick veneer.

FIGURE 5-59
Trim off end of flashing that extends out beyond veneer wall. (Brick Institute of America)

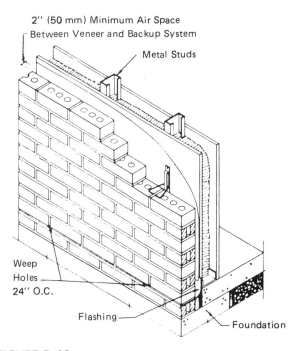

FIGURE 5-60
Weep holes must be located at the base of the brick veneer. (Brick Institute of America)

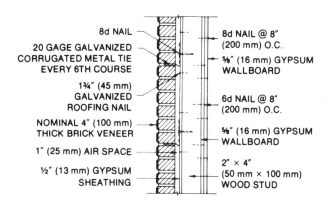

2-hr Fire Rated Brick Veneer Wall Assembly

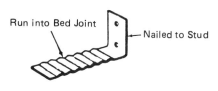

FIGURE 5-61
Metal ties are bent and the short vertical piece nailed to the support frame. The long horizontal part of the metal tie is placed between the brick courses. (Brick Institute of America)

rope wicks. The rod is removed after several courses are in place. The tubing should angle downward so water can flow out. The wicking or cotton rope is left in and acts as a wick to draw moisture out.

Metal Ties

Metal ties are used to fasten the brick veneer to the frame backing. Tie spacing requirements are dependent on the backup material, the size of the air space, and local building codes.

Metal Ties with Frame Construction

Corrugated metal ties are nailed to wood studs with corrosion-protected, 8-penny nails and then bent out so the metal tongue can run between brick in the bed joint. The tie should run into the joint at least two inches. Figure 5-61 shows the ties are bent out to fit into the bed joint. Wire ties, $\frac{3}{16}$-inch wide, are used to attach brick veneer to metal studs, as shown in Figure 5-60.

Figure 5-62 shows a section taken through a brick veneer wall attached to a wood frame wall. Note that flashing and weep holes are required over the top (head) of the window opening. Flashing and weep holes are also required at the window sill.

Metal Ties with Masonry Construction

Rectangular, U-shaped, or Z-shaped ties are used to attach brick veneer to masonry construction. The Z-shaped tie can only be used in conjunction with solid masonry units. Reinforced concrete uses wire anchors or flat dovetail ties.

Insulation

In some construction cases, insulation is inserted in the air space. A plastic foam sheet is often used. The metal ties go through the insulation to attach the veneer to the backing.

Electrical Boxes

Openings are left in the brick wall for exterior electrical outlets, as shown in Figure 5-63. Brick are cut short to allow room for the box.

Caulking

Caulking is required on the exterior of the building where masonry meets other materials; for example, around doors and windows. Figure 5-62 notes caulking points. If factory-assembled, prefabricated brick panels are used, caulking or sealing will be required between the panel joints. Silicone caulking is frequently used since it forms a tight waterproof joint and always remains elastic.

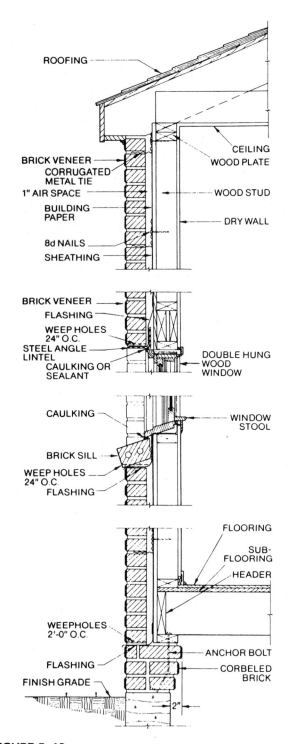

FIGURE 5-62

Brick veneer wall. Caulking is required around openings. (Brick Institute of America)

FIGURE 5-63
Cut brick short to make opening for exterior electrical outlets.

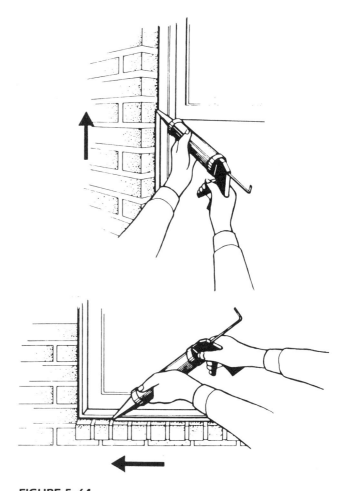

FIGURE 5-64
Caulking techniques. Caulk by pushing caulking gun so caulking flows into any openings around brick. (Illinois Department of Natural Resources)

From an energy saving viewpoint, caulking is extremely important. Without good caulking, heat can readily be lost during winter or gained during summer. Good, sound caulking can greatly reduce the heating and cooling bills for a house.

Figure 5-64 shows caulking being done on a window set in a brick wall. A caulking gun is used. The caulking cartridge fits into the gun. When the cartridge is empty, it is discarded and a new cartridge inserted. Note that caulking is *pushed* into the crack. This is the standard procedure. Figure 5-65 shows the technique; silicone rubber caulking is used here.

Some backer support will have to be inserted to stop the caulking from three-point adhesion. Figure 5-66 shows how filler is inserted. Oakum, fiberglass insulation, or insulation board strips can be used to fill any cracks before caulking.

The thickness of the bead made by the cartridge can be adjusted by the amount that is cut off the cartridge nozzle. The closer to the tip the cut is made, the thinner the width of the bead. The cut is made at an angle. This allows the cut

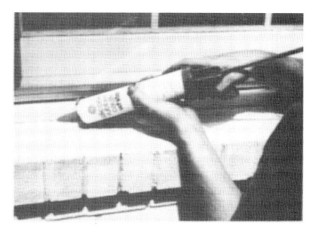

FIGURE 5-65
Silicone rubber caulking being applied around window in brick building. (General Electric Co.)

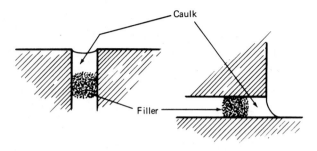

FIGURE 5-66
If opening to be caulked is wide, stuff filler into opening before caulking. (Illinois Department of Natural Resources)

face to run flush on the crack being filled when the cartridge is held at an angle during application (Figures 5-64 and 5-65).

Various caulking compounds are used. Silicone lasts the longest and is recommended for most uses. Butyl is especially recommended for masonry use.

Installation Techniques. The bead may be finished by running a special caulking tool over it or by finishing it with a concave jointer. Experiment with finishing techniques before trying one on the actual building. After cutting the tip, puncture the cartridge seal by running a long, clean nail into the tip. After using, wipe off any excess caulking on the tip. The cartridge can be sealed after use by inserting a large nail into the cartridge nozzle. Push the nail all the way in. This will prevent any caulking still in the cartridge from hardening or drying out. Colored caulking is also available and is sometimes used to match wood trim around windows or doors.

Cleaning

After the brick are laid, the face must be cleaned of mortar or other dirt. Any large mortar deposits should be cut off with the trowel when the brick are being laid. If a hardened mortar deposit is still left on the wall, rub off with a piece of broken brick. However, do not grind the broken brick into the brick being cleaned. Simply clean off any mortar deposits or tailings. A mason's brush is also used to remove dry mortar powder. Before cleaning with any cleaning agent, it's a good idea to try the agent on a small test area.

Cleanliness on the Job. Good workmanship and a professional job require that the mason plan the work to avoid mortar smears and dirt. An experienced mason, of course, should employ work methods and techniques that keep the face of the brick clean and relatively free of mortar droppings and splatter. Any mortar that falls on the brick should be immediately removed with the trowel. Use the following techniques to keep the brick clean:[1]

1. Cover brick on the site with plastic sheeting. Use plastic, boards, or plywood sheets to keep brick off the ground.

2. Protect the lower three or four feet of the brick wall with some covering. Plastic sheets, straw, or even sand can be used. This keeps off dirt and rain-splattered mud. Leave protection in place until *all* trade work is completed and landscaping is near completion.

3. Cover work at the end of the day to protect from dust or rain.

4. Scaffolds should be set away from the wall to allow room for mortar to fall to the ground. At the end of the work day, turn scaffold boards on edge. This prevents rain from splashing dirt on the brick face.

5. Practice good workmanship. Cut off all mortar droppings on the face of the wall with the trowel. Trowel off before the mortar sets. Set mortar can be removed with a piece of broken brick or a wooden board. If broken brick is used, do not grind the broken brick into the face brick. Brush the wall with a bricklayer's brush with medium soft hair.

---

[1]Information on cleaning new brickwork is given in the Brick Institute of America's "Technical Notes on Brick Construction: Cleaning Brick Masonry," (#20 Revised 1977), and from the Brick Association of North Carolina: "Good Practice for Cleaning New Brickwork."

Washing New Masonry Water is the safest and most effective cleaning agent. Washing should only be done after the mortar has set—wait at least seven days. Water should be hosed on and the wall scrubbed with a long-handled brush. All mortar droppings should be removed before washing. High pressure water cleaning is also used in larger jobs. Figure 5-67 shows cleaning methods recommended for new masonry.

Brick Category	Cleaning Method	Remarks
Red and Red Flashed	Bucket and Brush Hand Cleaning	Hydrochloric acid solutions, proprietary compounds, and emulsifying agents may be used.
	High Pressure Water	*Smooth Texture:* Mortar stains and smears are generally easier to remove; less surface area exposed; easier to presoak and rinse; unbroken surface, thus more likely to display poor rinsing, acid staining, poor removal of mortar smears.
	Sandblasting	
		Rough Texture: Mortar and dirt tend to penetrate deep into textures; additional area for water and acid absorption; essential to use pressurized water during rinsing.
Red, Heavy Sand Finish	Bucket and Brush Hand Cleaning	Clean with plain water and scrub brush, or *lightly* applied high pressure and plain water. Excessive mortar stains may require use of cleaning solutions. *Sandblasting is not recommended.*
	High Pressure Water	
Light Colored Units, White, Tan, Buff, Gray, Specks, Pink, Brown and Black	Bucket and Brush Hand Cleaning	*Do not use muriatic acid!!* Clean with plain water, detergents, emulsifying agents, or suitable proprietary compounds. Manganese colored brick units tend to react to muriatic acid solutions and stain. Light colored brick are more susceptible to "acid burn" and stains, compared to darker units.
	High Pressure Water	
	Sandblasting	
Same as Light Colored Units, etc., plus Sand Finish	Bucket and Brush Hand Cleaning	Lightly apply either method. (See notes for light colored units, etc.) *Sandblasting is not recommended.*
	High Pressure Water	
Glazed Brick	Bucket and Brush Hand Cleaning	Wipe glazed surface with soft cloth within a few minutes of laying units. Use soft sponge or brush plus ample water supply for final washing. Use detergents where necessary and acid solutions only for *very difficult mortar* stain. Do not use acid on salt glazed or metallic glazed brick. Do not use abrasive powders.
Colored Mortars	Method is generally controlled by the brick unit	Many manufacturers of colored mortars do not recommend chemical cleaning solutions. Most acids tend to bleach colored mortars. Mild detergent solutions are generally recommended.

FIGURE 5-67
Cleaning methods recommended for new masonry. (Brick Institute of America)

Testing Cleansing Agents. A wide number of cleansing agents are available for cleaning new masonry. No cleansing agent should be used unless the effect of its use is known. Select a test area on the wall of approximately 20 square feet and use the agent. Always follow manufacturer's recommendations on using any agent. The wall should usually be thoroughly wetted with water before use and thoroughly rinsed with water after use. Allow any test area to stand for one week before checking. If the wall shows no ill effects, you can assume the cleansing agent is *probably* safe to use. It's a good idea to check with other masons and even the brick manufacturers before using any cleansing agent.

Note: A wood or metal framework must be protected during the use of some cleansing agents. In all cases, observe the manufacturer's instructions on the safe use of a product. Wear eye protection such as goggles so fluid cannot get into your eyes. Wear rubber gloves.

Acid Solutions. Muriatic acid is frequently used to clean masonry walls. Muriatic acid is a mixture of hydrochloric acid and water. Hydrochloric acid dissolves mortar partially, so it is very effective. Acid should be mixed according to instructions on the acid container. *Caution: You must add acid to the water. (Never add water to acid!)* For normal cleaning, a ratio of 1 part acid to 9 parts water is commonly used to give a 10 percent solution.

The wall is always flushed with water before any acid treatment. Muriatic acid is then applied on the wet wall at the top. The solution is brushed on with a long-handled brush. Let set five to ten minutes before thoroughly rinsing with water. Figure 5–68 shows a wall being rinsed after treatment with muriatic acid. It is important that all the acid be removed. Otherwise, it will, over time, break down the mortar and even the brick. *Caution:* When cleaning with acid, wear goggles, rubber gloves, and old clothes.

FIGURE 5–68
Rinsing a brick wall with water after it has been cleaned with muriatic acid. (Pro So Co., Inc.)

Sandblasting. Sandblasting is sometimes used to clean new walls. The technique is more commonly used to clean old, blackened masonry walls. Sandblasting, however, can be very detrimental to a wall if not used properly or if used on softer brick. It's a good idea to test one or more areas before sandblasting the whole building.

Efflorescence

Efflorescence is caused by various minerals leaching out of the masonry units or the mortar. Water in the wall dissolves salts in the brick or mortar and the moisture is carried to the surface where it evaporates, leaving the salt residue. Several different efflorescences occur in brick masonry and each has its own remedy. Figure 5-69 notes the common causes of efflorescence and where it is commonly found.[2] Most efflorescent salts are water soluble and easily removed, usually with plain water.

White Efflorescence. White efflorescence or bloom is the most common type stain that occurs. It is caused by the leaching out of white, water-soluble salts. Bloom is simply removed by washing with clear water and a stiff brush.

Since bloom is caused by excess moisture, it's best that it be washed off when it is warm and dry. That way the moisture will not cause additional efflorescence.

Green Stain. Green stain is caused by vanadium salts that are leached out of the brick. Consult with the brick manufacturer on how best to remove the salt. Sodium hydroxide, a caustic base chemical, is normally used for removal.

Brown Stain. Brown stain is caused by deposits of manganese salts, usually found in colored mortars, or in the brick itself. The color of the stain runs from nearly black to a tan or gray. Manganese staining is usually the result of interaction with an acid, such as muriatic acid. Special compounds are available for its removal. Oxalic acid is sometimes used.

Stains

Stains are caused by external agents, such as paint, smoke, oil, or dirt. Welding splatter, for example, if it falls on brick will cause an iron stain.

A wide variety of commercial products are available for different stains. Follow manufacturer's instructions for the cleaning agent and always test a small area before doing the whole job.

Principal Effloresci	ng Salt	Most Probable Source
Calcium sulfate	$CaSO_4 \bullet 2H_2O$	Brick
Sodium sulfate	$Na_2SO_4 \bullet 10H_2O$	Cement-brick reactions
Potassium sulfate	K_2SO_4	Cement-brick reactions
Calcium carbonate	$CaCO_3$	Mortar or concrete backing
Sodium carbonate	Na_2CO_3	Mortar
Potassium carbonate	K_2CO_3	Mortar
Potassium chloride	KCl	Acid cleaning
Sodium chloride	$NaCl$	Sea water
Vanadyl sulfate	$VOSO_4$	Brick
Vanadyl chloride	$VOCl_2$	Acid cleaning
Manganese oxide	Mn_3O4	Brick
Iron oxide	Fe_2O_3 or $Fe(OH)_3$	Iron in contact or brick with black core
Calcium hydroxide	$Ca(OH)_2$	Cement

FIGURE 5-69
Common efflorescences and where they are commonly found. (Brick Institute of America)

[2]For additional information, refer to the Brick Institute of America's "Technical Notes on Brick Construction: Efflorescence Prevention and Control," #23A Revised, 1981.

CHAPTER REVIEW

QUESTIONS

1. List five steps to follow before starting work.

2. Describe how to test mortar for freshness and spreadability.

3. Describe how to load a trowel by cupping the mortar. Describe the clock method.

4. Describe how the mortar is thrown and how the mortar bed is furrowed.

5. What is thumbing the line? How is it avoided?

6. How far is the line set out from the face of the course?

7. Describe three things that may be done with mortar cut off from the mortar bed joint.

8. What is *buttering*? Describe how it is done.

9. Describe how a brick is laid.

10. What is "walling"? When is it done?

11. Describe at least two methods for locating the outside face of a brick wall.

12. What is dry layout? Why is it done?

13. Describe how the courses are leveled.

14. What is a corner lead?

15. What is racking?

16. How are adjustments made for out-of-plumb brick?

17. Why shouldn't brick be moved if the mortar has begun to set?

18. Why should opposite corner leads be the same height for each course?

19. What is a rake-back lead?

20. Describe how the mason's line is supported between corner leads.

21. How are line pins used?

22. What is a trig, how is it used, and how is it constructed?

23. Describe how masonry guides are used.

24. What is a closure? How is it made?

25. When striking a joint, tailings are raised. How are they removed?

26. Describe how veneer is fastened to a wood frame backing. To metal studs.

27. Where is caulking commonly required in an exterior masonry wall?

28. List five guidelines to follow to keep brickwork clean while it is being laid.

29. Describe three ways to clean new brickwork.

30. What is efflorescence and how is it caused? What is the most common type and how is it cleaned?

ACTIVITIES

1. To develop your basic manipulation skills, practice the following techniques:
   a. loading the trowel
   b. throwing the mortar
   c. furrowing the bed
   d. laying brick
   e. cutting off excess mortar from the bed joint
   f. buttering

2. Practice using the spirit level to check the horizontal level and vertical plumb of the brick in a course. Correct the position of the brick until they are level and plumb. Align the course with a straightedge or level.

3. As directed, lay out the following corner leads:
   a. single-wythe running bond
   b. double-wythe common bond

   Lay out leads to snapped chalk lines. Lay out the first course dry as a guideline.

4. Practice making closures in stretchers and header bond for a course of brick.

5. Check your work area and recommend at least three procedures you can follow to keep the brickwork clean during laying.

6. Use the elevation and plan views of the seven-course, one-wythe wall shown in Sketch A and
   a. write down the tools and materials needed to lay the wall.
   b. sketch elevation views of the leads you would build at each corner.
   c. using your sketch and the necessary materials, build the leads.
   d. align, level, and plumb leads.
   e. using mason's line, complete courses 1, 2, and 3. Align, level, and plumb.
   f. complete courses 4, 5, 6, and 7 so they and the wall are square and true.

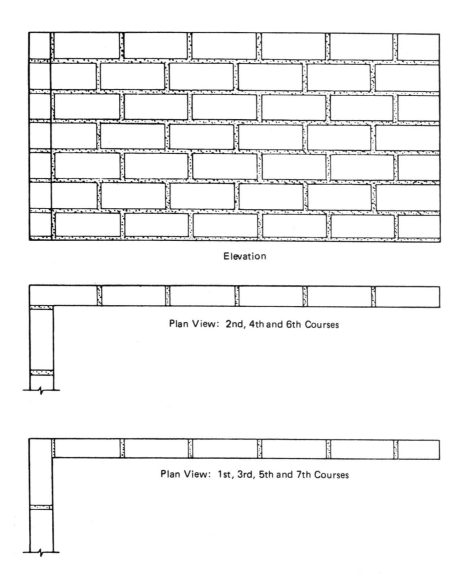

Elevation

Plan View: 2nd, 4th and 6th Courses

Plan View: 1st, 3rd, 5th and 7th Courses

SKETCH A

Chapter 6

BRICKWORK: ADVANCED AND SPECIALIZED

After studying this chapter you should be able to:

- Explain the construction and theory of different types of specialized brick construction: columns, piers, pilasters, chases, solid walls, cavity walls, reinforced brick masonry, corbelling, wall openings, lintels, arches, fireplaces, chimneys, paving, and steps.
- Build basic and specialized brick elements.

Once the basic techniques are learned, you can advance to more complex projects. This chapter provides detailed information on advanced masonry techniques, including columns, pilasters, cavity walls with reinforcement, corbelling, lintels, door and window openings, arches, fireplaces, and paving. Details and guidelines are given. Use these as a guide when working on a specific job project.

COLUMNS

Columns are vertical support members that support a large weight or load from above. Large or tall columns, and especially those designed to carry a considerable amount of weight, will be strengthened with reinforcing steel. Columns are supported by reinforced concrete footings. Column footings are either square or rectangular. Reinforcing bars may run up out of the footing to give strength to the base of the column.

Figure 6-1, top, shows two reinforced brick masonry columns. *Section views* through the columns are shown. Columns should always be built in an interlocking fashion. Each column ties to reinforcing bars or dowels in the footing (Figure 6-1, bottom). The reinforcing bars in the brick column are wired to the dowels projecting up from the reinforced concrete footing. Thick joints are used in the columns so the steel bars are completely surrounded by mortar. Grouting may be poured into the column around the center bats or brick. Note that joint reinforcement—a steel hoop—is used to give additional strength. The hoops are set in a full mortar bed and are wired to one of the vertical reinforcing bars. The steel reinforcement gives a very strong column that can support a great deal of weight. Figure 6-2 shows a reinforced column being constructed on the job. Note how the vertical steel is tied together. Grout is poured into the column at set intervals.

Figure 6-3 shows cross-sectional views of typical brick columns. Both reinforced (top) and unreinforced columns (bottom) are shown. Unreinforced brick columns carry light loads. Often the reinforced columns are made part of a free-standing wall, as a garden wall, and are non-load bearing.

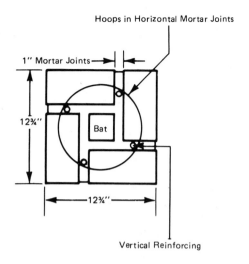

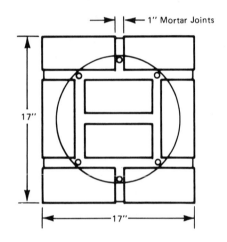

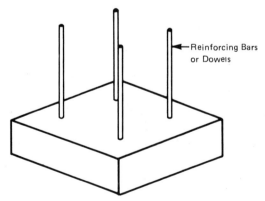

Square Reinforced Concrete Footing for Column

FIGURE 6-1
Construction of typical reinforced brick columns. Columns are supported by a footing. Vertical steel reinforcement is used in the columns; horizontal reinforcement is used in the brick joints. (*Top and center:* Brick Institute of America)

FIGURE 6-2
Brick reinforced column with six vertical steel bars. (Masonry Institute of America)

PIERS

Piers are like columns except they are shorter and frequently do not support a load. Piers are commonly used in garden walls at the ends of the wall, at corners, or at openings, such as gate posts. The piers in the garden wall serve to brace the wall panels. A garden wall with piers is sometimes called a pier and panel wall. Figure 6-4 shows a pier and panel garden wall. Piers allow a one-wythe wall four inches thick to be laid; they provide bracing and strength to the wall, as shown in Figure 6-4. The bond pattern is staggered so the wall is tied in from a different side in each course in an interlocking fashion. As you can see in the illustration, the pier and the wall panels are laid up at the same time. Free-standing piers must be capped to prevent water from entering at the top. Figure 6-5 shows a typical hollow pier. A four-inch wall would be laid up to the side of the pier.

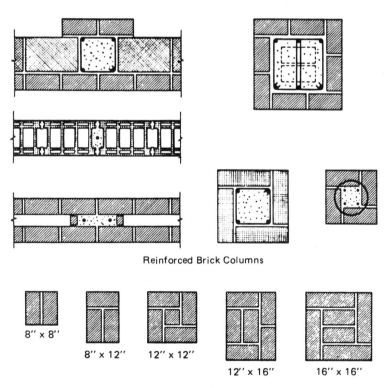

Reinforced Brick Columns

8" x 8"   8" x 12"   12" x 12"   12" x 16"   16" x 16"

Unreinforced Brick Columns

FIGURE 6-3
Top: Cross-sectional views of typical reinforced brick columns. *Bottom:* Cross-sectional views of typical unreinforced brick columns. (Brick Institute of America)

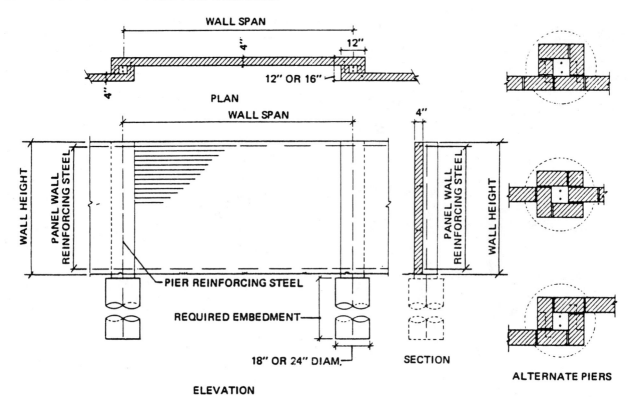

FIGURE 6-4

Pier and panel garden wall. (Brick Institute of America)

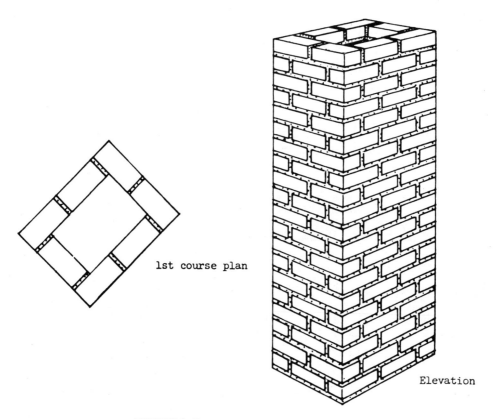

1st course plan

Elevation

FIGURE 6-5

Typical hollow pier. (Brick Institute of America)

PRACTICE: LAYING A HOLLOW BRICK PIER

Figure 6–5 shows a single, hollow brick pier, sized 16" × 20". This is a free-standing pier and is not integrated into a wall. The first course plan is shown. Note that odd courses repeat themselves; even courses repeat themselves. In actual practice, this hollow pier would require a cover or coping when completed. In the field, the pier would be built on a square footing and weep holes might be required. The following steps should be carried out when laying a hollow brick pier:

Step 1. Lay out the bed course dry to check layout. Use chalk lines for the outside faces of the brick.

Step 2. Lay the bed course on a 1-inch mortar bed. Check level of brick; check corners for 90° squareness. Use $\frac{3}{8}$-inch or $\frac{1}{2}$-inch joints.

Step 3. Lay second course following the pattern shown in the elevation view. Units should be laid so that head joints are offset to provide an interlocking connection.

Step 4. Lay odd and even courses to the top of the pier. Level, plumb, and square brick as the courses are being laid. Remove any dropped mortar off the face of the pier with the trowel. Avoid dropping any mortar inside the pier.

Step 5. After pier is finished, allow mortar to set until it is thumbprint hard; then finish with a concave joint.

Step 6. Clean any fins off the finished joints with the trowel. Clean brick surface with a bricklayer's brush. When mortar is set, the brick may be washed to remove any mortar.

PILASTERS

Pilasters are a kind of support column that are built into a masonry wall for extra strength. They project out from the wall to give additional bearing area. Pilasters are designed to receive loading directly from above, as from the end of a steel support beam.

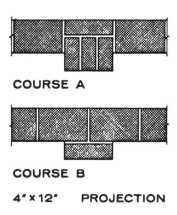

COURSE A

COURSE B

4" × 12"   PROJECTION

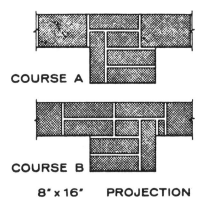

COURSE A

COURSE B

8" × 16"   PROJECTION

FIGURE 6–6
Typical brick pilasters. (Brick Institute of America)

Figure 6–6 shows typical pilasters. The brick is laid in an interlocking pattern so it is completely bonded into the wall. Note how the brick are laid so they are bonded into the wall. The first two courses are repeated over in sequence to the top of the wall.

Figure 6–6 shows brick pilaster layouts for a 4" × 12" projection (top) and an 8" × 16" projection (bottom). These are laid out to interlock with and be an integrated part of the bearing wall. Two courses are shown for each of the pilasters.

Reinforced pilasters are made by using vertical reinforcing bars. Figure 6–7 shows a heavily reinforced pilaster. Brick is laid around the steel reinforcement, then grout is poured in the space with the reinforcement.

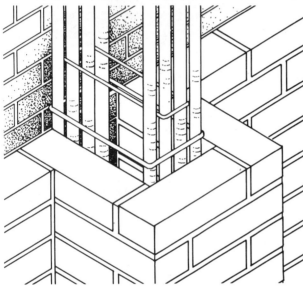

FIGURE 6-7
Steel reinforced brick pilaster. (*Top:* Masonry Institute of
America; *Bottom:* Brick Institute of America)

CHASES

Chases are recesses that are built back into the
wall. Chases are normally thought of as vertical;
however, horizontal chases are also constructed.
Chases are used to run electrical conduit and
plumbing piping and are constructed inside the
wall or floor. Figure 6–8 shows typical chases in a
brick wall. Recommended sizes are given. Since
the wall is set back (or hollowed out) for the chase,
reinforcement may be required to make up for the
loss of strength. In exterior walls, the back of the
chase should be dampproofed and insulated.

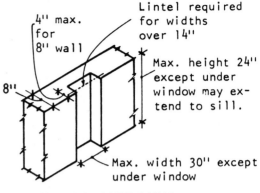

RECESS IN MASONRY WALL

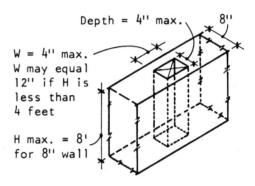

VERTICAL CHASE IN MASONRY WALL

FIGURE 6-8
Typical chases in brick wall. (HUD)

INTERSECTING WALLS

Intersecting brick walls are laid out so they tie together to form an integrated lateral support unit.
Brick units are laid so they interlock. Also, reinforcement ties may be used. Figure 6–9 shows
double-wythe, eight-inch intersecting walls laid
out so they interlock. The wythes in each wall are
separate and are tied together with metal Z-
shaped ties. The walls are constructed using standard running bond with joints broken so they
don't line up vertically.

PRACTICE: INTERSECTING WALLS

Practice by laying out the intersecting wall shown
in Figure 6–9. The layout plan for the first and

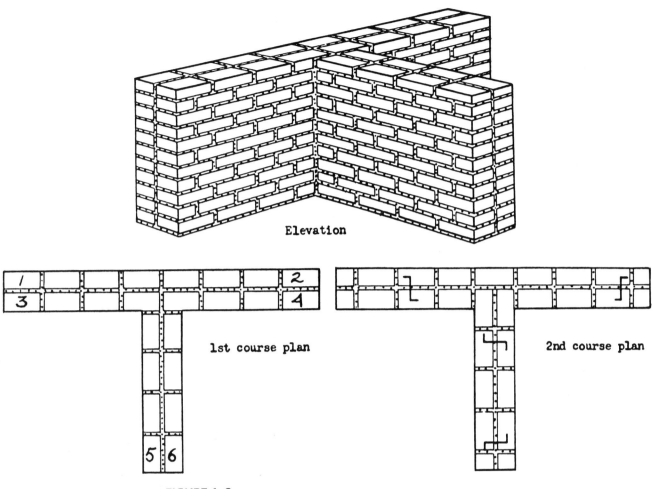

FIGURE 6–9
Two-wythe intersecting brick wall. (Brick Institute of America)

second courses is shown. This pattern is repeated for the height of the wall; i.e., 11 courses. Follow the steps below:

Step 1. Locate face of the walls on the floor. Snap a chalk line.

Step 2. Lay out the first course (Figure 6–9) with dry brick to identify and correct any problems.

Step 3. Spread mortar bed and lay out face wythe running from first brick to second brick. Align, level, and plumb the course of brick.

Step 4. Lay backing wythe running from third brick to fourth brick. Be sure to butter back side of brick where the backing wythe sets against the face course. This is called the collar joint and

should be completely filled. Align, level, and plumb. Check eight-inch wall thickness.

Step 5. Lay intersecting wall brick starting with fifth and sixth brick and running the course to the outside wall. Align, level, plumb, and check eight-inch wall thickness.

Step 6. Lay the second course following the layout plan. Align, level, and plumb.

Step 7. Set in the metal Z-shaped ties as shown on the second course layout plan. Set the metal ties in a mortar bed. Insert the other set of metal ties on the eighth course in the wall.

Step 8. Build small end-of-wall leads to serve as guides for the wall. Use corner blocks and string a mason's line.

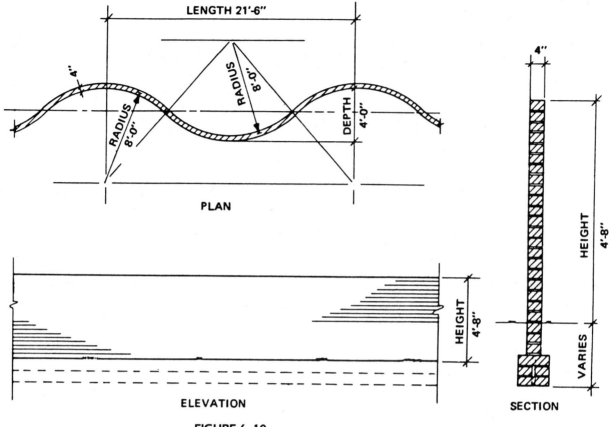

FIGURE 6–10

Serpentine wall. (Brick Institute of America)

Step 9. Complete the intersecting walls continuing the alternating layout pattern. Level and check plumb of the completed wall.

Step 10. Clean off any mortar splatter.

Step 11. When mortar is thumbprint hard, finish with a concave jointer. Do head joints, then bed joints. Use a sled jointer for the bed joints.

Step 12. Scrape off any mortar tailings left after finishing the joints. Clean wall by brushing with a bricklayer's brush.

SERPENTINE WALLS

Walls are frequently used as attractive architectural features outside the building. Solid, straight walls should present no special problem in layout. Some architects, however, design curving walls,

Figure 6–10, to give interest and variety to the grounds.

PRACTICE: LAYING A SERPENTINE WALL

Figure 6–10 shows the plans for making a typical serpentine wall. Note that brick footings are used. The curve is made by marking a radius from established points. Use a stout cord and a long sharpened slat or 1″ × 1″ to mark the curving line for the brick footing. Radius curves are drawn from three different points. The depth of the footings depends on the local frost line. After the footing is in, a carpenter's pencil, taped to the end of the slat or 1″ × 1″, can locate the line of the serpentine wall.

Note that the serpentine wall is only a one-wythe wall. The curving design of the wall gives

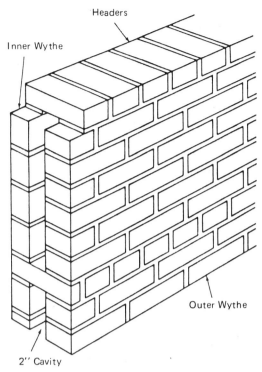

Cavity Wall Bonded with Brick Headers

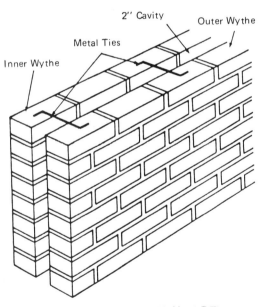

Cavity Wall Bonded with Metal Z Ties

FIGURE 6-11
Brick cavity walls. *Top:* Cavity wall bonded with headers.
Bottom: Cavity wall bonded with metal ties.

lateral support and strength to the design so the one wythe is stronger than a straight wall of the same thickness. The radius of the curve should be approximately two times the height of the wall above grade, here 4′-8″, and the depth of curvature should be no less than one-half the height. As shown, a radius of 8′-0″ is used.

CAVITY WALLS

Cavity wall construction is widely used today. As noted earlier, cavity walls are two-wythe walls with an opening between the two wythes. The opening between wythes is tied together with metal ties; cavity openings between wythes may have insulating material. Cavity wall construction is very popular because it can be used as a simple cavity wall, as a reinforced wall (with reinforcing steel and grouting), or as an insulated wall (foam plastic sheets or loose fill installed in the air space is commonly used). Because of the cavity, it has good resistance to sound transmission. It also has high fire resistance. Any moisture that gets into the wall falls to the bottom, is caught by the collection flashing, and drains out through the weep holes. The cavity, when used with insulation, forms a very effective thermal barrier.

As noted earlier, there are two types of cavity walls: one bonded with header brick and one bonded with metal ties. Almost all cavity walls are constructed today with metal ties. Figure 6-11 shows the two types of cavity walls; a 2-inch opening or cavity is shown. Cavity openings should not be greater that $4\frac{1}{2}$ inches or less than 2 inches in width.

Mortar

Laying the mortar bed for cavity walls differs from that of regular solid walls. It is important that mortar on the inside of the bed joint not fall into the cavity (Figure 6-12, top). A clean, clear cavity is required. Too much mortar may block any weep holes. Mortar from the bed joint should not extend too far into the cavity opening. Protruding bed joint mortar, or "fins," may form bridges that allow the passage of moisture across the opening. You should not cut mortar off from the inside face of the wall (Figure 6-12, top). This practice will cause some mortar to fall into the cavity. Rather

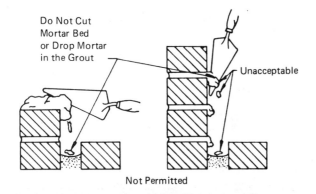

Correct

FIGURE 6–12

Top: NOT PERMITTED. Do NOT lay or cut mortar so it falls inside the cavity wall. *Bottom:* Correct method. Mortar that is squeezed out is plastered back on to the brick.

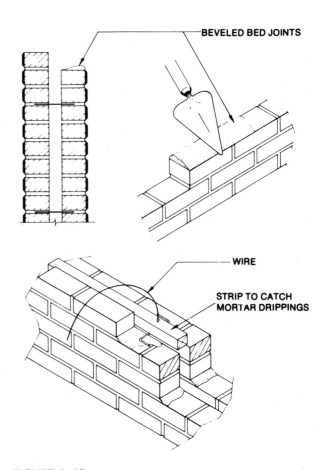

FIGURE 6–13

RECOMMENDED. Lay mortar so it is beveled and does not fall inside wall cavity. Use a wood strip to catch mortar droppings. (Brick Institute of America)

than cutting it off, flatten or plaster the mortar against the backs of the brick inside the cavity, as shown in Figure 6–12, bottom.

Two methods are used to prevent mortar from falling in the cavity or from protruding out too far from the interior face of the wall. One standard method is to bevel the bed joint, as shown in Figure 6–13, top. Beveling reduces the amount of mortar that squeezes out into the cavity. Note that the bed is not furrowed or, if furrowed, furrowed very lightly. Another method is to lay a strip of wood on the horizontal metal tie spacing in the cavity just beside the course being worked on (Figure 6–13, bottom). The strip of wood catches any mortar that is squeezed out and, at the same time, as it is pulled up it clears the inside of the cavity wall of excess mortar. The strip of wood is pulled up when the next horizontal row of ties is to be

installed. The wood strip is then repositioned on top of the ties.

Metal Ties

Metal ties are used to bond the two wythes together. Spacing of 24 to 36 inches on center horizontally and 16 inches on center vertically is commonly used. Most building codes require at least one metal tie for every $4\frac{1}{2}$ square feet of wall area. Figure 6–14 shows typical use of metal ties. Ties should be laid in a mortar bed on top of the course. It is important that the tie be well embedded and completely surrounded by mortar in the bed course. If a tie with a drip is used, the tie must be turned so the bend in the center (called a drip) points downward (Figure 6–15). This allows any

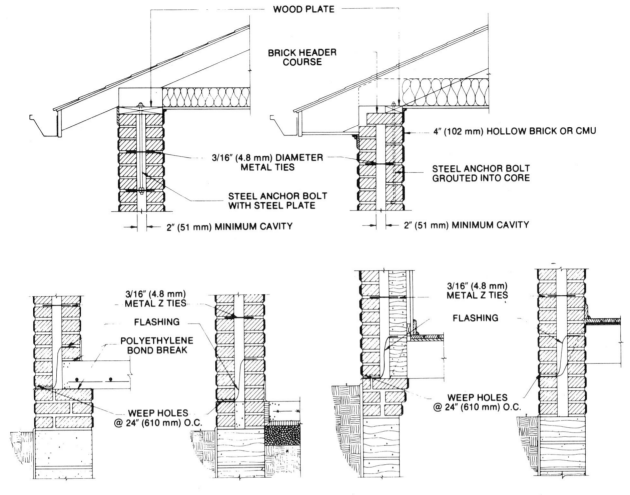

WOOD PLATE

BRICK HEADER COURSE

3/16" (4.8 mm) DIAMETER METAL TIES

STEEL ANCHOR BOLT WITH STEEL PLATE

2" (51 mm) MINIMUM CAVITY

4" (102 mm) HOLLOW BRICK OR CMU

STEEL ANCHOR BOLT GROUTED INTO CORE

2" (51 mm) MINIMUM CAVITY

3/16" (4.8 mm) METAL Z TIES

FLASHING

POLYETHYLENE BOND BREAK

WEEP HOLES @ 24" (610 mm) O.C.

3/16" (4.8 mm) METAL Z TIES

FLASHING

WEEP HOLES @ 24" (610 mm) O.C.

FIGURE 6-14
Typical use of metal ties in cavity wall. (Brick Institute of America)

water that condenses on the tie to run to the center (rather than back into the support wall) and drip into the cavity. Additional ties should be placed within 12 inches of openings and no more than 36 inches apart around the perimeter of openings, such as windows and doors. Figure 6-16 shows how metal ties should be used around windows.

Flashing

Flashing should be placed at the bottom of the cavity, over openings, and beneath sills. Metal or plastic is used, and it should run completely under the face wall. Flashing should be laid against the backing wall in a mortar bed and run into the bed

joint of the backing at least two inches, as shown in Figure 6-17, top. Figure 6-17, bottom, shows how flashing is used with a window sill. The flashing should fit under the window as shown. The recommended practice is to extend the flashing completely through the bed joint of the face brick until it projects outside slightly. The flashing projection outside should be turned down on the brick face to form a water drip.

Weep Holes

Weep holes are required at the base of the cavity wall just above the flashing (Figure 6-18). This allows any moisture that penetrates or condenses

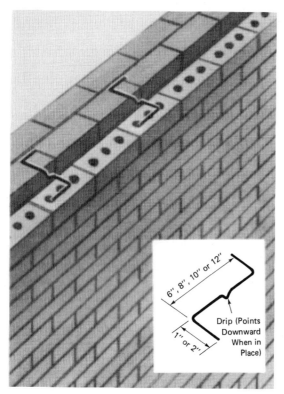

FIGURE 6-15

Drip point on metal tie should point downward when installed. (A.A. Wire Products Co.)

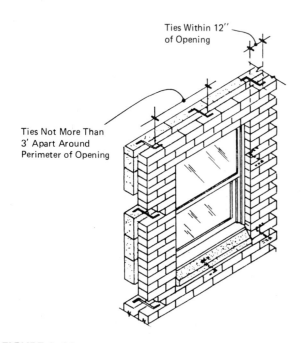

FIGURE 6-16

Opening in cavity wall. Place metal ties not more than three feet apart around and within twelve inches of opening. (U.S. Department of Housing and Urban Development)

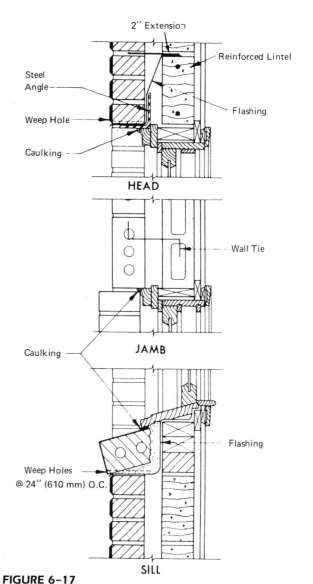

FIGURE 6-17

Section through cavity wall at window. Flashing is used around opening. (Brick Institute of America)

in the wall to flow outside. Weep holes are commonly located every 16″ or 24″ on center (O.C.) in the course immediately above the flashing. If the flashing does not extend through the wall at the base of the cavity, 16″ O.C. is recommended.

Weep holes are commonly made by omitting mortar from the head joint. Metal or plastic tubes are also used; they should tilt downward for easy water flow. Oiled rods can also be placed in the

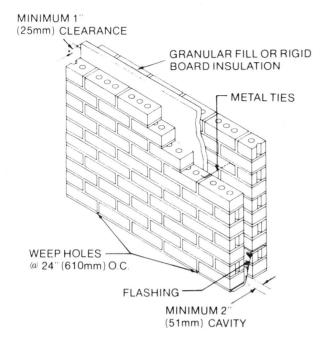

MINIMUM 1"
(25mm) CLEARANCE

GRANULAR FILL OR RIGID
BOARD INSULATION

METAL TIES

WEEP HOLES
@ 24" (610mm) O.C.

FLASHING

MINIMUM 2"
(51mm) CAVITY

FIGURE 6-18
Brick cavity wall with insulation. Weep holes are required at the base. (Brick Institute of America)

head joint. They should be removed before the mortar is completely set. The hole where the rod had been then serves as a weep hole for moisture flow. Rope or cotton cord may also be used. It extends completely through the joint and is left in place. The rope or cord acts as a wick to draw moisture out of the cavity.

Insulation

As noted, both loose insulation, such as water-repellent vermiculite or silicone-treated perlite, and rigid insulation are used in the cavity. When insulation is used, standard flashing and weep hole placement is still required. Loose insulation is poured into the cavity; rigid insulation is attached to the back of the cavity on the backing wythe. There should be a 1-inch air space between the rigid insulation and the back of the facing wythe (Figure 6-18). The flashing at the base should run behind the rigid insulation and into a bed course of the backing wythe.

Composite Cavity Wall

Composite cavity walls use two different types of building units for the wythes. A common type of composite cavity wall has face brick for the outside wythe and concrete block for the inside wythe. The same tie spacing as for cavity walls is suggested.

PRACTICE: LAYING A 10-INCH CAVITY WALL

Figure 6-19 shows a typical 10" cavity wall with a corner. In laying out the wall, follow the standard planning and layout procedure. This is a practice wall and no flashing is planned for in the design. Take care to keep your work clean and do *not* drop mortar into the cavity. Follow the steps below:

Step 1. Locate outside wall edges and snap chalk guidelines.

Step 2. Do a dry layout with the brick to identify any problems. Figure 6-19, bottom, shows the first course plan. Measure over 10 inches from the outside line to locate the inside line for the backing wythe. A two-inch cavity is used.

Step 3. Lay inside bed course running from bed brick 1 to bed brick 2. Work from both ends toward the middle. Lay mortar slightly thick for the bed joint; check plumb to be sure brick are vertically true. Take care to lay brick to the marked line. After laying, align and check horizontal level.

Step 4. Lay out bed brick 6, and the closure between brick 6 and 1. Align, plumb, and level. Measure to make sure corner is square; i.e., at a 90° angle.

Step 5. Cut three-quarter brick numbers 3, 4, and 5.

Step 6. Lay bed brick 3, 4, and 5 in mortar bed. Level and plumb brick. Measure distance to bed brick 3 and 4 to be sure the outside edge is located 10 inches from the inside face. Check corner by brick 2 and 5 to see that it is square.

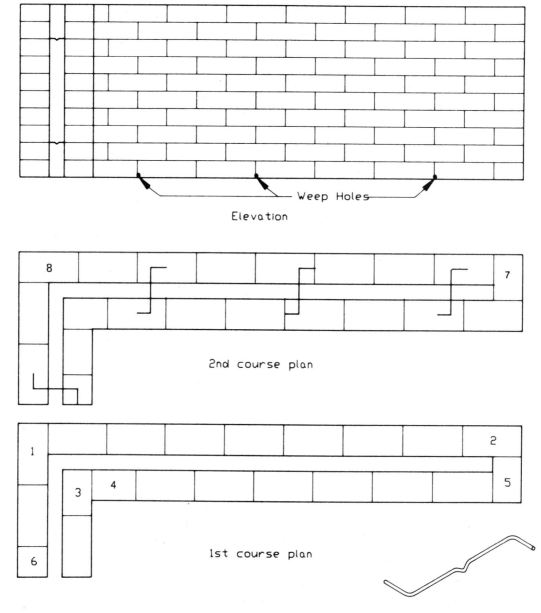

Elevation

2nd course plan

1st course plan

Note: Ties at 16' o.c. vertical and 36' o.c. horizontal staggered   Z Drip-Tie

FIGURE 6-19
Cavity wall: Ten-inch with metal ties. (Brick Institute of America)

Step 7. Lay brick between bed brick 4 and 5, and finish the leg off of bed brick 3. Level, plumb, and align. Check corners for square. Check 10-inch width of wall throughout.

Step 8. Leave the three weep holes in the head joints, as shown on the elevation view. Use empty head joints or use tubing or wicking such as a rope section.

Step 9. Cut three three-quarter brick for second course.

Step 10. Lay mortar bed. Bevel mortar bed to avoid dropping mortar in cavity. Lay three-quarter brick number 7 over right end of wall (over bed brick 2 and 5).

Step 11. Lay second course brick number 8 at other end of wall.

Step 12. Complete both face wythe and backing wythe following the procedure established for the first course. Plaster back any mortar that is squeezed out of the inside bed joints. Remember to bevel the inside of the mortar bed.

Step 13. Lay mortar for the four metal Z-shaped ties. Embed ties in the mortar, and locate as shown on the second course plan. Be sure that if a tie with a drip is used, the drip on the metal tie points downward.

Step 14. Build corner leads six courses high on each end of the wall.

Step 15. Finish wall to eighth course. Then embed metal Z-shaped ties, as noted on elevation view. Note that ties are offset from the ties on the second course.

Step 16. Use a 4-foot long 1″ × 2″ or 2″ × 2″ wood piece and attach wires at each end. This is used to catch any mortar inside the cavity and to finish the mortar flat.

Step 17. Complete the cavity wall. For practice, use the 1″ × 2″ or 2″ × 2″ wood piece inside the cavity to catch any mortar. Continue, however, to bevel the inside of the mortar bed before laying the brick. Square and align the wall. Remove any mortar splatter on the outside wall. Brush walls with bricklayer's brush.

Step 18. After the mortar has begun to set, finish the joints with a convex jointer. Check inside of the wall for mortar drippings. Make sure weep holes are clear.

REINFORCED BRICK MASONRY

In reinforced brick masonry (RBM), both vertical and horizontal steel reinforcing bars are used in the wall to give strength. Reinforced masonry can be used in high-rise buildings over three stories high. Cavity-type brick construction is used to make the reinforced brick walls. As explained earlier (Figures 4–55 and 4–56), steel reinforcing bars are positioned in the wall cavity and grout is poured or pumped in. In larger and heavier construction, the grout is normally pumped in. Grout should be well stirred before placing to avoid segregation of the aggregate. The steel reinforcement bars run both vertically and horizontally in the cavity.

Low-Lift Grouting

In low-lift grouting, only a few inches of grout are poured at any one time into the wall cavity. A "lift" is defined as the vertical height of a pour (placement) of grouting that is made at any one time. A vertical depth or lift of six inches to eight inches maximum can be poured in low-lift grouting. Figure 6–20 shows the recommended procedure for low-lift grouting with an opening or cavity of two inches or less. Note that steel reinforcing rods or dowels are already set in the concrete support base. The brick are laid on each side of the reinforcing bars. As the wall goes up, additional vertical reinforcing will be added and wired to the reinforcement already embedded in the concrete. Horizontal reinforcing bars and wall ties across the cavity space are also used.

Note in Figure 6–20 that the outside wythe is built up higher than the inside wythe. Pouring of grout is done from the inside, low wythe side. The higher, outside wythe can serve as a splash screen to prevent the grout from being accidentally splattered. Note that only a few inches are poured at a time, usually only a three-course height. Grout should be stopped 1½ inches below the top of the masonry. Avoid splashing grout on top of masonry units. Dried grout is detrimental to good joint bonding. Grout is brought in a bucket and poured in by hand (Figure 6–21). After pouring, the grout is puddled to consolidate it and to make sure it has flowed into all crevices (Figure 6–22). Puddling is done by working a stick back and forth and up and down in the grout. The recommended procedure is to have one mason pouring grout while the other is puddling.

Note: Placement of grout lifts should not be carried out too rapidly since excessive hydraulic pressure may cause the wall to blow out. If masonry units shift even slightly, the wall must be torn down and rebuilt. Place grout only after joint mortar has set. Wait at least three minutes between lifts. Grout crews should work at least 10 feet to 15 feet apart.

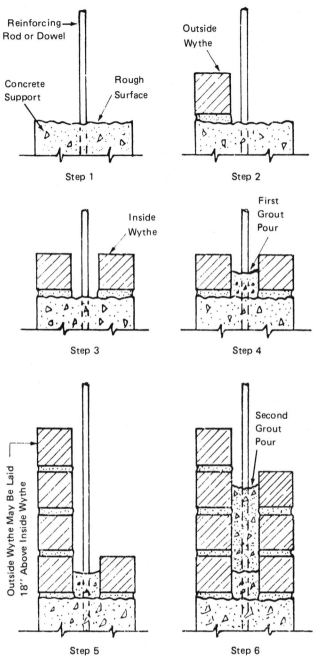

FIGURE 6-20
Low-lift grouting procedure. (Masonry Institute of America)

High-Lift Grouting

In heavier construction, much higher lifts are normally used. Cavity walls are laid to a considerable height; after they are cleaned and the mortar has set, grout is pumped into the cavity. Grout should not be poured until walls have been in place three days.

FIGURE 6-21
In low-lift grouting, grout is poured into the cavity from a bucket. *Top:* Scooping grout from grout tub. *Bottom:* Pouring grout into cavity. (*Top:* Masonry Institute of America; *Bottom:* Brick Institute of America)

FIGURE 6–22
Puddle the grout by working a stick up and down in the cavity to remove air pockets. (Masonry Institute of America)

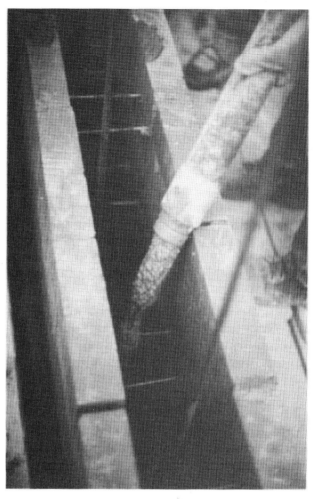

FIGURE 6–23
Pumping grout into wall cavity. (Masonry Institute of America)

Vertical brick dams are used to limit the displacement of the grout, as shown earlier in Figure 6–7, top. Large amounts of grout mixture are delivered to the construction site in ready-mix trucks. At the site, water is added to the grout mixture to thin it for pumping. The grout is then pumped up to the level where the cavity wall has been laid. Grout should be kept $1\frac{1}{2}$ inches below the top of masonry.

Figure 6–23 shows grouting being pumped into the brick wall cavity. Pumped grout may be poured as high as four feet at one time in the cavity. This is called high-lift grouting. Extreme care

must be taken so the wall does not bulge out or bow during high-lift grouting.

It is important that the steel bars be completely surrounded by the grout and that they not touch the walls. Bar positioners (as shown earlier in Figure 4–54) are used to position the vertical bars in the wall cavity. Wooden frames hold the bars. The spacing of the two wythes in reinforced brick masonry is wider than in cavity walls. Wythes are generally from 3 inches to 4 inches apart. Metal ties are use to keep the wythes from bowing or spreading during the grouting process.

RBM Techniques

After the grout is placed in the cavity, it is puddled or vibrated to remove any air voids. *Puddling* (Figure 6–22) is used in low-lift grouting and consists of working a stick or rod back and forth in the grout mixture. This assures that the grout has completely filled the cavity. In high-lift grouting, *vibrating* is done by a mechanical device which is stuck into the grout. This gives the same result—grout flows into all the spaces.

In grouted walls, of course, weep holes and flashing are not used at the base. Cleanouts, however, are required at the wall base in high-lift grouting. Cleanouts are made by leaving out every other brick at the bottom of one wythe (Figure 6–24, top). Note the polyethelene film and sand in the cleanout holes. In high-lift grouting, the projecting mortar fins inside the grout space are removed by a high pressure jet stream of water. After mortar droppings and debris are removed from the grout space, the cleanouts are sealed by mortaring in brick. After the cleanouts are sealed, grouting may begin. Mortar must be set, however, before high-lift grouting can start. High-lift grouting is done three to five days after the brick are laid. A dam is made to prevent grout from pouring out (Figure 6–24, bottom) by covering the just-sealed cleanout holes with a board and wedging with brick.

The mortar bed should be beveled to avoid, as much as possible, mortar being squeezed out of the bed joint into the cavity. The wall cavity must be kept clean and clear so the grout will flow in. Mortar should not be allowed to fall into the cavity. Mortar and grout should not be mixed together since it could lower the strength of the grouting.

CORBELLING

Corbelling is a masonry technique of widening or projecting out a masonry wall or part of a wall to form a decorative feature or a support shelf or ledge for building elements, such as a beam. Each brick course extends out further than the one below it. Corbelling is also used to widen a support wall. Figure 6–25 shows how an eight-inch founda-

Cleanouts

Cleanouts Closed by Covering with Board

FIGURE 6–24
Top: Cleanouts are made at the base of a cavity wall by leaving brick out. Bottom: Boards braced by brick are used to prevent grout from flowing out just-sealed cleanout holes. (Masonry Institute of America)

tion wall can be corbelled out to support a ten-inch cavity wall. In three courses, the support is corbelled out two inches to support the wall above. As a general rule, the brick (or any masonry unit) should not extend out more than one-third the width or one-half the height, whichever is less.

Since corbels must normally support a load, care must be taken in their construction. Headers are used to tie the corbel into the base. The top course must be a full header course, per building codes. Joints must be completely filled with mortar.

Figure 6–26 shows a simple corbel used on the outside of a chimney. This corbel is used to increase the thickness of the chimney and to improve its weathering resistance in high winds. The

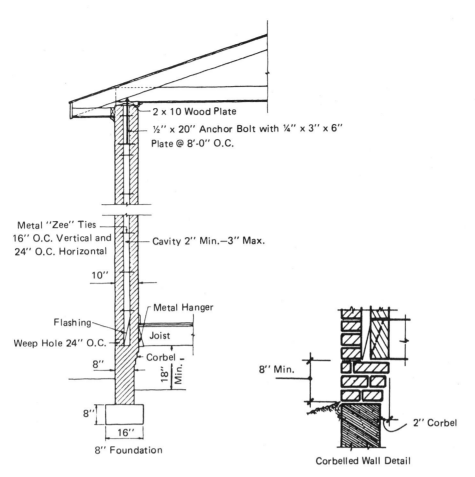

FIGURE 6-25
Corbelling used to widen wall from an eight-inch foundation wall to a ten-inch cavity wall. (*Left:* Brick Association of North Carolina)

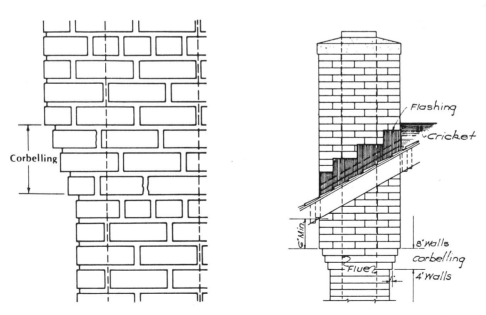

FIGURE 6-26
Corbelling used on chimney.

thicker walls are stronger. The first course of the corbel uses stretchers, the second course headers, and the third course uses three-quarter brick. Individual corbels shall not project out more than one inch, per codes, or more than one-third the width or one-half the height of the unit, whichever is less.

PRACTICE: CORBELLING A 12-INCH WALL

Figure 6–27 shows a 12-inch solid brick wall with a three-course corbel near the top. The corbel forms a shelf that projects out $2\frac{1}{4}$ inches beyond the face of the wall. The detail, Figure 6–27, shows that the corbel is laid out, projecting $\frac{3}{4}$ inch in each course. The first course of the corbel is made by using an extra head joint, over one-inch thick. Follow the steps below:

Step 1. Snap a guideline for the front of the wall.

Step 2. Lay out the first course in a dry run. Headers are used in the face wythe with a queen closure (brick split lengthwise) to the left. The right side uses a three-quarter brick. The back wythe is all stretchers with one header on the right. A bat or one-quarter brick is used to fill in on the right.

Step 3. Lay the first course in a thick mortar bed. Level and square the brick. Make sure they are aligned.

Step 4. Lay courses 2 to 6 as shown on the elevation. Level, square, and plumb the wall.

Step 5. Lay out remaining courses to the corbel. Course 7 repeats course 1. Courses 8 and 9 repeat courses 2 and 3. Level the courses and check the plumb.

Step 6. *Corbel course 1* (Wall course 10): Open the head joint and use a $1\frac{1}{8}$-inch joint to project the header course out $\frac{3}{4}$ inch, per detail. Check the level of the corbel.

Step 7. *Corbel course 2* (Wall course 11): Use stretchers in the front wythe, headers in the back

wythe, and bats between (see detail) to project out another $\frac{3}{4}$ inch. Check level.

Step 8. *Corbel course 3* (Wall course 12): Use stretchers on the front and back wythes; use three-quarter headers between the two wythes. The corbel should project out another $\frac{3}{4}$ inch.

Step 9. Build course 13 the same as course 1.

Step 10. Build course 14 per elevation.

Step 11. Finish all joints concave when mortar has set sufficiently (thumbprint hard). If this is a standing wall, as a garden wall, joints would be finished both front and back. (A coping or top would be required for an exposed, garden wall). Clean wall; trowel off tailings from mortar finish with trowel; brush wall with bricklayer's brush.

WALL OPENINGS

Openings in brick walls usually are made for windows and doors. The brick courses must be laid around openings so the brick are tight against the window or door frame. Also, a support sill must be built underneath the opening. This is very important, of course, for window openings. A support member, called a lintel, is required over all openings.

SILLS

Sills under doors are required before the door framework is put in place. Sills under exterior doors may be wood, metal, stone, or reinforced concrete. The door sill rests on top of the foundation, as shown in Figure 6–28. Of course, no brickwork is normally used under external doors. Once the sill is in, the door framework is set over the sill and braced.

Sills under windows, however, frequently use rowlock-positioned bricks. Figure 6–29 shows a rowlock sill course under a window. This is a brick veneer wall. Note that the rowlocks are tilted

A 3 COURSE CORBEL JOB ON A 12' WALL

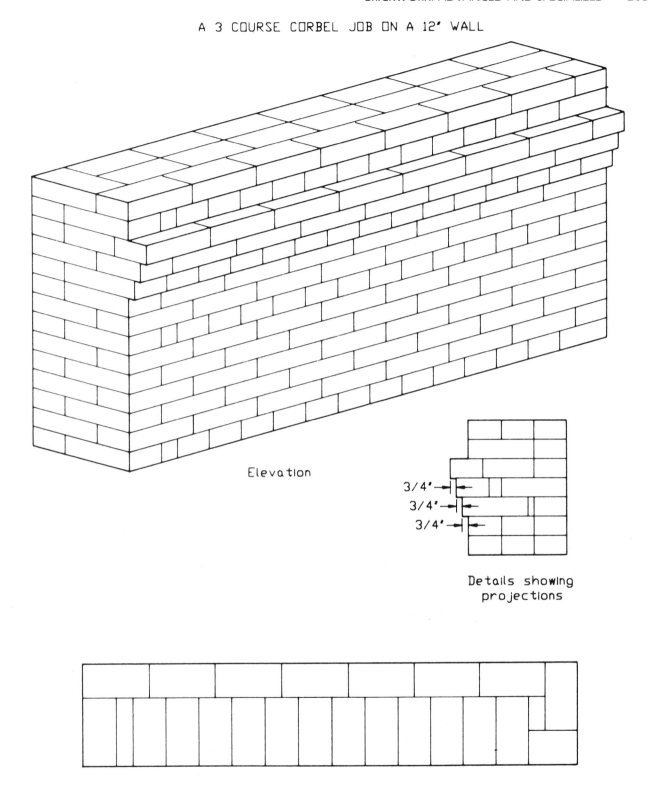

Elevation

3/4'→
3/4'→
3/4'→

Details showing
projections

1st course plan

FIGURE 6-27
Corbelling: 12-inch solid wall. (Brick Institute of America)

Use Five Wood Blocks on Each Side of
Door Frame to Anchor Frame

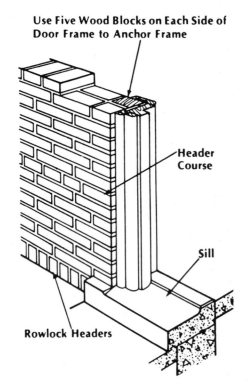

FIGURE 6-28
Sill and brickwork for door.

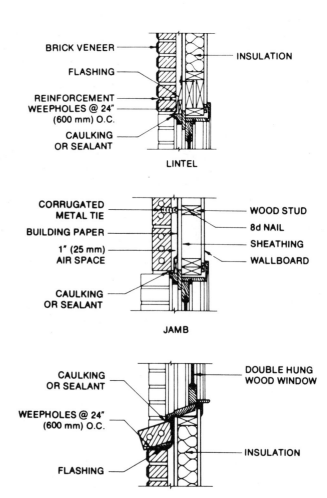

FIGURE 6-29
Sill and brickwork for window. (Brick Institute of America)

downward to allow water runoff and pitched a minimum of 15° from horizontal. The sill detail shows how the rowlocks are positioned under the window sill. Flashing is required. The flashing extends out to the brick wall exterior face and is set in a mortar bed. Mortar is also laid on top of the flashing to seat the rowlock brick. The flashing extends back into the window frame as shown. Weep holes, 24 inches on center, should be left between joints for the entire length of the sill.

Refer back to Figure 6-17 for information on a rowlock sill used in a cavity wall. Note in Figure 6-17 that three-quarter cut rowlocks are used.

JAMBS

Brickwork is laid up against the sides of the window or door framework. The window or door sides are called *jambs*. It is important that brickwork be

laid tight into the jambs, both to support the framework and to cut down air infiltration. (Of course, caulking at the jambs is required after the brick are in place.) Both Figures 6-28 and 6-29 show how the brick courses are laid up against the side at the jamb. The brick courses are started by laying the brick against the sides of the jamb framework; then the brick are laid working away from the jamb. Of course, the window or door frame must be plumbed to make sure it is aligned vertically before laying any brick along the jamb. It is important, therefore, that a dry layout be made of each course so the brick can be cut as needed to fit the bond and to lay against the framework. Figure 6-30 shows brick laid around a wood framework. After the brick are set, the framework is removed and the window is installed.

FIGURE 6–30
Brick laid around temporary window framework.

FIGURE 6–31
Brick and concrete block laid around metal door frame or buck.

The brick on the sides of the window and door opening are laid all the way to the top of the opening. It is very important that in laying the brick the thickness of the bed mortar be carefully planned so the top of the last course is even with the top or head of the window or door framework. This must be done so that the lintel across the top of the framework can bear or rest on the brick at each side of the opening. The brickmason's rule is used to check the height of the courses. If the height of the last course is too high or too low, the bed joint thickness must be adjusted. The top of the course should be no more than $\frac{1}{4}$ inch above the top of the window frame. *Note:* Take care to lay out the brick courses on each side of the opening so they are exactly the same height at the top. The top of the course should be finished smooth to form a bearing area for the ends of the lintel.

Figure 6–31 shows brick being laid up against the side of a metal doorframe or buck. The frame

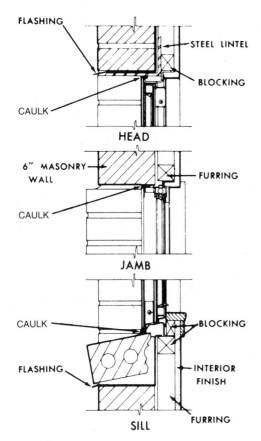

FIGURE 6–32
Double-hung window detail (sections) showing six-inch brick wall with aluminum, double-hung window. (Brick Institute of America)

is leveled and plumbed and braced in place. Note that the brick are mortared against the outside of the metal frame. Mortar is trowelled into the hollow frame sides. Height is critical since the top course must be level with the top of the doorframe. Height depends on bed joint thickness. Check height with the brick rule. Bed joint thickness must be planned and kept the same throughout.

Figure 6–32 shows a window detail or section on how the brick is laid for a six-inch brick wall. Sections for an aluminum, double-hung window are shown. The head and sill sections show a view looking from the side. The jamb section, however, shows a view of the jamb looking down from above. Note how caulking is used where the brick joins the window framework. A single steel angle lintel is used for the brick wall.

LINTELS

Lintels are horizontal support members which span doors and windows or other wall openings. Reinforced brick, stone, precast concrete, and structural steel are used. Wood is rarely used since it may deteriorate in the presence of lime and is not permitted by codes to support masonry. The type, size, and strength of the lintel used is selected by the architect to meet the load requirements for the wall opening. The lintel must not only carry the load of the wall above but also any part of a floor or other horizontal support attached, over the opening, to the wall, as in the case of a bearing wall. Care must be taken to assure the full structural strength of the lintel is attained.

Reinforced Brick

Reinforced brick lintels are constructed using reinforcing steel. Figure 6–33 shows, in end or section view, two lintels constructed using $\frac{3}{8}$-inch reinforcing bars. The bars run across the full width of the opening and extend over the end supports at least 24 inches into the brick wall. In Figure 6–33, left, running bond is used with reinforcing bars over the first and fourth courses. In Figure 6–33,

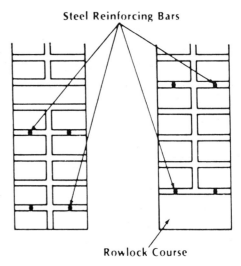

FIGURE 6–33
Reinforced brick lintels used over openings.

right, the bottom course over the opening is a rowlock course. The other courses use a running bond. The steel bars should be laid in a mortar bed and pressed down into the mortar; they should also be covered with mortar, and the mortar smoothed down. This assures that they are completely surrounded by mortar. A $\frac{1}{2}$-inch mortar joint is used with high strength, type N mortar. Mortar must always completely surround the steel. Complete all the course holding the reinforcing bars before laying the next course above the bars. This assures a good bond for the support course for the steel bars. The next course above the reinforcing steel bar is laid following the same procedure for regular brick without reinforcing steel.

Precast Reinforced Concrete

Cast reinforced lintels are also commonly used. Lintels are prefabricated to standard sizes and widths. They must be carefully mortared into the brick bond to form an integrated unit with the wall. Figure 6-34 shows a cross-sectional view of a precast reinforced concrete lintel used over a window. The ends of the concrete lintel rest on top of

a brick course in a mortar bed. Lintel ends extend at least eight inches past the opening onto the brick course. The architectural drawings will specify how far the lintel ends extend in the brick bond.

Cast-in-place reinforced concrete members are also used in masonry construction. Cast in place reinforced beams are rarely used as lintels, however.

Steel Lintels

Steel angle irons and I-beams are used across openings. Figure 6-35 shows how two angle irons are used. Note that brick must be cut to fit against the leg of the lintel. As much as $\frac{1}{2}$ inch may have to be chipped off the side of the brick. The ends of the angle bear on the brick at the sides of the opening. The lintel ends should bear at least 4 inches on the back course on each side of the opening (Figure 6-36). For heavier loads and for wide openings, the lintel ends may bear up to 12 inches on each side. Precaution must be taken when laying steel to allow for expansion. Metal expands much more than brick, so do not mortar in the ends. Leave at least $\frac{1}{4}$-inch space at each end of the steel lintels. If a cavity wall is built, two separate angles, as shown in Figure 6-37, are used.

Figure 6-38 shows an I-beam with a steel plate welded to the bottom. Again, the brick must be cut to fit against the support member, in this case the I-beam. Steel beams and plate lintels are used in solid brick walls with heavy loads or across openings greater than 8 feet.

ARCHES

Arches create a support over an opening, such as a walkway or doorway. Figure 6-39 shows the basic brick arches used. The jack arch is flat; all the others curve up. The semicircular arch is also called the Roman arch or the half-circle arch. Note in Figure 6-39 that arches are shown two different ways. This allows different bonding patterns to be shown. The jack arch, for example, shows both double (left) and single (right) brick patterns on the face.

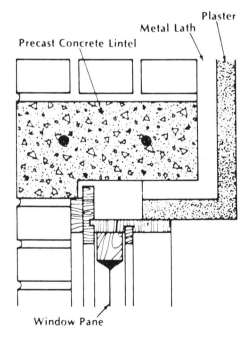

FIGURE 6-34
Precast reinforced concrete lintel.

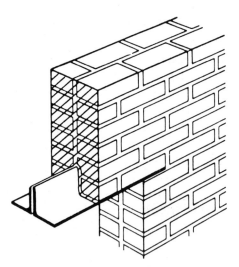

FIGURE 6–35
Angle irons used over openings.

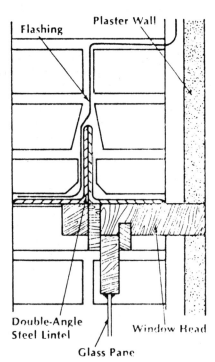

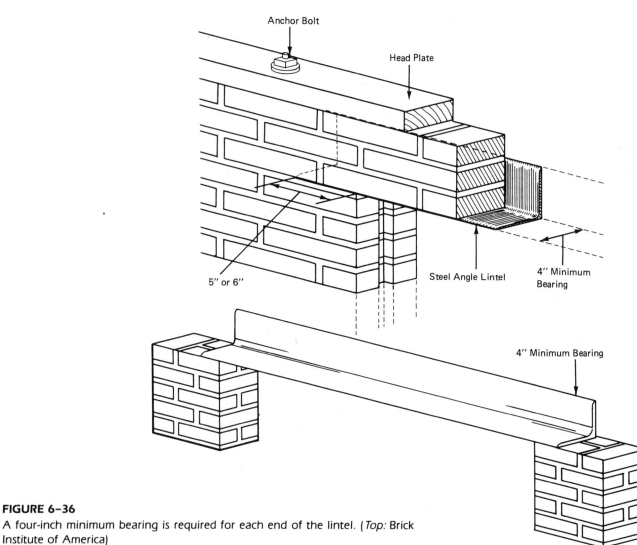

FIGURE 6–36
A four-inch minimum bearing is required for each end of the lintel. (*Top:* Brick Institute of America)

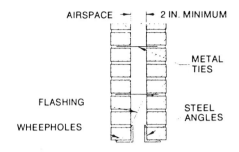

FIGURE 6-37
Angle iron used to support brick cavity wall opening. (Brick Institute of America)

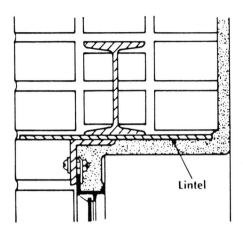

FIGURE 6-38
I-beam and steel plate used as lintel.

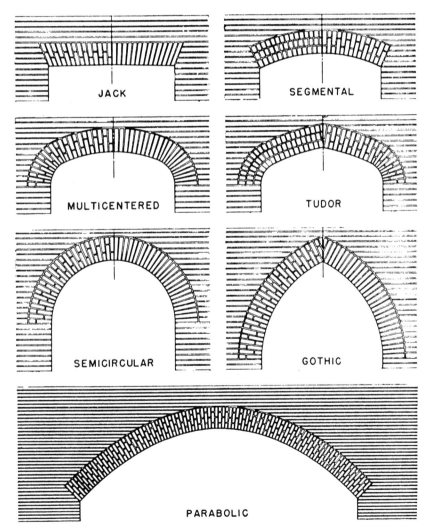

FIGURE 6-39
Typical brick arches. (Brick Institute of America)

Two major types of arches are recognized in design and construction: minor arches and major arches. *Minor arches* have an opening or span of six feet or less. They may have a uniform load of 1000 pounds per foot. Minor arches are those used over openings in residential and light commercial construction. *Major arches* have openings wider than six feet and have loading in excess of 1000 pounds per foot. The parabolic arch (Figure 6–39, bottom) is an example of a major arch. Parabolic arches are engineered arches used in larger and heavier construction.

Arch Specifications

The blueprints give detailed information on how to build the arch. The following information may be given on the detail drawings:

1. Masonry opening dimensions

2. Mortar joint thickness

3. Number of courses high

4. Bonding of arch (one, two, three piece)

5. Skewback angle

6. Type and texture of brick used

7. Radius (if applicable)

Figure 6–40 shows a jack arch with basic construction information detailed. The *bonding of the arch* refers to the number of brick used to create the

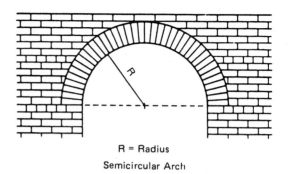

R = Radius
Semicircular Arch

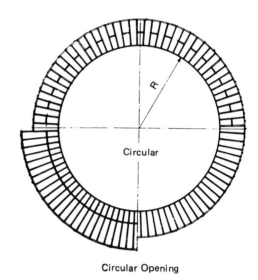

Circular

Circular Opening

FIGURE 6–41
Top: Semicircular arch. *Bottom:* Circular opening. (*Bottom:* Old Carolina Brick Co.)

height. Figure 6–40, right, shows a two-brick bond. Large arches may be several brick deep. The *skew angle* refers to the angle the brick make to the horizontal line. Brick ends are cut to fit the skew angle. The *radius* refers to a semicircular arch; Figure 6–41 shows how a radius (R) is measured for a semicircular arch (top) and for a circular opening (bottom). The course of brick following the curve of the arch is often referred to as the ring.

Arch Terminology

Arches are highly complex support elements that have evolved over centuries of practice and use. You should become familiar with some of the basic terms. Figure 6–42 illustrates an arch with basic terminology shown. This may appear complex and

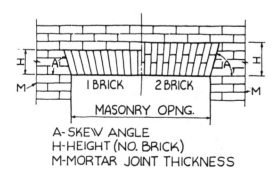

A- SKEW ANGLE
H- HEIGHT (NO. BRICK)
M- MORTAR JOINT THICKNESS

FIGURE 6–40
Jack arch and terminology. (Brick Association of North Carolina)

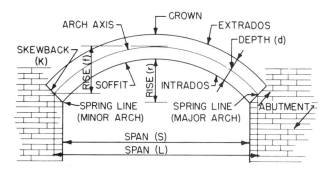

FIGURE 6-42
Arch and basic terminology. (Brick Institute of America)

confusing at first; however, these traditional terms are quickly learned.

Abutment.   The masonry support for the ends of the arch; also called the *piers.*

Arch axis.   Center line of the arch curve.

Crown.   The apex or top point of the arch.

Depth.   Top to bottom thickness of the arch.

Extrados.   Line running along the top edge of the arch.

Intrados.   Line running along the bottom edge of the arch.

Rise.   Rise is always a vertical distance. Arch rise (r) is measured from the line running from the bottom points of the arch to the high point of the intrados. (Rise is also calculated as the distance from the bottom point of the arch axis to the top point of the arch axis.)

Skewback.   Inclined surface of brick at each end of the arch.

Soffit.   The underside surface of the arch.

Span.   The horizontal distance across the masonry opening, or the clear span (S). Also the horizontal distance (L) between ends of the arch axis of the skewback.

Spring Line.   On a minor arch, the line where the skewback cuts the soffit. On a major arch, the intersection of the arch axis with the skewback.

Brick

Conventional brick are used in most arch construction. Since conventional brick are uniform in size, the thickness of the joint will vary from top to bottom, as shown in Figure 6-43. A sort of wedge-shaped joint is made. This results from the layout of the brick along a curving plane.

FIGURE 6-43
Note wedge-shaped joint made between brick in this fireplace arch. (Schaefer)

Special shaped brick, however, can be used. Shaped brick can be made by cutting on a power masonry saw. Shaped brick will, of course, allow an even masonry joint to be used. In some cases it is possible to order shaped brick from the brick manufacturer. Usually, shaped bricks are more expensive. Almost all arch construction and layout use conventional brick.

Arch Layout

Since the brick for the arch are laid overhead they can *not* stay in place in fresh mortar without support. A support base, called a *center,* is built and used to support the brick while they are being laid.

Figure 6–44 shows a semicircular arch laid on cut plywood centers. Two plywood pieces are cut for front and back and supported with a framework. The centers here are supported by loose masonry units until the arch is completely in place and the mortar is set—at least a week. When the brick are self-supporting, the support is removed.

Figure 6–45, bottom, shows another arch laid on a center. The brick are laid on top of the center to build the arch, as shown in Figure 6–45, top.

Centers, of course, must be exactly constructed to support the type of arch needed. A wide variety of arches are built and a support must be built for each one. Each center must exactly follow the curvature specified by the designer. Centers are made by cutting plywood pieces for the front and the back of the arches.

Remember that the center must be left in place until the mortar sets. Centers are constructed by carpenters following the architect's detail drawings. The bricklayer or the helper may assist in setting them in place. In any event, carefully check the center and the installation before laying any brick.

PRACTICE: LAYING A CIRCULAR ARCH

Figure 6–45 shows a circular or semicircular arch in a one-deep, rowlock pattern. Full rowlocks are used across the arch set on a solid, eight-inch wall.

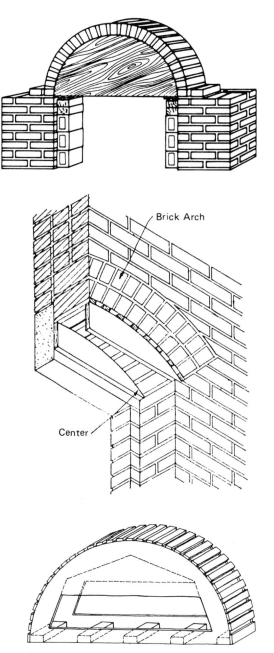

FIGURE 6–44
Shaped centers are used to support arch while it is being laid. (Bottom: Brick Associaton of North Carolina)

Two courses or rings of rowlocks are used in the arch. The two separate support abutments or piers must be constructed on each side before the center is installed. Note the radius stick that pivots from the center point underneath the arch. The radius stick is used to show the top (extrados) of the arch curve. It is marked for each course. After the center is in place, check the curve to make

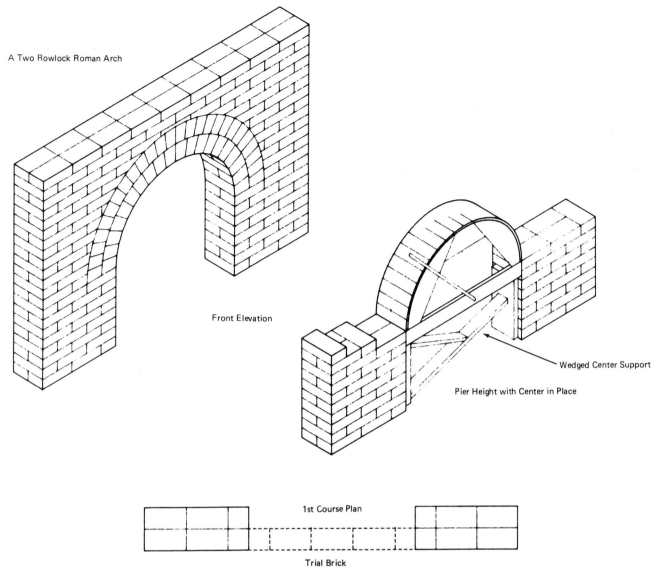

A Two Rowlock Roman Arch

Front Elevation

Wedged Center Support

Pier Height with Center in Place

1st Course Plan

Trial Brick

FIGURE 6-45
Circular arch with pier support. (Brick Institute of America)

sure it follows the detail drawings. Check the center for support. The support is designed so it is wedged in place and can easily be removed by knocking wedges apart.

It's a good idea before laying any brick to sketch out the relative position of the various brick used in the arch. Remember that the thickness of the joint will vary when brick are laid in an arch. Joints are thin at the soffit and thick at the top. Lay brick from both sides toward the center. As noted, piers should be built up on both sides, even to the bottom of the arch.

Dry Run

Lay out the arch brick in a dry run to determine how they will lay together in the first course or ring. One way to lay out the brick dry is to lay the center on its side on the ground, and then position the brick around the arch. This will show you the number of brick needed and the joint size. Joint thickness can be adjusted as needed so that the whole brick fits in. Pencil the joint location on the center as a guide. *Note*: You can also lay out the brick in a dry run on the center when it is in place.

Use wedge-shaped shims to hold the brick apart when placed on the curve of the center.

Placing Centers

Centers should be wedged in place and then plumbed and leveled. Check center in several places to make sure it is level throughout. Plumb the center front and back.

Laying Arch Brick

Lay from both ends. Remember that the head joint is thinner on the soffit end. No bed joint is used on the first course. Level and plumb brick as they are laid. Use the radius guide as a check on the brick position. A nail can be driven through the radius stick for each course as a guide to where the top of the brick should lay. Note that the *second* rowlock course is laid in a mortar bed. As a general rule, thin joints, normally $\frac{1}{4}$-inch, are used in arches.

Keystone

Normally an arch is designed with an odd number of brick or cut stones. This allows each side to be laid toward the center; the center brick or stone is called the *keystone*. Figure 6-46, for example, shows a brick rowlock arch with a cut stone used in the center as a keystone.

Finishing Wall

When the two courses of the rowlock arch are in place, leads should be continued up on both piers. Note that brick must be cut at an angle to fit against the curve at the top of the rowlock arch. These cut brick are called *creepers*. Use a foot rule to measure and mark the top and bottom lengths of the creepers. Creepers are cut on a masonry saw. Note that the angle of the creepers changes with each course. Lay in brick dry before cutting creepers.

Finish

After the wall is completed, clean and finish in the standard manner. Use concave joints. Do not remove the center until the mortar is completely set, which takes at least a week.

Tuckpointing

Since the bottom of the arch rested on the center, the joints will be rough and flush to the edge or face of the brick. These mortar joints may be finished by cutting the joint back $\frac{1}{2}$ inch and refilling. Then the joint may be concave finished.

FIREPLACES

Fireplaces are probably the most difficult structural element a bricklayer has to work with. Even

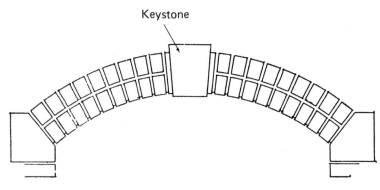

FIGURE 6-46
Arch with keystone.

when following the architect's detail drawings, the bricklayer may be called on to use his knowledge and experience to make a fireplace that is safe, workable, and has a good draft.

Figure 6–47 shows a section or cutaway view of a fireplace and chimney with the parts identified. The firebox or fire chamber is the area where the fire is built. It is lined with special firebrick. A damper controls the flow of smoke up the throat into the chimney flue. Some fireplaces, especially those over a basement, have an opening in the center of the back or inner hearth called an ash dump. The ash dump is opened to allow ashes to fall into the ash pit below the fire area. Note in Figure 6–47 that a special foundation or footing is required under the fireplace to support its weight. This is standard. The fireplace base is always located or built up from the reinforced concrete or masonry foundation.

Figure 6–48 shows brick fireplace details and how the parts are constructed. Note that a reinforced concrete slab is built under the outer hearth. This supports the masonry units in front of the fireplace.

For efficient fireplace design, a fresh air inlet is used, as shown in Figure 6–50. This allows outside air to be used for combustion and draft in the fireplace.

Most fireplaces are built with one single opening or face in the front. Fireplaces are also used with two or even three openings or faces, as shown in Figure 6–49. The detail drawings will show how the fireplace is to be built. The trade term for the fireplace opening is *face*.

Hearth

The hearth is the flat area on which the fire is built and a flat area or apron just in front of the fire area. The fire is built on the *inner hearth*; the area just in front of the fireplace is called the *outer hearth*. The inner hearth is made with firebrick. The outer hearth is commonly supported underneath by a reinforced concrete slab. It could also be supported by corbelled masonry. Figure 6–50 shows a fireplace with brick corbelling support under the outer hearth. With a fireplace opening of 6 square feet or less, the outer hearth should ex-

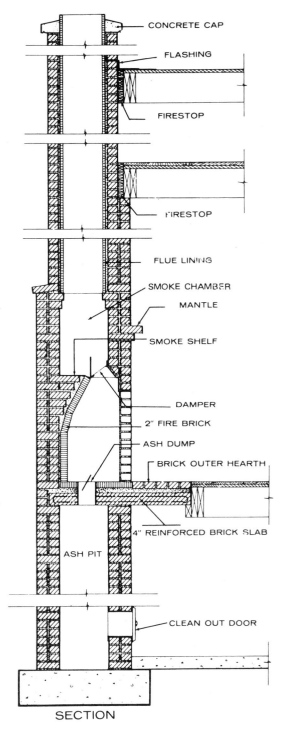

FIGURE 6–47
Brick fireplace and terminology. (Brick Institute of America)

tend at least 16 inches in front of the fireplace opening and at least 8 inches on each side of the opening. Various masonry units or flat stone are used to make the outer hearth.

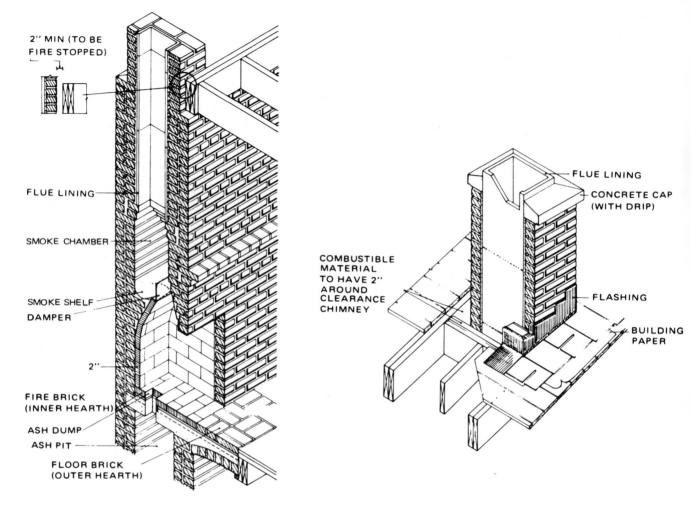

FIGURE 6-48
Brick fireplace details. (Brick Institute of America)

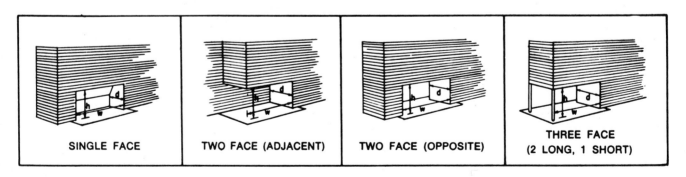

FIGURE 6-49
Basic fireplace openings or faces. (Brick Institute of America)

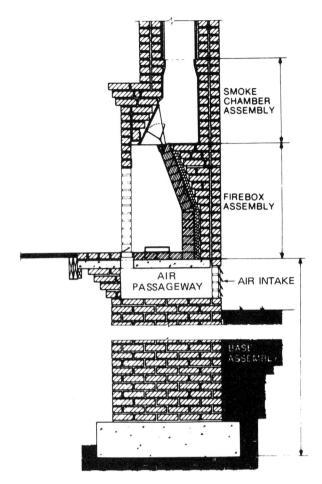

FIGURE 6-50
Fireplace with corbelled support under the outer hearth.
(Brick Institute of America)

FIGURE 6-51
Fireplace with raised hearth. (Brick Institute of America)

place is usually about two-thirds the height of the opening. The back of the fireplace is normally thirteen inches narrower than the front. This helps to guide the smoke toward the rear of the firebox or fire chamber where it then travels up through the throat and into the flue. Figure 6-52 gives recommended sizes to use when constructing the fireplace. The smoke chamber should be parged with fire-clay mortar (refractory mortar) on all sides. The firebox must be laid on all sides with firebrick. Codes require that fireplace walls and chimneys be separated from wood (or other combustible) construction by a two-inch air space.

A steel angle (lintel) is used to support the brick over the masonry opening. Figure 6-52 shows the location of steel lintel over the fireplace opening. Since steel angles expand much more than the brick, extra space must be provided for at each end of the angle for expansion. Fiberglass can be wrapped on the ends to provide expansion room (Figure 6-53). Angle ends should *not* be embedded in mortar.

Firebox or Combustion Chamber

The best fireplace construction uses a backup wall behind the firebrick. The backup wall of the firebox area is built with ordinary brick. Figure 6-54 shows the typical layout. Mortar fill is used to fill the void between the backup wall and the outside fireplace brick. A one-inch air space is left be-

In some cases a *raised hearth* is used, as shown in Figure 6-51. This is a design or architectural feature that creates a more attractive atmosphere in the room. The fire is raised to a higher level and is easier to see. The hearth must be tied to the raised fireplace to form an integrated whole. Some raised hearths may be enlarged and extended out on either side to form a seating area.

Fireplace Construction

As noted, the fireplace and the hearth are supported by a reinforced concrete slab and a footing or by corbelled masonry. The depth of the fire-

Conventional Fireplace Dimensions, Inches

A	B	C	D	E	F	G
24	24	16	11	14	19	8 x 12
26	24	16	13	14	21	8 x 12
28	24	16	15	14	21	8 x 12
30	29	16	17	14	24	12 x 12
32	29	16	19	14	24	12 x 12
36	29	16	23	14	27	12 x 12
40	29	16	27	14	29	12 x 16
42	32	16	29	14	32	16 x 16
48	32	18	33	14	37	16 x 16
54	37	20	37	16	45	16 x 16
60	37	22	42	16	45	16 x 20
60	40	22	42	16	45	16 x 20
72	40	22	54	16	56	20 x 20
84	40	24	64	20	61	20 x 24
96	40	24	76	20	75	20 x 24

Fireplace Details

Note: These Thumb Rules do not necessarily correspond to the above Conventional Fireplace Dimensions, but have proven, through experience, to work well for opening widths between 26" and 42".

Thumb Rules:

1) The height of the fireplace opening, (B), should be at least 6" less than the width of the fireplace opening, (A).

2) The back width of the firebox, (D), should be 1" less than the front width of the fireplace, (A)

3) The back height of the firebox, (E), should be no more than ½ the opening height of the fireplace, (B).

4) The height of the smoke chamber, (F), should be about equal to the height of the fireplace opening, (B).

Before building a fireplace and chimney, check with the local building codes.

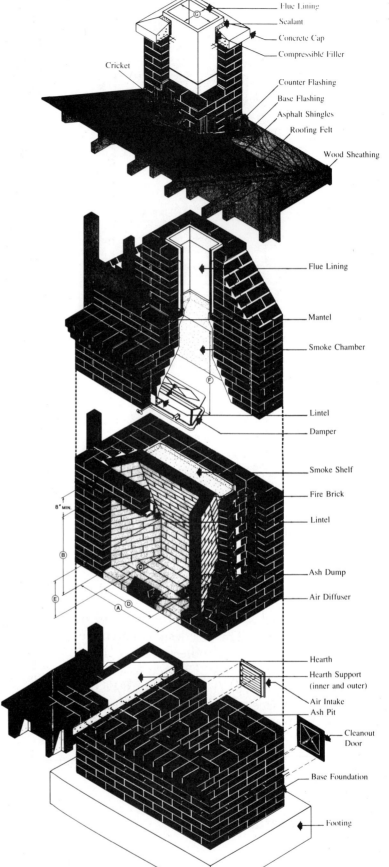

FIGURE 6–52

Recommended sizes for constructing a conventional fireplace. (Brick Institute of America)

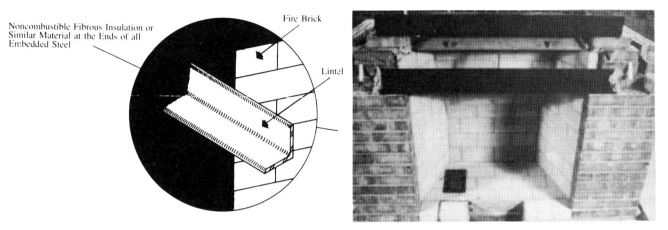

FIGURE 6-53
Steel lintel support is used over fireplace opening. Ends are wrapped in fiber insulation to allow expansion. (Brick Institute of America)

tween the backup wall and the firebrick. Fiberglass insulation is used to fill the air space between the backup wall and the firebrick. The firebrick is laid in with stretchers; the joints are broken.

Laying Firebrick

Be sure the firebrick is completely dry before laying in. Firebrick at least two inches thick must be used. Firebrick is laid with very thin joints. A special refractory mortar is used and mixed to a thin, watery consistency. Mortar is not troweled onto the firebrick. Rather, the firebrick is dipped into the mortar so all sides are covered except the exposed face. The firebrick is then immediately set into place. Use a bricklayer's hammer to tap the firebrick in so it is seated solidly. Firebrick should fit in very tightly to each other. Joints are broken so they do not line up. As noted, all sides of the fire box are laid with firebrick. A one-inch air space is left between the firebrick and the backup wall. The air space is filled from the top with fiberglass insulation after the walls have set. *Note:* No fire should be built in the fireplace for 30 days after it is built. This allows the mortar to completely dry out.

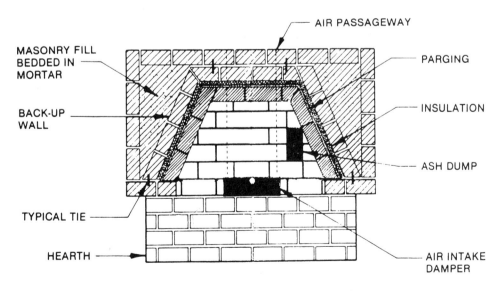

FIGURE 6-54
Firebox and combustion chamber layout. (Brick Institute of America)

Damper

Steel or cast iron dampers are used in all fireplaces to close off air flow when the fireplace is not in use. They are located in the throat just above the fire chamber. Dampers should be no less than eight inches above the fireplace opening. It is extremely important that a well-designed and tight-fitting damper be installed; otherwise air can flow in and out when the fireplace is not in use. Figure 6–52 shows a typical damper. Air flow can carry heat out of the house in winter or carry heat in during the summer. Various manufactured dampers are available, and they must be installed so they fit solidly and are airtight when closed. Figure 6–55 shows typical dampers. Follow the manufacturer's instructions for installation.

Dampers are installed in the forward part of the opening to the flue to allow room for the smoke shelf. Note that since the damper is metal, room must be provided for expansion when it is installed. The damper is sealed in the fresh mortar bed. Refractory mortar is used. A thin mortar bed is laid—just enough to level the damper and to

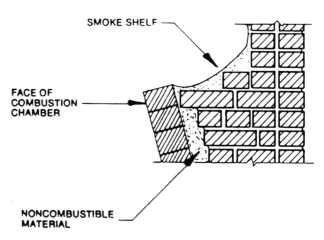

FIGURE 6–56
Smoke shelf. (Brick Institute of America)

create a seal to prevent smoke or air leakage. The damper is not embedded in the mortar; it is only seated.

Smoke Shelf

As mentioned, the smoke shelf is parged and lined with fire-clay mortar (refractory mortar). Figure 6–56 shows how the smoke shelf is formed and shaped. The smoke shelf is designed to allow the smoke to collect itself before going up the flue. However, the smoke shelf is primarily designed to prevent outside, down rushing air currents from forcing smoke back through the throat of the fire place and into the room. The curving shape of the smoke shelf is designed to turn any down rushing air currents back upward into the flue. The area above the smoke shelf is called the smoke chamber.

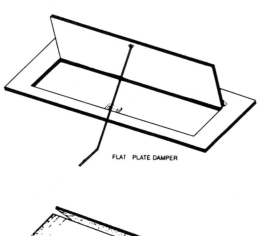

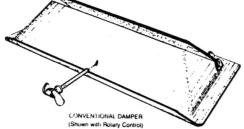

FLAT PLATE DAMPER

CONVENTIONAL DAMPER
(Shown with Rotary Control)

FIGURE 6–55
Typical dampers used in fireplace. (Brick Institute of America)

Flues

The flue starts just above the smoke chamber and continues all the way to the top of the chimney, as shown in Figure 6–47. Special flue tile is used to line the inside of the chimney. The tile is laid end to end with refractory mortar. By code, the flue tile must be at least $\frac{5}{8}$-inch thick. Flue linings must be able to resist temperatures of at least 1800°F

(980°C) without cracking. The flue tile liners should be surrounded by at least four inches of solid masonry. A flue is required for each fireplace or each heating element vented through the chimney.

The flue tile is installed as the chimney is built up. The flue liner is installed before the chimney brick are laid around it. One flue liner section is installed ahead of the brickwork. Sections are two feet long. End-to-end close fitting joints are required on the flue tile. The inside

must be left smooth so soot does not collect. A one-inch air space is required between the flue tile and the surrounding masonry.

Figure 6–57 shows how the flue liners are placed inside a brick chimney. Note that a chimney wall at least four inches thick is required around the flue. Note that the flue liner and chimney brick are sealed at the top of the chimney. Figure 6–57, bottom, shows how the base of the flue liner is supported. The brick end is corbelled over to support the base of the liner at the top of the smoke chamber.

In earthquake areas, such as California, steel reinforcement is required in the support around the flue liner. Figure 6–58 shows steel reinforcements used around a single and double flue brick chimney. This type of construction is required in seismic zones such as in California.

Chimneys

The chimney is made by laying masonry units around the flue (or flues). Nominal four-inch thick brick are used. (If a flue liner is not used, eight-inch thick walls must be used around the flue.)

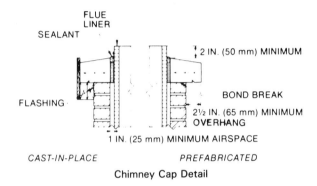
Chimney Cap Detail

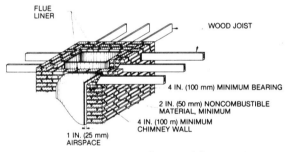
Chimney Used as a Structural Support

FIGURE 6–57
Flue liner installation details. (Brick Institute of America)

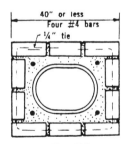
Single Flue Chimney

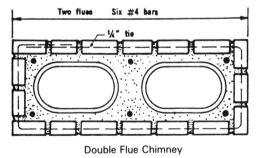
Double Flue Chimney

FIGURE 6–58
Reinforcement used in chimneys in earthquake areas. (Masonry Institute of America)

Figure 6–57 shows details on chimney construction.

In earthquake areas, as shown in Figure 6–58, the chimney brick are laid around the flues. Grout or mortar is poured into the void between the brick and the flue liner; vertical steel reinforcing rods are used in the void. Ties are used around the perimeter of the chimney every 18 inches vertically. The metal $\frac{1}{4}$-inch ties are set in the chimney

course bond. A $\frac{3}{8}$-inch tie or two $\frac{1}{4}$-inch ties may be used at 24-inch vertical intervals, instead of the single $\frac{1}{4}$-inch ties at 18-inch intervals.

For chimneys *outside* the building, anchors are used to secure the chimney to the building framework. Figure 6–59 shows how a single flue outside chimney is attached to the framework. The $\frac{1}{4}$-inch steel anchor straps are embedded in the grout around the flue; the other ends are bolted or screwed to the floor joists. The outside chimney is anchored at each floor and at the upper ceiling or roof line.

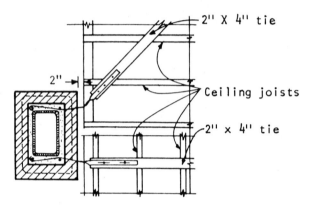

FIGURE 6–59
Anchor straps are used to anchor the outside chimney to the building framework.

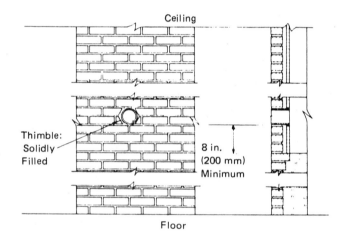

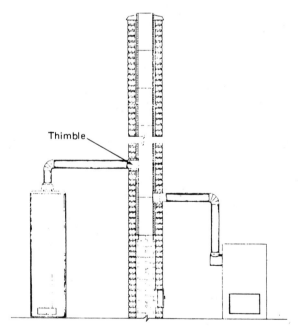

FIGURE 6–60
Appliance chimney with thimbles. (*Top and left: Brick Institute of America*)

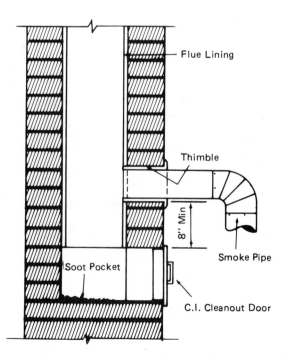

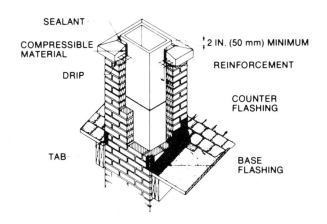

FIGURE 6–61
Flashing details of chimney. (Brick Institute of America)

Thimbles

Thimbles are used for appliance chimneys; that is, all chimneys that are not used with fireplaces. Appliance chimneys may serve only one or two appliances, such as a furnace or a boiler. They will have an opening to receive the smoke pipe from the appliance. A thimble fits into the opening into the side of the chimney and flue. The hole in the flue liner should be at least eight inches above the bottom edge of the flue lining. Boiler putty or asbestos cement is used to seat the thimble in the opening. The opening around the thimble must be completely sealed; it must be as airtight as possible. Metal smoke pipes from appliances, such as a furnace or boiler, connect into the chimney us-

ing the thimble (Figure 6–60). A cleanout door is installed at the base of the appliance chimney for removing soot.

Flashing

Where the chimney exits through the roof, flashing is required. The flashing is bonded to the side of the chimney and runs underneath the roof covering. Figure 6–61 shows flashing around the chimney. Note how flashing runs under the shingles. The top of flashing is bent and inserted into the brick joint. Flashing always overlaps each other. Flashing should be tuckpointed into the brick joint.

Chimney Cap

The top of the chimney should be finished with a cast-in-place or prefabricated concrete chimney cap, as shown in Figure 6–57, top. The cap is sloped to allow water runoff. Caps are recommended because they are moisture-tight.

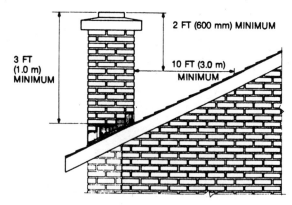

FIGURE 6–62
Chimney height guidelines. (Brick Institute of America)

Chimney Height

Most codes require that the chimney height either be three feet above the highest point where the chimney comes through the roof *or* two feet higher than any portion of the roof within ten feet of the chimney. Figure 6–62 shows chimney height guidelines.

Note: When there are two or more flues in a chimney, they must not be finished to the same height. If they are at the same height, smoke or fumes from one flue could be sucked down another flue. Allow for a distance of six inches between the tops of different flues.

Smoke Test

Once the chimney is completed, it should be tested for tightness and design. A smoke test can be made by burning crumpled paper in the opening to the chimney. This can be done by holding a crumpled piece of newspaper in your hand, but wear leather gloves! If there is a good draft, the smoke will be drawn into the thimble. If there is a poor draft, then the chimney is not high enough and should be built higher. The same test can be made in a fireplace. Remember, however, that a wood fire should not be burnt in the fireplace until the mortar is completely dry, which is approximately one month after completion.

The smoke test can also be used to check for tightness of the flue. Cover the top of the flue with a wet blanket, and then build a smoky paper fire. Any opening in the flue or masonry will show up in smoke leaks. Any leaks should be corrected immediately. There should be *no leaks!*

MANUFACTURED FIREPLACES

Metal, factory-built fireplaces are also used. Like all masonry fireplaces, the metal fireplace must be supported with a concrete footing. Also, prefabricated or pre-engineered fireplaces with designed masonry units are also used. The firebox of the fireplace is laid up with specially designed, modular refractory components, as shown in Figure 6–63, left. Once the manufactured fireplace is installed, it is surrounded with a veneer of brick. Figure 6–63, right, shows a manufactured metal fireplace installed. Manufactured fireplaces may use a fan to circulate heat from the fire. Round steel flues are often used for the metal fireplace.

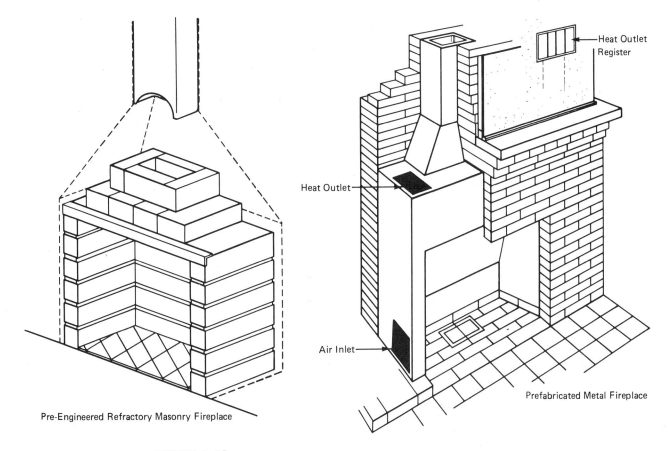

Heat Outlet Register

Heat Outlet

Air Inlet

Pre-Engineered Refractory Masonry Fireplace

Prefabricated Metal Fireplace

FIGURE 6–63
Manufactured fireplaces. (*Left:* Thermal Energy Storage Systems, Inc.)

PRACTICE: LAYING A ONE-FLUE CHIMNEY

Figure 6–64 shows a simple, one-flue appliance chimney with a thimble and cleanout door. This design is used to practice some of the layout techniques of chimney construction. A cleanout door is used at the base of the chimney to remove any soot that falls to the bottom. Two rectangular 8″ × 8″ × 24″ tile flue liners are used. A thimble hole is prepared in the bottom flue liner. The thimble hole is cut in the tile by standing the tile on end and packing it with sand. Using a compass, locate and draw a circle on the side of the tile for the thimble. Cut a small hole in the center of the circle with a chisel. Use a tile hammer or light brick hammer and tap away the tile inside the circle. (Since this is a practice chimney stack, dummy

flue liners made out of wood could be used.) Follow the steps below to lay a one-flue chimney:

Step 1. Lay bed course in full mortar bed. Align and level brick and check squareness of corner.

Step 2. Lay course 2, breaking joints as shown in the illustration. Note that only two course layouts are used, those for course 1 and course 2. Odd (course 1) and even (course 2) patterns are repeated to the top of the chimney.

Step 3. Lay courses 3 to 5 as shown and mortar in the cleanout door. Manufactured cleanout doors have flanges on the sides to receive the mortar and the side of the brick.

Step 4. Lay courses 6 to 8 as shown on the elevation and section views. Note the four cut

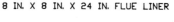
8 IN. X 8 IN. X 24 IN. FLUE LINER

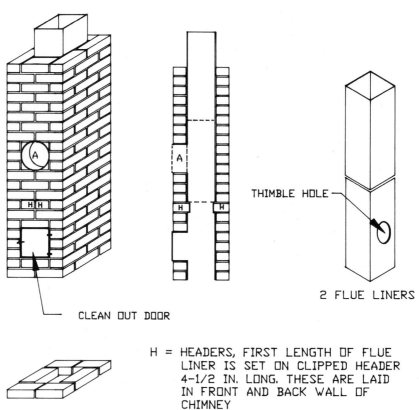

CLEAN OUT DOOR

THIMBLE HOLE

2 FLUE LINERS

H = HEADERS, FIRST LENGTH OF FLUE
    LINER IS SET ON CLIPPED HEADER
    4-1/2 IN. LONG. THESE ARE LAID
    IN FRONT AND BACK WALL OF
    CHIMNEY

A = THIMBLE

ISOMETRIC PLAN OF FIRST COURSE

FIGURE 6-64
One-flue chimney with thimble. (Brick Insitute of America)

headers, marked "H," used in course 8 to support the flue linings. Two headers each are used front and back. Course 8 is laid in around the base of the flue lining with the thimble hole. Use a level to check the plumb of the sides of the chimney stack.

Step 5. Continue and lay courses 9, 10, and 11. These are needed to support the headers in course 8 when the liner is installed. Allow mortar to set before going on.

Step 6. Set in the flue liner with the thimble. Lay refractory mortar on the headers and set the liner in. Carefully plumb the liner. Clean off

any mortar that is squeezed out over the end of the liner.

Step 7. Continue the courses to and around the thimble. Ordinarily, the sides of the liner are not mortared to the brick in an appliance chimney. A space is left between the lining and the inside chimney walls, except at the base support. Depending on the size of the thimble used, you will have to cut brick to fit around the opening. Set the thimble in a thick bed of mortar and cut off the excess. Refractory mortar should be used. Mortar must completely surround the thimble so there is no air space. Cut off excess mortar; strike the inside of the lining smooth of mortar.

Step 8. Lay the second flue liner to the top end of the first liner. Refractory mortar should be used. The mortar joint should be struck smooth inside the liner. Plumb the liner.

Step 9. Continue the brick bond to near the top of the second liner as shown. Approximately six inches of the liner top is left exposed. This leaves enough height to finish the chimney. The chimney top is finished by installing a chimney cap and sealing the space between the inside of the cap opening and the side of the flue liner.

PAVING BRICK

Brick paving is used both inside for floors and outside for patios, sidewalks, driveways, and so forth. Special, very hard paving brick is recommended since it will wear better. Two types of paving are used: mortared and mortarless.

Mortared Paving

In mortared paving, the brick are set in a mortar that is laid on top of a concrete base; the joints between the brick are also mortared. Mortared paving is commonly referred to as *rigid paving* because it is set on top of a reinforced concrete slab.

Figure 6–65 shows brick laid in mortar on a reinforced concrete base. The concrete slab is set on a gravel base for drainage. A $\frac{1}{2}$-inch mortar bed is used on top the slab to level and bond the brick to the base. Note in Figure 6–65 that a brick edging is used at the side of the brick paving. Edging is always used around the perimeter of the paved area.

A type M mortar is used between the brick. If brick are set wide apart, the brick are buttered with the mortar and set together. More commonly, the brick are set close together, around $\frac{1}{4}$ inch apart. Sand and dry cement are then swept between the cracks. A broom is used to sweep the dry sand and cement mixture between the brick cracks. When the cracks are full of the dry mixture, the area is sprayed with a fine mist of water until the brick and mortar mixture are thoroughly wet. This is an easy way to make the mortar joints. However, the bond between the units will be less strong than that of units buttered in mortar.

Note: Any brick paving that is laid outside must be laid at a slope so the water will run off. Walks and driveways should be slightly higher down the center. This will allow water to run off both sides. The high point in the center of the driveway is called the *crown*.

Mortared paving can also be used for floors inside the building, as shown in Figure 6–66. Here the brick floor is laid over a rough floor supported by wood joists. The mortar bed is laid over a poly-

FIGURE 6–65
Paving brick laid in mortar over reinforced concrete base. (Brick Institute of America)

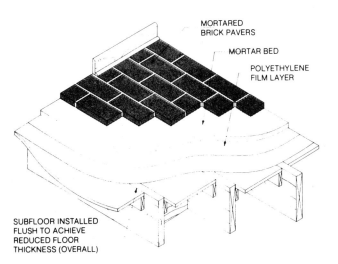

MORTARED
BRICK PAVERS

MORTAR BED

POLYETHYLENE
FILM LAYER

SUBFLOOR INSTALLED
FLUSH TO ACHIEVE
REDUCED FLOOR
THICKNESS (OVERALL)

FIGURE 6–66
Paving brick laid in mortar over wood frame. (Brick Institute of America)

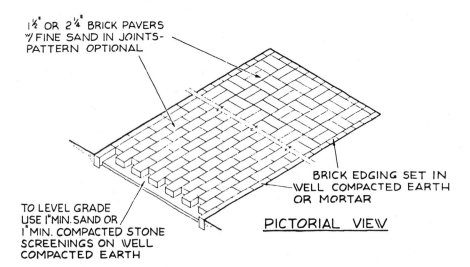

1½" OR 2¼" BRICK PAVERS
⅍FINE SAND IN JOINTS-
PATTERN OPTIONAL

BRICK EDGING SET IN
WELL COMPACTED EARTH
OR MORTAR

TO LEVEL GRADE
USE 1"MIN. SAND OR
1"MIN. COMPACTED STONE
SCREENINGS ON WELL
COMPACTED EARTH

PICTORIAL VIEW

FIGURE 6-67
Mortarless paving brick are laid in sand base over compacted earth. (Brick Association of North Carolina)

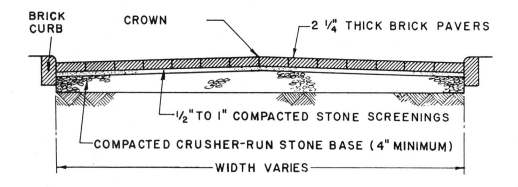

BRICK
CURB

CROWN

2¼" THICK BRICK PAVERS

½" TO 1" COMPACTED STONE SCREENINGS

COMPACTED CRUSHER-RUN STONE BASE (4" MINIMUM)

WIDTH VARIES

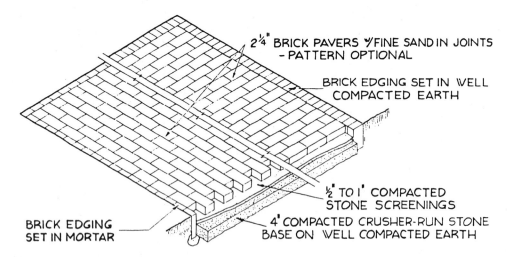

2¼" BRICK PAVERS ⅍FINE SAND IN JOINTS
- PATTERN OPTIONAL

BRICK EDGING SET IN WELL
COMPACTED EARTH

½" TO 1" COMPACTED
STONE SCREENINGS

BRICK EDGING
SET IN MORTAR

4" COMPACTED CRUSHER-RUN STONE
BASE ON WELL COMPACTED EARTH

FIGURE 6-68
Driveway laid with mortarless paving brick. (Brick Association of North Carolina)

ethylene film. Brick are laid in with buttered mortar joints.

Mortarless Paving

In mortarless paving, the brick are set on a sand or compacted stone base. The sand or crushed stone base is commonly called a *flexible base*. Mortarless paving is commonly referred to as *flexible paving*. Flexible brick paving allows surface water to seep into the subgrade. Figure 6–67 shows a brick sidewalk or patio set on a sand base. Two different brick patterns are shown. About an inch of sand is used. Sand is brushed into the cracks between the brick. You can spray the paving with a fine mist of water to compact the sand in the joints. Note that a brick edging is used along the side of the sidewalk or patio. Edging is essential and must be used in paving; otherwise the brick will move and spread apart.

Figure 6–68, top, shows a cross-sectional view of a driveway laid with mortarless brick. Crushed stone is used as a bed. Note how the center of the driveway is raised to make the crown. Crowns are required on all driveways to allow water runoff. Any large brick area must be sloped so water will run off. Figure 6–68, bottom, shows two different

brick patterns commonly used for driveways. Note in Figure 6–68 that curbs are used on each side of the driveway. The brick are packed tight against each other and then sand is scattered over the top and swept into the cracks. Figure 6–69 shows a driveway being laid. Note that the mason hammers the brick tight to each other. Tightness prevents movement or shifting. Note also that a line is used as a guide in laying the brick.

Mortarless paving can also be used inside, either on a wood or a concrete slab base. Figure 6–70 shows mortarless brick paving laid on a wood floor (top) or on a concrete slab (bottom). Asphalt roofing felt layers are used as a base. Fine sand is swept between the brick joints.

Mortarless paving brick are also laid into an asphalt or bituminous setting bed. This type of setting bed is called a *semi-rigid base*. The asphalt bed is normally poured over a concrete base or slab, as shown in Figure 6–71. The paving brick are set into the bituminous setting and leveling bed in the same way as into sand or crushed rock. No mortar is used; brick pavers are installed hand-tight. Sand may be used to fill in any cracks left between the brick. Bituminous bases are used for paving brick in public areas. Brick pavers are also laid over an existing asphalt base; for example, an asphalt driveway or roadway.

FIGURE 6–69
Laying paving brick in driveway. (Brick Association of North Carolina)

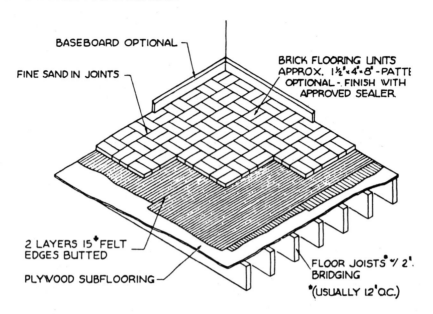

BASEBOARD OPTIONAL

FINE SAND IN JOINTS

BRICK FLOORING UNITS
APPROX. 1½"×4"×8" -PATTE
OPTIONAL - FINISH WITH
APPROVED SEALER.

2 LAYERS 15° FELT
EDGES BUTTED

PLYWOOD SUBFLOORING

FLOOR JOISTS °×2'.
BRIDGING

°(USUALLY 12'O.C.)

BRICK FLOOR ON WOOD SUPPORT SYSTEM

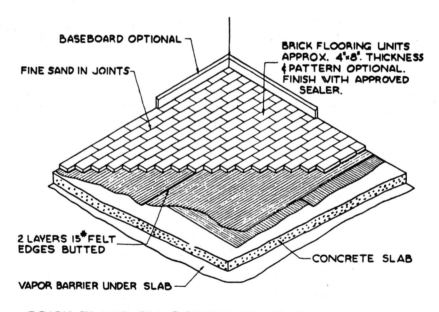

BASEBOARD OPTIONAL

FINE SAND IN JOINTS

BRICK FLOORING UNITS
APPROX. 4"×8". THICKNESS
& PATTERN OPTIONAL.
FINISH WITH APPROVED
SEALER.

2 LAYERS 15° FELT
EDGES BUTTED

CONCRETE SLAB

VAPOR BARRIER UNDER SLAB

BRICK FLOOR ON CONCRETE SLAB

FIGURE 6-70
Mortarless paving brick laid over wood floor (*top*) and concrete slab (*bottom*).
(Brick Association of North Carolina)

Brick Patterns

A wide number of brick patterns may be used, often in combination with each other. Figure 6-72 shows some of the common patterns used.

Note how the circular and running bond patterns can be combined together for an effective, eye-appealing design. Figure 6-73 shows an attractive, well-designed use of a basic brick pattern for an inner-city park, fountain, and walkway.

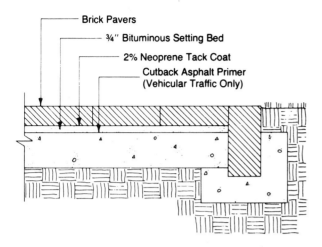

FIGURE 6-71
Brick pavers laid on bituminous setting bed. (Brick Institute of America)

Laying Hints

The key condition for laying brick pavers is the proper preparation of the base. A well-drained base is essential to any brick paving. In wet areas, use crushed gravel under the concrete slab for mortared paving. Always slope the concrete slab or the sand so that there is drainage. A slope of $\frac{1}{8}$-inch or $\frac{1}{4}$-inch per foot is usually sufficient. A driveway should have a crown in the center. Always use an edging around the brick paving.

When laying, use a straightedge to check that the brick lay level with each other. A line can be stretched to show where the top of the brick should run. Start laying at a corner and work toward another corner. Tap the brick down so they are solidly set into the base. A 2″ × 4″ or 2″ × 6″ can be laid over several brick, and they can be tapped down together. This assures that they

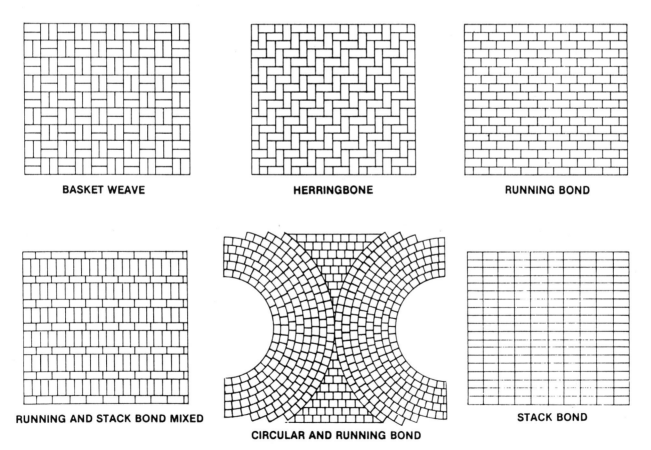

BASKET WEAVE   HERRINGBONE   RUNNING BOND

RUNNING AND STACK BOND MIXED   CIRCULAR AND RUNNING BOND   STACK BOND

FIGURE 6-72
Common paving patterns. (Brick Institute of America)

FIGURE 6–73
Paving brick used for walkway in park. (Higgins Brick Co.)

are even and level to each other; it also prevents damage to the brick. The board protects the brick from the hammer. When tapping individual brick, tap with the hammer handle end. If one brick is low in a mortarless paving, you can always take it out and add more sand underneath it.

Mortarless brick paving can be used as soon as its completed. Mortared paving should not be used until the mortar has completely set.

PRACTICE: LAYING BRICK PAVING

Figure 6–74 shows a simple running bond confined in a set area, as for a small patio or outdoor cooking area. A wooden box is made from 2″ × 6″s for the practice; the box is square, designed to hold five brick lengths. The size of the box will

vary, depending on the size of the brick used. Note that the floor slopes down from the top right to the bottom and left. The high, top right corner is $\frac{3}{4}$ inch above the top of the box; the bottom right corner is $\frac{1}{2}$ inch above; the top left corner is $\frac{1}{4}$ inch above; and the bottom left corner is level with the top of the box. Careful layout will be necessary to achieve these specifications. The brick are laid mortarless in a sand base. After all brick are laid, sand will be brushed into the joints. Follow the steps below to lay brick paving:

Step 1. Box should be almost filled with sand. Shift sand to form high sides, to the front and top right. Roofing felt or polyethylene film can be used to form a more even bed.

Step 2. Place brick in all four corners; position according to the layout shown in Figure 6–74. Measure height of corner brick above the top of the boards. Add or remove sand to reach the re-

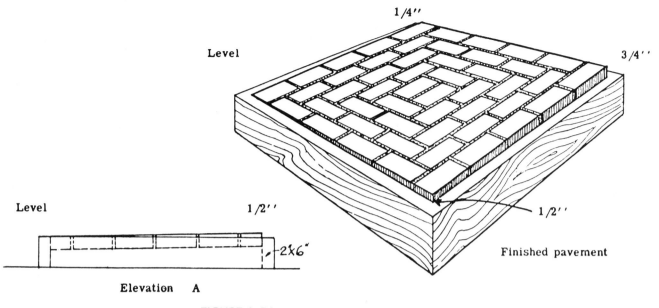

FIGURE 6-74
Brick paving project. (Brick Institute of America)

quired height. Sand should be even inside the box, sloping toward the low corner. Elevation A shows the slope on the left side.

Step 3. Lay brick as shown on the outside completely around the box. Check level with a straightedge. String can be stretched from corner to corner to make sure all brick are even.

Step 4. Continue laying courses of brick and checking slope and evenness.

Step 5. Finish paving area with the two closure brick in the center. Check level.

Step 6. Finish by brushing sand into the joints between the brick. Fill all cracks and sweep off any sand left over.

STEPS

Brick steps are used mostly outside with brick sidewalks and walkways. Brick steps are frequently used at the front entrance of brick houses, as shown in Figure 6-75. They are also used inside the building when brick paving is used. All steps

have two parts: the tread and the riser. The *tread* is the horizontal surface you step on; the *riser* is the vertical support for the tread. The tread should be at least 12 inches wide.

FIGURE 6-75
Brick step used at house entry. (Brick Institute of America)

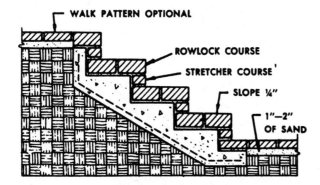

FIGURE 6–76
Brick steps laid over concrete foundation. (Brick Institute of America)

Brick steps are laid on a concrete base or composed completely of brick or masonry. Figure 6–76 shows brick steps laid over a stepped concrete foundation. Curbs are built on both sides of the steps, although the curb on the near side has been removed to show the construction. Brick are laid in mortar spread over the concrete base. Treads are made by laying brick flat, side by side.

The steps run directly into the brick sidewalk, which is laid in a running bond pattern.

Figure 6–77 shows much more complex brick steps. These are decorative stairs used at the main entrance to a house. The 12-inch treads are made with rowlock brick. Rowlocks are laid over flat brick to give a 7-inch riser on the step. Note the complexity of the corners of the tread. This would be difficult to cut and lay. Cutting with exact angles would have to be done on a masonry saw. However, this complex corner is made using 8″ × 8″ × 4″ factory-made corners available from most brick manufacturers. A type S mortar is specified for these brick steps.

SOLAR THERMAL STORAGE

Masonry walls and floors (both masonry units and reinforced concrete) also play a very important role in solar heating. The mass of the masonry wall

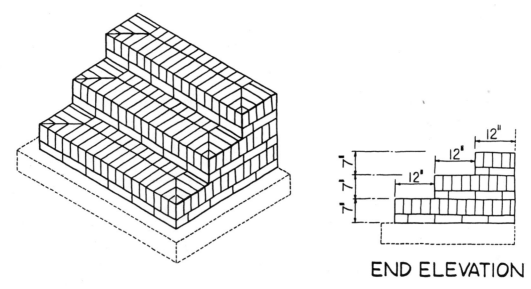

FIGURE 6–77
Decorative brickwork used for entry steps. (Brick Association of North Carolina)

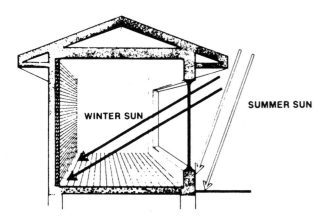

FIGURE 6-78
Direct passive solar heating. Heat is stored in the brick thermal wall at the rear. (Illinois Department of Energy Conservation)

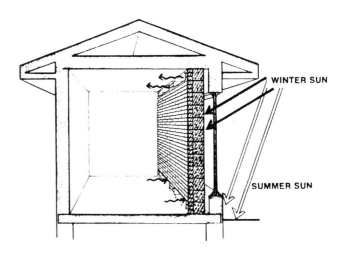

FIGURE 6-79
Indirect passive solar heating. Sun's heat is collected in the thermal wall by the window. (Illinois Department of Energy Conservation)

or floor is used to store the sun's heat. The sun's heat is stored in the masonry mass during the daylight hours; this is called thermal storage. At night, the heat stored in the masonry radiates out to heat the living area. Figure 6-78 shows a simple passive solar heating layout. During the daylight hours, the heat is collected in the brick masonry mass or thermal storage wall at the rear. At night the collected heat radiates out to warm the area. The windows of the building must be oriented southward, of course, to take advantage of the low winter sun. Figure 6-79 illustrates the same principle using a massive brick storage wall located alongside the window area. Again, during the day the heat of the sun is collected in the thermal storage wall. The wall radiates out heat to warm the area at night. Vents or openings are designed into the wall to allow heat flow and circulation around the wall and into the living area. Of course, it is very important that the window glass area be well insulated to prevent heat loss through the glass during the night. Most passive solar heating designs require an insulative covering over the glass area at night. This prevents heat loss. Figure 6-80 shows a detail of a brick thermal storage wall.

A typical use of a masonry thermal wall is shown in Figure 6-81. Here a greenhouse is used with a thermal wall behind it. This type of construction is called a sunspace.

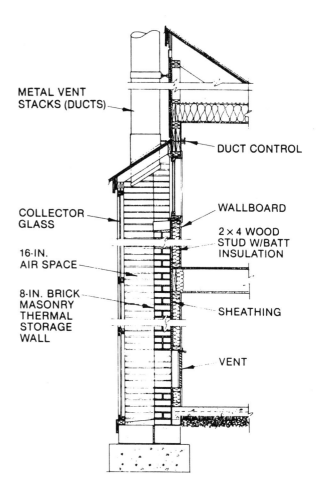

FIGURE 6-80
Brick thermal storage wall. (Brick Institute of America)

FIGURE 6-81
Sunspace with thermal storage wall. (U.S. Department of Energy)

CHAPTER REVIEW

QUESTIONS

1. What is a brick column? How does it support a load? How is reinforcement used?

2. What is a pier? How are piers used in garden walls?

3. What is a pilaster? How is it used?

4. What is a chase?

5. How are intersecting walls laid together?

6. How are cavity walls built?

7. What special techniques are used with mortar in cavity wall construction?

8. How are weep holes made in cavity walls?

9. How is insulation used in cavity walls?

10. What is RBM? How are RBM elements made?

11. What is low-lift grouting?

12. What is high-lift grouting?

13. What is corbelling and why is it used?

14. What are sills? Jambs? Heads?

15. How are brick laid to the jambs?

16. What kinds of lintels are used over openings?

17. How are lintels installed over openings?

18. Describe how steel lintels are installed. What precautions must be taken when installing steel lintels?

19. What specifications are used to describe the type of arch needed?

20. Identify the following arches:

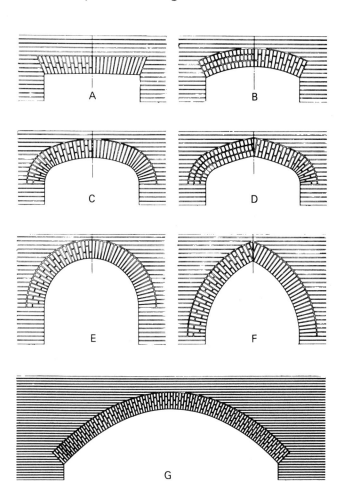

21. What is the skew angle?

22. Define the following terms: crown, extrados, intrados, rise, soffit, span.

23. Write the missing terms used to describe an arch:

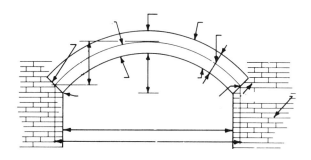

24. How are joints made in arches using conventional brick?

25. What are centers? How are they used?

26. How can a dry run be made for the first course of the arch?

27. What are creepers?

28. Why may tuckpointing be done in an arch?

29. Identify the missing terms used to identify a fireplace:

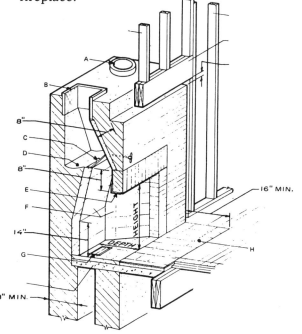

30. How is a fireplace supported?

31. What is the hearth?

32. Describe how firebrick are laid in the fire chamber.

33. What is the smoke shelf? How is it constructed and what is its purpose?

34. What precautions must be followed in installing the angle iron lintel and in placing the metal damper?

35. How is flue tile reinforced in the chimney?

36. Describe how a single flue appliance chimney and flue are constructed.

37. What support or anchorage is needed for chimneys built on the outside of the house?

38. What is a thimble? Why is it used? How is it installed?

39. Describe how chimney tops are finished.

40. Describe how mortared paving is installed Mortarless paving.

ACTIVITIES

1. Practice your bricklaying knowledge and techniques with the projects covered earlier in this chapter.
   a. Hollow brick pier (Figure 6–5)
   b. Intersecting wall (Figure 6–9)
   c. 10″ cavity wall (Figure 6–19)
   d. Corbelled 12-inch wall (Figure 6–27)
   e. Circular arch (Figure 6–45)
   f. One-flue chimney (Figure 6–64)
   g. Floor paving (Figure 6–74)

2. Sketch A shows a solid garden wall laid out in a diamond pattern. The diamonds are made using dark brick. Cut brick and lay out the bed course dry before laying in mortar. Lay a four-course lead at each end of the wall. Finish courses and lay another four-course lead; repeat this procedure until the wall is completed. Align, level, and plumb the wall as you work on it.

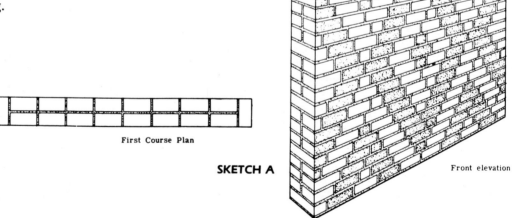

First Course Plan

SKETCH A

Front elevation

3. Sketch B shows the layout for running bond paving. Locate the four corner bricks to the levels shown. Use a straightedge as a guide between corners. When completed, fill joints with sand and sweep off the surface.

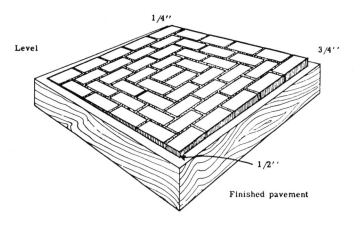

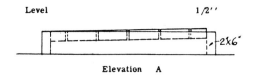

Elevation   A

SKETCH B

Chapter 7

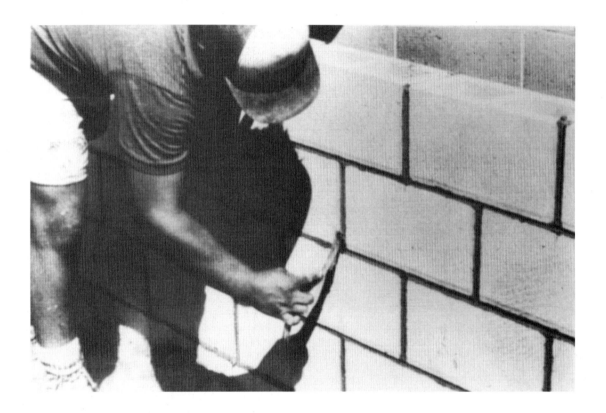

CONCRETE BLOCK MASONRY

After studying this chapter you should be able to:

- Describe and demonstrate the basic techniques for working with concrete block.
- Demonstrate the techniques of aligning, leveling, and plumbing.
- Explain the construction and installation techniques for columns, piers, pilasters, recesses and chases, anchor bolts, bond beams, joist ends, beams, dry bond, capping, flashing, control joints, fireplaces, and paving.
- Explain how reinforced concrete block walls are constructed.
- Explain how wall openings are laid in concrete block walls.
- Explain how insulation is used in concrete block walls.

FIGURE 7-1
To work efficiently, you need a well laid out work area. Mortar and block must be located within easy reach. (Non-Stop scaffolding)

Concrete block is widely used in commercial and industrial construction. Often, the concrete block is used for backing for other exteriors or finishes such as brick or tile. Decorative concrete block or grill block is also very popular for garden walls or sun screens. Many of the techniques for building with block are the same as for brick. However, many building techniques are unique to concrete block and they must be studied separately. As with any trade, the most important aspect of the job is good planning and organization. Good planning starts with the layout of the concrete block and mortar at your work station. Figure 7-1 shows work areas laid out for efficient work. Both mortar and concrete block should be within easy reach and should not require you to walk away from where you are working. Always plan your job before starting work.

BASIC TECHNIQUES

Concrete block is placed in the same manner as other masonry units. The face edge of the wall or other building element is located on the footing and a chalk line is snapped to show the edge. Corners are located by dropping a plumb bob down from surveyed building lines. They are located by batter boards at the corners, as shown earlier in Figures 5-20 to 5-23. A chalk line is snapped from corner to corner to locate the face edge of the wall. Figure 7-2 shows concrete block laid to the corner.

Most concrete block walls are laid in a running bond with joints broken and centered. When laying block, the voids must fall so vertical reinforcement, if used, can run up through the block (Figure 7-3). Stacked bond is also used with reinforcement. Stack bond is frequently used outside as a decorative wall. Mortar joints are laid with a $\frac{3}{8}$-inch thickness.

Dry Run

Corners and outside wall lines are established by locating and snapping chalk lines. These guidelines are used when laying the block. Lay out the block dry in the first course to check any problems. Leave about $\frac{3}{8}$-inch between block for the

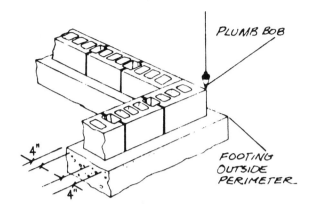

FIGURE 7-2
Block is laid to guidelines marked on the footing or slab.
(American Plywood Association)

FIGURE 7-3
Block laid out so vertical steel reinforcement runs up
through center of the cells or cores. Space is left here between the block so a steel column can be placed.

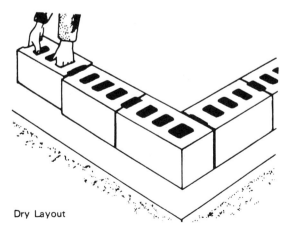

Dry Layout

FIGURE 7-4
Dry layout of block is made working from the corner. (National Concrete Masonry Association)

head joint. This is done by inserting a $\frac{3}{8}$-inch board
or piece of plywood between the block. The cor-
ner, as shown in Figure 7-4, should be laid with a
corner block that has a plain end. Other block in
the wall are the standard stretcher block with two
ears at each end.

Cutting

Laying out the first course of the wall in a dry run
allows you to prepare for or correct any problems.
If concrete block must be cut, use a hammer and
chisel or a masonry saw. If a hammer and chisel are
used, mark, with a pencil, a line on both sides of
the block where the break should be made. Then,
tapping the chisel with a hammer, cut a score following the line. Score on both sides. Keep tapping
at the score line until the block breaks (Figure
7-5). Take your time. On the job, and in trade
work, a masonry saw (Figure 7-6) is commonly
used. Always mark where the saw cut should be
made. Half-length concrete block units are available and should be used when needed to avoid unnecessary cutting. Always wear eye protection
when cutting.

Mortar

Mortar for concrete block is mixed stiffer than
other mortars, as for brick. The reason for this is

FIGURE 7-5
Breaking block with chisel and hammer. (National Concrete
Masonry Association)

FIGURE 7-6
Cutting block with masonry saw. (National Concrete Masonry Association)

FIGURE 7-7
Furrowing mortar bed for concrete block. (National Concrete Masonry Association)

that a stiffer mortar is needed to support the weight of the block.

Mortar Bed

A trowel-load of mortar is cut from the mortar pile in the same manner as for brick. A full bed course is laid and furrowed for the first course of concrete block (Figure 7–7). A much wider mortar bed is required for block than for brick. Lay the bed about 1-inch thick and about 2 inches wider than the block being laid. Lay out a bed long enough for two or three blocks. The second and subsequent courses, however, only have mortar laid for the face shell of the block, as shown in Figure 7–8. This is called *face shell bedding*. Note that mortar is *not* laid for the cross webs in concrete block walls. (Full mortar bedding, however, including the cross webs, is sometimes required for concrete block laid into columns, piers, and pilasters.) The head joint is made by buttering the face shell ends or ears. Use about $\frac{3}{4}$ inch of mortar. Figure 7–8, top, shows how the ends are buttered. The block with buttered ends is then laid into the mortar bed and shoved into place against the block already in place.

There is one requirement in laying block that should be followed. Since the block are made in molds, the side on the bottom of the mold is

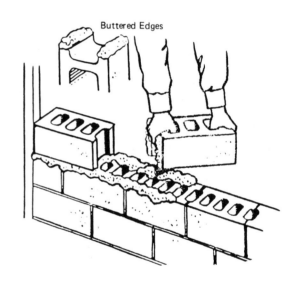

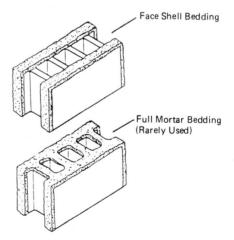

Buttered Edges

Face Shell Bedding

Full Mortar Bedding (Rarely Used)

FIGURE 7-8
Laying mortar on the block. (*Top:* Marshalltown Trowel Company; *bottom:* National Concrete Masonry Association)

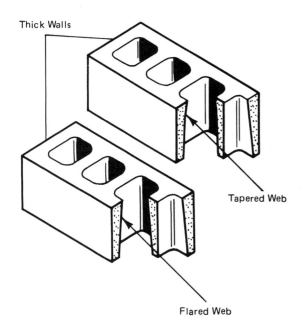

FIGURE 7–9
The thicker or flared side of the block is always laid facing upward. (National Concrete Masonry Association)

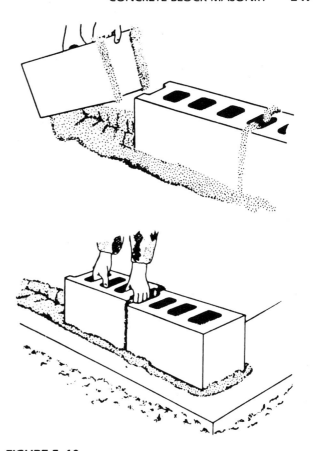

FIGURE 7–10
The block is held by the cross webs while being positioned into place.

slightly smaller than the side at the top of the mold. This allows the completed block to be easily removed from the mold. The side with the thicker or wider face shell or web should be facing upward. This allows a wider base for mortar and makes it easier to lay the next block on top of the wider bed for a good seat and bond. Figure 7–9 shows how the concrete block size or thickness varies. The shell and web will either be tapered or flared, depending on the type of mold used when casting. The wider or flared side should always be laid facing up.

Remember: The second course and all other higher courses have mortar placed only on the outside face shell. Cross webs are not normally mortared.

Laying the Block

The block is laid into the base mortar following the chalk guidelines and the dry layout. A wide bed mortar base is required for concrete block. Pick up the block by the cross webs, as shown in Figure 7–10, and position into place. *Remember:* Pick the block up on the bed that has the thicker cross web and face shell. This side must face up

when laid. It is easier to lift the block holding onto the thick side. Cut off excess mortar from the bed joints and use for the next head joint. Figure 7–11 shows a cross-sectional view of the block set in the

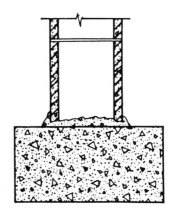

FIGURE 7–11
The bed mortar should extend out beyond the sides of the block.

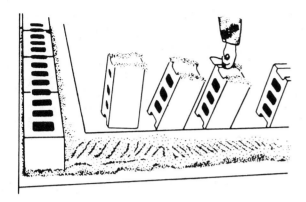

FIGURE 7–12
For efficiency, you can butter three or four block at once and then lay in sequence.

mortar bed. Note that the mortar extends well beyond the face shell of the block.

When laying block, it saves time to lay out a full mortar bed for several block and butter the ends on three or four block, as shown in Figure 7–12. Use a thick, buttered joint of approximately 3/4 inch. Buttering saves time since you can quickly lay several buttered block at a time, one after the other.

When laying the block, keep the buttered end pointed upward until it is moved just over and beside where it is to be laid. Then lower it into place and shove it gently against the end of the already laid block. When doing this, tip the block slightly toward you so you can see the outside edge of the block on which you are laying. This helps as a guide when aligning on the course below. When handling the block, move with a slow, steady motion; set the block down and shove it into place gently. Careful movements are important to prevent the buttered mortar from falling off. If it does fall off, re-butter and try again.

Note: Unlike brick, concrete block is always laid dry. Never hose or wet down concrete masonry units. Always keep covered on the job so they are not exposed to rain or snow.

Trowel Techniques

On the job, the mason always uses the most efficient, fastest technique. Try these tested techniques:

1. Lay a long mortar bed of at least five or six block.

2. Butter the block ends or ears and lay in the block.

3. Cut off the squeezed mortar. Use this mortar for buttering. For efficiency, try buttering the already laid block. Butter both ears. This way you can lay in an unbuttered block.

Note: It is important *not* to return excess mortar to the mortar pile. Use it on mortar units to be laid. Either butter the laid unit or butter a unit to be laid.

4. When buttering the ears of a stretcher block, butter with *one* trowel-load. Cut half of a trowel load on one ear; then cut the other half on the other ear. This technique may take some practice.

5. Solid or four-inch block can be buttered like large brick. Butter on the end before laying. Lay four-inch solid block in a furrowed bed.

Note: When first learning basic techniques, study your movements to try to find the fastest and most efficient method. Better yet, watch an experienced mason while he is working. Carefully study his motions and techniques—then copy his methods. Start out slowly; then work up to speed. Have your work techniques and finished work checked to make sure you are doing it right.

Checking Layout

After laying three or four block, the alignment of the block should be checked, as shown in Figure 7–13, top left. Use a level or straightedge for aligning. Use a level to check the level (Figure 7–13, bottom) and plumb (Figure 7–13, right). (When leveling, check both lengthwise and crosswise for each block.) Correct any misalignment by tapping with the trowel to level or align.

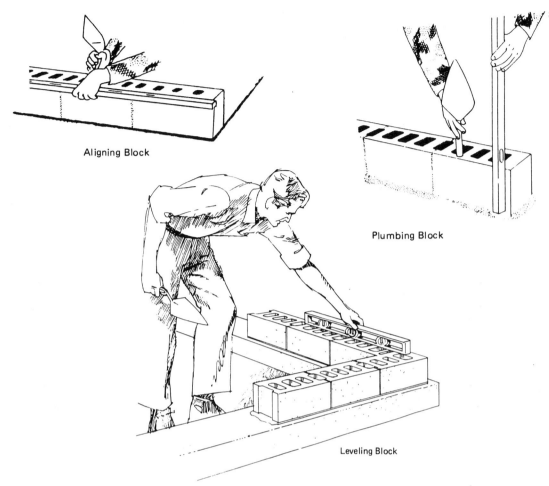

Aligning Block

Plumbing Block

Leveling Block

FIGURE 7-13
After several block are laid, check alignment, plumb, and level. (*Bottom:* Hyde Manufacturing Company)

Laying Leads

Corners should be carefully built up with leads to serve as a guide for the courses. Running bond is used and the corner block alternated from each side or leg of the lead, as shown in Figure 7-14. This allows head joints to center over the middle of stretcher block above and below. Take care to align, level, and plumb each corner. Figure 7-15 shows a completed lead being checked. Also, you should measure the height to be sure each corner has the same height. Figure 7-16 shows height and location of bed joints being checked with a story pole. Bed joint markings are made eight inches apart. The racking can be checked by laying a level or straightedge diagonally along the

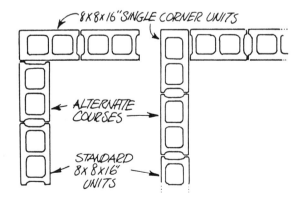

FIGURE 7-14
Corner block alternate from course to course. (National Concrete Masonry Association)

FIGURE 7-15
Checking vertical plumb of completed lead. (National Concrete Masonry Association)

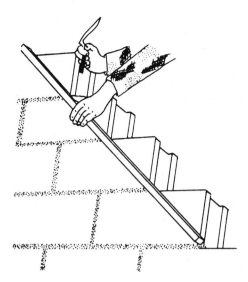

FIGURE 7-17
Racking the blocks.

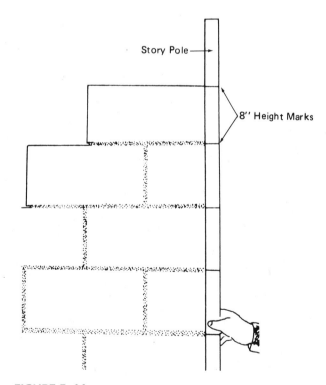

FIGURE 7-16
Checking corner height and bed joint location with story pole. Pole is marked with 8″ height marks.

outside corners of the block, as shown in Figure 7-17. Check the square of the corner with a right angle square. Opposing corners or leads should be exactly in line with each other. The chalk line should guarantee that leads are on line with each other.

Mason's Line

Once the two corner leads are constructed, a mason's line is stretched between the two corners (Figure 7-18). The block between the two leads is laid using the line as a guide (Figure 7-19). Lay to $\frac{1}{16}$ inch from the top of the line.

Closure

At the center of the course, between the two leads, the closure is made by buttering both ends of the block *and* the ends of the stretcher block already in place (Figure 7-20). This assures that the head joints will be completely filled with mortar. Lay the block in slowly and carefully to avoid knocking the mortar off the buttered ends. If any voids or openings are left in the head joints, trowel in additional mortar.

FIGURE 7-18
A mason's line is stretched between the two corners to serve as a course guide. (Portland Concrete Association)

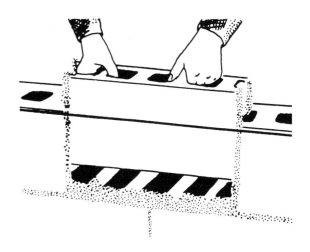

FIGURE 7-20
Closure. Butter mortar both on the closure block ends *and* the block already in place.

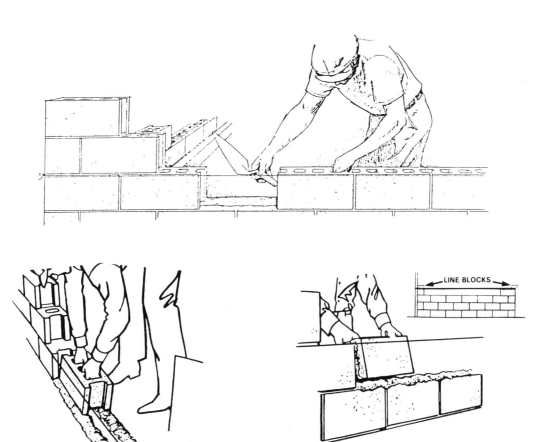

FIGURE 7-19
Block is laid between the two leads using the mason's line as a guide. (*Top:* Hyde Manufacturing Co.; *bottom:* Marshalltown Trowel Co.)

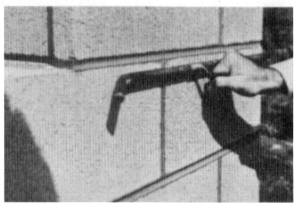

FIGURE 7-21
Striking the mortar joints. (*Top:* Genstar Lime Co.; *bottom:* National Concrete Masonry Association)

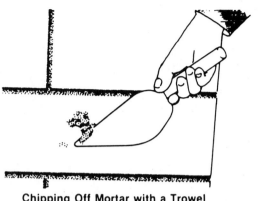

Chipping Off Mortar with a Trowel

Chipping Off Mortar with a Piece of Broken Block

Striking Joints

After the mortar is thumbprint hard, the joints are struck. Vertical joints are struck first (Figure 7-21, top); then the horizontal joints (Figure 7-21, bottom) are struck. When striking the horizontal joints, use a long jointer, at least 22 inches long, such as a sled runner. Concave joints are normally used.

Cleaning

When laying the block, any mortar droppings or splatter on the face of the concrete block face should be scraped off with the edge of the trowel and thrown away (Figure 7-22, top). Dried mortar can be loosened and scraped off with a piece of

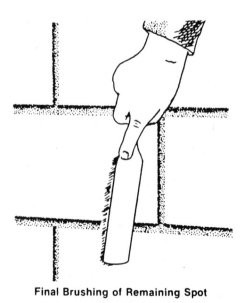

Final Brushing of Remaining Spot

FIGURE 7-22
Cleaning the block.

broken block (Figure 7–22, center). Don't, however, rub the block piece so hard it scratches off the block face or wears into the block surface. Dirt and mortar powder on the block face should be brushed off with a stiff mason's brush (Figure 7–22, bottom).

Use the trowel to trim off the tailings or burrs left after the joints are finished. Figure 7–23 shows tailings being removed.

Caution: Acid solutions should not be used on concrete masonry since the cement material in the block is susceptible to acid attack. Also, because of the porosity of the concrete material, the block wall is *not* washed with water. During construction, the concrete masonry element should be covered and protected from rain or snow. Once wet, it can take some time for concrete masonry units to dry out. Also, wetted concrete masonry units are subject to efflorescence. In very hot, dry weather, however, when the block is hot to the touch, a fine fog spray may be used for cooling. Check with the manufacturer for recommendations on the removal of any stains on exposed walls.

FIGURE 7–23
Trowelling off burrs made when finishing the joints. (National Concrete Masonry Association)

COLUMNS AND PIERS

Columns are vertical support members; they carry part of the building load imposed directly from

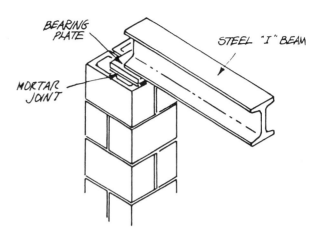

FIGURE 7–24
Column or pier supports the end of the steel beam. (National Concrete Masonry Association)

above. Piers are short columns that are sometimes used to support residential foundation beams. Figure 7–24 shows how a typical column or pier is designed to support the end of a steel I-beam. Both columns and piers are normally reinforced with reinforcing steel. Steel may be used in grouted cells in the block or in the hollow center of special column block.

Figure 7–25 shows the construction of typical reinforced concrete masonry columns. Either standard two cell masonry block or special column or pilaster units are used. Four vertical reinforcing rods are used in each of the columns shown. In addition, horizontal or lateral ties are used to give additional strength.

Figure 7–26 shows a pictorial view of a column using reinforcing steel in the center. The four vertical reinforcing rods are tied and held together with horizontal or lateral ties. The vertical rods and the horizontal (lateral) ties are normally wired together as a unit, to the specific size and length specifications required for the column. This prepared reinforcement is called a *cage* and is made separately. After the base, concrete masonry units are laid for the column. The wired reinforcement cage is then lifted into and positioned inside the masonry units. Grouting is then placed inside the column to cement in the reinforcement.

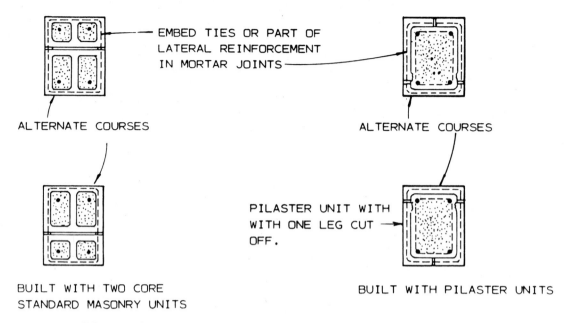

FIGURE 7–25
Reinforced concrete masonry columns. (National Concrete Masonry Association)

Note: As called out on Figure 7–26, if no cleanouts are provided to allow mortar and debris to be removed at the bottom of the column, then low-lift grouting is used. Low-lift grouting for a reinforced concrete masonry column allows a lift (grouting depth) of up to four feet.

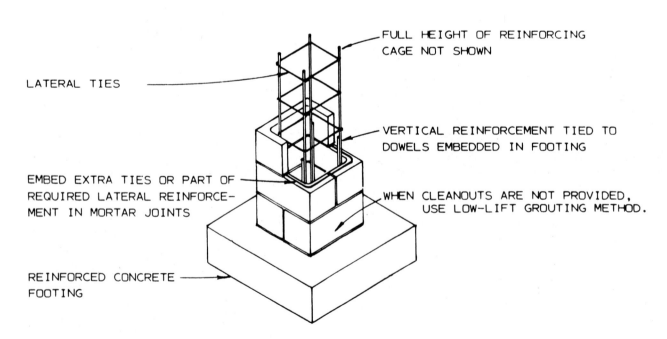

FIGURE 7–26
Reinforced concrete masonry column. (National Concrete Masonry Association)

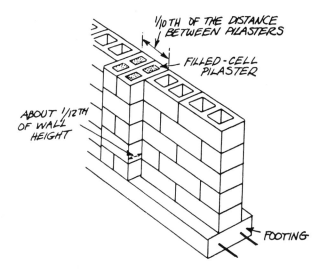

FIGURE 7-27
Typical concrete masonry pilaster. (National Concrete Masonry Association)

PILASTERS

Pilasters are similar to columns except they are integrated with and built into a wall. Pilasters are used to provide an enlarged support base for a beam or girder end. Figure 7-27 shows a typical pilaster used with a concrete block bearing wall. Two-cell, grouted concrete block are laid into the walls. Figure 7-28 shows a typical reinforced pilaster; both vertical and horizontal (lateral) reinforcement is used. The reinforcement is integrated to and tied to the bearing wall. In this case, a continuous bond beam is used in the wall. Grout or concrete flows from the wall into the pilaster to form a unit.

RECESSES AND CHASES

Recesses and chases are hollow spaces left in the wall. These openings are generally thought of as vertical, especially in masonry walls, but they may also be horizontal. Figure 7-29 shows a typical recess in a concrete block wall. A metal duct is installed in the opening. The duct could be used for warm air flow. Recesses are also used for running electrical conduit or for plumbing pipes. A half-thickness partition block is used to finish the wall behind the recess opening.

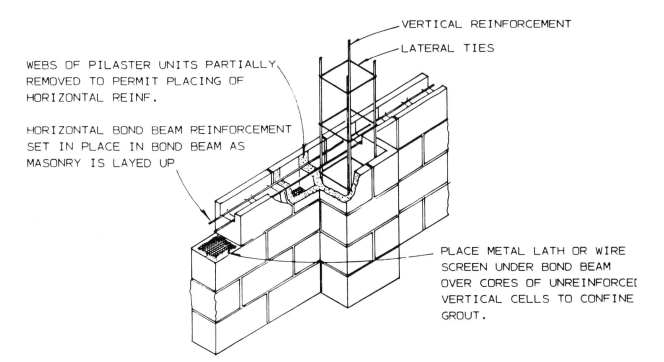

FIGURE 7-28
Reinforced concrete masonry pilaster. (National Concrete Masonry Association)

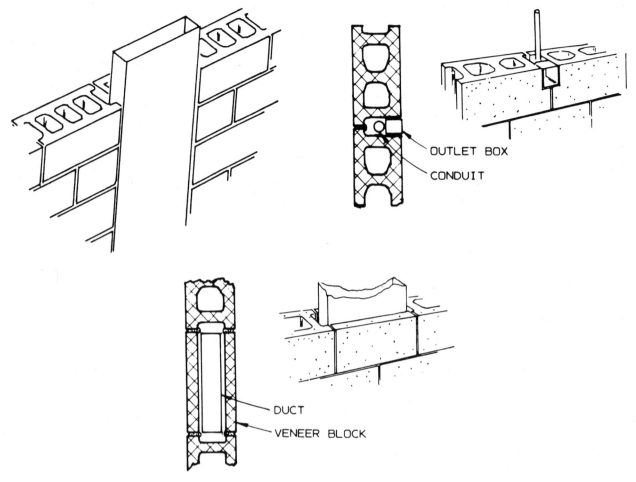

FIGURE 7-29
Recesses or chases in concrete block wall. (National Concrete Masonry Association)

ELECTRICAL OUTLET OPENINGS

Electrical conduit or cable is frequently run inside the concrete block cells. Openings must be made in the face shell of the block to allow electrical outlets to be installed. A masonry saw is used to cut the side cuts needed in the block. A hammer and chisel are then used to score and break off the face shell. Figure 7–30 shows how a block can be cut for the wiring of outlets. Only the face shell of the block is cut so the wiring can exit. Electrical wiring is also run on the face of the concrete block wall between furring strips and under finished wallboard.

FIGURE 7-30
Electrical outlet openings. (National Concrete Masonry Association.)

ANCHOR BOLTS

As shown in Figure 7-31, anchor bolts are used to bolt down a sill at the top of a wall. Anchor bolts are embedded in the block cells; a wire screen or wire lath is used at the bottom of the concrete block to hold the grouting that is poured into the block cell to hold the anchor, as shown in Figure 7-31. The anchors extend through two block courses and are commonly located every six feet on center (O.C.). In areas subject to earthquakes (seismic zones), codes specify closer spacing O.C.

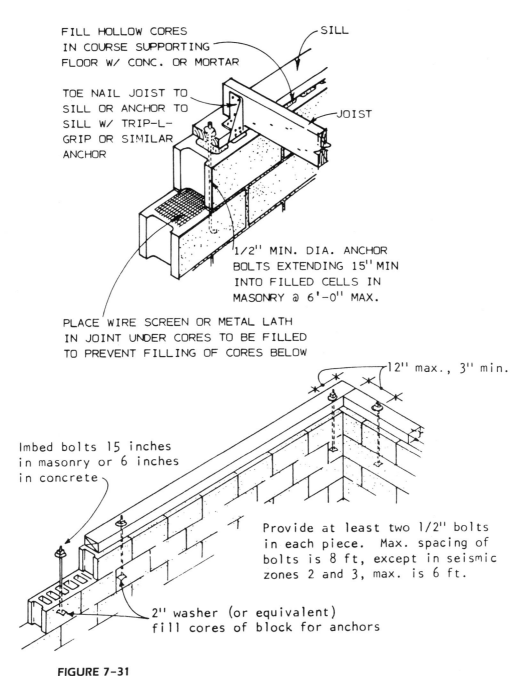

FILL HOLLOW CORES IN COURSE SUPPORTING FLOOR W/ CONC. OR MORTAR

SILL

TOE NAIL JOIST TO SILL OR ANCHOR TO SILL W/ TRIP-L-GRIP OR SIMILAR ANCHOR

JOIST

1/2'' MIN. DIA. ANCHOR BOLTS EXTENDING 15'' MIN INTO FILLED CELLS IN MASONRY @ 6'-0'' MAX.

PLACE WIRE SCREEN OR METAL LATH IN JOINT UNDER CORES TO BE FILLED TO PREVENT FILLING OF CORES BELOW

12'' max., 3'' min.

Imbed bolts 15 inches in masonry or 6 inches in concrete

Provide at least two 1/2'' bolts in each piece. Max. spacing of bolts is 8 ft, except in seismic zones 2 and 3, max. is 6 ft.

2'' washer (or equivalent) fill cores of block for anchors

FIGURE 7-31
Use of anchor bolts at top of concrete block wall. (*Top:* National Concrete Masonry Association; *bottom:* U.S. Department of Housing and Urban Development)

WALLS

As mentioned earlier, concrete block walls are usually built with running bond (Figure 7–32). When building the wall, unfinished ends are normally stepped or racked (Figure 7–32, top), or sometimes an unfinished wall may be toothed (Figure 7–32, bottom) although this is not usually recommended. Walls that cannot be completed during the work shift are left with a shaped temporary end so it is easy to continue work the next day. With racked or toothed ends, the courses are already established and it is a simple matter to continue the courses.

Concrete block walls that are built higher than eight feet to ten feet should have temporary bracing until the mortar sets. Figure 7–33 shows

FIGURE 7–33
Temporary bracing is used to hold the completed wall.

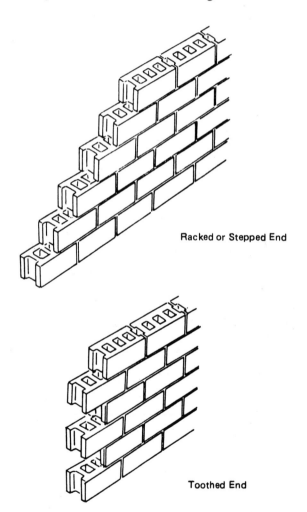

Racked or Stepped End

Toothed End

FIGURE 7–32
Unfinished wall ends may be racked (*top*) or toothed (*bottom*). (National Concrete Masonry Association)

types of temporary bracing used on block walls. Bracing is required on *both* sides of the wall. The bottom of the bracing is set in the earth, weighted, or butted against a cross support. Figure 7–33, top, shows typical supports wedged into place. The bottom end is butted against a wooden piece nailed into the concrete floor. Bracing is left in place until the floors are in place and the mortar is completely set.

REINFORCED WALLS

As shown earlier (Figures 4–40 to 4–43 and Figure 4–56), both vertical and horizontal steel reinforcement is used in concrete block walls. Figure 7–34

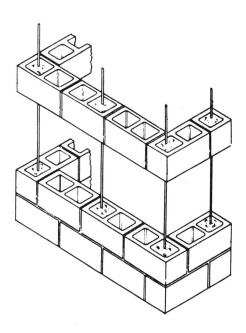

PREFABRICATED HORIZONTAL JOINT
REINFORCEMENT IN HORIZONTAL
MORTAR JOINTS. AT SPACING
AS REQUIRED

shows horizontal joint reinforcement used with vertical steel bars. This shows typical reinforced concrete masonry construction. Horizontal joint reinforcement is embedded in mortar in the bed joint and then covered with additional mortar. It is important that the metal does not come into contact with the block. Vertical steel reinforcement is inserted into the cells or cores, which are then filled with grout. The vertical bars must not touch the sides of the opening.

Figure 7–34, bottom, shows how vertical reinforcing bars are arranged in the block cells of a small single-wythe, 8″ wall. The vertical bars are tied (wired) to dowels or bars set in the footing and projecting up into the block. Depending on the wall size, bars can be installed on 16″, 24″, 32″, or 40″ centers.

Figure 7–35 shows concrete block laid in stack bond. As noted, this bond by itself is very weak and is used in decorative walls, especially garden walls. With horizontal joint reinforcement, however, the bond strength is greatly increased. Horizontal joint reinforcement is used every second course, as noted in the figure.

When using joint reinforcement, be sure that reinforcing steel is completely surrounded by mortar. Horizontal reinforcing steel is laid in a mortar

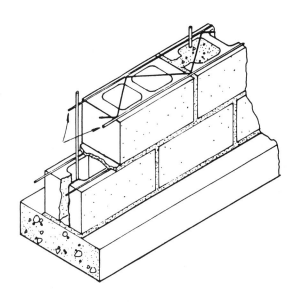

HORIZONTAL JOINT REINFORCEMENT USED
IN LIEU OF BOND BEAMS TO PROVIDE
LATERAL REINFORCEMENT

FIGURE 7–34
Typical steel reinforcement used in concrete block construction. (*Top:* National Concrete Masonry Association; *bottom:* Masonry Industry Advancement Committee)

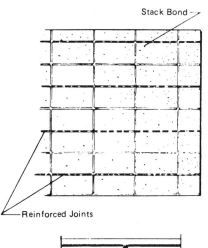

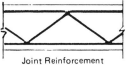

FIGURE 7–35
Joint reinforcement used in stack bond.

bed. Additional mortar is then laid on top. This assures that the steel is completely surrounded by mortar.

Low-Lift Grouting

In low-lift grouting, concrete block walls are only built to a low height before grouting is poured into the steel reinforced cells or cores. Only selected cells are grouted and no more than four feet (vertical depth) can be poured at any one time. Figure 7-36 shows typical low-lift grouting. The grout is frequently poured in by hand from buckets, especially on small jobs.

High-Lift Grouting

High-lift grouting is used on large building projects. A full story of grouting may be poured at one

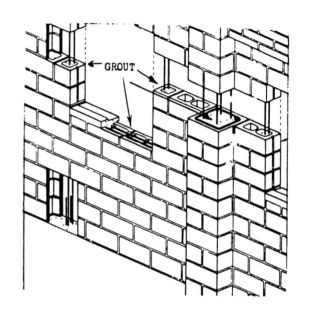

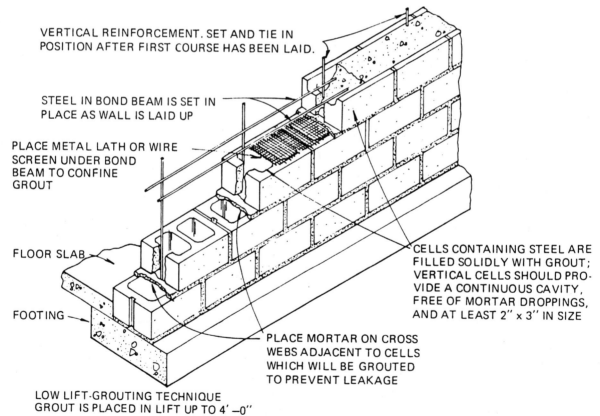

VERTICAL REINFORCEMENT. SET AND TIE IN POSITION AFTER FIRST COURSE HAS BEEN LAID.

STEEL IN BOND BEAM IS SET IN PLACE AS WALL IS LAID UP

PLACE METAL LATH OR WIRE SCREEN UNDER BOND BEAM TO CONFINE GROUT

FLOOR SLAB

FOOTING

CELLS CONTAINING STEEL ARE FILLED SOLIDLY WITH GROUT; VERTICAL CELLS SHOULD PROVIDE A CONTINUOUS CAVITY, FREE OF MORTAR DROPPINGS, AND AT LEAST 2" x 3" IN SIZE

PLACE MORTAR ON CROSS WEBS ADJACENT TO CELLS WHICH WILL BE GROUTED TO PREVENT LEAKAGE

LOW LIFT-GROUTING TECHNIQUE GROUT IS PLACED IN LIFT UP TO 4'-0"

FIGURE 7-36
Typical low-lift grouting in concrete block construction. (National Concrete Masonry Association)

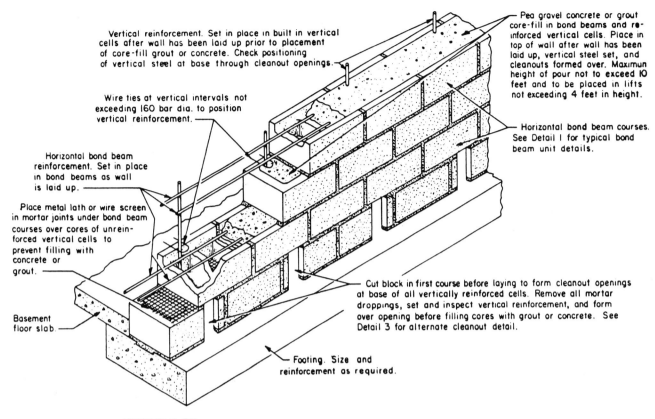

Vertical reinforcement. Set in place in built in vertical cells after wall has been laid up prior to placement of core-fill grout or concrete. Check positioning of vertical steel at base through cleanout openings.

Wire ties at vertical intervals not exceeding 160 bar dia. to position vertical reinforcement.

Horizontal bond beam reinforcement. Set in place in bond beams as wall is laid up.

Place metal lath or wire screen in mortar joints under bond beam courses over cores of unrein-forced vertical cells to prevent filling with concrete or grout.

Basement floor slab.

Pea gravel concrete or grout core-fill in bond beams and re-inforced vertical cells. Place in top of wall after wall has been laid up, vertical steel set, and cleanouts formed over. Maximum height of pour not to exceed 10 feet and to be placed in lifts not exceeding 4 feet in height.

Horizontal bond beam courses. See Detail 1 for typical bond beam unit details.

Cut block in first course before laying to form cleanout openings at base of all vertically reinforced cells. Remove all mortar droppings, set and inspect vertical reinforcement, and form over opening before filling cores with grout or concrete. See Detail 3 for alternate cleanout detail.

Footing. Size and reinforcement as required.

FIGURE 7-37
Typical high-lift grouting in concrete block construction. (National Concrete Masonry Association)

time. Grouting is pumped in. Figure 7-37 shows typical high-lift grouting. Openings are left at the base of the wall so mortar dropping and other debris can be cleaned out before grouting. After cleaning, the openings are mortared and closed with concrete block.

Take care when laying the concrete block to wipe mortar off the inside of the cell or core openings. Mortar that protrudes into the cell, as shown in Figure 7-38, will interfere with the grouting pumped into the cement block during high-lift grouting. Mortar fins inside the block cells are removed with a trowel as the wall is built.

BOND BEAMS

Very strong reinforced walls can be created using bond beams. Bond beams are made using special beam or lintel block. Figure 7-36 shows uses of

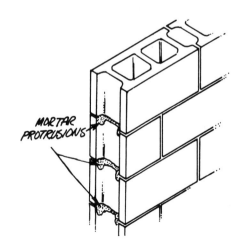

MORTAR PROTRUSIONS

FIGURE 7-38
Mortar protrusions or fins in cells that are to be grouted should be removed as the wall is built. (National Concrete Masonry Association)

lintel block to make the bond beam. The open-top block are designed to take horizontal reinforcement, and they are then filled with grout or cement. Figure 7–36, bottom, and Figure 7–37 show bond beams used in a reinforced concrete block wall. Bond beams are required in areas subject to earthquakes.

INTERSECTING WALLS

Intersecting concrete block walls are tied together by using metal anchors (as was shown in Figures 4–45 and 4–50). Metal lath or wire mesh (Figure 4–45) or strap anchors (Figure 4–50) are used to anchor the walls together. Figure 7–39 shows the use of a strap anchor. Joint reinforcement can also be used, as shown in Figure 7–40, right. This shows nonload bearing partitions tied together. The detail at Figure 7–40, left, shows how the block wall is anchored to a concrete wall using a dovetail anchor.

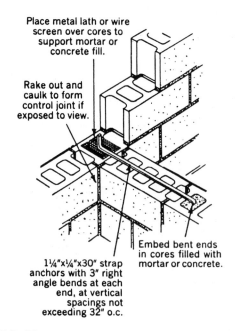

FIGURE 7–39
Strap anchor used to tie intersecting block walls. (National Concrete Masonry Association)

FLOOR SUPPORT

Joists frame onto the block walls and must have at least a three-inch bearing. Figure 7–41 shows how joist ends bear on the top of a masonry wall. Half block are used on the outside wall face, beyond the joist ends; short, half units, called hollow bridging units, are used between the joists. Note that the joist ends are cut at an angle to provide a fire cut. The fire cut prevents the top of the joist from acting as a pry if it were to burn through and fall.

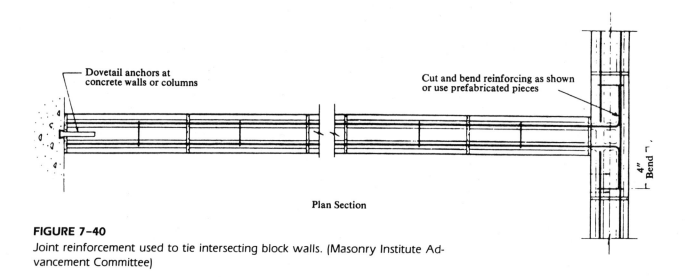

FIGURE 7–40
Joint reinforcement used to tie intersecting block walls. (Masonry Institute Advancement Committee)

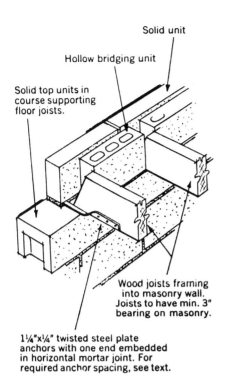

FIGURE 7–41
Joist anchors are used to tie joists to block walls. (National Concrete Masonry Association)

CORBELLING

A corbel can be built into walls 12 inches or more in thickness. Projection for each corbel course should not exceed one inch. Total corbel projection should not be more than one-third the total wall thickness when the corbel supports a structural member. A corbel projection up to 6 inches may be used for support of a chimney built into a wall.

BEAM POCKETS

When support beams are used at the foundation, pockets or recesses should be left at the top of the foundation wall. The pocket or recess receives the end of the beam or girder. Figure 7–42 shows a beam pocket in a concrete block wall. Notched block are used to form the pocket.

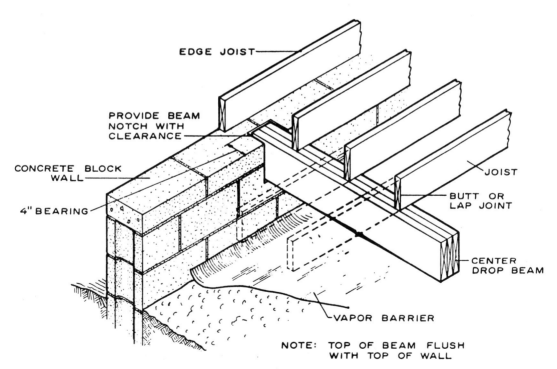

FIGURE 7–42
Beam pocket in concrete block wall.

INCORRECT

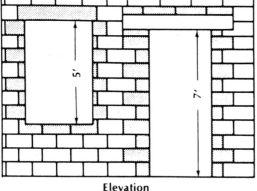

Elevation

Shaded Portion = Cut Masonry Units

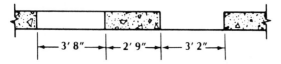

├── 3' 8" ──┤── 2' 9" ──┤── 3' 2" ──┤

FIGURE 7–43
WRONG. Poor planning requires unnecessary cutting of block units.

Correct

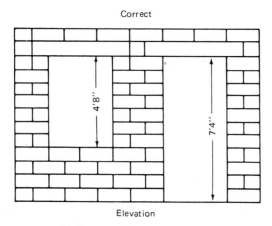

Elevation

All Masonry = Full or Half-Size Units

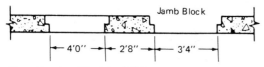

Jamb Block

├── 4'0" ──┤── 2'8" ──┤── 3'4" ──┤

Note: Based on 8" x 8" x 16" Concrete Block.

Jamb Block

FIGURE 7–44
CORRECT. Good planning allows whole or half block to be used.

OPENINGS

Openings in walls, such as windows or doors, create special problems since the opening must be laid to exact size. The opening may be built and the window or door frame may then be installed, or the block may be laid around a framework already in place. Lintels are always required over any opening.

When laying the block to openings, it is very important that the block be laid out and planned so units do not have to be cut or at least cut only infrequently. Figure 7–43 shows what can result from poor planning. Note in the shaded area all the block that must be cut. This is a time-consuming and uneconomical practice. Figure 7–44 shows good planning and how standard full-length or half-length block can be used. This, of course, saves a great deal of time and work. Note also in Figure 7–44 that special *jamb block* (shown in section view) are used around the window and door openings. The jamb block have a recess cut in to receive the window and door frames.

Special jamb or sash block with a slot or key down their end are also used, as shown in Figure 7–45. Here the jamb block are first laid up around a wooden frame. The wooden frame is then removed, and a metal window frame is installed. The metal window frame has flanges on the sides (jambs) that slide down the slots on the jamb block.

Figure 7–46 shows concrete block laid up to receive a metal window. A concrete window sill is in place. The precast concrete window sill is installed *after* the block for the window opening is in place, as shown in Figure 7–47. Note that flashing is required under the window sill to prevent water entry. The metal window fits into the window opening, and caulking is used to seal off any moisture, as shown by the detail drawings.

Figure 7–48 shows a bond beam used as a lintel over the opening. Here the metal door frame is in place. Note that the lintel block has a slot or key in the bottom into which the metal frame fits. In this case, the metal frame is set in place, aligned, and plumbed. The concrete block are then laid around it. If the metal frame is not in place when the lintel is installed, bracing must be used to support the concrete block lintel until the

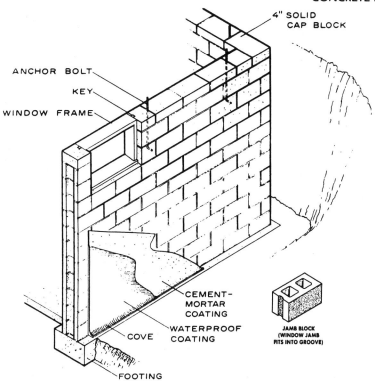

FIGURE 7-45
Jamb block are used at window opening in the block wall.

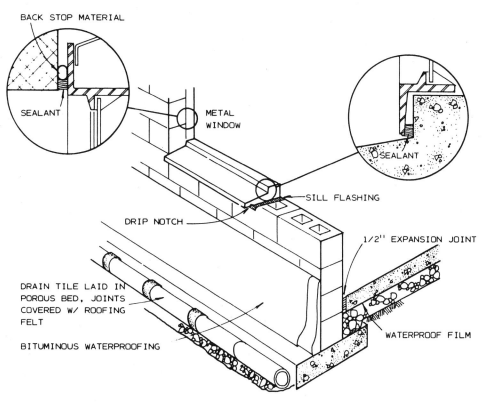

FIGURE 7-46
Installation of window in block wall. (National Concrete Masonry Association)

FIGURE 7-47
Installing precast concrete window sill. (National Concrete Masonry Association)

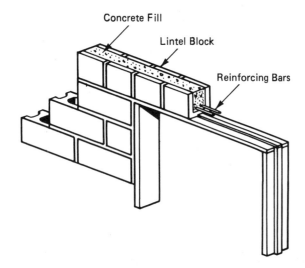

FIGURE 7-48
Bond beam used as lintel over opening.

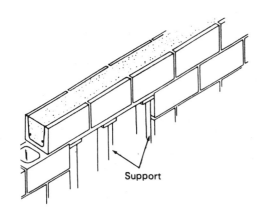

FIGURE 7-49
Bracing for bond beam. (National Concrete Masonry Association)

mortar is completely set. Figure 7-49 shows bracing used under a bond beam.

Precast reinforced concrete lintels and steel angle irons or I-beams are also commonly used over openings as lintels. Figure 7-50 shows a precast concrete lintel installed over a door opening.

A typical window detail or section, as in Figure 7-51, is used to show exactly how the window fits into the opening. It is very important that dimensions be very exactly followed when laying up the opening; otherwise, the metal window won't fit in. Take careful measurements when building the opening.

Vent openings are left in the foundation walls of houses with crawl spaces. This allows air to flow through the crawl space and circulate between the ground and the wooden floor, which

FIGURE 7-50
Precast concrete lintel installed over opening. (National Concrete Masonry Association)

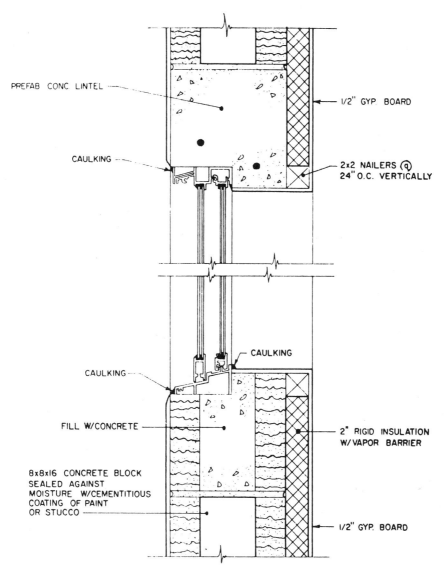

FIGURE 7-51
Window detail or section shows how window fits into opening.

prevents moisture buildup. Metal vents or screens are used in the wall. Figure 7-52 shows a foundation wall with a vent or screen. The floor plans and elevation will show where vents are required. Vents are always required on opposite sides of the foundation to allow crossflow of air. Vents or screens are sized to replace one full block in the wall, as shown in Figure 7-52. Special metal vent boxes may be used and are laid in the mortar in the same way as an ordinary block.

VENEER, CAVITY, AND COMPOSITE WALLS

As shown in earlier chapters, concrete block is frequently used as the backing wythe for a brick veneer. A composite block and brick wall is also common, as are block and brick cavity walls. (Refer back to Figures 4-40 and 4-42, for example.) This is a common practice. The separate wythes are al-

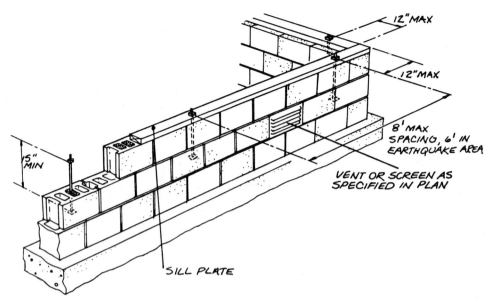

FIGURE 7–52
Foundation wall with vent. (American Plywood Association)

ways tied together with wire ties or steel anchors (veneer) or steel joint reinforcement or anchors (composite walls).

Any veneer, of course, is non-load bearing. A veneer rests on a foundation and is attached to the load bearing backing wall. A composite wall is composed of two separate wythes made of two different types of material (such as block and brick) that are laid together to form a single, load bearing unit. Cavity walls have a space or cavity between the two wythes. Insulation is often used in the cavity. Figure 7–53 shows a masonry cavity wall with foam plastic insulation between the concrete block backing and the brick face.

INSULATION

The use of insulation in masonry construction is increasing today. Loose-fill insulation is frequently poured into the concrete block cells to increase the resistance to heat transfer. Additional insulation, of course, reduces heating and cooling costs. Figure 7–53 shows how foam plastic insulation sheets are used in the space between the two wythes. Use of insulation in veneer and cavity wall is a common practice.

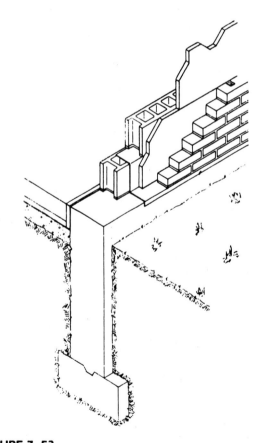

FIGURE 7–53
Masonry concrete block and brick wall with plastic foam insulation. (United States Gypsum Co.)

Sheet insulation is also commonly used on the outside of concrete block basement walls. Insulation should run from the footing to the top of the foundation wall. Insulation may also be used on the inside of the wall, but outside use is more effective and is recommended.

If basement walls are uninsulated on the outside, *furring strips* should be used on the inside wall, as shown in Figure 7–54. Here, vertical wood strips are nailed into the concrete block with masonry nails. The horizontal wood strips are installed every 24″ O.C. Wallboard is then attached to the furring strips. The furring strips are needed to remove the wallboard from the masonry surface which, because no outside insulation is used, may be cold and cause water condensation. The space between the furring strips is sometimes filled with fiberglass insulation. The space is also used to run electrical wiring.

DRY BOND

Dry bond is the laying of masonry units without any mortar. This practice is used with concrete block walls and has been proven successful over the years. Figure 4–24 illustrated this practice. It

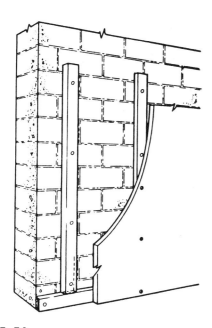

FIGURE 7–54
Furring strips used on inside of concrete block wall. Interior drywall or wallboard is then nailed to furring strips. (National Gypsum Co.)

has been thoroughly tested and is generally approved by building codes.

WATERPROOFING

Basement walls must be damp proofed or waterproofed. This is done by finishing the outside face of the wall with special mortars and bituminous coatings. This practice was illustrated in Figure 4–25. Figures 7–45 and 7–46 show waterproofing techniques. The standard practice is to trowel on a coating of cement mortar over the outside wall. Then, when the mortar is dry, a coating of asphalt or other waterproofing is applied.

CAPPING

No hollow masonry wall supporting joists or girders should be used without filling the top block with grout or capping with a solid block or a 2-inch wood plate. Figure 7–55 shows when capping is required at the top of a concrete block wall. Capping is not required if, as shown in Figure 7–55, bottom, the top of the wall is covered by a wood plate. Either the top concrete block are grouted (Figure 7–55, middle) or a solid masonry cap (Figure 7–55, top) is mortared in place. Figure 7–45 showed solid cap block laid in at the top of a wall.

COPING

Any exposed masonry wall, such as a garden wall or a parapet must have coping. Precast reinforced concrete caps or copings are commonly used on top of exposed walls; four-foot coping sections are used and are laid in mortar on top of the wall, as shown in Figure 7–56. Flashing is required under the coping.

FLASHING

As discussed in Chapter 4, flashing is required in masonry work over and under openings, at the base of the veneer, and under wall capping. Fig-

Capping is always
required when rafter
or joist is supported
directly on hollow
masonry walls.

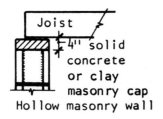

Capping is always
required when girders
are supported on
hollow masonry walls.

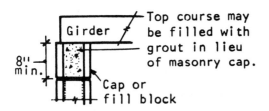

Capping is not
required when
rafter or joist
is supported by
a plate.

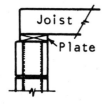

FIGURE 7-55
Capping is required at top of concrete block wall.

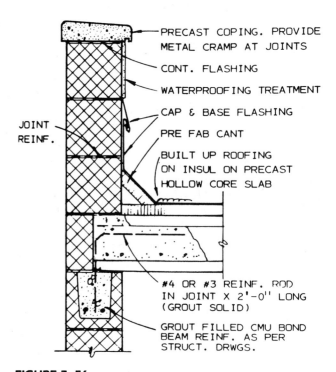

FIGURE 7-56
Precast coping used at top of concrete block wall. (National Concrete Masonry Association)

ures 4-50 to 4-62 showed the use of flashing in a masonry building. Figure 4-56 shows the location of flashing under the precast coping and where the parapet meets the roof. Figure 7-57 shows how the flashing is installed at the parapet area. The detail shows how the end of the flashing is worked back into the bed joint between the concrete block.

CONTROL JOINTS

As discussed earlier, control joints are built into concrete block walls to control random cracking caused by contraction and thermal expansion. Refer back to Figures 4-63 to 4-67 for guidelines on the use and construction of control joints in a masonry building. Control joints are located and noted by the architect on the blueprints. Remember that the control joint runs from the footing to the top of the wall. Figure 7-58 shows control joint details. Control joints are used at

- changes in wall height or thickness;

- construction joints in foundation, roof, and floors;

- chases and recesses for piping, columns, fixtures, and so forth;

- abutment of wall and columns;

- return angles in L-, T-, and U-shaped structures; and

- one or both sides of wall openings.

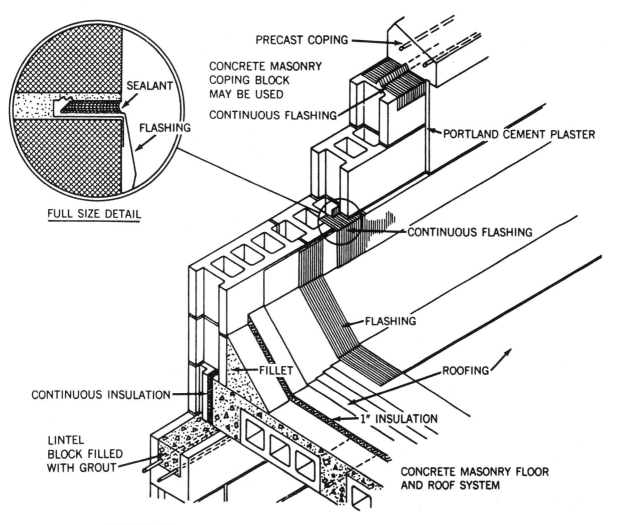

FULL SIZE DETAIL

SEALANT

FLASHING

PRECAST COPING

CONCRETE MASONRY
COPING BLOCK
MAY BE USED

CONTINUOUS FLASHING

PORTLAND CEMENT PLASTER

CONTINUOUS FLASHING

FLASHING

ROOFING

FILLET

1" INSULATION

CONTINUOUS INSULATION

LINTEL
BLOCK FILLED
WITH GROUT

CONCRETE MASONRY FLOOR
AND ROOF SYSTEM

FIGURE 7–57
Flashing used in concrete block wall. (National Concrete Masonry Association)

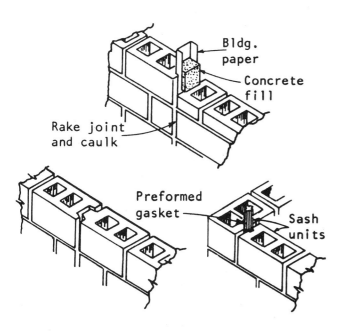

Bldg.
paper

Concrete
fill

Rake joint
and caulk

Preformed
gasket

Sash
units

FIGURE 7–58
Typical control joints in a concrete block wall. (*Left:* National
Concrete Masonry Association)

FIGURE 7-59

Caulking raked back control joint. (National Concrete Masonry Association)

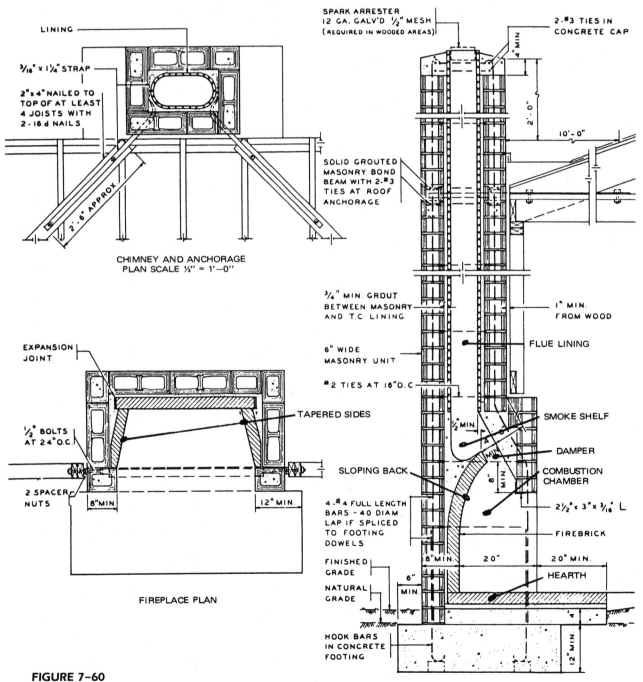

LINING

³⁄₁₆" × 1¼" STRAP

2" × 4" NAILED TO TOP OF AT LEAST 4 JOISTS WITH 2 - 16 d NAILS

2'-6" APPROX

CHIMNEY AND ANCHORAGE PLAN SCALE ½" = 1'-0"

EXPANSION JOINT

½" BOLTS AT 24" O.C.

2 SPACER NUTS

8" MIN.

12" MIN.

TAPERED SIDES

FIREPLACE PLAN

SPARK ARRESTER 12 GA. GALV'D ½" MESH (REQUIRED IN WOODED AREAS)

2 - #3 TIES IN CONCRETE CAP

4" MIN

2'-0"

10'-0"

SOLID GROUTED MASONRY BOND BEAM WITH 2 - #3 TIES AT ROOF ANCHORAGE

¾" MIN. GROUT BETWEEN MASONRY AND T.C. LINING

6" WIDE MASONRY UNIT

#2 TIES AT 16" O.C.

1" MIN. FROM WOOD

FLUE LINING

½" MIN.

SMOKE SHELF

DAMPER

COMBUSTION CHAMBER

2½" × 3" × ³⁄₁₆" L

FIREBRICK

SLOPING BACK

8" MIN

4 - #4 FULL LENGTH BARS - 40 DIAM. LAP IF SPLICED TO FOOTING DOWELS

FINISHED GRADE

NATURAL GRADE

6" MIN.

8" MIN.

20"

20" MIN.

HEARTH

HOOK BARS IN CONCRETE FOOTING

12" MIN.

VERTICAL SECTION

FIGURE 7-60

Concrete block used in fireplace and chimney construction.

272

All control joints are raked back from the block face and caulked, as shown in Figure 7–59. Note how the half block are used to allow the control joint to run from the bottom to top of the wall.

FIREPLACES AND CHIMNEYS

Fireplaces are sometimes built using four-inch concrete block. The same techniques are used as for brick (described in Chapter 6). Figure 7–60 shows plans for building a concrete block fireplace and chimney. Naturally, the combustion chamber must be lined with firebrick using refractory mortar. As shown, the concrete block at the corners have vertical steel reinforcement and are grouted.

The outside chimney is anchored to the floor joists with steel straps for support.

CONCRETE PAVING

Concrete masonry paving units are widely used in patios, sidewalks, and driveways. Because of their size, they are quicker to install than brick paving units. Figure 3–49 showed a few different types of concrete masonry paving units. Interlocking patterns are often used to form a tighter, more rigid finished floor. Concrete masonry paving units are installed in the same way as brick paving. Either mortared or mortarless paving is used. Figure 7–61 shows concrete paving units laid out; these are interlocking paving units used for driveways.

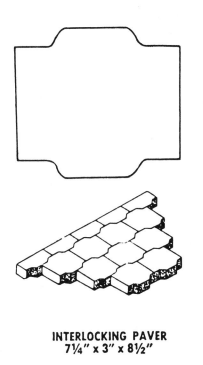

INTERLOCKING PAVER
7¼" x 3" x 8½"

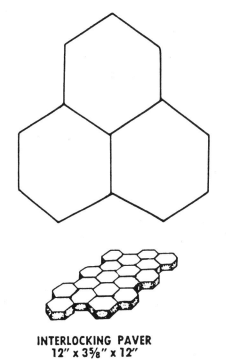

INTERLOCKING PAVER
12" x 3⅝" x 12"

FIGURE 7–61
Typical concrete paving block. (Concrete Masonry Association of California and Nevada)

CHAPTER REVIEW

QUESTIONS

1. Describe two methods of cutting concrete block. What safety precautions should be followed?

2. What is face shell bedding?

3. Which side or bed of the concrete block should be laid facing up?

4. What is buttering? How is the stretcher block buttered?

5. Describe how the concrete block courses are checked for trueness.

6. How is closure made in a block course?

7. What is the procedure for cleaning a block wall?

8. Describe how concrete block reinforced columns are constructed.

9. What is a pilaster? How is it constructed?

10. How are wall recesses made?

11. Describe how anchor bolts are installed.

12. How are unfinished walls left so the next day's work can be easily completed?

13. When are concrete block walls braced? How long is the bracing left?

14. Describe one way concrete block walls are reinforced.

15. What is a bond beam? How is it used?

16. Describe one way intersecting walls are tied together.

17. Describe how joist ends are received and supported by concrete block walls.

18. What is a beam pocket?

19. Describe at least one way of laying block up around a window or door opening.

20. What is the difference between veneer and composite construction?

21. What kinds of insulation are used in concrete masonry construction?

22. What are furring strips? Where and why are they used?

23. What is dry bond? How is it constructed?

24. Describe how basement walls are waterproofed.

25. Where should concrete block walls be capped? What kind of capping is used?

26. List and describe at least four places flashing is used in a masonry wall.

27. What are control joints? List six places control joints are used in concrete block construction.

28. What type of concrete block is sometimes used in fireplace and chimney construction?

29. What are the advantages of interlocking concrete paving units?

ACTIVITIES

1. Obtain a two-cell concrete block stretcher and
   a. measure and write down its thickness, height, and length (T × H × L) in inches.
   b. measure the thickness of the cross web on each bed. What is the difference between the cross web on the thick side and the thin side?

2. Snap right angle corner guidelines and, using several concrete block, including both stretchers and corner block, lay out a corner lead three courses high. Use Figure 7–13, bottom, as a guide for the first course of the corner lead. Use chalk lines as a guide. Leave $\frac{3}{8}$ inch between block for head joints. When completed, align and check for squareness and plumb. Mark location of each head joint on the foundation.

3. Practice buttering the ears on stretcher block. Test your buttered ears by laying them against other stretcher block. Make $\frac{3}{8}$-inch joints and check for mortar fullness. Cut off excess mortar and use to butter the next block.

4. Lay out, in an appropriate mortar bed, a corner bed course identical to Figure 7–13, bottom.

Start with a wide bed approximately one-inch deep. Square corner; align, level, and plumb the block.

5. Continue building the corner lead started in #4. Lay out the second and third courses. Align block, square corner, and check work for level and plumb. Check the diagonal alignment on the rack. (See Figure 7–17 for reference.)

6. For further practice, an opposing lead similar to the one completed in #5 can be laid. Three courses can then be laid between the two corner leads. Use corner block and mason's line as a guide. *Note:* Be sure the distance between the two leads can be filled with standard-size block. Check by laying a dry run of block between the two leads.

Chapter **8**

BLUEPRINT READING

After studying this chapter you should be able to:
- Explain the relationship of blueprints and specifications.
- Define the types of blueprints: A, S, M, and E.
- Explain what scale is and how it is noted on the blueprint.
- Explain visualization and how it works.
- Define and identify the line conventions of object line, centerline, hidden line, break lines, cutting plane line.
- Explain what an orthographic view is.
- Define elevation and explain how an elevation is drawn.
- Explain what window schedules and door schedules are and how they work.
- Explain what a plan view is and how it is made.
- Explain how sections are made and how they are viewed.
- Recognize and identify symbols and abbreviations used on blueprints.
- Recognize the Construction Specification Institute (CSI) division format.
- Analyze a set of blueprints for architectural, structural, mechanical, and masonry information.

Blueprint reading is the key to successful masonry work. You can be an excellent technician. You can lay straight and even brickwork or perfectly aligned and finished concrete block. In short, the job can look great! However, if it is not located correctly, or the dimensions are not accurate (e.g., openings are off center), the excellent craftsmanship is wasted. To be a professional job, it must meet specifications and be exactly what the architect asked for.

Not being able to read blueprints is a kind of illiteracy. You have to be told everything that needs to be done. This helplessness is absolutely unnecessary. With a little practice and study, you can become competent in interpreting blueprints. You can feel secure that you have crafted the job exactly to specifications.

BLUEPRINTS AND SPECIFICATIONS

Each masonry job will have *working drawings* or *blueprints* and written guidelines, called *specifications*. The two parts work together. Blueprints show what the job looks like; specifications give written instructions. Specifications describe in writing the working conditions and quality of work. Work to be done and specific materials to be used are spelled out.

Blueprints and specifications work together to give information on how to build a structure. If there is a conflict between the blueprints and the written specifications, the written specifications have the greater authority. Specifications take precedence. Of course, if there is a difference between the blueprints and the specifications, the architect should be consulted.

READING BLUEPRINTS

Each trade reads blueprints to get specific information on how their part of the job is to be built. Blueprints are copies of the architect's original working drawings. They have blue lines on a white background. They are bound together, usually in a roll, and are available right at the job site (Figure 8-1). They are constantly referred to to make sure each masonry detail is located and laid correctly.

In residential construction, only a few blueprint sheets are needed to show how to do the job. In commercial and industrial construction, however, a great number of sheets are required. In larger sets of blueprints, the prints may be identified by the type of information they show. General architectural prints are labeled "A" for architectural, "S" for structural, and "M" for mechanical prints. On larger projects, a separate set of electrical blueprints, labeled "E," are sometimes prepared. The letter designation of the print is located in the title box, usually in the lower right-hand corner, as shown in Figure 8-2. The designation "S" means that a structural print is shown. "S3 of 6" means this is structure print #3 of 6 prints in the set. In commercial construction, there are separate sets for architectural, structural, and mechanical blueprints. They are all bound together, in sequences, in one set of project blueprints (Figure 8-1). The mason will have to consult both the architectural and structural prints to find all the information needed to build a masonry element. As noted, on residential prints, architectural, structural and mechanical blueprints are all together on a few prints.

Note that the title box (Figure 8-2) also identifies the job and the kind of information shown on the print; for example, elevation or floor plan. Always check the title box of the print to determine exactly what you are looking at.

Basic Blueprints

Most blueprints show just a few different types of drawings. Figure 8-3 shows the different drawings used on blueprints. The key drawing is the *floor plan*. You should always check the basic floor plan first to get a quick overall view of the shape of the building and the type of construction. When the drafter draws the blueprints, the first floor plan is drawn first and then other views are related to this basic plan. Floor plans include the foundation plan, or basement plan, first floor plan, second

FIGURE 8–1
Blueprints show how the job is to be done. They are the mason's most important tool.

floor plan, and so forth, and the roof plan. Other key blueprints that the mason works with are the plot plan or site plan, elevations, and sections and details.

Plot Plan

The plot plan or site plan locates the structure on the site.

I HEREBY CERTIFY THAT THIS PLAN, SPECIFICATION, OR REPORT WAS PREPARED BY ME OR UNDER MY DIRECT SUPERVISION AND THAT I AM A DULY REGISTERED ARCHITECT UNDER THE LAWS OF THE STATE OF ILLINOIS	PROPERTY DESCRIPTION: LOT 7, BLOCK I, BURR OAKS, 2ND ADDITION, GOLDEN HILLS	
DATE _____ REG. NO.	ADDRESS: JOB NO. 84 DOGWOOD AVENUE NEW VALLEY, ILLINOIS 8022	
DATE: 4/25/88	FIRST FLOOR PLAN	PROJECT: 8712	SHEET S 3 OF 6 SHEETS
DRWN: DB		
CHKD: E.A.A.	SCALE: $\frac{1}{4}$"=1'-0"	

FIGURE 8–2
The title box identifies the blueprint. (Comteck)

Foundation Plan

The foundation plan (or basement plan) shows the top of the support for the building. This plan is very important to the mason since he lays masonry units on the top of the foundation.

Elevations

Elevations show what each side of the building looks like. They show the type of siding or masonry units used and locate windows and doors.

Sections and Details

Sections show cross-cut views of different parts of the building. Sections are extremely important to the mason since they show location and detail on masonry walls. Details are large scale views of dif-

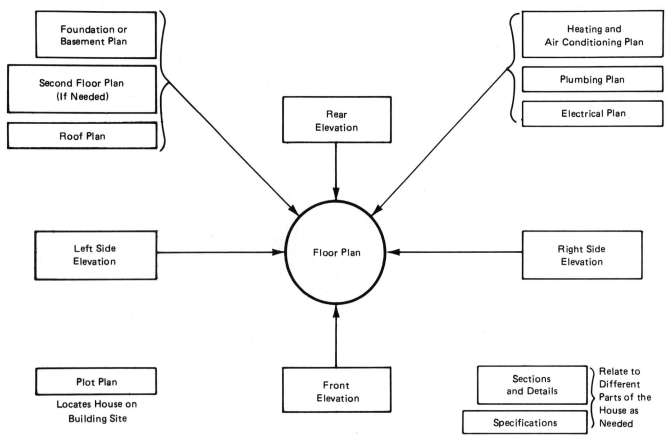

FIGURE 8–3
Basic blueprints. The floor plan is the key blueprint. (Comteck)

ferent building elements. Scale relates to how large the drawing is made in relation to the size of the actual building. Details show very detailed information on how the masonry units are laid.

Scale

Obviously, drawings cannot be drawn the same size as the building. The drawings are made, therefore, to some exact ratio or scale to the actual structure. The most common scale used is $\frac{1}{4}'' = 1'-0''$, or $\frac{1}{4}$ inch = 1 foot, 0 inches. Each $\frac{1}{4}$ inch drawn on the blueprint represents exactly one foot ($1'-0''$) on the actual building. Commercial structures are drawn at a smaller scale of $\frac{1}{8}'' = 1'-0''$. Sections and details are drawn to a larger scale. Larger scales of $\frac{3}{4}'' = 1'-0''$, $1\frac{1}{2}'' = 1'-0''$, and $3'' = 1'-0''$ are used. Sometimes very detailed

architectural features are drawn *full size* and labeled F.S. The scale at which a drawing is made is noted just under the drawing. If all the drawings on a blueprint sheet are the same size, the scale will be noted in the title box.

VISUALIZATION

Visualization relates to being able to see or imagine how the building looks. Visualization is done by first studying the plans and elevations and then putting them together mentally to "see" the complete structure. Figure 8–4 illustrates this basic and important concept. By looking at the plan (top) view and the elevations, the viewer in Figure 8–4 can imagine the completed structure.

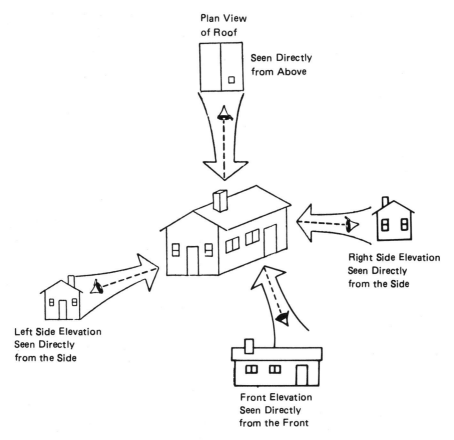

FIGURE 8–4
Study the plan view and the elevations to visualize what the structure looks like.
(Comteck)

DRAWING CONVENTIONS

When first viewing a blueprint, the great number of different lines may be confusing. Much of this initial confusion can be cleared up if you understand the line conventions used by the drafter. Once the basic drafting lines are recognized, you can immediately recognize what the drawing is trying to show. Figure 8–5 shows all of the lines used in drafting. These line conventions are universal; they are used in all areas of drafting.

Object Lines

Shows outside line or outline of the building or structural element.

Centerlines

Used to show the center of something, as the center of a window opening.

Hidden Lines

Hidden lines show the edge of a building or structural element that *cannot* be seen in the specific view shown. Footings are commonly shown with hidden lines since the edge of the footing is underground and cannot be seen.

Break Lines

Break lines show where a large structural element is broken off; the drawing is not completed.

LINES USED TO DRAW THE OBJECT

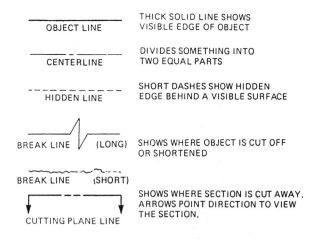

LINES USED TO DIMENSION THE OBJECT

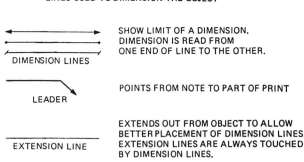

FIGURE 8–5
Line conventions used on blueprints. (Comteck)

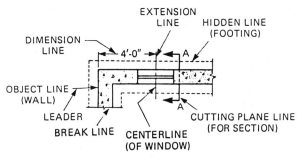

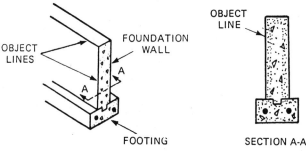

FIGURE 8–6
Sample use of lines on blueprint. (Comteck)

Cutting Plane Lines

The cutting plane line is the heaviest line used in the blueprint. It is very important since it shows where sections are taken. The arrowheads point the direction in which to view the completed section drawing.

Dimension Lines

Other lines, as shown in Figure 8–5, bottom, are used to dimension the structure. They show the limit of a dimension or point to some part of the drawing.

Figure 8–6 shows a typical use of basic lines. A plan or top view of a part of a foundation is shown. Note that the heavy object lines are used to show the outside edge or surface of the foundation wall.

ELEVATIONS

Elevations, as shown in Figure 8–7, show the outside walls of a building. They are drawn looking straight at the different sides of the building. Drawings made looking straight at the side of the structure, or looking straight down on the floor, are called *orthographic views.*

Elevations are identified by their relation to the front entrance (front, rear, left, right) or by compass direction (North, South, East, West).

Figure 8–7 shows four simple house elevations. The elevation that shows the front door is called the Front Elevation. Note that brick veneer is used on the outside of the house. Foundation and footings are shown with dashed hidden lines since they are not visible in the elevation views. A brick, single-flue chimney is also built into the house. Elevations are very important since they show the locations of all doors and windows. Head heights of the windows are dimensioned on the elevations. The actual size of the different windows are given on separate schedules or tables.

The letters A, B, C, D, and E shown on the

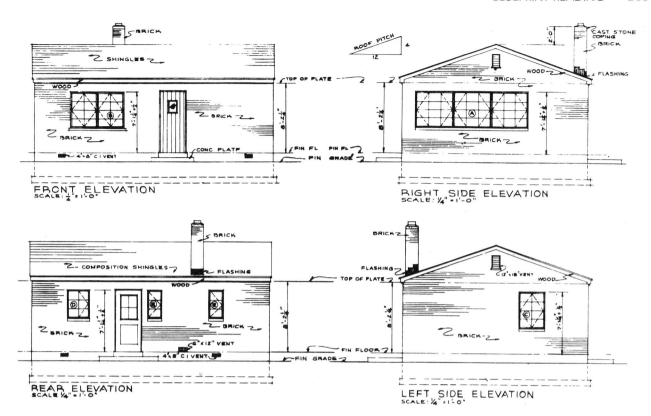

FIGURE 8–7
Elevations for a brick house.

windows (Figure 8–7) refer to the window schedule where the exact window sizes are given. The window head height and the window sizes given in the window schedules are used when laying out the brick veneer wall. The floor plan for the house gives the rest of the information needed for locating the window and door openings.

Figure 8–8 shows the elevation for a concrete block house. A running bond is specified: 8″ × 8″ × 16″ nominal size concrete block are used. Concrete sills are used under the windows. Again, letters on the windows refer to a window schedule. Doors have numbers that refer to a door schedule. Figure 8–9 shows the window schedule and door schedule for this house. Door and window sizes are very important, of course. The masonry units cannot be laid until the exact exterior window and door frame size is known. Again, refer to the floor plan to pick up house and opening dimensions.

Window Symbols

Figure 8–10 shows commonly used window conventions and material symbols. Window swing is indicated by a dashed "V." The point of the "V" points to the side of the window with the hinge. The direction of slide on sliding windows is indicated with arrows. The material symbols used on elevations are shown in Figure 8–10, right. Brick may be shown by detailing each individual brick. However, brick detailing is rarely done since it takes too long. The simplified symbol for brick is parallel horizontal lines. Figure 8–7 shows the use of the simplified symbol for brick. The simplified symbol for brick is almost identical to the symbol for wood siding. The two symbols need not be confused since notes or callouts on the elevation will specify the type of siding or masonry units used.

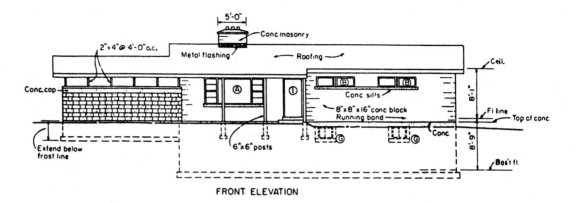

FRONT ELEVATION

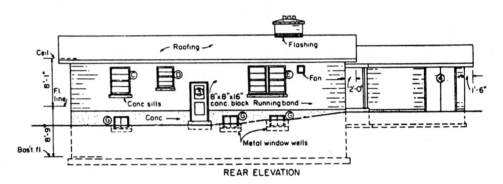

REAR ELEVATION

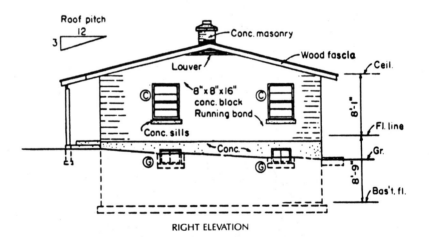

RIGHT ELEVATION

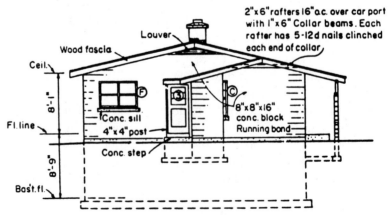

LEFT ELEVATION

FIGURE 8-8
Elevations for a concrete block house.

WINDOW SCHEDULE

Mark	Size Width	Height	Description	No. Req.
Ⓐ	2'-0" x 4'-6"		Double hung	2
	5'-8" x 4'-6"		Fixed	1
Ⓑ	3'-4" x 1'-4"		Twin awning	2
Ⓒ	3'-4" x 4'-6"		Double hung	4
Ⓓ	2'-8" x 3'-2"		" "	1
Ⓔ	3'-4" x 4'-6"		Twin double hung	1
Ⓕ	5'-4" x 2'-10"		Awning	1
Ⓖ	2-8⅞ x 1-10¾		2 Lt - 15x20 glass	7

Basement sash metal - all other wood
All operating sash screened

DOOR SCHEDULE

Mark	Size	Description
①	3'-0" x 6'-8" x 1¾"	Flush panel - exterior
②	3'-0" x 6'-9" x 1⅛"	Screen
③	3'-0" x 6'-8" x 1¾"	One panel - exterior glazed
④	2-2'-6" x 6'-8" x ¾"	T & G with battens
⑤	3'-0" x 6'-9" x 1⅛"	Screen
⑥	2'-4" x 6'-8" x 1⅜"	Flush panel - interior
⑦	2'-8" x 6'-8" x 1⅜"	" " "
⑧	3'-0" x 6'-8" x 1⅜"	" " "
⑨	2'-6" x 4'-0" x ¾"	Plywood
⑩	Accordion type doors as indicated on plan	
	Sliding doors are indicated for closets	

FIGURE 8–9
Window and door schedules (Refer to Figure 8–8 elevations.)

FOUNDATION PLANS

Foundation plans show views looking straight down on the exposed foundation. A drawing made looking straight down on the structure is called an *orthographic view* or *plan view*. Orthographic views always look straight at the surface of the building; they are always two-dimensional. Both elevation views and plan views are orthographic. Plan views are a type of orthographic view that is made looking straight *down* on a surface. There are plot plans, roof plans, foundation plans, basement plans, first floor plans, second floor plans, and so forth. They all look straight down on the structure. The use of the term "plan" may be confusing. In general use, "plans" are taken to mean all the drawings needed to build something, such as a house or, say, a drill press. In strict and more accurate technical use, a "plan" is a two-dimensional drawing made looking straight down on a structure or an object.

Foundation plans show exposed views of the foundation. Figure 8–11 shows how a foundation plan is made. You must imagine that an imaginary cutting plane (top left) is passed through the house and the house is removed from the foundation (top right) to expose the foundation. The drafter then draws a two-dimensional plan view of the foundation, as shown in Figure 8–11, bottom left.

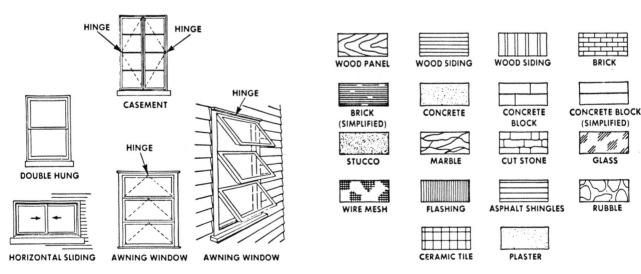

FIGURE 8–10
Window conventions and symbols. (Comteck)

Pictorial View   Cut-Away to Show Foundation Plan

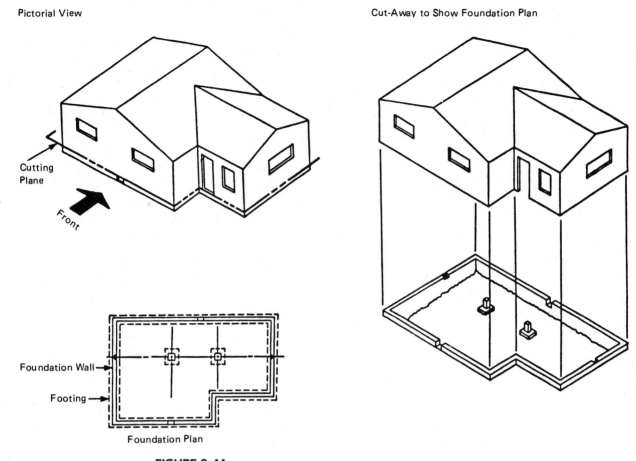

FIGURE 8-11
Foundation plan shows exposed view of the support. (Comteck)

Foundation plans show major structural elements, such as footings (with dashed, hidden lines), bearing walls, foundation walls, support piers, beams, and beam pockets.

FLOOR PLANS

Floor plans, like foundation plans, are two-dimensional orthographic views made looking straight down on the exposed floor. Figure 8-12 shows how floor plans are made. An imaginary cutting plane is passed through the house and the top of the house is removed. The floor plan view shows the layout of the exposed walls.

As mentioned, the first floor plan is the key blueprint in the set of drawings. The drafter draws the first floor plan first and then uses it for drawing other plans and elevations. Critical dimensions for locating openings are picked up from the first floor plan.

Floor plans are drawn for each floor. The floor plan drawn for the second floor is called the "second floor plan." Plans for the third floor are called the "third floor plan," and so forth.

Floor Plan Symbols

Figure 8-13 shows the material symbols used on the exposed floor plan walls. You should learn the

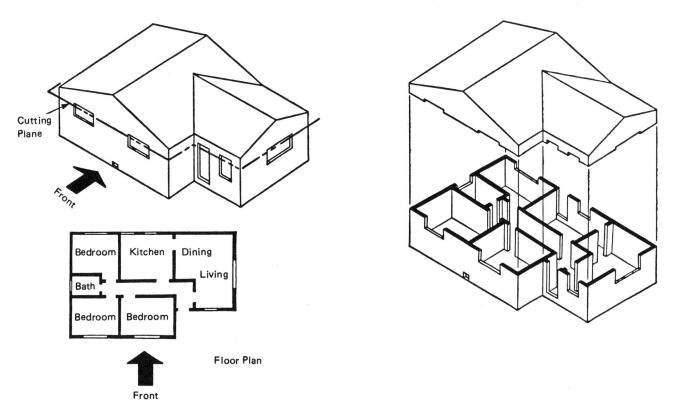

FIGURE 8-12
Floor plan shows exposed view of floor area. (Comteck)

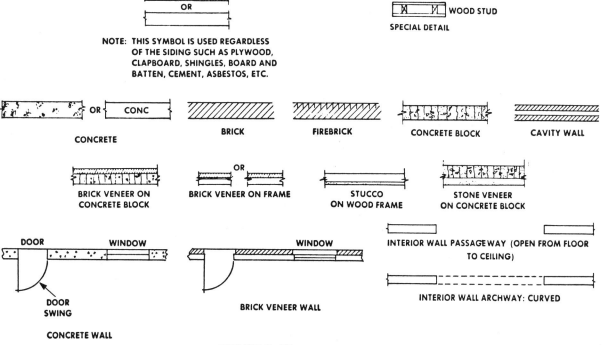

FIGURE 8-13
Floor plan symbols. (Comteck)

symbols for brick and concrete block. Notes are used to clarify the material used so there should be no confusion.

SECTIONS

Sections show vertical cross-cut views (two-dimensional orthographic views) of walls and other structural elements. A cutting plane line is used to show where the section is taken. Sections may be taken anywhere in a building.

Figure 8–14, left, shows how a cutting plane line is run through a window elevation. The arrows at the end of the cutting plane line point the direction to view the section (Figure 8–14, right). It is important to know from what direction to view or relate the section since the view often differs, depending on which direction it faces. Figure 8–14, Section A-A (right) shows the head and sill section of the window. The section is viewed (as directed by the arrows) looking to the right.

Figure 8-15 shows how the cutting plane line and arrows are used. Often a "balloon" is used with the cutting plane line. The top section of the balloon identifies the section or detail; the bottom section notes on what blueprint sheet it is shown.

Figure 8–16 shows some of the great variety of different cutting plane lines that are used. If no arrow is used on the cutting plane line (right), the completed section can be viewed either way. Note in Figure 8–16, top left, that the balloon may use additional identification. The top section of the balloon identifies the section number; the bottom left identifies *where* (from what sheet) the section was taken; and the bottom right of the balloon notes what sheet the section is *shown* on. This convention is used on commercial blueprints.

House Section

Figure 8–17 shows how a house section is taken. Cutting plane line A-A shows where the section is taken. The arrows point to the right so the completed section, Section A-A, is viewed looking to the right.

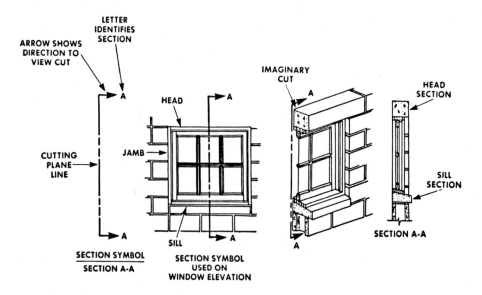

FIGURE 8-14
Cutting plane line shows where section is taken and from what direction to view it.

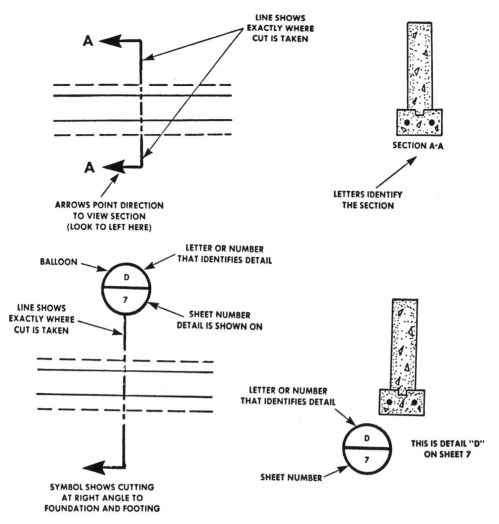

FIGURE 8-15
Use of cutting plane line. (Comteck)

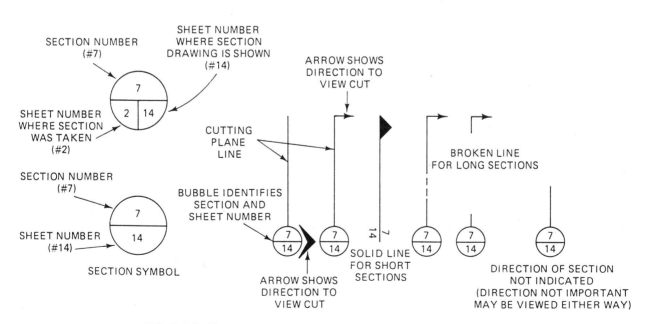

FIGURE 8-16
The balloon on the cutting plane line identifies the section. (Comteck)

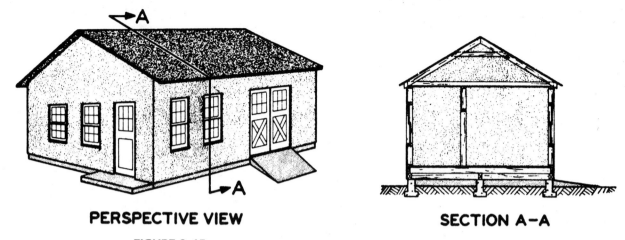

PERSPECTIVE VIEW   **SECTION A–A**

FIGURE 8-17
House section. Section is viewed from the direction the arrows point.

Wall Section

For the mason, the wall section is one of the most important drawings in a set of blueprints. It is important because it shows the details of the wall construction. Figure 8–18 shows how wall sections are taken. They run from the foundation to the roof. Figure 8–19 shows a typical wall section in a brick veneer house. Note that a great deal of essential information is given on the construction of the concrete block foundation and the brick veneer. For the mason, this detail is essential.

Section Symbols

Figure 8–20 shows symbols used on section views. The material wall symbols for sections are identical to the material wall symbols for plan views. This is logical since both plan views and sections show cross-cut views of the wall. Figure 8–21 relates the use of material symbols to plan views, sections, and elevations. Note that plan view symbols and section symbols are identical. Figure 8–22 shows section symbols used for steel reinforcement. A note will spell out size, length, and placement.

DETAILS

A detail, as already explained, is any large scale view. Section views, if drawn large, are sometimes referred to as details. On large projects, a whole sheet may be used just to show details. Details may be located using a bubble and cutting plane line, as shown in Figure 8–16.

MECHANICAL SYMBOLS

Although the mason is not responsible for reading mechanical drawings, it is useful to have a working knowledge of some of the basic symbols. Figure

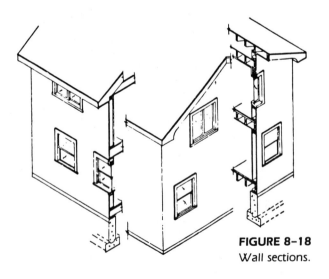

FIGURE 8-18
Wall sections.

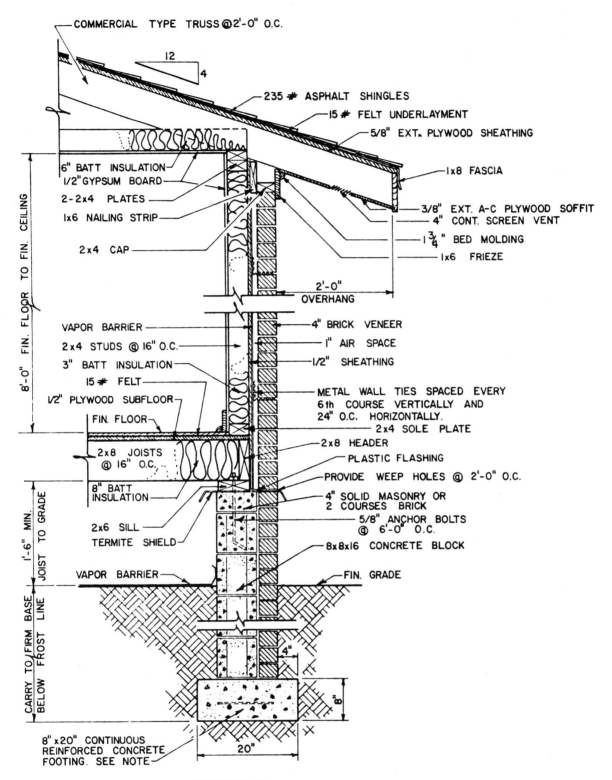

COMMERCIAL TYPE TRUSS @ 2'-0" O.C.

12
4

235 # ASPHALT SHINGLES
15 # FELT UNDERLAYMENT
5/8" EXT. PLYWOOD SHEATHING

6" BATT INSULATION
1/2" GYPSUM BOARD
2-2x4 PLATES
1x6 NAILING STRIP
2x4 CAP

1x8 FASCIA

3/8" EXT. A-C PLYWOOD SOFFIT
4" CONT. SCREEN VENT
1 3/4" BED MOLDING
1x6 FRIEZE

2'-0"
OVERHANG

8'-0" FIN. FLOOR TO FIN. CEILING

VAPOR BARRIER
2x4 STUDS @ 16" O.C.
3" BATT INSULATION
15 # FELT
1/2" PLYWOOD SUBFLOOR
FIN. FLOOR

4" BRICK VENEER
1" AIR SPACE
1/2" SHEATHING

METAL WALL TIES SPACED EVERY
6th COURSE VERTICALLY AND
24" O.C. HORIZONTALLY.
2x4 SOLE PLATE
2x8 HEADER
PLASTIC FLASHING
PROVIDE WEEP HOLES @ 2'-0" O.C.
4" SOLID MASONRY OR
2 COURSES BRICK
5/8" ANCHOR BOLTS
@ 6'-0" O.C.
8x8x16 CONCRETE BLOCK

2x8 JOISTS
@ 16" O.C.

8" BATT
INSULATION

2x6 SILL
TERMITE SHIELD

VAPOR BARRIER

FIN. GRADE

1'-6" MIN. JOIST TO GRADE
CARRY TO FIRM BASE BELOW FROST LINE

4"

8"

8" x 20" CONTINUOUS
REINFORCED CONCRETE
FOOTING. SEE NOTE

20"

FIGURE 8-19
Typical wall section for brick veneer house.

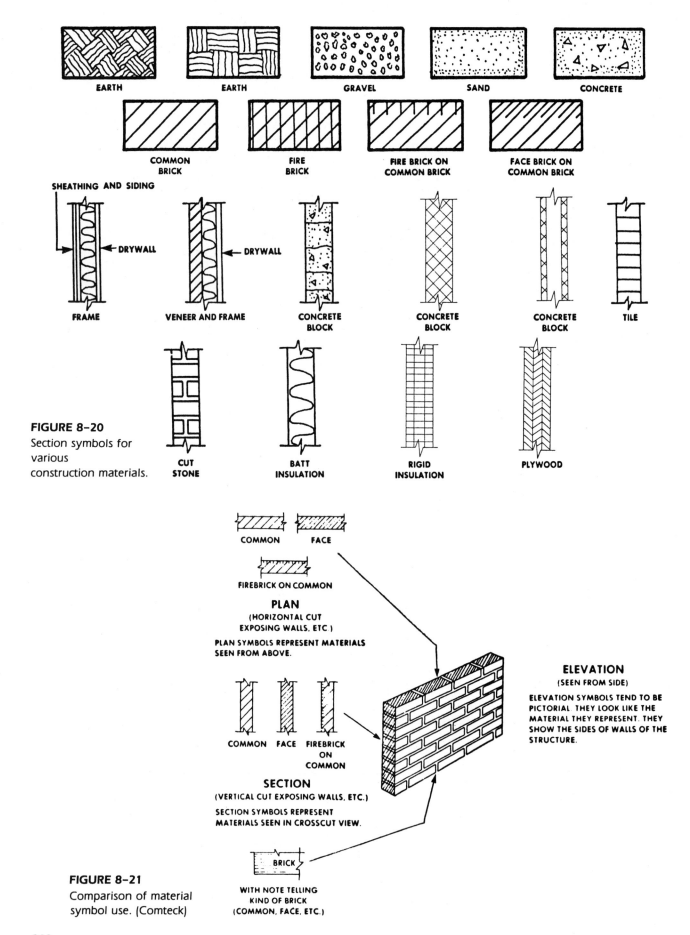

EARTH EARTH GRAVEL SAND CONCRETE

COMMON BRICK FIRE BRICK FIRE BRICK ON COMMON BRICK FACE BRICK ON COMMON BRICK

SHEATHING AND SIDING

← DRYWALL

← DRYWALL

FRAME VENEER AND FRAME CONCRETE BLOCK CONCRETE BLOCK CONCRETE BLOCK TILE

CUT STONE BATT INSULATION RIGID INSULATION PLYWOOD

FIGURE 8–20
Section symbols for various construction materials.

COMMON FACE

FIREBRICK ON COMMON

PLAN
(HORIZONTAL CUT EXPOSING WALLS, ETC.)

PLAN SYMBOLS REPRESENT MATERIALS SEEN FROM ABOVE.

COMMON FACE FIREBRICK ON COMMON

SECTION
(VERTICAL CUT EXPOSING WALLS, ETC.)

SECTION SYMBOLS REPRESENT MATERIALS SEEN IN CROSSCUT VIEW.

BRICK

WITH NOTE TELLING KIND OF BRICK (COMMON, FACE, ETC.)

ELEVATION
(SEEN FROM SIDE)

ELEVATION SYMBOLS TEND TO BE PICTORIAL. THEY LOOK LIKE THE MATERIAL THEY REPRESENT. THEY SHOW THE SIDES OF WALLS OF THE STRUCTURE.

FIGURE 8–21
Comparison of material symbol use. (Comteck)

292

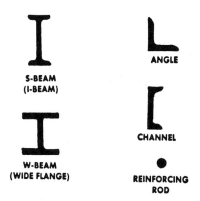

FIGURE 8-22
Section symbols for steel.

8-23 shows a few common symbols for plumbing and heating specifications (top) and electrical specifications (bottom). Many of the plumbing and heating symbols are pictorial; that is, they look like the thing they symbolize. The mason is required to locate openings for mechanical, plumbing, and electrical runs.

ABBREVIATIONS

You will run across a great number of different abbreviations on the blueprints you work with. Most of the abbreviations will be used on notes that

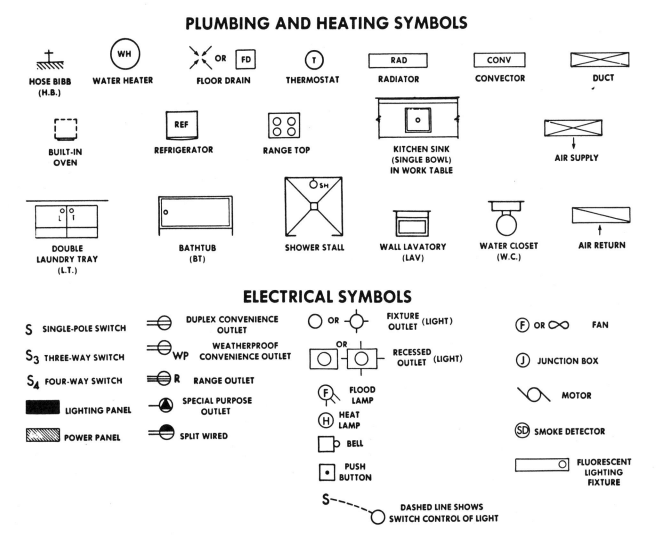

FIGURE 8-23
Symbols for plumbing, heating, and electrical specifications.

often point to different parts of the structure. You can usually figure out what the abbreviation means by where it is used or by how it relates to the structural element. Figure 8–24 shows some of the more commonly used abbreviations. Until you are familiar with blueprints, you may want to refer to this for help. Be warned, however, that the use of abbreviations is not consistent. Architects vary so you may still have some problems as you work with different sets of blueprints. Remember, though, how the abbreviation is used on the blueprint is the key to its meaning.

SPECIFICATIONS

As noted, specifications are written information on building a structure. The technical specifications may be very shcrt or they may run for hundreds of pages. For larger or more complex construction, specification standards have been developed by the Construction Specification Institute (CSI). CSI has developed a complete format for use in all areas of construction. Construction work is organized into the following 17 key areas:

Division 0—Bidding and Contract Requirements
Division 1—General Requirements
Division 2—Site Work
Division 3—Concrete
Division 4—Masonry
Division 5—Metals (Architectural and structural)
Division 6—Wood and Plastics
Division 7—Thermal and Moisture Protection
Division 8—Doors and Windows
Division 9—Finishes
Division 10—Specialties
Division 11—Equipment
Division 12—Furnishings
Division 13—Special Construction
Division 14—Conveying Systems
Division 15—Mechanical
Division 16—Electrical

Division 4 covers masonry work. The major discussions are broken down into sections that give further work details. Division 4, for example, is broken down into the following 8 major sections:

DIVISION 4—MASONRY

04050	MASONRY PROCEDURES
04100	MORTAR
04150	MASONRY ACCESSORIES
04200	UNIT MASONRY
04400	STONE
04500	MASONRY RESTORATION AND CLEANING
04550	REFRACTORIES
04600	CORROSION RESISTANT MASONRY

Each of these sections is further broken down on the actual specification.

A typical set of masonry specifications will spell out the conditions of the work on the job, including:

1. *Quality of workmanship*—how accurate and plumb the masonry wall should be. For example, "Do not exceed $\frac{1}{4}$ inch in 10-foot variation from plumb."

2. *Job conditions*—protection of masonry materials and protection of work from weather.

3. *Materials*—specific cements, mortars, limes, and aggregates to be used. Water should be clean, potable, and free from harmful acids, alkalies, or organic materials.

4. *Mortar mix*—type and proportion of mortars used.

5. *Execution of work*—preparing units and laying masonry walls and so forth. Information on joint thickness and tooling of joints is included.

6. *Expansion and control joints*—required for brick and concrete block, respectively.

7. *Flashing*—required.

8. *Repairing, pointing, and cleaning*—required.

Term	Abbreviation	Term	Abbreviation
Above Finish Floor	A.F.F.	Dimension	DIM
Anchor Bolt	A.B.	Ditto	DO
Acoustic	AC	Divided	DIV
Angle	∠	Double	DBL
Architectural Terra Cotta	ATC	Drawing	DWG
Asphalt	ASPH	Drywall	D.W.
Basement	BSMT	Each	EA
Beam	BM	Elevation	EL
Beveled	BEV	End to End	E to E
Bituminous	BIT	Existing	EXIST
Block	BL or BLK	Expansion	EXP
Bottom	BOT	Expansion Joint	EXP JT or E.J.
Brick	BRK	Exterior	EXT
Building	BLDG	Face Brick	F.B.
Building Line	B.L.	Facing Tile	F.T.
Caulking	CLKG	Finished	FIN
Cast Iron	CI	Finish Floor	FIN. FL
Cast Stone	CS	Firebrick	FB BK
Ceiling	CLG	First Floor Elevation	F.F.E.
Cement	CEM	Flashing	FL
Center	CTR	Floor	FL
Center to Center	C/C or C.C.	Footing	FTG
Centerline	CL or ℄	Foundation	FDN or FOUND
Chimney	CHIM		
Column	COL	Full Size	F.S.
Concrete	CONC	Galvanized	GALV
Concrete Block	CONC BLK	Gauge	GA
Concrete Masonry	C.M. or C/M	Girder	GDR
Concrete Masonry Unit	CMU	Glass Block	GL BL
Construction	CONST	Glazed Structural Unit	G.S.U.
Continuous	CONT	Grade	GR
Control Joint	C.J. or CONT JT	Grade Line	G.L.
		Ground	GRD
Damp proofing	DP	Head	HD
Detail	DET	Height	HT
Diagonal	DIAG	Horizontal	HORIZ
Diameter	DIA or D or φ	Inclusive	INCL

FIGURE 8-24

Reading blueprints. Abbreviations commonly used on the job.

Term	Abbreviation	Term	Abbreviation
Inside Diameter	I.D.	Reinforced	RNF or REINF
Insulation	INS or INSUL	Reinforced Concrete	R/C
Interior	INT	Reinforced Concrete Masonry	RCM
Jamb	JMB	Riser	R
Joint	JT	Rod	RD
Joist	J or JT	Rough Opening	R.O.
Length	L or LGTH	Round	RND or φ
Level	LEV	Rough	RGH
Limestone	LS	Scale	SC
Long	L or LG	Section	SECT
Manufacturer	MFR	Sheet Metal	S.M.
Masonry	MAS	Siding	SDG
Masonry Opening	M.O.	Sill	S or SL
Material	MTL or MAT	Similar	SIM
Maximum	MAX	Soffit	SOF
Metal	MET	Specification	SPEC
Millimeter	mm or MIL	Square	SQ
Minimum	MIN	Standard	STD
Miscellaneous	MISC	Steel	STL
Modular	MOD	Stone	ST
Nominal	NOM	Suspended	SUSP
Number	NO. or #	Symmetrical	SYM
On Center	O.C.	Temperature	T or TEMP
Opening	OPNG	Thick	THK
Opposite	OPP	Through	THRU
Outside Diameter	O.D.	Tongue and Grooved	T & G
Over	OVR	Top of Curb	TC
Overhead	OVHD or O.H.	Top of Foundation	T.O.F.
Plats	PL or ℙL	Top of Slab	TSL
Position	POS	Top of Wall	T/W or TW
Pound	LB or #	To Weather	T.W.
Precast	PC	Tread	T
Prefabricated	PREFAB	Typical	TYP
Prefinished	PFN	Underground	UG
Radius	R		
Recessed	R		

FIGURE 8-24   (Continued)

Term	Abbreviation
Unfinished	UNF or UNFIN
Vertical	VERT
Waterproof	WP
Waterproofing	WPFG
Weatherproof	WP
Weephole	WH
Weight	WT
Welded Wire Fabric	W.W.F.
Width	W or WD or WDTH
With	W/
Without	W/O

FIGURE 8-24 *(Continued)*

READING BLUEPRINTS

Pages 300 to 304 show basic blueprints for a three-bedroom brick veneer house. A full basement, open on two sides, can also be used as a living area. The following blueprint information is provided:

- Sheet 1. Exterior Elevations
- Sheet 2. Basement and Foundation Plan
- Sheet 3. First Floor Plan
- Sheet 4. Wall Sections
- Sheet 5. Interior Elevations, Electrical Key, and Door and Window Schedules.

To introduce you to the amount of information that can be picked up from blueprints, a brief overall analysis of the house is covered.

Foundation

The full basement (Sheet 2) shows the house support and support for the first floor.

Footing. A continuous 8″ × 20″ reinforced concrete footing runs around the house. The wall section (Sheet 4) shows that #4 ($\frac{1}{2}$-inch) reinforcing bars are used in the footing.

An 8″ × 16″ × 16″ pad footing (Sheet 4) is used under the 4-inch steel columns in the basement. Again #4 steel rebars are used.

An 8″ × 24″ × 24″ pad footing (Sheet 2) is used under the brick chimney (section drawing not shown).

Footings are used under the foundation supporting the front and rear entrance stoops. The basement entry has a 4-inch reinforced concrete slab (Sheet 2-section drawings not shown).

Basement wall footings are shown with hidden lines on the elevation views (Sheet 1).

Foundation Walls. The house foundation walls are constructed using concrete block (Sheet 4). Concrete block 12 inches thick is used below grade. Standard 8-inch thick block is used above grade. The 8-inch concrete block above grade exposes the 12-inch block that is used to support the brick veneer. The wall section (Sheet 4) shows this simple relationship.

A 4-inch solid concrete cap is placed on the top of the 8-inch blocks (Sheet 4).

The 4-inch brick veneer is attached to the 2″ × 4″ stud wall with metal wall ties (Sheet 4).

Basement Floor. The basement floor has a 4-inch concrete slab reinforced with 6″ × 6″ number 10 welded wire mesh (Sheet 2). A minimum 4-inch gravel fill is placed under the slab (Sheet 4). The Wall Section (Sheet 4) shows the detail of the floor construction.

House Support. The foundation walls along with a 6″ × 12″ beam support the superstructure or main part of the house. See Sheet 2.

The built-up beam runs down the center of the house. Three 2″ × 12″ timbers form the nominal 6″ × 12″ inch beam. (The actual size of the beam is $4\frac{1}{2}$″ × $11\frac{1}{2}$″.) The 43′-9″ beam is supported by three steel columns. Sheet 4, Wall Section, shows house support details. Beam ends extend over the concrete block foundation top.

Both the wood beam and the foundation walls are supported by footings.

The 2" × 6" sill is attached to the foundation wall with $\frac{5}{8}$-inch anchor bolts, 6'-0" O.C. See Wall Section, Sheet 4.

House Framing

Platform Floor. The platform floor is constructed of 2" × 10" floor joists running 16" O.C. Joists are doubled under the first floor partitions. Joists run from the foundation wall over to the 6" × 12" beam. The joists frame into the side of the beam (Sheet 4) and are supported by joist hangers. Sheet 2 shows joist information. Sheet 3 shows the location of partitions on the first floor.

Brick Veneer. A wood frame with brick veneer is used for the outside walls. The wall section, Sheet 4, shows construction details. The platform wall has 2" × 4" studs, 16" O.C. Insulation is placed between the studs. The brick veneer is tied to the frame wall with metal wall ties spaced every sixth course vertically and 24" O.C. horizontally.

Flashing is used through the brick veneer at sill height. Weep holes are left in the veneer base 24" O.C. (Sheet 4). Weep holes allow moisture drainage from the veneer wall.

Partitions. Location of all interior partitions are shown on the First Floor Plan and the Basement Plan. Conventional frame walls are used. Since no specific indication is made, you assume the walls are 2" × 4", 16" O.C. Wall heights are shown on Elevations and on the Wall Section.

Windows. Window locations are shown on the First Floor Plan and the Elevations. The types and sizes of windows are indicated on the Window Schedule, Sheet 5. *Letter* symbols are used to indicate window types.

Doors. Door locations are shown on the First Floor Plan. Exterior doors are also shown on Elevation Views. The Door Schedule (Sheet 5) gives the type and size of the different doors. Doors are indicated on the Floor Plan by *number* symbols.

Exterior Finish. Exterior finish is shown on elevation. Brick veneer is used on all walls. Gable ends have a wood siding with gable vents built in. The roof has #235 asphalt shingles. Wrought-iron railings are used at front and rear first floor entrances.

Interior Finish. Interior finish is shown on Interior Elevations (Sheet 5) and on the Wall Section (Sheet 4). The Wall Section spells out interior wall and ceiling finish ($\frac{1}{2}$-inch gypsum board) and floor ($\frac{3}{4}$-inch plywood subfloor, #15 felt and finish floor).

Ceiling. Ceiling framing and finish is shown on the Wall Section. The ceiling is held by the bottom chord of the roof trusses. Insulation is used between the trusses.

Stairs. A one-quarter turn wooden stairway runs from the first floor to the basement, as shown on Sheet 2. A total of 14 risers are used. The stairs are enclosed on the first floor but are open, with railing, in the basement. The stairway is supported by a 4" × 4" wood post in the basement. This is a conventional, carpenter-built stairway. No detail is provided.

Roof. The Wall Section shows roof framing and finish information. Trusses are used on 2-foot centers. Exterior plywood sheathing is used to cover the roof. Felt underlayment is used over the plywood; asphalt shingles finish off the roof.

Insulation. Insulation is used between outside studing and between ceiling trusses. Four-inch batt insulation is used in outside walls and 6-inch batt insulation is used between trusses.

Mechanical Information

Mechanical information is shown on First Floor and Basement plans. Mechanical information is referred to as HVAC: Heating, Ventilating, and Air Conditioning.

H.V.A.C. Very little heating and cooling information is shown. Since a chimney is provided, you can assume that an oil or gas-fired furnace is used. Either forced warm air or hot water is used. This is a general set of blueprints designed for different locations and different types of heating.

Vents from over the range and from the dryer run through the rear wall: First Floor Plan, Rear Elevation, and Kitchen Elevation #1.

The soil stack is shown in the bathroom wall by a circle (First Floor Plan). The elevations show where the chimney and plumbing stack vent are located.

Plumbing. Locations of plumbing fixtures are shown in plan views. The Rear Elevation shows the stack vent location. The soil pipe for the bathroom is shown as a small circle in the bathroom wall (First Floor Plan). The soil pipe wall should be 6 inches thick to allow room for the 4-inch soil pipe.

Electrical. Electrical fixtures and outlets are shown by symbol on the plan views. Outside entrance lights are shown on the front and rear elevations.

House Expansion

Future growth is planned into the basic house design. The First Floor Plan and Right Elevation show the location of the 14'-0" × 26'-10" garage and storage area.

Masonry Work

Once you have analyzed the structural framework of the building, it is easy to understand the required masonry work. Sheet 1 gives the information on the position of wall openings and the size of windows and exterior doors. Sheet 2 shows the top of foundation walls. The brick veneer is located flush to the outside edge of the foundation wall top. The wall section (Sheet 4) shows the relationship of the foundation top and veneer. The wall section also shows how the veneer is attached to the wood frame wall.

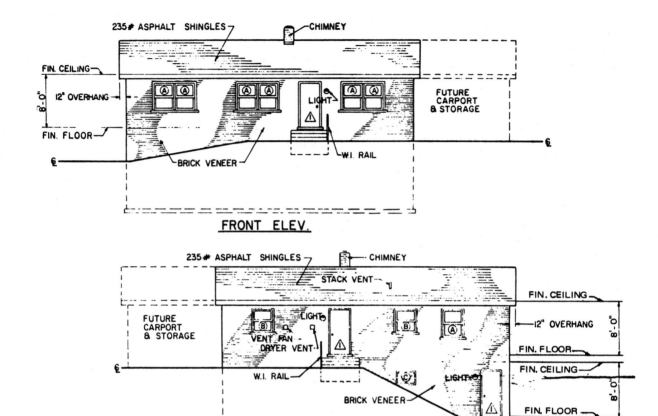

235# ASPHALT SHINGLES — CHIMNEY

FIN. CEILING

12" OVERHANG

8'-0"

FIN. FLOOR

LIGHT

FUTURE CARPORT & STORAGE

BRICK VENEER

W.I. RAIL

FRONT ELEV.

235# ASPHALT SHINGLES — CHIMNEY

STACK VENT

FUTURE CARPORT & STORAGE

VENT FAN
DRYER VENT

LIGHT

W.I. RAIL

BRICK VENEER

LIGHT

FIN. CEILING

12" OVERHANG

8'-0"

FIN. FLOOR

FIN. CEILING

8'-0"

FIN. FLOOR

REAR ELEV.

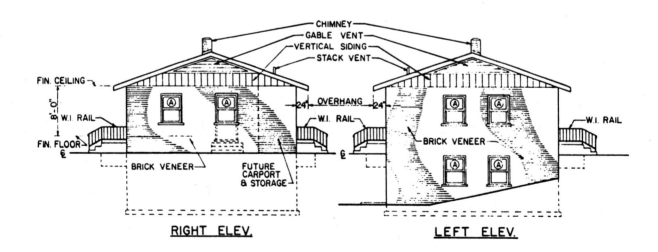

CHIMNEY
GABLE VENT
VERTICAL SIDING
STACK VENT

FIN. CEILING

8'-0"

W.I. RAIL

FIN. FLOOR

BRICK VENEER

24" OVERHANG 24"

W.I. RAIL

W.I. RAIL

FUTURE CARPORT & STORAGE

BRICK VENEER

W.I. RAIL

RIGHT ELEV.

LEFT ELEV.

ELEVATIONS

SHEET 1

BASEMENT & FOUNDATION PLAN.

SHEET 2

FIRST FLOOR PLAN

SHEET 3

302

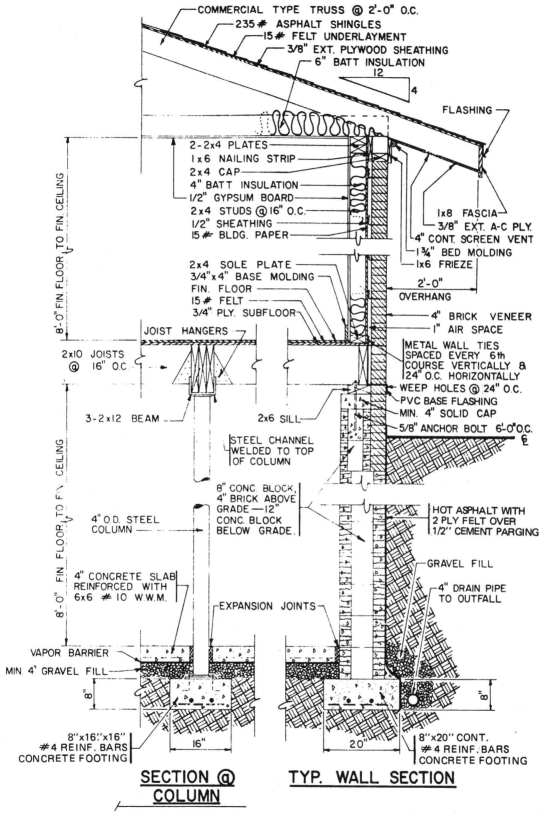

COMMERCIAL TYPE TRUSS @ 2'-0" O.C.
235 # ASPHALT SHINGLES
15 # FELT UNDERLAYMENT
3/8" EXT. PLYWOOD SHEATHING
6" BATT INSULATION

12
4

FLASHING

2-2x4 PLATES
1x6 NAILING STRIP
2x4 CAP
4" BATT INSULATION
1/2" GYPSUM BOARD
2x4 STUDS @ 16" O.C.
1/2" SHEATHING
15 # BLDG. PAPER

1x8 FASCIA
3/8" EXT. A-C PLY.
4" CONT. SCREEN VENT
1 3/4" BED MOLDING
1x6 FRIEZE

2'-0"
OVERHANG

2x4 SOLE PLATE
3/4"x4" BASE MOLDING
FIN. FLOOR
15 # FELT
3/4" PLY. SUBFLOOR

4" BRICK VENEER
1" AIR SPACE

8'-0" FIN. FLOOR TO FIN CEILING

JOIST HANGERS

METAL WALL TIES
SPACED EVERY 6th
COURSE VERTICALLY &
24" O.C. HORIZONTALLY
WEEP HOLES @ 24" O.C.
PVC BASE FLASHING
MIN. 4" SOLID CAP
5/8" ANCHOR BOLT 6'-0"O.C.

2x10 JOISTS
@ 16" O.C.

3-2x12 BEAM
2x6 SILL

STEEL CHANNEL
WELDED TO TOP
OF COLUMN

8" CONC. BLOCK,
4" BRICK ABOVE
GRADE —12"
CONC. BLOCK
BELOW GRADE.

HOT ASPHALT WITH
2 PLY FELT OVER
1/2" CEMENT PARGING

4" O.D. STEEL
COLUMN

GRAVEL FILL

4" DRAIN PIPE
TO OUTFALL

4" CONCRETE SLAB
REINFORCED WITH
6x6 # 10 W.W.M.

8'-0" FIN. FLOOR TO FIN. CEILING

EXPANSION JOINTS

VAPOR BARRIER
MIN. 4" GRAVEL FILL

8"

8"

8"x16"x16"
4 REINF. BARS
CONCRETE FOOTING

16"

20"

8"x20" CONT.
4 REINF. BARS
CONCRETE FOOTING

SECTION @ COLUMN

TYP. WALL SECTION

SHEET 4

303

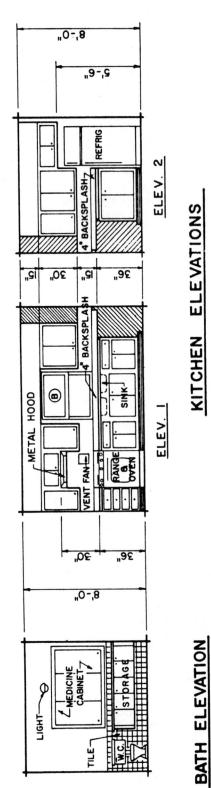

KITCHEN ELEVATIONS

ELEV. 1

ELEV. 2

BATH ELEVATION

DOOR SCHEDULE		
MARK	SIZE	TYPE	Nº REQD
△1	3'-0"x6'-8"	WOOD SOLID CORE, EXTERIOR	3
△2	2'-8"x6'-8"	WOOD HOLLOW CORE, INTERIOR	4
△3	4'-0"x6'-8"	WOOD LOUVERED BIFOLD	4
△4	2'-0"x6'-8"	" "	2
△5	2'-6"x6'-8"	" "	1
△6	3'-0"x6'-8"	FOLDING PARTITION	1

W.H. = WATER HEATER
VTR = VENT THROUGH ROOF

ELECTRICAL KEY	
MARK	TYPE
S	SINGLE POLE SWITCH
S₃	THREE WAY SWITCH
	DUPLEX CONVENIENCE OUTLET
	RANGE OUTLET
	SPECIAL PURPOSE OUTLET
	CEILING OUTLET
	CEILING OUTLET W/PULL SWITCH
	WATERPROOF WALL OUTLET
	FLUORESCENT FIXTURE

WINDOW SCHEDULE		
MARK	SIZE	TYPE	Nº REQD
Ⓐ	3'-0"x4'-0"	WOOD DOUBLE HUNG	13
Ⓑ	3'-0"x3'-4"	"	2
Ⓒ	3'-0"x2'-0"	ALUMINUM HOPPER	1

NOTE : CHECK LOCAL CODES BEFORE STARTING CONSTRUCTION

SHEET 5

CHAPTER REVIEW

QUESTIONS

Write answers on separate piece of paper.

1. How do blueprints and specifications work together?

2. In case of conflict, which has the most authority—blueprints or specifications?

3. What do the designations A, S, M, or E mean when used on blueprints?

4. What would the designation "M1 of 3" mean if used in a blueprint?

5. What does the designation of ¼" = 1"–0" mean?

6. What does the designation F.S. mean?

7. Define object lines, centerlines, hidden lines, break lines, and cutting plane lines.

8. Explain what an orthographic view is and how it is made.

9. Explain how elevations are drawn.

10. What are plan views? How are they made?

11. How are door and window schedules used?

12. How are foundation plans and floor plans made?

13. How are section views made?

14. What division of the CSI specifications covers masonry?

15. Refer to the figure below and identify the types of lines used.

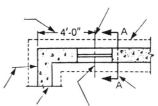

16. From what direction should you look at or view Section A-A (below) in the foundation section?

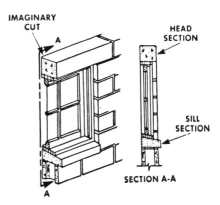

17. Identify the section number (below), what sheet the section is taken from, and what sheet the section is located on.

18. Identify the mechanical symbols below:

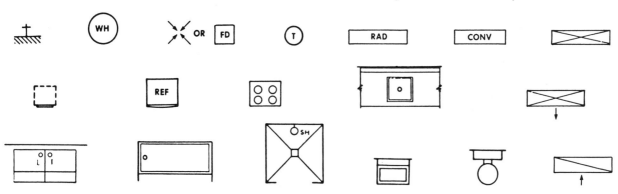

19. Identify the material symbols below:

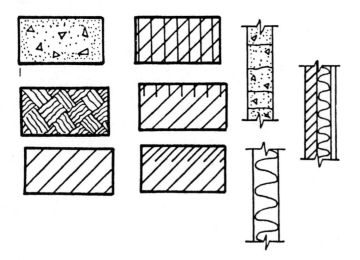

20. Write out the meaning of the abbreviations:

A.F.F.	C.M.	O.D.
A.B.	CMU	℞
BSMT	C.J.	φ
BEV	EXP 3T	SOF
BLK	F.B.	ST
B.L.	FBRK	T.O.F.
CLG	F.F.E.	TYP
CEM	FL	UNF
C.C.	JT	WP
℄	M.O.	WF
CHIM	MTL	W.W.F.
CONC	NOM	W/O
	O.C.	

TRADE TEST

Reading blueprints for Exterior and Interior Details. (Refer to the set of blueprints, sheets 1 to 5, on pages 300 to 304.)

1. The chimney is located in the _____ elevation roof side.

2. The brick veneer goes all the way to the roof line. True or False.

3. The outside electric light by the back door is located
   a. to the left of the door.
   b. over the door.
   c. to the right of the door.
   d. beside the left window.

4. Gable vents are located at both ends of the house. True or False.

5. How many horizontal rows of tile are used on the bathroom wall?

6. One bathroom light is located on the wall over the _____.

7. How high is the back splash in the kitchen?

8. The doors under the kitchen sink
   a. open from the right side.
   b. open from the left side.
   c. open from the center with hinges on the outside.
   d. are sliding.

9. The Bath Elevation shows the
   a. front wall.
   b. rear wall.
   c. left wall.
   d. right wall.

10. The front door is hinged on the _____.

11. All of the windows in the front are _____. (Describe and give size.)

12. The rear basement window is _____. (Describe and give size.)

13. What size is the basement door?

14. What size is the first-floor bathroom door?

15. Which elevation has only four double-hung windows?

TRADE TEST

Reading blueprints for structural support and framing. (Refer to the blueprint sheets 1 to 5 on pages 300 to 304.

1. What size is the foundation wall footing?

2. What size is the column footing?

3. What size is the chimney footing?

4. What kind of reinforcement is used in the 4-inch basement slab?

5. The built-up 6-inch × 12-inch beam is supported by
   a. three steel columns and pilasters.
   b. three steel columns with pad footings.
   c. three steel columns and foundation wall tops.
   d. steel columns and joist hangers

6. Floor joists run
   a. from foundation walls to the building beam.
   b. between partitions.
   c. from wall to wall.
   d. between foundation walls and column supports.

7. The outside of the stair platform is supported by _____.

8. Front and rear stoops are constructed of _____.

9. First floor partitions are supported by the floor platform with
   a. 4-inch × 4-inch posts.
   b. steel columns.
   c. double joists.
   d. special cross bridging.

10. The brick veneer is tied to the frame walls and supported on _____.

11. The built-up beam is held to the steel columns with _____.

12. The floor joists are nailed into the side of the built-up beam and are held by _____.

13. The 2-inch × 6-inch sill under the platform rests on a _____.

14. The outside of the frame house walls has
    a. 1/2-inch gypsum board.
    b. 1/2-inch plywood sheathing with building paper.
    c. #30 felt.
    d. #235 asphalt shingles.

15. The roof trusses are supported by
    a. a brick wall.
    b. ceiling joists.
    c. interior partitions and gypsum board.
    d. two, 2-inch × 4-inch plates on top of the wall.

16. Roof trusses are spaced _____.

17. Attic venting is provided by a
    a. ceiling fan.
    b. stack vent.
    c. screen vent in cornice and gable vents.
    d. screen vent in cornice and roof fan.

18. The roof slope is _____.

19. The roof cornice overhang is _____.

20. The roof gable overhang is _____.

Chapter 9

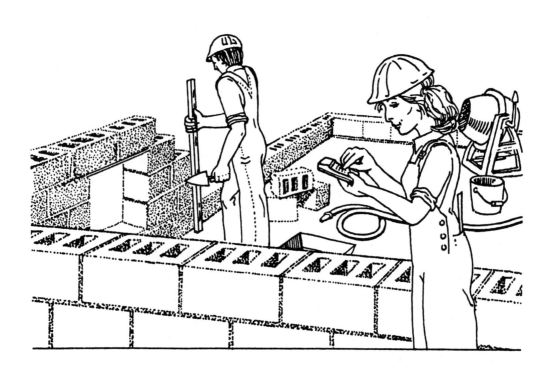

MASONRY MATH
AND ESTIMATING

After studying this chapter you should be able to:
- Read and use the inch rule.
- Explain and use layout and measuring conventions.
- Work with feet and inches.
- Work with fractions.
- Work with decimals.
- Estimate brick and concrete block needs.
- Estimate mortar needs.

With today's hand-held calculators, it is a simple matter to perform calculations and estimate materials needed. This presumes, of course, that you are familiar with the basic principles involved. If you don't understand the basics, you will not understand how to use the calculator properly nor will you be able to quickly verify the accuracy of any calculator answer.

A math test is provided at the end of this chapter. It's a good idea to take this test first, before reviewing the basics covered in this chapter. Take the test, and then check your answers. The test answers are given at the end of the chapter. Make a list of the answers you missed on the test. These will identify areas of weaknesses. Take care to review the math in the areas where you are weak.

READING AN INCH RULE OR TAPE

Much of the masonry work on the job presumes you can accurately read an inch rule. Without this basic and simple skill, you cannot do a professional job. Review these basics to make sure you understand the use of the inch rule. Both folding rules and steel tapes are used on the job. As noted in Chapter 2, you should use a folding rule with brick spacing or modular spacing divisions.

Figure 9-1 shows how an inch is divided into 16 parts. Each part represents 1/16 of an inch, written as 1/16′. When reading the tape, you don't have to count the number of spaces. As shown in Figure 9-2, the short marks represent 1/16ths, medium short marks are 1/4ths, and 1/2-inch marks are longer. The inch marks are longest and have a number representing a whole inch. Figure 9-3 shows an inch rule with various readings marked. One foot, of course, is 12 inches. In technical usage, one foot is commonly written as 1′-0″; 13 inches is written as 1′-1″; 14 inches as 1′-2″, and so forth. If inch fractions are used, they are written in the same manner. For example, 1 foot, 3 1/2 inches is written as 1′-3 1/2″.

When using the folding rule, always be sure to put one end flat against one side of the distance being measured. Figure 9-4 shows an opening being measured. With one end square against one

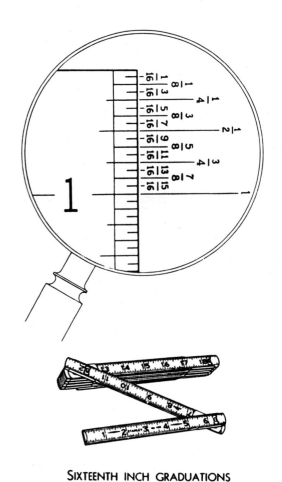

FIGURE 9-1
Reading the inch rule. (Stanley Works)

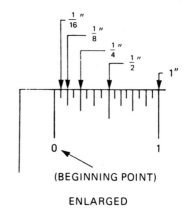

FIGURE 9-2
Inch is divided into fractions.

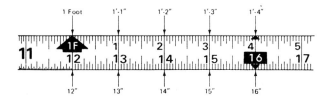

FIGURE 9-3
Sample readings on ruler.

side, read the inch measure looking down on the rule. Figure 9-5 shows the use of a mason's rule with standard brick spacings. As shown, place one end evenly at the base of the wythe.

LAYOUT AND MEASURING CONVENTIONS

Most architects show dimensions on blueprints following standard conventions. Figure 9-6 shows standard layout and dimensioning conventions. Wood frame construction is dimensioned to the outside face of the stud; any outside sheathing or finish is ignored. This is useful to the carpenter since he knows exactly where to locate the outside face of the studs. This same convention is followed when dimensioning brick veneer. Dimensions are given to the outside face of the wood studs. The mason, when he studies a set of blueprints for a brick veneer house, knows that the house dimensions shown do *not* include the brick veneer. The outside face of the brick will be be-

FIGURE 9-4
Measuring an opening. (Stanley Works)

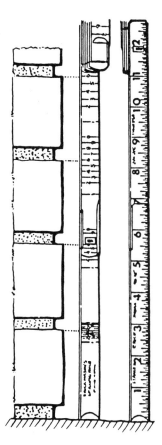

FIGURE 9-5
Measuring with mason's rule. (Brick Institute of America)

yond the dimensions shown. The mason knows to add on the depth or thickness of the brick unit plus the one-inch air space between the veneer and the wood frame. He then knows where to locate the face of the veneer. Openings in frame construction or veneer are dimensioned to the centerline of the opening.

Solid masonry, such as that in a double-wythe wall or reinforced concrete, is dimensioned to the outside face and also across the wall thickness. Openings in solid masonry, such as windows or doorways, are dimensioned up to the edge of the opening and also across the opening. Solid masonry walls and openings are critical. They can't be easily torn down and moved, so it's customary to use two dimensions. Figure 9-7 illustrates standard dimensioning procedures for frame, veneer, and solid masonry walls and openings.

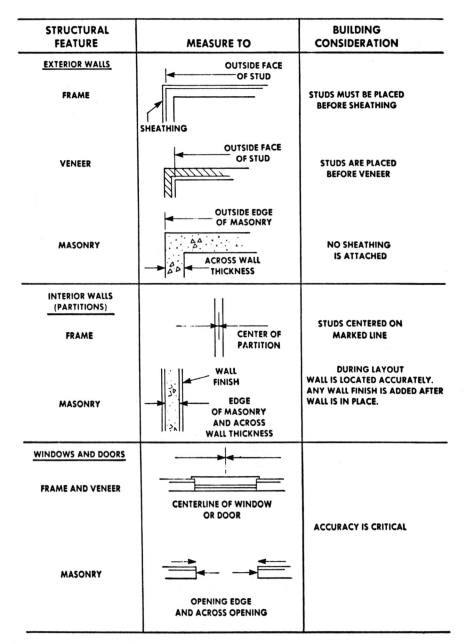

STRUCTURAL FEATURE	MEASURE TO	BUILDING CONSIDERATION
EXTERIOR WALLS FRAME	OUTSIDE FACE OF STUD SHEATHING	STUDS MUST BE PLACED BEFORE SHEATHING
VENEER	OUTSIDE FACE OF STUD	STUDS ARE PLACED BEFORE VENEER
MASONRY	OUTSIDE EDGE OF MASONRY ACROSS WALL THICKNESS	NO SHEATHING IS ATTACHED
INTERIOR WALLS (PARTITIONS) FRAME	CENTER OF PARTITION	STUDS CENTERED ON MARKED LINE
MASONRY	WALL FINISH EDGE OF MASONRY AND ACROSS WALL THICKNESS	DURING LAYOUT WALL IS LOCATED ACCURATELY. ANY WALL FINISH IS ADDED AFTER WALL IS IN PLACE.
WINDOWS AND DOORS FRAME AND VENEER	CENTERLINE OF WINDOW OR DOOR	ACCURACY IS CRITICAL
MASONRY	OPENING EDGE AND ACROSS OPENING	

FIGURE 9–6
Standard layout and measuring conventions. (Comteck)

WORKING WITH FEET AND INCHES

On the job you will have to work with feet and inches—adding together or subtracting different measurements or dimensions. As noted, the foot has 12 inches. Most inch measurements are converted to feet and inches. You divide inches by 12 to get feet. For example, a 40-inch measurement would be converted to 3'–4": 40" ÷ 12" = 3' plus 4" left over, or 3'–4". You should know the basics of doing feet and inch calculations by hand. There are, of course, hand-held calculators that will do feet and inch calculations (Figure 9–8).

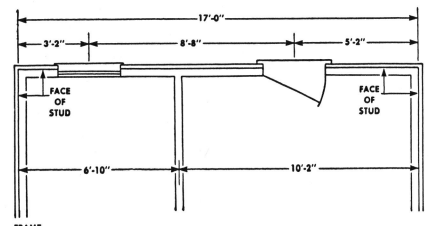

FRAME
EXTERIOR DIMENSIONS: TO OUTSIDE OF STUD FACE.
INTERIOR DIMENSIONS: TO CENTER OF STUD (FRAME PARTITION).

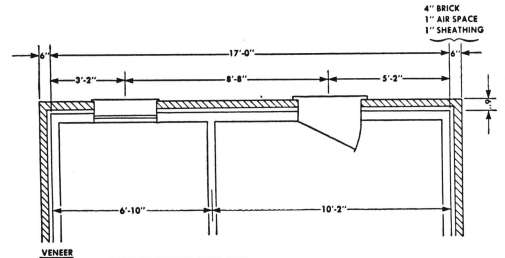

VENEER
EXTERIOR DIMENSIONS: TO OUTSIDE OF STUD FACE.
INTERIOR DIMENSIONS: TO CENTER OF STUD (FRAME PARTITION).

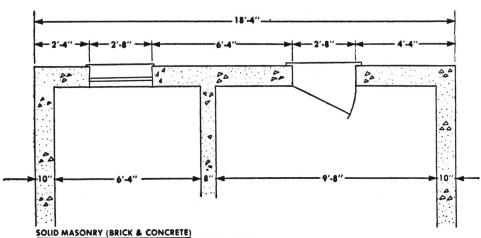

SOLID MASONRY (BRICK & CONCRETE)
EXTERIOR DIMENSIONS: TO OUTSIDE FACE OF MASONRY.
INTERIOR DIMENSIONS: TO OUTSIDE FACE OF SOLID MASONRY.
 TO CENTER OF STUD (FRAME PARTITION).

FIGURE 9–7
Typical dimensioning practices. (Comteck)

FIGURE 9–8
Working on the job. (State of New Jersey, Department of Education, Division of Vocational Education)

Addition

You will often have to add feet measures. For example, if you wanted to add 2'–3" plus 1'–7", you would write it out as

$$
\begin{array}{r}
2'\text{–}3'' \\
+\ 1'\text{–}7'' \\
\hline
=\ 3'\text{–}10''
\end{array}
$$

Another example is

$$
\begin{array}{r}
6'\text{–}10'' \\
+\ 3'\text{–}8'' \\
\hline
=\ 9''\text{–}18''\ \text{or}\ 10'\text{–}6''
\end{array}
$$

Here the 18 inches is converted to 12 inches (one foot) plus 6 inches. The extra foot is added to the 9 feet to get 10 feet, plus the left over 6 inches or 10'–6".

Subtraction

Subtraction is also fairly simple. For example

$$
\begin{array}{r}
3'\text{–}10'' \\
-\ 1'\text{–}8'' \\
\hline
=\ 2'\text{–}2''
\end{array}
$$

Another example is

$$
\begin{array}{r}
4'\text{–}8'' \\
-\ 2'\text{–}11'' \\
\hline
\end{array}
$$

which is converted to

$$
\begin{array}{r}
3'\text{–}20'' \\
-\ 2'\text{–}11'' \\
\hline
=\ 1'\text{–}9''
\end{array}
$$

Since 11 inches cannot be subtracted from 8 inches, you bring another foot or 12 inches over to get 3'–20" which can then be easily subtracted.

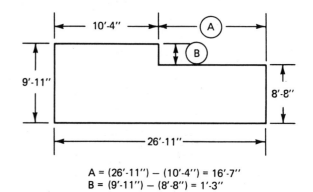

A = (26'-11") – (10'-4") = 16'-7"
B = (9'-11") – (8'-8") = 1'-3"

FIGURE 9–9
Finding missing dimensions.

You will frequently have to work with blueprints or measurements on the job to pick up missing dimensions. Knowing how to add and subtract feet and inches is critical. Figure 9–9 shows a figure with missing dimensions A and B. You can find dimension A by subtracting the two known dimensions: $(26'-11'') - (10'-4'') = 16'-7'$. Dimension B is also found by subtracting known dimensions: $(9'-11'') - (8'-8'') = 1'-3''$.

Division

When dividing feet and inches, each is divided separately. For example

1. $6'-3'' \div 2 = 3' - 1\frac{1}{2}''$

2. $11'-1'' \div 4 = 2\frac{3}{4}'$ and $\frac{1}{4}''$ or $2'$ and $9''$ plus $\frac{1}{4}'' = 2'-9\frac{1}{4}''$. The $\frac{3}{4}'$ converts to $9''$.

3. $8'-3'' \div 4 = 2'-\frac{3}{4}''$

Always convert any fraction of a foot to inches. Some examples are as follows:

1. $10'-4'' \div 3 = 3\frac{1}{3}'$ and $1\frac{1}{3}''$ or $3'-5\frac{1}{3}''$ (convert $\frac{1}{3}'$ to $4''$)

2. $4'-2'' \div 5 = \frac{4}{5}'$ and $\frac{2}{5}''$ or

(convert $\frac{4}{5}'$ to inches $\dfrac{4 \times 12}{5} = \dfrac{48''}{5} = 9\frac{3}{5}''$)

$9\frac{3}{5}''$ and $\frac{2}{5}'' = 9\frac{5}{5}''$ or $10''$

Multiplication

Feet and inches are multiplied separately. For example

1. $4'-2'' \times 3 = 12'-6''$

2. $1'-2'' \times 14 = 14'$ and $28''$ or $16'-4''$ ($28''$ converts to $2'-4''$)

3. $3'-2\frac{1}{4}'' \times 5 = 15'$ and $10\frac{5}{4}''$ or $15'-11\frac{1}{4}''$ ($\frac{5}{4}''$ converts to $1\frac{1}{4}''$)

FRACTIONS

Fractions are parts of a whole. For example, $\frac{1}{4}$th is one part of a whole divided into four parts; $\frac{1}{8}$th is one part of a whole divided into eight parts. Figure 9–10, top, illustrates this basic and simple concept. Fractions can be easily understood by working with an inch rule. Figure 9–10, bottom, shows an inch broken into parts: two $\frac{1}{2}$ parts or fractions equal a whole or 1 inch; four $\frac{1}{4}$ parts or fractions equal a whole; eight $\frac{1}{8}$ parts or fractions equal a whole.

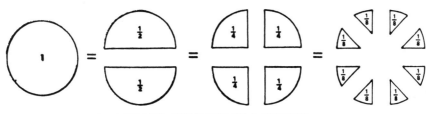

FRACTIONS ARE PART OF A WHOLE
$\frac{8}{8} = \frac{4}{4} = \frac{2}{2} = 1$

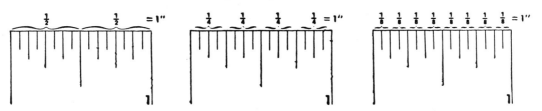

FIGURE 9–10
Fractions are part of a whole. (Comteck)

Adding or Subtracting Fractions

Fractions can be added or subtracted if their bottom number, called a denominator, is the same. For example, ¼ + ¼ can easily be added to equal ²⁄₄ or ½. In adding or subtracting, only the top part of the fraction, the numerator, is added, the bottom, or denominator, always stays the same—that is, they must have a *common denominator*. For example,

1. ⅛ + ²⁄₈ + ⁴⁄₈ = ⅞
2. ³⁄₁₆ + ¹⁄₁₆ + ⁵⁄₁₆ + ²⁄₁₆ = ¹¹⁄₁₆

On the other hand, ³⁄₁₆ + ⅛ + ½ *cannot* be added together because their denominators are different. (They can be added if their denominators are changed so they are the same: ³⁄₁₆ + ²⁄₁₆ + ⁸⁄₁₆ = ¹³⁄₁₆.)

Common Denominator

As noted, you can only add or subtract fractions if their denominators are the same. When they are different, they must be changed so they are the same or "common." For example, you can't add 1/2 + 1/4. However, you can change 1/2 to 1/4ths by multiplying both the top *and* the botom by 2: 1/2 × 2/2 = 2/4. The fraction 2/4 has exactly the same value as 1/2; 2/4 reduces to 1/2. You can add 2/4 + 1/4 = 3/4.

You can change any fraction to another fraction with a different denominator by multiplying by a whole number fraction. For example, 2/2 equals 1; likewise 3/3, 4/4, 5/5, 6/6, and so on are all equal to *one*. Multiplying by a whole number fraction changes both the denominator and numerator but does not change the *value* of the fraction.

Some common denominators are not so obvious. For example, if you wanted to add 1/3 + 1/4 you would have to find a common denominator for both fractions. You can find a common denominator by multiplying the two denominators together: 3 × 4 = 12. If both fractions were converted to fractions whose denominators equal 12, they could be worked with. You can always find a

common denominator between two fractions by multiplying them together. To convert 1/3 to 12ths, multiply by 4/4:

$$1/3 \times 4/4 = 4/12$$

To convert 1/4 to 12ths, multiply by 3/3:

$$1/4 \times 3/3 = 3/12$$

With the common denominator of 12, you can now add the two fractions:

$$4/12 + 3/12 = 7/12$$

Some examples are

1. 3/16 + 1/8 + 1/2 =
convert 1/8 to 2/16 (multiply by 2/2)
convert 1/2 to 8/16 (multiply by 8/8)
Then, 3/16 + 2/16 + 8/16 = 13/16

2. 5/8 – 1/16 =
convert 5/8 to 10/16 (multiply by 2/2)
Then, 10/16 − 1/16 = 9/16

3. (3/8 + 1/16 + 1/4) − 1/32 =
3/8 to 12/32 (multiply by 4/4)
1/16 to 2/32 (multiply by 2/2)
1/4 to 8/32 (multiply by 8/8)
Then, (12/32 + 2/32 + 8/32) − 1/32 =
22/32 − 1/32 = 21/32

Reducing Fractions

Any fraction should be reduced to its lowest common denominator. It is easier to work with. For example, 4/8 should be reduced to 1/2—it has the same value. Of course, there may be layout situations where you would want to, in this case, work with the 4/8 measure rather than 1/2. If you had a fraction of 32/64 or 128/256, on the other hand, you would certainly want to reduce them. They both reduce to 1/2.

Fractions are reduced by dividing both the top and bottom numbers by the same number. For example, with the fraction 4/8, divide both the top and bottom by 4 to get 1/2. With 128/256, divide the top and bottom by 128 to get 1/2. For example

1. 6/8 converts to 3/4 (divide by 2/2)

2. 12/16 converts to 3/4 (divide by 4/4)

3. 8/64 converts to 1/8 (divide by 8/8)

4. 6/10 converts to 3/5 (divide by 2/2)

Improper Fractions

An improper fraction is a fraction that contains a whole number; that is, is equal to more than 1. For example, 8/4 is an improper fraction. It reduces to 2; divide the bottom (denominator) into the top (numerator) to reduce the fraction.

Examples are

1. 3/2 converts to 1-1/2 (divide 2 into 3). The 3/2 can be seen as 2/2 + 1/2, the 2/2 converts to 1, therefore 1-1/2.

2. 9/4, converts to 2-1/4 (divide 4 into 9). The 9/4 can be seen as 4/4 + 4/4 + 1/4 or 2-1/4.

3. 8/5 converts to 1-3/5 (divide 5 into 8). The 8/5 can be seen as 5/5 + 3/5 or 1-3/5.

Multiplication

Multiplication of fractions is very simple: Multiply both the denominators *and* numerators together. For example

1. 1/2 × 1/4 = 1/8

2. 3/4 × 2/4 = 6/16 = 3/8

3. 3/16 × 3/5 = 9/80

4. 4/5 × 2/3 × 3/4 = 24/60 = 2/5

Multiplying a fraction by a whole number is equally straightforward. For example, 1/8 × 4 = 4/8 = 1/2. For purposes of multiplication, the whole number 4 is written as 4/1.

Division

Division is done by inverting or turning over the fraction that is being divided (the divisor) into another number and then multiplying. For example

2/3 ÷ 1/2 converts to 2/3 × 2/1 = 4/3 = 1⅓
1/2 ÷ 2/3 converts to 1/2 × 3/2 = 3/4

It is very important to be clear which fraction is the one that is doing the dividing. Some examples are

1. 1/5 ÷ 1/4 converts to 1/5 × 4/1 = 4/5

2. 1/4 ÷ 1/5 converts to 1/4 × 5/1 = 5/4 = 1-1/4.

3. 4/5 ÷ 1/3 converts to 4/5 × 3/1 = 12/5 = 2⅖

4. 5/6 ÷ 1/8 converts to 5/6 × 8/1 = 40/6 = 6⅘ = 6⅔

It may be confusing to invert the fraction doing the dividing. Here's how it works. Say you want to divide 1/2 by 1/4 You are actually asking how many 1/4's there are in 1/2.

1/2 ÷ 1/4 = 1/2 × 4/1 = 4/2 = 2

There are two 1/4 fractions in the fraction 1/2; in other words, 1/4 goes into 1/2 two times.

Dividing a fraction by a whole number is easy. For example, to divide 1/8 by 4, write

1/8 ÷ 4/1 converts to 1/8 × 1/4 = 1/32

DECIMALS

Most technical calculations today are done with decimals. Decimals are formed on the base of 10—multiples of 10 or divisions of 10. A *decimal point* is used to determine the value of any number. Where the decimal point is placed determines the place value. For example

First decimal place   0.1 = 1/10
Second decimal place   0.01 = 1/100
Third decimal place   0.001 = 1/1000

When the decimal point is just in front of a number, as 0.1, then the number is in 10ths—the decimal 0.1 represents 1/10. This is called the *first decimal place*. If the decimal point is placed two spaces to the left of the number, as in 0.01, then the number is in 100ths—the decimal 0.01 represents 1/100. This is called the *second decimal place*. The *third decimal place* is written as 0.001, representing 1/1000. This process can be continued indefinitely.

Converting Fractions to Decimals

In masonry work, the accuracy required is usually no more than 1/16 of an inch. Fractions in 1/16ths can easily be converted to decimal by dividing 16 into 1. The fraction 1/16 has a decimal equivalent of .0625. Figure 9–11 shows decimal equivalents of common fractions, all given in 1/16ths. *Rule:* To find a decimal equivalent of a fraction, always divide the bottom number (denominator) into the top number (numerator). For example, 1/2 converts to 1 ÷ 2 or 0.5.

Decimal rulers are available for working with decimals. For example, decimal inch rulers divided into 0.1-inch increments are commonly available. These are *not* used on the masonry job, however. The mason's ruler divided into 1/16ths of an inch is still universally used.

Decimals are used in masonry calculations and in estimating. Decimal measures are shown on hand calculators.

Converting Inches to Decimal Feet

Inches can be quickly converted to decimal feet by dividing the inch measure by 12. For example, 3 inches converts to 0.25 feet. Three inches actually represents 3/12 of a foot.

$$3''/12'' = 0.25'$$

Fraction	Decimal
1/16	.0625
1/8	.125
3/16	.1875
1/4	.25
5/16	.3125
3/8	.375
7/16	.4375
1/2	.5
9/16	.5625
5/8	.625
11/16	.6875
3/4	.75
13/16	.8125
7/8	.875
15/16	.9375

FIGURE 9–11
Decimal equivalents of fractions.

Some examples are

1. 8″ = 8″/12″ or 0.667′
2. 4⅛″ = 4.125″/12 or 0.34375′

Remember that 1/8 = 0.125.

The number 0.34375 represents an accuracy that would not be required in masonry work. You would normally round the five place decimal to three places, or 0.344.

Rounding Off

In masonry calculations, as in estimating, the answer is normally rounded off to the third place. Rounding off is done by either increasing or leaving the same the last significant digit, depending on what the next digit is.

Rule 1. If the next number is 5 or larger, the last significant number is raised by one. Example: 0.7436 is rounded off to three places as 0.744.

Rule 2. If the next number is 4 or smaller, the last significant number is unchanged. Example: 0.7434 is rounded off to three places as 0.743.

The following are examples of rounding off to *three* places:

$$0.7465 = 0.747$$
$$0.7455 = 0.746$$
$$0.8421 = 0.842$$
$$0.8425 = 0.843$$
$$0.8426 = 0.843$$

The following are examples of rounding off to *two* places:

$$0.7465 = 0.75$$
$$0.7455 = 0.75$$
$$0.8021 = 0.80$$
$$0.867 \ = 0.87$$
$$0.9375 = 0.94$$

Adding and Subtracting

Adding and subtracting with decimals is like any ordinary number calculation except it is very important to *line up* the decimal point. For example, in addition

$$
\begin{array}{r}
8.20 \\
22.125 \\
44.562 \\
+ \ 0.75 \\
\hline
75.637
\end{array}
$$

and in subtracting

$$
\begin{array}{r}
28.75 \\
- \ 4.18 \\
\hline
24.57
\end{array}
$$

Multiplication

Multiplication is the same for decimals as for ordinary numbers. You must, however, take care to move the decimal place. For example, in the mul-

tiplication of 4.44 × 0.42, each number being multiplied has two places. The answer, after multiplication, must have four places.

$$
\begin{array}{rl}
4.44 & \text{(two places)} \\
\times 0.42 & \text{(two places)} \\
\hline
1.8648 & \text{(four places)}
\end{array}
$$

Round off to three places to 1.865.
For example

$$
\begin{array}{rl}
2.0625 & \text{(four places)} \\
\times 0.125 & \text{(three places)} \\
\hline
0.2578125 & \text{(seven places)}
\end{array}
$$

Round off to three places to 0.258.

Division

In division, you move the decimal point to the right so the dividing number is a whole number. The number being divided has its decimal point moved to the right an equal number of places. For example, if you wanted to divide 0.6875 by 0.125, you would move the decimal place on 0.125 over three places to get a whole number, or 125. Also, you move the decimal over three places on the 0.6875 to get 687.5. Therefore,

$$0.125 \, \overline{\smash{)}0.6875}$$

is changed to

$$125 \, \overline{\smash{)}687.5}^{\,5.5}$$

Take care to locate the decimal point exactly in the answer so it reflects the new position.
For example

$$4.8125 \div 68.75$$

$$6875 \, \overline{\smash{)}481.25}^{\,0.07} \quad \text{Locate decimal point}$$

Move Decimal Point Over Two

Move Decimal Point Over Two To Make Whole Number

ESTIMATING

Masonry estimating involves finding out how many masonry units or how much mortar is needed to do a job. Estimates should always be a little high to allow for waste. At least 5 percent should be added to brick or block estimates. Figure from 10 percent to 25 percent extra for mortar. The size of masonry units and the dimensions of the building, including all opening sizes, are picked up from the blueprints.

Brick Estimating

Brick is estimated by the square foot method. Before determining the area covered, you should determine four things:

1. Brick type
2. Brick dimensions
3. Brick pattern
4. Joint thickness

Brick type and size are picked up from the specifications. Brick pattern is shown on the elevations and is often noted in the specifications. Joint thickness may be noted on the specifications and is commonly given on the wall section. There are three basic joint thicknesses: $\frac{1}{4}$ inch, $\frac{3}{8}$ inch, and $\frac{1}{2}$ inch. Bed and head joints are usually $\frac{3}{8}$ inch or $\frac{1}{2}$ inch. Collar joints may vary from $\frac{3}{4}$ inch to 2 inches.

Square Footage. The square footage needed is calculated for each brick wall. For a veneer wall without openings, this is simply the length of the wall times the height. This gives the total square footage of the wall. If the wall has openings, simply calculate the square footage of the openings and subtract that from the overall square footage of a wall. If a solid, double-wythe wall is used, multiply the square footage by two.

A brick wall, for example, that is 22 feet long and 6 feet high would have 6' × 22' or 132 square feet. If there was a 2-foot by 4-foot opening you would subtract 8 square feet (2' × 4') from the total square footage of the wall: $132 - 8 = 124$ square feet. If this was a one-wythe wall you would have 124 square feet of brick. If a solid, two-wythe wall was being built, you would have twice as much (124 × 2) or 248 square feet of brick wall.

If you know the total square footage being covered *and* the brick size and joint thickness, you can arrive at the number of brick needed for the wall. This is done for every wall. After all walls are calculated, you then add a percentage for waste.

Brick Size. If in the 124 or 248 square foot wall in the example above, a brick size and joint thickness are given, you can calculate the number of brick needed. Assume that a nonmodular $3\frac{3}{4}$-inch × $2\frac{1}{4}$-inch × 8-inch standard brick with a $\frac{1}{2}$-inch head and bed joint is specified.

Step 1. Find the surface area of the brick in inches *plus* the $\frac{1}{2}$-inch joints, as shown in Figure 9–12. The height is $2\frac{1}{4}$ inches; add $\frac{1}{2}$ inch for the bed joint, and it equals $2\frac{3}{4}$ inches. The length is 8 inches; add $\frac{1}{2}$ inch for the head joint, and it equals $8\frac{1}{2}$ inches.

$$2\frac{3}{4}'' \times 8\frac{1}{2}'' = 2.75 \times 8.5'' = 23.375 \text{ sq. in.}$$

which is rounded off to 23.38 sq. in.

Step 2. Find the number of brick per square foot of wall. A square foot is 12 inches × 12 inches or 144 square inches. A brick with the mortar joint is 23.38 square inches. The number of brick per square foot is

$$\frac{144 \text{ sq. in.}}{23.38 \text{ sq. in.}} = 6.159 \text{ or } 6.16$$

Step 3. Calculate the number of brick in the wall. If there are 124 square feet: 124 × 6.16 = 763.84 or 764 brick. Always round off a part of a brick, no matter how small, to a whole brick. If there are 248 square feet: 248 × 6.16 = 1527.68 or 1528 brick.

Step 4. Add a waste factor of 5 percent: 764 brick plus 5 percent = 764 + 38.2 or 764 + 39 = 803 brick. For 1528 plus 5 percent: 1528 + 76.4 or 1528 + 77 = 1605 brick. In practice, you should

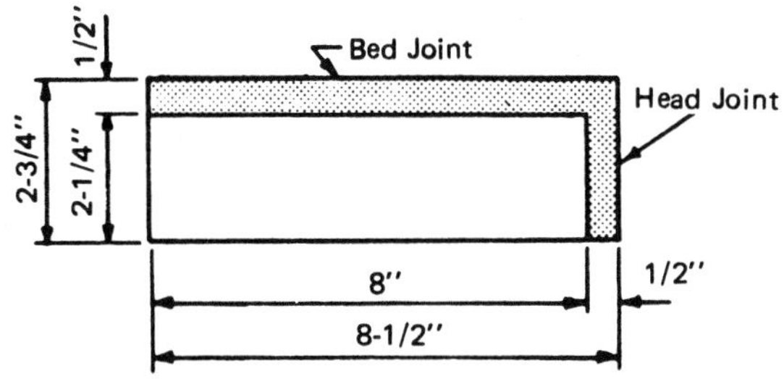

2-3/4" x 8-1/2" = 23.38 Square Inches

FIGURE 9–12
Calculating brick sizes, brick surface area plus mortar for joints.

determine all the square footage and all the brick needed for the house before adding on 5 percent for waste. Remember, however, that brick are commonly packaged in cubes of 500 or 525 brick. Most contractors or estimators would order brick based on multiples of 500, which is the number of standard or modular brick in a cube.

Tables are available showing number of nonmodular brick (in running bond) per hundred square feet. Figure 9–13 shows a table with the number of brick per 100 square feet (in a one-wythe wall) already worked out. The $3\frac{3}{4}'' \times 2\frac{1}{4}'' \times 8''$ brick, for example, is calculated at 616 brick per 100 square feet with a $\frac{1}{2}$-inch joint. This exactly duplicated the calculation made that showed 6.16 brick per square foot or 616 per 100 square feet. Once the total square footage is known, it is a simple matter to calculate the number of brick.

Figure 9–14 shows a table for calculating modular brick. The number of brick per 100

Nominal Size of Brick in. (t h l)	Number of Brick per 100 sq ft	Cubic Feet of Mortar: Per 100 Sq Ft, ⅜-in. Joints	Per 100 Sq Ft, ½-in. Joints	Per 1000 Brick, ⅜-in. Joints	Per 1000 Brick, ½-in. Joints
4 x 2⅔ x 8	675	5.5	7.0	8.1	10.3
4 x 3⅕ x 8	563	4.8	6.1	8.6	10.9
4 x 4 x 8	450	4.2	5.3	9.2	11.7
4 x 5⅓ x 8	338	3.5	4.4	10.2	12.9
4 x 2 x 12	600	6.5	8.2	10.8	13.7
4 x 2⅔ x 12	450	5.1	6.5	11.3	14.4
4 x 3⅕ x 12	375	4.4	5.6	11.7	14.9
4 x 4 x 12	300	3.7	4.8	12.3	15.7
4 x 5⅓ x 12	225	3.0	3.9	13.4	17.1
6 x 2⅔ x 12	450	7.9	10.2	17.5	22.6
6 x 3⅕ x 12	375	6.8	8.8	18.1	23.4
6 x 4 x 12	300	5.6	7.4	19.1	24.7

FIGURE 9–14
Modular brick and mortar required for single-wythe walls in running bond (no allowances for breakage or waste). (Brick Institute of America)

square feet (in a one-wythe wall) are calculated for running bond. Again, once you know the total square footage coverage, it is a simple matter to calculate the number of brick. Remember to always add 5 percent for waste.

Both Figures 9–13 and 9–14 give calculations based on running (or stack) bond. When other bonds, such as those using headers, are used, additional brick may be required.[1] Figure 9–15 shows correction factors needed for different bonds with headers and for garden wall bonds.

[1]For further information, use the Brick Institute of America's Technical Notes on Brick Construction, #10 Revised, "Estimating Brick Construction," 1971.

Size of Brick in. (t h l)	With ⅜-in. Joints: Number of Brick per 100 Sq Ft	With ⅜-in. Joints: Cubic Feet of Mortar per 100 Sq Ft	With ⅜-in. Joints: Cubic Feet of Mortar per 1000 Brick	With ½-in. Joints: Number of Brick per 100 Sq Ft	With ½-in. Joints: Cubic Feet of Mortar per 100 Sq Ft	With ½-in. Joints: Cubic Feet of Mortar per 1000 Brick
2¾ x 2¾ x 9¾	455	3.2	7.1	432	4.5	10.4
2⅝ x 2¾ x 8¾	504	3.4	6.8	470	4.1	8.7
3¾ x 2¼ x 8	655	5.8	8.8	616	7.2	11.7
3¾ x 2¾ x 8	551	5.0	9.1	522	6.4	12.2

FIGURE 9–13
Nonmodular brick and mortar required for single-wythe walls in running bond (no allowances for breakage or waste). (Brick Institute of America)

Bond	Correction Factor [1]
Full headers every 5th course only	1/5
Full headers every 6th course only	1/6
Full headers every 7th course only	1/7
English bond (full headers every 2nd course)	1/2
Flemish bond (alternate full headers and stretchers every course)	1/3
Flemish headers every 6th course	1/18
Flemish cross bond (Flemish headers every 2nd course)	1/6
Double-stretcher, garden wall bond	1/5
Triple-stretcher, garden wall bond	1/7

[1] Note: Correction factors are applicable only to those brick which have lengths of twice their bed depths.

FIGURE 9–15

Bond correction factors for walls of Figure 9–13 and 9–14. (Add to facing and deduct from backing.) (Brick Institute of America)

Cubic Feet of Mortar Per 100 Sq Ft of Wall		
¼-in. Joint	⅜-in. Joint	½-in. Joint
2.08	3.13	4.17

Note: Cubic feet per 1000 units = $\dfrac{10 \times \text{cubic feet per 100 sq ft of wall}}{\text{number of units per square foot of wall}}$

FIGURE 9–16

Cubic feet of mortar for collar joints. (Brick Institute of America)

Mortar Calculations. As shown in Figures 9–13 and 9–14, the cubic feet of mortar needed is calculated based on the different brick sizes and the thickness of the mortar joint. The amount needed is given for 100 square feet of brick or per 1000 brick. For example, it would take 4.2 cubic feet of mortar (Figure 9–14) to lay 100 square feet of brick sized $4'' \times 4'' \times 8''$ with a $\frac{3}{8}$-inch mortar joint.

Collar joints require additional mortar. Figure 9–16 shows the mortar required per 100 square feet of wall for different thicknesses of collar joints. Remember, a waste factor from 10 percent to 25 percent is added to the mortar required.

Masonry Calculators. The Brick Institute of America has developed a manual, sliding calculator called the Brick Masonry Estimator for calculating brick and mortar needed for different walls. See Figure 9–17.

Concrete Block Estimating

Concrete block is estimated in the same way as brick except different sizes are used. Joint thickness in concrete masonry units is normally $\frac{3}{8}$ of an inch.

Estimating Block. The number of concrete block required is determined by calculating the first course and then using this number for the higher courses. Calculations are based on a standard nominal $8'' \times 8'' \times 16''$ block. The number of block around the foundation of the structure is figured. You can do this by determining the total perimeter, minus openings. The floor plan or foundation plan gives the needed wall measurements. You can calculate the total footage. Multiply by 12 to get total inches and then divide by 16, the length of the concrete block. This should be the number of blocks needed for the first course. Each course would need an equal number of block.

An easier method is to use a standard table, as shown in Figure 9–18. Figure 9–18 is based on a nominal $8'' \times 8'' \times 16''$ block. This gives the number of block around different-sized foundations. For example, if you were laying blocks around the perimeter of a 22-foot × 36-foot building without any openings, the total number of block needed would be 85. This includes all four sides. If you multiplied this number by the number of courses in the wall, you would get the number of blocks needed, assuming no openings.

You can determine the number of courses needed by dividing eight inches into the total height of the wall. The wall height must, of course, be converted into inches. An easier way is to use Figure 9–19. This gives the number of

BRICK MASONRY ESTIMATOR

BRICK INSTITUTE OF AMERICA

TABLE I
Single Wythe Walls in Running Bond

	BRICK SIZE — in.			BRICK PER 100 SQUARE FEET	
	t	h	l		
MODULAR (nominal)	4	2⅔	8	675	
	4	3⅓	8	563	
	4	4	8	450	
	4	5⅓	8	338	
	4	2⅔	12	450	
	4	3⅓	12	375	
	4	4	12	300	
	4	5⅓	12	225	
	6	2⅔	12	450	
	6	3⅓	12	375	
	6	4	12	300	
	8	4	12	300	
				⅜" JOINT	**½" JOINT**
NON-MODULAR (actual)	3	2¼	8¾	532	505
	3	2¾	9⅝	481	457
	3	2¾	9¾	457	433
	3	2¾	10	529	500
	3¾	2¼	8	655	616
	3¾	2¾	8	551	522

TABLE II
Single Wythe Walls in Running Bond

	BRICK SIZE — in.			CUBIC FEET OF MORTAR PER 1000 BRICK	
	t	h	l	⅜" JOINT	½" JOINT
MODULAR (nominal)	4	2⅔	8	8.1	10.3
	4	3⅓	8	8.6	10.9
	4	4	8	9.2	11.7
	4	5⅓	8	10.2	12.9
	4	2⅔	12	11.3	14.4
	4	3⅓	12	11.7	14.9
	4	4	12	12.3	15.7
	4	5⅓	12	13.4	17.1
	6	2⅔	12	18.5	22.6
	6	3⅓	12	18.1	23.4
	6	4	12	19.1	24.7
	8	4	12	25.9	33.6
NON-MOD. (actual)	3	2¼	8¾	7.6	9.7
	3	2¾	9⅝	8.2	11.1
	3	2¾	9¾	8.4	11.3
	3	2¾	10	8.2	11.1
	3¾	2¼	8	8.8	11.7
	3¾	2¾	8	9.1	12.2

TABLE III

MORTAR	
TYPE	PROPORTION (by volume)
M	1 : ¼ : 3
S	1 : ½ : 4½
N	1 : 1 : 6
O	1 : 2 : 9

© 1975, PERRYGRAF, LA, CA 91324-3552 Printed in U.S.A

Instructions:

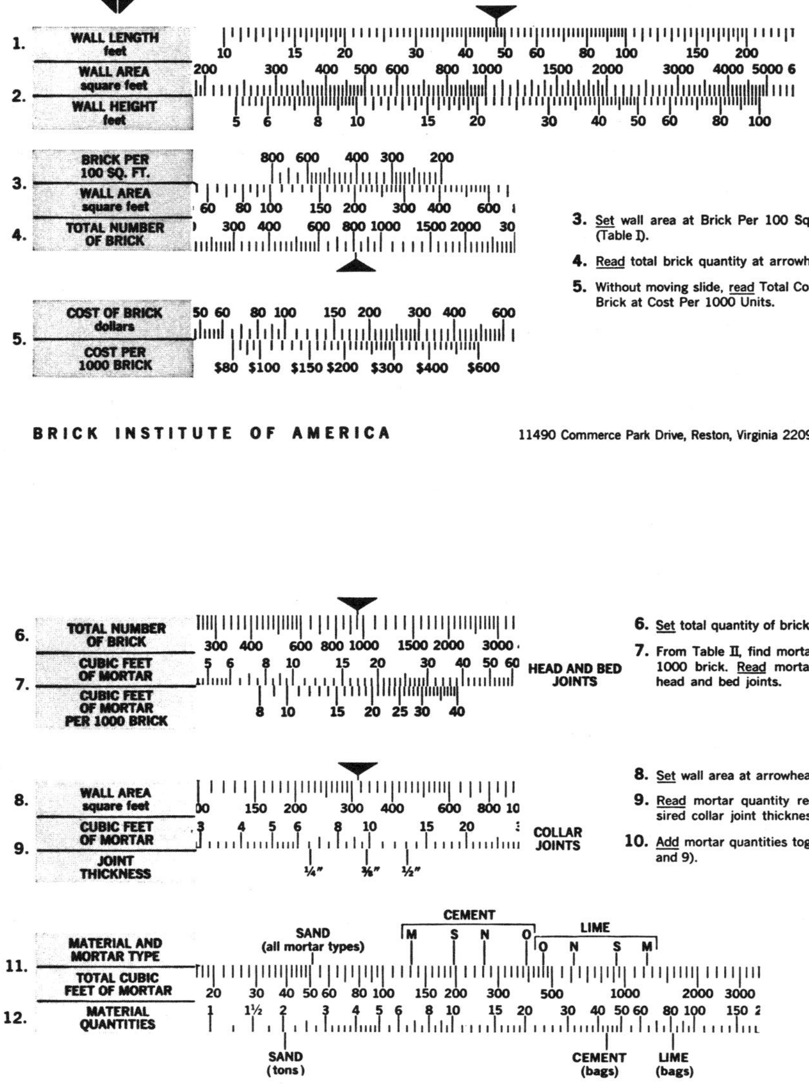

1. Set wall length at arrowhead.
2. Read wall area at wall height.

3. Set wall area at Brick Per 100 Sq. Ft. (Table I).
4. Read total brick quantity at arrowhead.
5. Without moving slide, read Total Cost of Brick at Cost Per 1000 Units.

6. Set total quantity of brick at arrowhead.
7. From Table II, find mortar quantity per 1000 brick. Read mortar quantity for head and bed joints.
8. Set wall area at arrowhead.
9. Read mortar quantity required for desired collar joint thickness.
10. Add mortar quantities together (steps 7 and 9).

11. Set total mortar quantity at appropriate index for sand, cement and lime (top of window). Separate settings are required for each material.
12. Read total material quantities at proper index (bottom of window).

Note: No allowances for waste or breakage are included in Tables I and II or mortar quantity scales. Breakage and waste allowances of 5% of brick quantity and from 50% to 100% of mortar are common.

BRICK INSTITUTE OF AMERICA

11490 Commerce Park Drive, Reston, Virginia 22091

Scale labels:
- WALL LENGTH feet
- WALL AREA square feet
- WALL HEIGHT feet
- BRICK PER 100 SQ. FT.
- WALL AREA square feet
- TOTAL NUMBER OF BRICK
- COST OF BRICK dollars
- COST PER 1000 BRICK
- TOTAL NUMBER OF BRICK
- CUBIC FEET OF MORTAR
- CUBIC FEET OF MORTAR PER 1000 BRICK — HEAD AND BED JOINTS
- WALL AREA square feet
- CUBIC FEET OF MORTAR — COLLAR JOINTS
- JOINT THICKNESS
- MATERIAL AND MORTAR TYPE
- TOTAL CUBIC FEET OF MORTAR
- MATERIAL QUANTITIES — CEMENT (bags), LIME (bags), SAND (tons)

FIGURE 9–17

Brick masonry estimator. (Brick Institute of America)

			Number of Block Per Course For Solid Walls of Various Sizes																		
Size In Feet	2	4	6	8	10	12	14	16	18	20	22	24	26	28	30	32	34	36	38	40	
2	4	7	10	13	16	19	22	25	28	31	34	37	40	43	46	49	52	55	58	61	
4	7	10	13	16	19	22	25	28	31	34	37	40	43	46	49	52	55	58	61	64	
6	10	13	16	19	22	25	28	31	34	37	40	43	46	49	52	55	58	61	64	67	
8	13	16	19	22	25	28	31	34	37	40	43	46	49	52	55	58	61	64	67	70	
10	16	19	22	25	28	31	34	37	40	43	46	49	52	55	58	61	64	67	70	73	
12	19	22	25	28	31	34	37	40	43	46	49	52	55	58	61	64	67	70	73	76	
14	22	25	28	31	34	37	40	43	46	49	52	55	58	61	64	67	70	73	76	79	
16	25	28	31	34	37	40	43	46	49	52	55	58	61	64	67	70	73	76	79	82	
18	28	31	34	37	40	43	46	49	52	55	58	61	64	67	70	73	76	79	82	85	
20	31	34	37	40	43	46	49	52	55	58	61	64	67	70	73	76	79	82	85	88	
22	34	37	40	43	46	49	52	55	58	61	64	67	70	73	76	79	82	85	88	91	
24	37	40	43	46	49	52	55	58	61	64	67	70	73	76	79	82	85	88	91	94	
26	40	43	46	49	52	55	58	61	64	67	70	73	76	79	82	85	88	91	94	97	
28	43	46	49	52	55	58	61	64	67	70	73	76	79	82	85	88	91	94	97	100	
30	46	49	52	55	58	61	64	67	70	73	76	79	82	85	88	91	94	97	100	103	
32	49	52	55	58	61	64	67	70	73	76	79	82	85	88	91	94	97	100	103	106	
34	52	55	58	61	64	67	70	73	76	79	82	85	88	91	94	97	100	103	106	109	
36	55	58	61	64	67	70	73	76	79	82	85	88	91	94	97	100	103	106	109	112	
38	58	61	64	67	70	73	76	79	82	85	88	91	94	97	100	103	106	109	112	115	
40	61	64	67	70	73	76	79	82	85	88	91	94	97	100	103	106	109	112	115	118	
42	64	67	70	73	76	79	82	85	88	91	94	97	100	103	106	109	112	115	118	121	
44	67	70	73	76	79	82	85	88	91	94	97	100	103	106	109	112	115	118	121	124	
46	70	73	76	79	82	85	88	91	94	97	100	103	106	109	112	115	118	121	124	127	
48	73	76	79	82	85	88	91	94	97	100	103	106	109	112	115	118	121	124	127	130	
50	76	79	82	85	88	91	94	97	100	103	106	109	112	115	118	121	124	127	130	133	
52	79	82	85	88	91	95	97	100	103	106	109	112	115	118	121	124	127	130	133	136	
54	82	85	88	91	94	97	100	103	106	109	112	115	118	121	124	127	130	133	136	139	
56	85	88	91	94	97	100	103	106	109	112	115	118	121	124	127	130	133	136	139	142	
58	88	91	94	97	100	103	106	109	112	115	118	121	124	127	130	133	136	139	142	145	
60	91	94	97	100	103	106	109	112	115	118	121	124	127	130	133	136	139	142	145	148	

FIGURE 9-18
Standard 16-inch concrete masonry. (National Concrete Masonry Association)

courses needed for different wall heights. An eight-inch high block is used.

A quick way to determine the number of 16-inch long block for any set length is to multiply the number of feet by 0.75. This takes into account the length of the block (16 inches) with mortar. For example, if you wanted to know the number of 16-inch block in a course 20 feet long: 20 × 0.75 = 15 block.

Multiply the number of block in a course by the number of courses to determine the total number of block needed. Make adjustments for any openings required. When the total number needed is determined, add 5 percent for waste.

Figures 9–20 and 9–21 show the number of block needed based on the square footage method. Figure 9–20 shows the number of different size block needed for 100 square feet. Be sure

(Height of unit 7-5/8")
(Joint thickness 3/8")

Height	No. of courses
8"	1
1'4"	2
2'0"	3
2'8"	4
3'4"	5
4'0"	6
4'8"	7
5'4"	8
6'0"	9
6'8"	10
7'4"	11
8'0"	12
8'8"	13
9'4"	14
10'0"	15
10'8"	16
11'4"	17
12'0"	18
12'8"	19
13'4"	20
16'8"	25
20'0"	30
23'4"	35
26'8"	40
30'0"	45
33'4"	50

FIGURE 9-19

Concrete masonry courses by height. (National Concrete Masonry Association)

Nominal Height and Length of Units in Inches	Number of Units Per 100 Sq. Ft.
8 x 16	112.5
8 x 12	150.0
5 x 12	221.0
4 x 16	225.0
2 1/4 x 8*	675.0
4 x 8**	450.0
5 x 8***	340.0
2 x 12****	600.0
2 x 16****	450.0

*Modular Concrete Brick (2 1/4 x 3 5/8 x 7 5/8).
**Jumbo Concrete Brick (3 5/8 x 3 5/8 x 7 5/8).
***Double Concrete Brick (4 7/8 x 3 5/8 x 7 5/8).
****Roman Concrete Brick: (1 5/8 x 3 5/8 x 11 5/8)
(1 5/8 x 3 5/8 x 15 5/8).

FIGURE 9-20

Concrete masonry requirements for 100 square feet of wall area. (Wall is assumed to be one masonry unit in thickness.) (National Concrete Masonry Association)

Wall Description	Number of Masonry Units Per 100 Sq. Ft.	
	Exterior Wythe	Interior Wythe
COMPOSITE WALLS 4-in. concrete brick plus 4-in. block:		
Masonry Bonded	772	97.0
Wire Ties	675	112.5
4-in. concrete brick plus 8-in. block:		
Masonry Bonded	868	97.0
Wire Ties	675	112.5
CAVITY WALLS 4-in. concrete brick plus 4-in. block	675	112.5
4-in. block plus 4-in. block	112.5	112.5

FIGURE 9-21

Number of concrete masonry units required for 100 square feet of various composite or multi-wythe walls. (National Concrete Masonry Association)

Nominal Height and Length of Units in Inches	Cu. Ft. of Mortar Per 100 Sq. Ft.
8 x 16	6.0
8 x 12	7.0
5 x 12	8.5
4 x 16	9.5
2 1/4 x 8*	14.0
4 x 8**	12.0
5 x 8***	11.0
2 x 12****	15.0
2 x 16****	15.0

*Modular Concrete Brick (2 1/4 x 3 5/8 x 7 5/8).
**Jumbo Concrete Brick (3 5/8 x 3 5/8 x 7 5/8).
***Double Concrete Brick (4 7/8 x 3 5/8 x 7 5/8).
****Roman Concrete Brick: (1 5/8 x 3 5/8 x 11 5/8)
(1 5/8 x 3 5/8 x 15 5/8).

FIGURE 9-22
Mortar requirements for 100 square feet of concrete masonry wall area. (Wall is assumed to be one masonry unit in thickness.) (National Concrete Masonry Association)

to subtract any openings. Figure 9-21 shows the number of block needed in composite or multi-wythe walls.

Estimating Mortar. The amount of mortar required is based on the size of the concrete block. Figure 9-22 shows cubic foot mortar requirements per 100 square feet using different size block. When calculating the square feet in a wall (length × height), be sure to subtract any openings. Figure 9-23 shows mortar requirements for composite or multi-wythe walls. Allow 10 percent for waste.

The cubic feet of mortar can be converted to cubic yards by dividing by 27. There are 27 cubic feet in a cubic yard. For example, if you needed 125 cubic feet of mortar, you could convert this to cubic yards: 125/27 = 4.63 cubic yards. Mortar is commonly mixed by the cubic yard. Figure 9-24 shows the amount of different ingredients needed to mix one cubic yard of mortar.

Wall Description		Cu. Ft. of Mortar Per 100 Sq. Ft.
COMPOSITE WALLS 4-in. concrete brick plus 4-in. block:		
	Masonry Bonded	18.0
	Wire Ties	18.0
4-in. concrete brick plus 8-in. block:		
	Masonry Bonded	13.5
	Wire Ties	18.0
CAVITY WALLS 4-in. concrete brick plus 4-in. block		15.0
4-in. block plus 4-in. block		12.0

FIGURE 9-23
Mortar required for 100 square feet of various composite or multi-wythe concrete masonry walls. (National Concrete Masonry Association)

Mortar Type, A.S.T.M.: C 270	Sand, damp, loose volume	Cementitious Materials (bags of material or cubic feet)*		
		Portland Cement	Masonry Cement	Lime
Type M	1.0 cy	4.5	4.5	-
Type M	1.0 cy	7.5	-	2.0
Type S	1.0 cy	3.0	6.0	-
Type S	1.0 cy	6.0	-	3.0
Type N	1.0 cy	-	9.0	-
Type N	1.0 cy	4.5	-	4.5
Type O	1.0 cy	-	9.0	-
Type O	1.0 cy	3.0	-	6.0

*Cementitious materials are usually one cubic foot volume per bag.

FIGURE 9-24

Quantities of materials for a cubic yard of concrete masonry mortar. (National Concrete Masonry Association)

ESTIMATING PROBLEMS

1. You are required to build a two-wythe garden wall 36 feet long; the wall is 6 feet high. Running bond with $\frac{3}{8}''$ mortar joint is used with metal ties. How many $4'' \times 2\frac{2}{3}'' \times 8''$ brick would be required? How many $4'' \times 2\frac{2}{3}'' \times 12''$ brick?

2. How much mortar would be required for the garden wall using $4'' \times 2\frac{2}{3}'' \times 8''$ brick with a $\frac{1}{2}$-inch joint and $\frac{1}{4}$-inch collar joint?

3. A 4-foot high concrete block foundation is to be built for a 22-foot × 36-foot structure. No openings are needed. How many $8'' \times 8'' \times 16''$ concrete block are required?

4. How many cubic feet of mortar are required for the concrete block foundation? How many cubic yards?

CHAPTER REVIEW

MASONRY MATH REVIEW

Write the correct answer on a separate piece of paper. Correct answers are given at the end of the chapter. Check your own work.

1. A = ____
2. B = ____
3. C = ____
4. D = ____

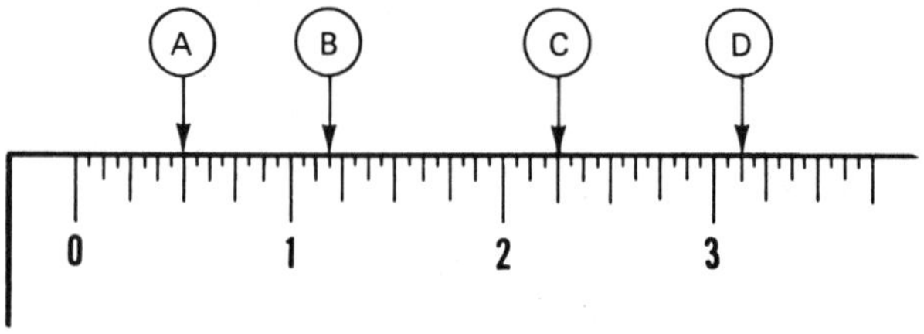

5. Add: 1′–4″ + 12′–4″
6. Add: 20′–3″ + 7′–10-1/2″ + 2′–0-1/2″
7. Add: 8′–4″ + 1′–6″ + 14′–0″
8. Subtract: (8′–8″) – (2′–4″)
9. Subtract: (10′–2″) – (4′–10″)
10. Subtract: (9′–0″) – (7′–2-1/2″)
11. Multiply: 7′–2″ × 4
12. Multiply: 6′–1-1/2″ × 5
13. Divide: 9′–4″ ÷ 3
14. Divide: 16′–2″ ÷ 8
15. Add: 1/4 + 1/8
16. Add: 5/16 + 1/2 + 5/8
17. Subtract: 3/16 – 1/8
18. Subtract: 12-1/2 – 7/16
19. Multiply: 2/3 × 1/2
20. Multiply: 1/2 × 1/3 × 1/4
21. Divide: 1/5 ÷ 1/3
22. Divide: 3/5 ÷ 1/2
23. Convert: 3/16 to a decimal
24. Multiply: 0.1875 × 0.24
25. Divide: 0.875 ÷ 0.0625

MASONRY MATH REVIEW—ANSWERS

Note: Always mark inch or foot symbols if appropriate.

1. 1/2″
2. 1 3/16″
3. 2 1/4″
4. 3 1/8″
5. 13′–8″
6. 29′–14″ or 30′–2″
7. 23′–10″
8. 6′–4″
9. 5′–4″
10. 1′–9 1/2″
11. 28′–8″
12. 30′–7 1/2″
13. 3′–1 1/3″
14. 2′–1/4″
15. 3/8
16. 23/16 or 1 7/16
17. 1/16
18. 12 1/16
19. 2/6 or 1/3
20. 1/24
21. 3/5
22. 6/5 or 1 1/5
23. 0.1875
24. 0.045
25. 14

Appendix

REFERENCE TABLES AND CHARTS

TABLE 1.
Height of Courses Using $2\frac{1}{4}$-Inch Brick, $\frac{3}{8}$-Inch Joint (Facing Brick)

Courses	Height, ft and in	Courses	Height, ft and in	Courses	Height, ft and in	Courses	Height, ft and in	Courses	Height, ft and in
1	0 $2\frac{5}{8}$	21	4 $7\frac{1}{8}$	41	8 $11\frac{5}{8}$	61	13 $4\frac{1}{8}$	81	17 $8\frac{5}{8}$
2	0 $5\frac{1}{4}$	22	4 $9\frac{3}{4}$	42	9 $2\frac{1}{4}$	62	13 $6\frac{3}{4}$	82	17 $11\frac{1}{4}$
3	0 $7\frac{7}{8}$	23	5 $0\frac{3}{8}$	43	9 $4\frac{7}{8}$	63	13 $9\frac{3}{8}$	83	18 $1\frac{7}{8}$
4	0 $10\frac{1}{2}$	24	5 3	44	9 $7\frac{1}{2}$	64	14 0	84	18 $4\frac{1}{2}$
5	1 $1\frac{1}{8}$	25	5 $5\frac{5}{8}$	45	9 $10\frac{1}{8}$	65	14 $2\frac{5}{8}$	85	18 $7\frac{1}{8}$
6	1 $3\frac{3}{4}$	26	5 $8\frac{1}{4}$	46	10 $0\frac{3}{4}$	66	14 $5\frac{1}{4}$	86	18 $9\frac{3}{4}$
7	1 $6\frac{3}{8}$	27	5 $10\frac{7}{8}$	47	10 $3\frac{3}{8}$	67	14 $7\frac{7}{8}$	87	19 $0\frac{3}{8}$
8	1 9	28	6 $1\frac{1}{2}$	48	10 6	68	14 $10\frac{1}{2}$	88	19 3
9	1 $11\frac{5}{8}$	29	6 $4\frac{1}{8}$	49	10 $8\frac{5}{8}$	69	15 $1\frac{1}{8}$	89	19 $5\frac{5}{8}$
10	2 $2\frac{1}{4}$	30	6 $6\frac{3}{4}$	50	10 $11\frac{1}{4}$	70	15 $3\frac{3}{4}$	90	19 $8\frac{1}{4}$
11	2 $4\frac{7}{8}$	31	6 $9\frac{3}{8}$	51	11 $1\frac{7}{8}$	71	15 $6\frac{3}{8}$	91	19 $10\frac{7}{8}$
12	2 $7\frac{1}{2}$	32	7 0	52	11 $4\frac{1}{2}$	72	15 9	92	20 $1\frac{1}{2}$
13	2 $10\frac{1}{8}$	33	7 $2\frac{5}{8}$	53	11 $7\frac{1}{8}$	73	15 $11\frac{5}{8}$	93	20 $4\frac{1}{8}$
14	3 $0\frac{3}{4}$	34	7 $5\frac{1}{4}$	54	11 $9\frac{3}{4}$	74	16 $2\frac{1}{4}$	94	20 $6\frac{3}{4}$
15	3 $3\frac{3}{8}$	35	7 $7\frac{7}{8}$	55	12 $0\frac{3}{8}$	75	16 $4\frac{7}{8}$	95	20 $9\frac{3}{8}$
16	3 6	36	7 $10\frac{1}{2}$	56	12 3	76	16 $7\frac{1}{2}$	96	21 0
17	3 $8\frac{5}{8}$	37	8 $1\frac{1}{8}$	57	12 $5\frac{5}{8}$	77	16 $10\frac{1}{8}$	97	21 $2\frac{5}{8}$
18	3 $11\frac{1}{4}$	38	8 $3\frac{3}{4}$	58	12 $8\frac{1}{4}$	78	17 $0\frac{3}{4}$	98	21 $5\frac{1}{4}$
19	4 $1\frac{7}{8}$	39	8 $6\frac{3}{8}$	59	12 $10\frac{7}{8}$	79	17 $3\frac{3}{8}$	99	21 $7\frac{7}{8}$
20	4 $4\frac{1}{2}$	40	8 9	60	13 $1\frac{1}{2}$	80	17 6	100	21 $10\frac{1}{2}$

TABLE 2.
Height of Courses Using 2¼-Inch Brick, ½-Inch Joint (Building Brick)

Courses	Height, ft and in	Courses	Height, ft and in	Courses	Height, ft and in	Courses	Height, ft and in	Courses	Height, ft and in
1	0 2¾	21	4 9¾	41	9 4¾	61	13 11¾	81	18 6¾
2	0 5½	22	5 0½	42	9 7½	62	14 2½	82	18 9½
3	0 8¼	23	5 3¼	43	9 10¼	63	14 5¼	83	19 0¼
4	0 11	24	5 6	44	10 1	64	14 8	84	19 3
5	1 1¾	25	5 8¾	45	10 3¾	65	14 10¾	85	19 5¾
6	1 4½	26	5 11½	46	10 6½	66	15 1½	86	19 8½
7	1 7¼	27	6 2¼	47	10 9¼	67	15 4¼	87	19 11¼
8	1 10	28	6 5	48	11 0	68	15 7	88	20 2
9	2 0¾	29	6 7¾	49	11 2¾	69	15 9¾	89	20 4¾
10	2 3½	30	6 10½	50	11 5½	70	16 0½	90	20 7½
11	2 6¼	31	7 1¼	51	11 8¼	71	16 3¼	91	20 10¼
12	2 9	32	7 4	52	11 11	72	16 6	92	21 1
13	2 11¾	33	7 6¾	53	12 1¾	73	16 8¾	93	21 3¾
14	3 2½	34	7 9½	54	12 4½	74	16 11½	94	21 6½
15	3 5¼	35	8 0¼	55	12 7¼	75	17 2¼	95	21 9¼
16	3 8	36	8 3	56	12 10	76	17 5	96	22 0
17	3 10¾	37	8 5¾	57	13 0¾	77	17 7¾	97	22 2¾
18	4 1½	38	8 8½	58	13 3½	78	17 10½	98	22 5½
19	4 4¼	39	8 11¼	59	13 6¼	79	18 1¼	99	22 8¼
20	4 7	40	9 2	60	13 9	80	18 4	100	22 11

TABLE 3.
Quantities of Materials Required for Brick Walls*

Wall Area, sf	Wall Thickness, in							
	4		8		12		16	
	Number of Bricks	Mortar, cf	Number of Bricks	Mortar, cf	Number of Bricks	Mortar, cf	Number of Bricks	Mortar, cf
1	6.17	.08	12.33	.2	18.49	.32	24.65	.44
10	61.7	.8	123.3	2	184.9	3.2	246.5	4.4
100	617	8	1,233	20	1,849	32	2,465	44
200	1,234	16	2,466	40	3,698	64	4,930	88
300	1,851	24	3,699	60	5,547	96	7,395	132
400	2,468	32	4,932	80	7,396	128	9,860	176
500	3,085	40	6,165	100	9,245	160	12,325	220
600	3,712	48	7,398	120	11,094	192	14,790	264
700	4,319	56	8,631	140	12,943	224	17,253	308
800	4,936	64	9,864	160	14,792	256	19,720	352
900	5,553	72	10,970	180	16,641	288	22,185	396
1,000	6,170	80	12,330	200	18,490	320	24,650	440

*Quantities are based on ½-inch thick mortar joint. For ⅜-inch thick joint use 80% of these quantities.

TABLE 4.
Nominal Heights of Modular Concrete Masonry Walls in Courses

Number of Courses	Nominal Height of Concrete Masonry Walls	
	Units 7⅝" High and ⅜" Thick Bed Joints	Units 3⅝" High and ⅜" Thick Bed Joints
1	8"	4"
2	1' 4"	8"
3	2' 0"	1' 0"
4	2' 8"	1' 4"
5	3' 4"	1' 8"
6	4' 0"	2' 0"
7	4' 8"	2' 4"
8	5' 4"	2' 8"
9	6' 0"	3' 0"
10	6' 8"	3' 4"
15	10' 0"	5' 0"
20	13' 4"	6' 8"
25	16' 8"	8' 4"
30	20' 0"	10' 0"
35	23' 4"	11' 8"
40	26' 8"	13' 4"
45	30' 0"	15' 0"
50	33' 4"	16' 8"

Note: For concrete masonry units 7⅝" and 3⅝" in height laid with ⅜" mortar joints. Height is measured from center to center of mortar joints.

TABLE 5.
Nominal Lengths of Modular Concrete Masonry Walls in Stretchers

Number of Stretchers	Nominal Length of Concrete Masonry Walls	
	Units 15⅝" Long and Half Units 7⅝" Long with ⅜" Thick Head Joints	Units 11⅝" Long and Half Units 5⅝" Long with ⅜" Thick Head Joints
1	1' 4"	1' 0"
1½	2' 0"	1' 6"
2	2' 8"	2' 0"
2½	3' 4"	2' 6"
3	4' 0"	3' 0"
3½	4' 8"	3' 6"
4	5' 4"	4' 0"
4½	6' 0"	4' 6"
5	6' 8"	5' 0"
5½	7' 4"	5' 6"
6	8' 0"	6' 0"
6½	8' 8"	6' 6"
7	9' 4"	7' 0"
7½	10' 0"	7' 6"
8	10' 8"	8' 0"
8½	11' 4"	8' 6"
9	12' 0"	9' 0"
9½	12' 8"	9' 6"
10	13' 4"	10' 0"
10½	14' 0"	10' 6"
11	14' 8"	11' 0"
11½	15' 4"	11' 6"
12	16' 0"	12' 0"
12½	16' 8"	12' 6"
13	17' 4"	13' 0"
13½	18' 0"	13' 6"
14	18' 8"	14' 0"
14½	19' 4"	14' 6"
15	20' 0"	15' 0"
20	26' 8"	20' 0"

NOTE: Actual wall length is measured from outside edge to outside edge of units, and equals the nominal length minus ⅜" (one mortar joint).

TABLE 6.
Unit Weights and Quantities for Modular Concrete Masonry Walls

Actual Unit Sizes (Width × Height × Length, in)	Nominal Wall Thickness, in	For 100 sf of Wall			For 100 Concrete Units	
		Number of Units	Average Weight of Finished Wall		Mortar** cf	Mortar*** cf
			Heavyweight Aggregate, lb*	Lightweight Aggregate, lb*		
3⅝ × 3⅝ × 15⅝	4	225	3,050	2,150	13.5	6.0
5⅝ × 3⅝ × 15⅝	6	225	4,550	3,050	13.5	6.0
7⅝ × 3⅝ × 15⅝	8	225	5,700	3,700	13.5	6.0
3⅝ × 7⅝ × 15⅝	4	112.5	2,850	2,050	8.5	7.5
5⅝ × 7⅝ × 15⅝	6	112.5	4,350	2,950	8.5	7.5
7⅝ × 7⅝ × 15⅝	8	112.5	5,500	3,600	8.5	7.5
11⅝ × 7⅝ × 15⅝	12	112.5	7,950	4,900	8.5	7.5

Notes: Table based on ³⁄₈-inch mortar joints.
 *Actual weight within ± 7% of average weight.
 **Actual weight within ± 17% of average weight.
***With face-shell mortar bedding. Mortar quantities include 10% allowance for waste.
Actual weight of 100 sf of wall can be computed by formula W (N) + 150 (M) where: W = actual weight of a single unit
N = number of units for 100 sf of wall
M = cf of mortar for 100 sf of wall

TABLE 7.
Average Concrete Masonry Units and Mortar per 100 sq ft of Wall

DESCRIPTION, SIZE OF BLOCK (in.)	THICKNESS WALL (in.)	WEIGHT PER UNIT (lb.)	NUMBER OF UNITS PER 100 SQ. FT. OF WALL AREA	MORTAR (cu. ft.)	WEIGHT, POUNDS PER 100 SQ. FT. OF WALL AREA
8 X 8 X 16	8	50	110	3.25	5850
8 X 8 X 12	8	38	146	3.5	6000
8 X 12 X 16	12	85	110	3.25	9700
8 X 3 X 16	3	20	110	2.75	2600
9 X 3 X 18	3	26	87	2.5	2500
12 X 3 X 12	3	23	100	2.5	2550
8 X 3 X 12	3	15	146	3.5	2550
8 X 4 X 16	4	28	110	3.25	3450
9 X 4 X 18	4	35	87	3.25	3350
12 X 4 X 12	4	31	100	3.25	3450
8 X 4 X 12	4	21	146	4	3500
8 X 6 X 16	6	42	110	3.25	5000

TABLE 8.
Lintel Sizes for 8-Inch and 12-Inch Walls

Wall Thickness, in	Span				
	3 Ft		4 Ft* Steel Angles	5 Ft* Steel Angles	6 Ft* Steel Angles
	Steel Angles	Wood			
8	2-3 × 3 × ¼	2 × 8 / 2-2 × 4	2-3 × 3 × ¼	2-3 × 3 × ¼	2-3½ × 3½ × ¼
12	3-3 × 3 × ¼	2 × 12 / 2-2 × 6	3-3 × 3 × ¼	3-3½ × 3½ × ¼	3-3½ × 3½ × ¼

	7 Ft* Steel Angles	8 Ft* Steel Angles
	2-3½ × 3½ × ¼	2-3½ × 3½ × ¼
	3-4 × 4 × ¼	3-4 × 4 × 4¼

*Wood lintels should not be used for spans over 3 feet since they burn out in case of fire and allow the brick to fall.

TABLE 9.
Concrete Reinforced Lintels with Stirrups for Wall and Floor Loads

SIZE OF LINTEL		CLEAR SPAN OF LINTEL FT.	REINFORCEMENT		WEB REINFORCEMENT NO. 6 GAGE WIRE STIRRUPS. SPACINGS FROM END OF LINTEL – BOTH ENDS THE SAME
HEIGHT IN.	WIDTH IN.		TOP	BOTTOM	
7 5/8	7 5/8	3	NONE	2 – 1/2-IN. ROUND	NO STIRRUPS REQUIRED
7 5/8	7 5/8	4	NONE	2 – 3/4-IN. ROUND	3 STIRRUPS, SP. :2,3,3 IN.
7 5/8	7 5/8	5	2 – 3/8-IN. ROUND	2 – 7/8-IN. ROUND	5 STIRRUPS, SP. :2,3,3,3,3 IN.
7 5/8	7 5/8	6	2 – 1/2-IN. ROUND	2 – 7/8-IN. ROUND	6 STIRRUPS, SP. :2,3,3,3,3,3 IN.
7 5/8	7 5/8	7	2 – 1-IN. ROUND	2 – 1-IN. ROUND	9 STIRRUPS, SP. :2,3,3,3,3,3,3,3 IN.

PORTLAND CEMENT ASSOCIATION

Table 10.
Rumford Fireplace Dimensions[a,b]

Finished Fireplace Opening						Rough Brick Work					Flue	Angle	Throat and Smoke Shelf		
A	B	C	D	E	F[c]	G	H	I[c]	J	K	L × M	N	O	P	R
36	32	16	16	16	28	4	44	19½	27	14	12 × 16	A-48	4	12	10
40	32	16	16	16	28	4	48	19½	29	16	16 × 16	A-48	4	12	14
40	37	16	16	16	33	4	48	19½	29	16	16 × 16	A-48	4	12	14
40	40	20	20	20	32	4	48	23½	29	16	16 × 16	A-48	4	12	14
48	37	16	16	16	33	4	56	19½	36	18	16 × 20	B-60	4	12	14
48	40	20	20	20	32	4	56	23½	36	18	16 × 20	B-60	4	12	14
48	48	20	20	20	40	4	56	23½	36	18	20 × 20	B-60	4	12	16
54	40	20	20	20	32	4	66	23½	45	23	20 × 20	B-72	4	12	16
54	48	20	20	20	40	4	66	23½	45	23	20 × 20	B-72	4	12	16
54	54	20	20	20	46	4	66	23½	42	21	20 × 24	B-72	4	12	16
60	48	20	20	20	40	4	72	23½	45	24	20 × 24	B-72	4	12	16

[a]These approximate dimensions based on historic data of Rumford Fireplace Construction; as is true with all fireplaces, successful performance is experimental.

[b]These dimensions have been developed from the following formulae. These formulae may also be used for opening dimensions other than those listed. Minimum dimensions are taken from the CABO one- and two-family dwelling code, 1986 ed.

A = Fireplace opening width, in.
B = Fireplace opening height, in. where: ⅔ A < B ≤ A
C = D = E where: ⅓ B ≤ C ≤ ½ B
F = B − E + P, where: P = 12 in. minimum
G = 4 in.
H = A + B in. for A ≤ 48 in.; A + 12 in. for A > 48 in.
I = C + 3½ in. minimum when fire brick are laid as shiners or C + 5½ in. when fire brick or common brick are laid as stretchers.
J = K/u, where 0.50 ≤ u ≤ 0.58
K = ½ (H − M)

L × M > 1/10 (A × B)
N = A = 3 × 3 × 3/16″ angle (number denotes length, in.)
   B = 3½ × 3 × ¼″ angle
O = Nominal brick thickness.
P = 12 in. minimum.
Q = 8 in. minimum when A × B < 864 in²; 12 in. minimum when A × B ≥ 864 in².
R = Smoke shelf width (flue opening length, in.)
S = 8 in. minimum when fire brick lining is used; 10 in. minimum when common brick lining is used.
T = 16 in. minimum when A × B < 864 in².; 20 in. minimum when A × B ≥ 864 in².

[c]Minimum dimensions

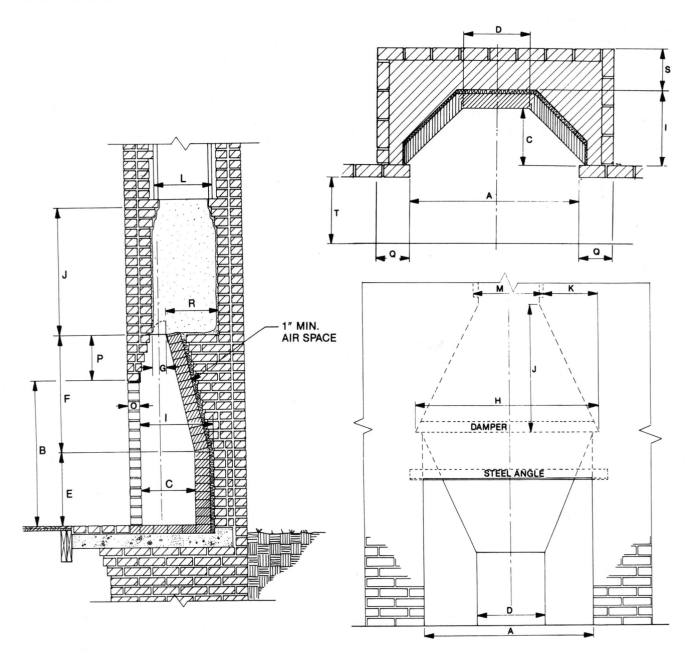

Courtesy of Brick Institute of America

TABLE 11.
Average Specific Gravities and Unit Weights[1]

Material	Specific Gravity	Unit Weight in Pounds Per Cubic Foot
Portland Cement	3.15	94
Lime	2.25	40
Water	1.00	62.4

[1] Values for sand are not listed because they vary considerably. Obtain precise values from laboratory tests (or from supplier).

Courtesy of Brick Institute of America

TABLE 12.
Material Quantities Per Cubic Foot of Mortar

Material	Quantities by Volume				Quantities by Weight			
	Mortar Type and Proportions by Volume				Mortar Type and Proportions by Volume			
	M	S	N	O	M	S	N	O
	1:¼:3	1:½:4½	1:1:6	1:2:9	1:¼:3	1:½:4½	1:1:6	1:2:9
Cement	0.333	0.222	0.167	0.111	31.33	20.89	15.67	10.44
Lime	0.083	0.111	0.167	0.222	3.33	4.44	6.67	8.89
Sand	1.000	1.000	1.000	1.000	80.00	80.00	80.00	80.00

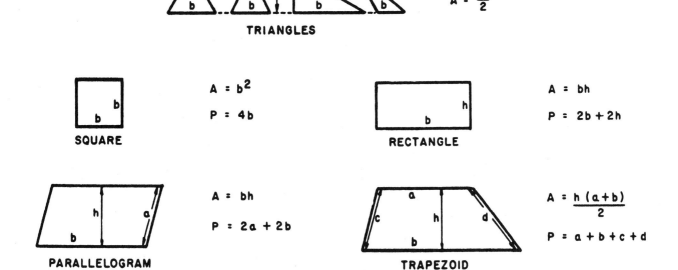

TABLE 13.
Metric and Customary Measure Conversions

Quantity	Convert from	To	Multiply by
Length	inch	millimetre (mm)	25.4*
	inch	centimetre (cm)	2.54*
	foot	metre (m)	0.304 8*
	yard	metre	0.914 4*
	chain	metre	20.116 8
	mile (statute)	kilometre (km)	1.609 347
	mile (nautical)	kilometre	1.852*
	millimetre (mm)	inch	0.039 370
	centimetre	foot	0.032 808
	metre	foot	3.280 840
	metre	yard	1.093 613
	kilometre	mile (statute)	0.621 370
Area	square inch	square centimetre (cm^2)	6.451 600*
	square foot	square metre (m^2)	0.092 903
	square yard	square metre	0.836 127
	square centimetre	square inch	0.155 000
	square metre	square foot	10.763 91
	square metre	square yard	1.195 99
Volume	cubic inch	cubic centimetre (cm^3)	16.387 06
	cubic foot	cubic metre (m^3)	0.028 317
	cubic yard	cubic metre	0.764 555
	cubic centimetre	cubic inch	0.061 024
	cubic metre	cubic foot	35.314 66
	cubic metre	cubic yard	1.307 951

*Exact value

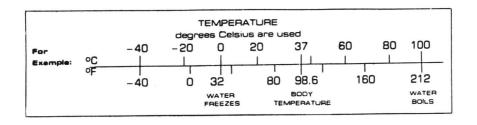

GLOSSARY

Absorption. Amount of water a masonry unit will absorb when completely submerged in either cold or boiling water for a set length of time. Absorption amount is expressed as a percentage weight increase.

Absorption Rate. Weight of water absorbed by masonry unit (usually a brick) in one minute. See also *initial rate of absorption*.

Accelerator. Material added to mortar to speed up setting time.

Active solar heating. Indirect solar heating; solar heat is circulated mechanically (by pump or fan) from solar collectors outside the building.

Adhesion. Ability of mortar to stick to masonry unit.

Admixture. Material added to mortar to change the character of the mortar. Admixture may change color or may speed up or slow down setting time.

Adobe Brick. Unit made of clay with asphaltic material sometimes added; unit is sun-hardened.

Aggregate. Material, such as sand or gravel, that is added to mortar.

Anchor Bolt. Threaded bolt placed in grouted masonry unit opening (or in concrete wall top) used to fasten wood sill, beam, or other structural support to wall top.

Angle Iron. A structural iron angle shaped like an "L", used for lintels to support masonry over openings, such as doors or windows.

Apprentice. Individual indentured (contracted) to a training program run by a Joint Apprenticeship and Training Committee (JATC) in the building trades. See *journeyman*.

Arch. Curved structural support across the top of an opening.

Area Wall. Masonry wall surrounding an area.

Arris. Sharp edge or corner made where two surfaces or sides meet.

Ashlar. A squared or rectangular cut stone used in building.

ASTM. American Society for Testing and Materials; a standards organization for testing materials.

Backfill. Filling around finished building foundation; masonry units filled in within an arch; masonry units between structural members; masonry units built between two faces or behind a facing.

Backhand. Laying brick by facing wall from outside and moving backward while laying brick. See *forehand, overhand*.

Backing Up. Laying brick inside a masonry wall after the facing wall has been laid.

Backup. Masonry wall behind the face wall.

Bat. A brick piece; broken brick. Often a half brick.

Batter. Sloping back of the outer side of a masonry wall; as the sloping back of a retaining wall to withstand the hydrostatic (water) pressure that builds up behind the wall. The opposite of *corbel*.

Beam. Horizontal structural support member.

Bearing. Surface area that holds weight or load of a building member.

Bearing Plate. Steel plate placed under beam ends or column base, that is used to distribute the weight of the structural member.

Bearing Wall. Wall that supports part of the building weight above it in addition to its own weight. Opposed to a *non-bearing wall*.

Bed. The bottom side of a brick or block as it has been laid in the wall.

Bed Joint. Horizontal mortar bed on which masonry unit is laid.

Belt Course. Layer or row of masonry units at the same level.

Block. Concrete block.

Bond. Pattern of laid masonry units; adhesion between mortar and masonry units; tying together parts of two or more wythes of masonry walls by overlapping masonry units.

Bond Beam. Horizontal masonry units filled with concrete and laid with steel reinforcing rods designed to form a continuous beam to reinforce the wall.

Bond Stone. Stone or masonry unit that projects back from the facing wall into a backup wall; designed to tie the two walls or wythes together. Unlike a header, the bond stone may *not* project completely through the two walls or wythes.

Bonder. Bonding unit.

Breaking Joints. Laying of masonry units in a pattern so head joints do *not* line up on top of each other in successive courses; staggered joints.

Brick. Rectangular masonry unit, with or without cores (holes), made by firing shaped clay unit in a kiln. Various brick are available: acid-resistant, adobe, angle, arch, building, clinker, common, dry press, economy, engineered, facing, fire, floor, gaged, jumbo, modular, Norman, pawing, Roman, salmon, SCR, sewer, soft-mud, and stiff-mud.

Brick and Brick. Laying brick with very little mortar between units; brick touch with only enough mortar to fill irregularities in the surface between units.

Building Brick. Brick used for general construction; also called common brick. Defined by ASTM C62.

Burning the Joint. Mortar joint that is tooled after the mortar has partially set and is hard; the hardness of the mortar rubs off metal from jointer, leaving dark streaks.

Buttering. Spreading mortar on a masonry unit with a trowel before it is laid.

Buttress. Vertical masonry support arm or projection built onto the front of a wall to provide support and stability.

Caulking. Process of sealing cracks around doors, windows, or other openings in a wall; the sealing material itself.

Cavity Wall. A two-wythe wall. Wythes are separated from each other by a small air space; air space is at least two inches wide and may be filled with insulation. Walls or wythes are connected with metal ties. Also called a *hollow wall*.

C/B Ratio. Ratio of amount of cold water absorbed by a brick to the amount of boiling water absorbed. Indicator of how brick will react to freezing and thawing cycle. Also known as saturation coefficient.

Cell. Hole in a masonry unit; cell is defined as a void with a cross-sectional area greater than $1\frac{1}{2}$ square inches. See also *core*.

Cement. Also called *portland cement*.

Cement Masonry. Concrete construction; placing of concrete for footing, floors, walls, and so forth. Work is done by a cement mason.

Centering. Temporary framework used to support masonry units being laid in arch. Also called *center*.

Ceramic Glaze. Glass-like coating fused onto the face of a tile or brick. May be colored or clear.

Ceramic Tile. Thin tile with glass-like face set into adhesive or mortar; tile is set by tile setter, not a mason.

Ceramic Veneer. Terra cotta units held in place by grout and anchors or by adhesive.

Chase. Set back or recess built into a wall; used for piping, electrical runs, ductwork.

Chimney. Brick or stone structure that holds flues for the fireplace.

Cleanout. Opening in a wall base used for cleaning out fallen mortar. Also opening at base of fireplace for cleaning out ashes.

Clinker Brick. A very hard-burned brick whose shape is distorted or bloated due to nearly complete vitrification.

Clip. Cut brick piece or section.

Closer. The last brick or concrete block laid in the course. Also called *closure, closure brick, closure block.*

CMU. Concrete masonry unit.

Column. Vertical support member.

Common Brick. Building brick. (Defined by ASTM C62.)

Composite Wall. Masonry wall with wythes of different materials, as brick and block.

Compression. Downward crushing load or strain on a wall or beam, as on the top of a lintel.

Concrete Block. Molded masonry unit made of concrete; may be solid or with cells.

Concrete Brick. Small size, solid concrete block.

Control Joint. Vertical joint made in the wall to allow for shrinkage movement. Prevents random cracking of the wall caused by contraction. Term used with concrete building units such as concrete block. See also *expansion joint.*

Coping. Masonry cap on top of a wall or pier; wall top covering.

Corbel. A shelf or ledge built out from the face of a masonry wall; several courses that project out further and further as they go higher. The opposite of *batter.*

Core. Opening in a brick; core is defined as a void with a cross-sectional area equal to or less than 1 ½ square inches. See also *cell.*

Course. Horizontal row of masonry units.

Crowding the Line. Masonry units laid so they touch the guideline; an unacceptable practice.

Crown. High point or apex of a curving arch.

Cull. Reject; below standard. Masonry unit that does not meet standards or specifications.

Cupping the Mortar. Cutting and rolling the mortar off the mortar board with a trowel.

Curtain Wall. Non-bearing wall built between columns or piers; can be entirely outside of building frame.

Cut Brick. Brick cut to length to fit in course. See *king closure, queen closure, bat.*

Damp Course. Layer of impervious material to prevent entrance of moisture.

Damp Proofing. Treatment of masonry wall surface to retard passage of moisture.

Dimensioned Stone. Stone cut to standard sizes.

Drip. Projecting brick course or other material below a window to allow water run off away from the wall. Also, a slot cut on the bottom of the projection; slot prevents water from running back under the projection. Also, a bend in a metal tie used in cavity walls; the drip collects any moisture and allows it to fall in the center.

Dry Bonding. Laying of masonry units without the use of mortar between the joints.

Dry Joint. Joint without mortar.

Dwarf Wall. A wall or partition which does not extend to the ceiling.

EBM. Engineered Brick Masonry; design is based on structural analysis.

Efflorescence. Powder or stain that forms on mortar or concrete; usually caused by moisture leaching out salts from the material in the masonry.

Element. A masonry or building structural unit.

Expansion Joint. Joint or separation made between different materials that have different expansion rates, as between a concrete floor and a column base or wall. A filler strip is placed in the joint. The term is used in relation to brick building units. See also *control joint.*

Extrados. The outer curve on a curving masonry arch; opposed to intrados.

Face. The exposed surface of a wall or masonry unit; also, the surface of a unit designed to be exposed in the finished masonry. Also, the opening of a fireplace.

Face Brick. Select grade of brick used on the outside of a wall; also called a facing brick. (Defined by ASTM C216.)

Face Wall. Masonry wall exposed to view.

Facing. Part of an exterior masonry wall; finished surface.

Fat Mortar. Mortar that is sticky and adheres to the trowel; contains a high percent of cementitious materials. Opposite of *lean mortar.*

Field. Expanse of brickwork or blockwork between openings or structural supports.

Fire Brick. Brick made of fire-resistant clay; used to line the firebox area of a fireplace.

Fire Wall. Any wall designed to resist the spread of fire. Walls are rated by the length of time they can resist fire.

Flagstone. A natural, flat stone used in walkways. One stone is a flag.

Flashing. Sheet metal or plastic used at breaks in a building where water might leak in. Flashing is run under the building material to create a barrier.

Flash Set. Very rapid set or hardening of mortar.

Flue. Passage that carries off smoke from a fireplace; flue is lined with tile.

Footing. Support for wall, column, or pier.

Forehand. Laying brick by facing wall from outside and moving forward while laying brick. See *backhand, overhand.*

Frog. Small depression or indentation in the bed of a brick.

Frost line. Depth at which the earth freezes at a specific location.

Furring. Wood or metal strips fastened to the inside of a masonry wall as a base for interior finish.

Furrowing. Small indentation cut into the mortar bed by a trowel; prepares the mortar bed for the brick.

Glass Block. Square or rectangular, hollow, pressed glass building units.

Glazing. A fired, glass-like finish.

Glazed Structural Tile. Structural tile with glazed finish. See also *prefaced masonry.*

Green. Fresh mortar; mortar that has not set.

Grounds. Nailing strips placed in masonry walls as a means of attaching trim or furring.

Grout. Mortar of pouring consistency used to fill masonry voids in building units or to fill between masonry walls. A liquid mortar. Made of portland cement, lime, aggregates, and water. See *high-lift grouting, low-lift grouting.*

G.S.U. Glazed Structural Unit.

Hard to the Line. Masonry units set too close to the guideline.

Harsh Mortar. Mortar that is difficult to spread.

Hawk. A small *mortar board.*

Head. Top of door or window frame.

Head Joint. Vertical mortar joint.

Header. Masonry unit laid flat on its bed surface with end facing out; often used to tie two wythes together.

Headway. Clear space under an arch.

Hearth. Floor of a fireplace; flat area in front of fireplace.

Heat Sink. Masonry wall for storage of the sun's heat; used in passive solar heating. A *thermal storage wall.*

High-Lift Grouting. Grouting of hollow wall after it is built fairly high; grout is poured in lifts (heights) of around four feet. See *low-lift grouting.*

Hod. V-shaped, long-handled carrier for mortar.

Hog. Improper wall laying, where one end of the wall has more courses than the other end, although both ends are the same height. Caused by different masons working on wall ends.

Hollow Brick. A masonry unit of clay or shale in which the net cross-sectional area in any plane parallel to the bearing surface is not less than 60 percent of its gross cross-sectional area measured in the same plane. (ASTM Specification C652.)

Hollow Wall. A *cavity wall.*

Hydrated Lime. Quicklime treated with water; used in masonry mortar. Also called *slaked lime.*

Initial Rate of Absorption. Weight of water absorbed by a brick calculated in grams per 30 square inches of contact surface when brick is partially submerged in water for one minute.

Initial Set. Beginning of mortar set.

Insulation. Material that resists heat flow; used on masonry wall to help prevent heat loss or heat gain.

Intrados. Inner or bottom curve on an arch; opposed to *extrados.*

IRA. Initial rate of absorption.

Jamb. Side of a window or door frame.

Joint. Edge or surface where two masonry units are laid together; the mortar-filled space between two masonry units.

Jointing. Finishing of masonry joints. A metal jointer is used to smooth down and remove mortar. Also called *tooling.* Flush, weathered, concave, V, and raked joints are used; a struck joint is also used but is susceptible to moisture and freezing.

Joint Reinforcement. Steel reinforcement that is placed in a masonry unit joint.

Journeyman. Craftsman or tradesman who has completed and passed an apprenticeship in a trade.

Keystone. The center brick or center stone in an arch.

Kiln. Oven for firing brick or tile.

King Closure. Closure made using a brick with one corner cut off diagonally to give one two-inch end and one full-width end.

Laitance. Surface layer fines in concrete or mortar brought to top by excess water in the mix.

Lap. Distance one masonry unit extends over another.

Lateral Support. Side support for a wall or other structural member.

Lateral Thrust. Strain or pressure from the side, horizontal load; for example, on the outside of the base of a round arch.

Lead. Built-up masonry corner used as a guide in laying a wall. Normally two corners or leads, connected by a line, are laid up as a guide. See also *rake-back lead*.

Lean Mortar. A difficult-to-spread mortar that is deficient in cementitious materials. Opposite of *fat mortar*.

Leaner. Less cement.

Lift. Height of grout (or concrete) placed at one time from one pour.

Lime. Quicklime (calcium oxide). Made by burning off calcium dioxide from limestone.

Lime Putty. Quicklime with water added to make a paste.

Lintel. Horizontal structural unit (beam) over an opening; support member over a door or window opening.

Load. Weight, strain, or pressure on a structural unit or element.

Low-Lift Grouting. Grouting of wall as it is built; grout is poured in lifts (heights) of six inches to eight inches. See *high-lift grouting*.

Mantel. Shelf over and above the fireplace opening. Stone or brick may be used.

Manufactured Stone. Artificial stone made from textured and colored concrete to simulate natural stone; used in veneer work.

Mason. Skilled specialist and journeyman who works with and lays brick, concrete block, and stone. Special-ties are identified as brickmason, blockmason, and stonemason.

Masonry. Art and craft of laying masonry units of brick, concrete block, glass block, structural tile, and stone. Also, construction of units of such materials as clay, shale, concrete, glass, gypsum, or stone, set in mortar. The following are different types of masonry: (1) *hollow masonry*—units in which the voids exceed 25 percent of the cross-sectional area; (2) *solid masonry*—units in which the voids do not exceed 25 percent of the cross-sectional area at any plane parallel to the bearing surface; and (3) *modular masonry*—units manufactured to a nominal four-inch module size or a multiple of four inches.

Masonry Cement. A pre-packaged cement used in place of portland cement and lime.

Masonry Reinforcement. A means of increasing strength by using steel reinforcing rods, wire mesh or fabric, steel ties, joint reinforcement, pilasters, or buttresses.

Masonry Unit. Building unit of fired clay, shale, concrete, glass, gypsum, or stone. Unit is set in mortar.

Membrane. Thin, unbroken sheet applied to a wall for waterproofing.

Modular. Construction or manufacture of building units to a four-inch module size or a multiple of four inches.

Moisture Protection. Safeguarding of living units against penetration or passage of water, water vapor, and dampness.

Mortar. Plastic mixture of cementitious materials, sand (aggregate), and water; used as a bed and for cementing masonry units in place. Sometimes called *mud*.

Mortar Board. Square board used by mason to hold mortar ready for use on the job. Also called a *hawk*.

Mud. A common name for mortar.

Muriatic Acid. Acid solution used for cleaning masonry work. A solution of hydrochloric acid.

Nominal Dimension. The size of a building unit in place with mortar, as opposed to the actual, measured size of the building unit.

Non-Bearing Wall. Wall that does *not* support any of the building weight or load but carries only its own weight. See also *bearing wall*.

Ornamental Brick. Brick with a glazed surface.

Ornamental Terra Cotta. Shaped or sculptured terra cotta building units.

Outer Hearth. Flat apron in front of the fireplace opening; may be brick, stone, tile, cement, or other noncumbustible material.

Overhand Work. Laying of brick from inside a wall.

Panel (Masonry). Building unit constructed of masonry units. Masonry panel is delivered to the job in one unit and is hoisted into place in the building.

Parapet. Wall section that extends above the roof; normally associated with a flat roof.

Parge. Cement mortar used for parging.

Pargeting. *Parging.*

Parging. Process of applying a coat of mortar to masonry construction, especially used for masonry walls. Also, the cement mortar coat itself.

Partition. Interior wall; a non-bearing wall.

Party Wall. Wall between two separate living areas; a common wall.

Passive Solar. Direct heating by the sun's rays. No mechanical means is used to circulate the heat.

Paver. Special brick, adobe, tile, stone, or solid concrete unit used for floors, walks, and patios. Concrete pavers are shaped with interlocking sides.

Paving. Laying flat masonry units in ground. Also, placing of concrete on the ground.

Paving Brick. Brick especially suitable for use in pavements (ASTM Specification C902).

Pick and Dip. Technique of bricklaying. Mason picks up a brick at the same time he dips mortar (for laying the brick) with his trowel.

Pier. A short masonry or concrete column supporting the foundations of the floor structure in spaces without a basement. Pier may be freestanding or bonded at its sides to other masonry or concrete. A masonry column used to support a garden wall. A freestanding column.

Pilaster. A pier or column forming part of a masonry or concrete wall, partially projecting from it and bonded to it. Designed to receive joist or beam load.

Plinth. Base for a column, usually square-shaped.

Plumb. Exactly vertical. Measured with a plumb line.

Pointing. Filling mortar into the joint with a trowel after the masonry units are laid; filling of raked-out joints.

Post. Vertical support member.

Prefabricated Brick Masonry. Assembling of masonry units away from the actual structure; completed panel is then hoisted into place. See *panel.*

Prefaced Masonry. Concrete block with face glazing. See also *glazed structural tile.*

Puddling. Settling of grout in masonry wall by agitating the mixture with a stick or rod; designed to remove air voids in the grout.

Quarry. Open stone or clay pit.

Quarry Masonry. Rough quarry stone. Wall built of rough quarry stone.

Queen Closure. Closure made by using less than half of a brick. The brick itself is a cut brick having a nominal horizontal face dimension of two inches.

Quicklime. Caustic lime made of calcium oxide (CaO) made by heating carbon dioxide (CO_2) off limestone. Used to make a fine putty by adding water (slaking). Also called lime, hot lime.

Quoin. Large squared stone or brick set at the corner formed by two masonry walls. Projects out from the corner in some cases.

Racking. Laying or stepping back each higher masonry course.

Raggle. Groove or slot in a masonry unit; slot is cut along one side to receive the edge of the flashing. Also called a *reglet.*

Rack Back. To set back, as to set back a brick or block course from the lower one. Rack back is normally the distance of one-half the length of the masonry unit.

Rack-Back Lead. Several masonry courses laid up in the center of a wall as a guide. Each higher course is racked back from the lower one. See also *lead.*

Rake Out. To remove broken or fresh mortar.

Raked Joint. Masonry joint where mortar is removed or tooled back in the joint.

Raking. Cleaning out mortar from a joint; both fresh mortar and old, broken mortar may be removed.

Ranging the Corner. Aligning two corners by a line stretched from each corner or lead.

RBM. Reinforced Brick Masonry.

RGBM. Reinforced Grouted Brick Masonry.

Reglet. A *raggle.*

Reinforced Masonry. Masonry with reinforcing steel and/or grout used in the wall.

Retaining Wall. Wall built to hold earth in place.

Retarder. Mortar additive that slows down setting.

Retemper. To remix mortar by adding more water.

Return. A surface turned back from the face or principle surface.

Revertment. Parging or facing on a masonry wall for protection.

Rich Mortar. Mortar high in cementitious material.

Rip Block. Concrete block not of full height.

Rise. Vertical direction.

Rowlock. Masonry units laid on face edge with end facing out. Also spelled *rolok*.

Rubbed Joint. Flush mortar joint; joint is rubbed flat to the face of the masonry units.

Rubble. Rough, irregular stone.

Rubble Masonry. Masonry wall built with rubble stone; rubblework.

Rubblework. Masonry using rubble stone.

Run. Horizontal direction.

Rustic. Brick with rough, lined pattern on the face.

Sag. To bend down; to fall below a horizontal line.

Sailor. Brick laid on end with the large or bed side facing outward.

Sand. Fine aggregate; sand is a very fine aggregate of quartz.

Sandblasting. Cleaning masonry wall by blowing a stream of sand on the wall.

Saturation Coefficient. See *C/B Ratio.*

Scratch Coat. First or base coat of a two-coat plastering or parging. Coat is scratched to form a good bonding surface for the finished coat.

Screen Wall. Wall with special screen block that have open design.

Serpentine. Curving, as a wall that curves back and forth.

Set. Hardening of mortar. In *initial set,* mortar reaches a partial strength; in *final set,* the full specified hardness is attained.

Setting. Laying masonry units in place.

Setting Up. Hardening of mortar.

Shiner. Brick set on the face side with the large or bed side facing out.

Shop Drawings. Drawings made by masonry contractor or manufacturer showing details of masonry construction.

Shoved Joint. Joint made by shoving end of one brick against another in the mortar bed.

Sill. Bottom of a window or door frame.

Skew. To twist back or lean; to incline.

Skewback. Inclined surface at end of arch where arch joins the supporting wall.

Slack to the Line. Masonry units set too far back from the guideline.

Slaking. Adding water to hydrate lime.

Slaked Lime. Quicklime with water added.

Slurry. Runny or liquid cement mixture; used for thin-coating a masonry surface. See *wash.*

Slushed Joints. Joint that is filled after the brick is laid; joint is filled in with the trowel. (This is considered an unprofessional practice.)

Smoke Test. Checking a masonry fireplace and chimney by building a fire in the fireplace and closing the flue top. Smoke will flow out of any cracks or openings.

Soffit. Underside, as the underside of a cornice or arch, or the underside of a run of stairs.

Solar Heating. Heating by the sun's rays. *Active solar* uses mechanical means, such as a pump or a fan, to move heated liquid or air from a solar collector to inside the building. *Passive solar* uses direct heating by the sun's rays. Direct solar heat may be stored in masonry walls for interior heating when the sun is no longer visible.

Solar Collectors. Panels located outside the building that catch the sun's rays. A liquid or air inside the collector is heated and then pumped or blown inside the building for heating.

Solar Orientation. Facing of building's windows or solar collectors toward the south for solar heating in the cold months.

Solar Screen. A masonry wall with openings that is used as a sun screen.

Solar Storage. Storage of solar heat in rock or in a masonry wall or floor; *thermal storage.*

Soldier. Brick or concrete block set on end with face oriented toward the outside.

Spall. Small stone used in rubble masonry. Also, small masonry or stone chips that break off the rock or masonry unit, as from freezing or thawing or from a hammer blow.

Span. Distance between two supports.

Spandrel. Triangular area on each side of an arch. Also, a support unit between columns or piers.

Specifications. Written description of work to be done, quality of work, and type of materials. Also called specs.

Splay. Slanted or beveled surface.

Split. To split or break a masonry unit lengthwise parallel to the bed side.

Stiff Mortar. Low water mortar; a drier mortar.

Stone Masonry. Art and craft of laying stone in mortar.

Storypole. Stick or pole marked with key masonry heights that is used as a guide when laying corners.

Stretcher. Masonry unit laid lengthwise on its bed; the face side faces out.

Striking. Tooling or jointing a mortar joint.

Stringing Mortar. Spreading out a mortar bed for the laying of several units.

Struck Joint. Mortar joint that has been finished with a trowel and is bevelled in at the bottom.

Structural Clay Unit. Fired masonry unit such as a brick or tile.

Suction Rate. Ability of a material, such as a brick, to absorb water. Also called *initial rate of absorption.*

Sun Space. Area of building designed to be heated by the sun's rays.

Surface Bonding. Method of laying concrete block in a wall without mortar in the joints; wall is coated with a special surface bonding mortar containing fiberglass.

Synthetic Stone. *Manufactured stone.*

Tailing the Lead. Aligning masonry courses on a corner so they are straight and level.

Temper. Adding water to mortar; to moisten and mix to a proper consistency.

Template. Shaped pattern or guide used when forming or laying brick to follow a specific shape.

Tender. Laborer who helps a mason, for example, by bringing mortar or brick.

Tension. Strain tending to pull material apart, as on the bottom of a lintel or beam. A stretching force.

Terra Cotta. Fired clay building units usually with vitreous (glass-like) colored finish on face.

Thermal Storage Wall. Masonry storage wall for passive solar heat. Masonry wall is heated during the day by direct sunlight; at night heat radiates out of the wall to warm the living area. A masonry floor area is also used for heat storage.

Throat. Opening at top of fireplace through which the smoke flows.

Throwing the Mortar Joint. Applying mortar to the end of a brick with a sweeping or throwing motion.

Tie. Masonry unit or metal piece used to tie walls together or used to tie a masonry wall to some other structural base.

Tier. A wythe.

Tile. Hollow masonry unit made of fired clay, shale, fire clay, or some mixture of these.

Tile Setter. One who sets tile.

Tile Setting. Setting of tile into an adhesive or mortar bed by a tile setter.

Tooling. Compressing, shaping, or finishing of mortar joints with a special finishing tool. See also *jointing.*

Toothing. Temporary wall end where alternate stretchers project out. Projecting masonry units are called *tooths.*

Tree Wall. Circular masonry wall built around the base of a tree to hold back the surrounding earth.

Trig. Device used for supporting a line at the center of a wall.

Trig Brick. The brick that holds the trig.

Trim. Masonry or stone facings; sills or coping.

Trimming. Cutting of stone or masonry units on different sides to a specified dimension or shape.

Tuckpointing. Refilling of old masonry joints that have been raked out and cleaned.

Veneer. Separate wythe of masonry units that has no structural value and is attached to the structural face of the building or another wall. A non-bearing wall attached to another wall or structural base.

Vitrified. Glassy in appearance. A fired clay that has been fused together. Commonly used on the face of terra cotta units.

Voids. Openings, cells, cores, or holes in a masonry unit.

Voussoir. Wedge-shaped masonry unit or stone used in laying a curved arch.

Wall. Vertical structural member. Various masonry walls constructed are: apron, area, bearing, cavity, composite, curtain, dwarf, enclosure, exterior, faced, fire, foundation, hollow, panel, parapet, party, perforated, reinforced, retaining, solid masonry, spandrel, veneered.

Wall Panel. Wall unit made by laying masonry units in place away from the building; panel is delivered to the site and hoisted in place.

Wall Tie. Metal tie used to tie or join wythes together or to fasten veneer to a structural base.

Wall Tie, Cavity. A rigid, corrosion-resistant metal tie which bonds two wythes of a cavity wall. It is usually steel, $\frac{3}{16}$ inches in diameter and formed in a "Z" shape or a rectangle.

Wall Tie, Veneer. A strip or piece of metal used to tie a facing veneer to the backing.

Wash. Washing or painting on a thin slurry of cement or mortar on a masonry wall face; designed to prevent entrance of moisture.

Washing Down. Cleaning of masonry wall by washing with water, with muriatic acid and water, or with proprietary cleaning solutions.

Waterproofing. Surfacing or treating of masonry wall to prevent or retard moisture or water entry.

Water Retentivity. Mortar designed to hold water to prevent rapid loss to masonry units with high degree of absorption or suction.

Water Table. Projection of the base masonry slightly out from the bottom of the wall.

Weathering. Decaying of masonry units or mortar through the effect of the weather.

Web. Solid wall section between cores in a masonry unit; commonly used to describe the solid wall between concrete block cells.

Weep Holes. Openings in masonry joints left at the base of a masonry wall so moisture may run out.

Wind. A bend or twist, a curve or warp.

Winning. Digging and mining of clay or shale for use in the manufacturer of brick and tile.

Wire Mesh. Metal reinforcing fabric.

Working Drawings. Blueprints of the structure being built.

Working Overhand. Working a double-wythe wall from one side only.

Working to One's Hand. Working from a corner based on whether a mason is left-handed or right-handed. It is easier for a right-handed mason to lay units working from the left corner to the center; a left-handed mason works easiest working from the right corner.

Wythe. Vertical wall or tier of masonry units one-unit thick. The thickness of masonry separating flues in a chimney. Also called *withe* or *tier*.

INDEX